INSIGHT GUIDE

SCOTLAND

APA PUBLICATIONS

Part of the Langenscheidt Publishing Group

ABOUT THIS BOOK

Editorial

Project Editor
Josephine Buchanan
Editorial Director
Brian Bell

Distribution

UK & Ireland
GeoCenter International Ltd
The Viables Centre
Harrow Way
Basingstoke
Hants RG22 4BJ
Fax: (44) 1256-817988

United States
Langenscheidt Publishers, Inc.
46–35 54th Road
Maspeth, NY 11378
Fax: (718) 784-0640

Worldwide
APA Publications GmbH & Co.
Verlag KG (Singapore branch)
38 Joo Koon Road
Singapore 628990
Tel: (65) 865-1600
Fax: (65) 861-6438

Printing

Insight Print Services (Pte) Ltd
38 Joo Koon Road
Singapore 628990
Tel: (65) 865-1600
Fax: (65) 861-6438

©1999 APA Publications GmbH & Co.
Verlag KG (Singapore branch)
All Rights Reserved
First Edition 1984
Fourth Edition (updated) 1999

CONTACTING THE EDITORS
Although every effort is made to provide accurate information in this publication, we live in a fast-changing world and would appreciate it if readers would call our attention to any errors or outdated information that may occur by writing to us at:
Insight Guides, P.O. Box 7910, London SE1 8ZB, England.
Fax: (44 171) 620-1074.
e-mail:
insight@apaguide.demon.co.uk

This guidebook combines the interests and enthusiasms of two of the world's best known information providers: Insight Guides, whose titles have set the standard for visual travel guides since 1970, and Discovery Channel, the world's premier source of nonfiction television programming.

The editors of Insight Guides provide both practical advice and general understanding about a destination's history, culture, institutions and people. Discovery Channel and its Web site, www.discovery.com, help millions of viewers explore their world from the comfort of their own home and encourage them to explore it firsthand.

How to use this book

The book is carefully structured to convey an understanding of Scotland and its culture and to guide readers through its sights and attractions:

◆ The Features section, with a yellow colour bar, covers the country's history and culture in lively authoritative essays written by specialists.

◆ The Places section, with a blue bar, provides full details of all the sights and areas worth seeing. The chief places of interest are coordinated by number with specially drawn maps.

◆ The Travel Tips section, with an orange bar, at the back of the book, offers a convenient point of reference for information on travel, accommodation, restaurants and other practical aspects of the country. Information may be located quickly by using the index printed on the

back cover flap, which also serves as a convenient bookmark.

The contributors

This new edition was edited by **Josephine Buchanan**, putting her Scottish ancestry to good use. It was fully updated by **Roger Smith**, the former editor of *Great Outdoors* magazine, who lives in Galashiels. He has written or edited more than 20 books on Scottish themes.

The current edition builds on the original one produced by **Brian Bell**, who is now Insight's editorial director. A journalist with wide experience in newspapers and magazines, Bell was attracted to Insight's philosophy that a country's "warts" should not be omitted from a guidebook.

A leading contributor – of the chapters on Edinburgh, the age of rebellion, modern Scotland, Scots geniuses, tartan and hunting – is **George Rosie**, who began his career

in Dundee with publisher D.C. Thomson. Rosie moved to London and joined the *Sunday Times* in 1974, but has since returned to Scotland and writes about it from the inside for newspapers and TV.

Other Scottish journalists to have contributed to this guide include **Julie Davidson**, who wrote five of the Places chapters (Glasgow, the Southwest, Forth and Clyde, the West Coast and the East Coast), and Glasgow-born **Marcus Brooke**, who wrote the chapters on Skye, the Outer Hebrides and Orkney, as well as those on Highland games, festivals, golf, Edinburgh architecture and the feature on castles and abbeys. Also from Glasgow is the novelist and artist **Naomi May**, who wrote the chapters on Scottish art and religion.

Two contributors to *The Scotsman* – **Alastair Clark** and **Conrad Wilson** – add their insight to the music and food of Scotland, whilst **Stuart Ridsdale**, **Roland Collins**, and **Dymphna Byrne** share their enthusiasm for the Borders, Central Scotland and the Hebrides. **Andrew Eames**, who wrote the features on crofting and Highland flora and fauna, is a journalist and author of *Four Scottish Journeys*.

Insight Guides are as much about people as places and **Christopher Smout** offers a refreshing alternative to the myth of Highlanders and Lowlanders, drawing on his expertise as the author of the *History of the Scottish People*. Remaining chapters – on the Scottish character, early history, whisky, and Shetland – are written by Bell.

The book's main photographer, Edinburgh-based **Douglas Corrance**. was formerly principal photographer for the Scottish Tourist Board and is now published all over the world.

Map Legend

– –	State Boundary
– – –	Region Boundary
–·–·–	National Park/ Nature Reserve
– – – –	Ferry Route
Ⓜ	Metro
✈	Airport: International/ Regional
🚍	Bus Station
Ⓟ	Parking
❶	Tourist Information
✉	Post Office
♱	Church/Ruins
☾	Mosque
✡	Synagogue
♜	Castle/Ruins
∴	Archaeological Site
⋒	Cave
★	Place of Interest

The main places of interest in the Places section are coordinated by number with a full-colour map (e.g. ❶), and a symbol at the top of every right-hand page tells you where to find the map.

INSIGHT GUIDES
SCOTLAND

CONTENTS

Maps

Introduction

History

Features

The monument at Glenfinnan, where Bonnie Prince Charlie raised the Stuart banner in 1745

Travel Tips

Places

THE SCOTTISH CHARACTER

A confusing mix of dourness and humour, the Scots are unanimous only when identifying the common cause of their problems: England

Natives of Scotland, it has been said, consider themselves as Scots before they think of themselves as human beings, thus establishing a clear order of excellence. This attitude, naturally enough, wins them few popularity points from the rest of the human race and none at all from their nearest neighbour, England. Indeed, English literature is so peppered with anti-Scots aphorisms that the cumulative impression amounts to national defamation.

"I have been trying all my life to like Scotchmen," wrote the essayist Charles Lamb, "and am obliged to desist from the experiment in despair." P.G. Wodehouse was no kinder: "It is never difficult," he wrote, "to distinguish between a Scotsman with a grievance and a ray of sunshine." And Dr Samuel Johnson, whose tour of the Hebrides in 1773 was immortalised by his Scottish biographer James Boswell, produced the most enduring maxim: "The noblest prospect that a Scotchman ever sees is the high road that leads him to England".

Shotgun marriage

It is a road that many have taken: an estimated 20 million people of Scots descent, one of the most inventive peoples on earth, are scattered throughout every continent – four times as many as live in Scotland itself. Yet an unease towards the English, a suspicion that they are their social superiors, has for centuries blighted the Scots psyche. The union of the two countries in 1707, after centuries of sporadic hostility, was regarded by most Scots as a shotgun marriage and more than 280 years have scarcely diluted the differences in outlook and attitude between the ill-matched partners.

It is an old tune, often played. When the future Pope Pius II visited the country in the 15th century, he concluded: "Nothing pleases

PRECEDING PAGES: rolling countryside in the Borders; Scottish thistle; red deer; Edinburgh Castle from Princes Street Gardens.
LEFT: on guard at Blackness Castle.
RIGHT: stall holder in Paddy's Market, Glasgow.

the Scots more than abuse of the English". In that respect, the Scots resemble England's other close neighbours, the French, with whom they have intimate historical connections.

Both share an outspokenness, which the English mistake for rudeness. Both are proud peoples, a characteristic which, in the case of the

Scots, the English translate as ingratitude. "You Scots," the playwright J.M. Barrie once had one of his characters say, "are such a mixture of the practical and the emotional that you escape out of an Englishman's hand like a trout." Barrie, the creator of Peter Pan, was a Scot himself and often cast a cynical eye over his fellow countrymen. "There are few more impressive sights in the world," he declared, "than a Scotsman on the make."

It is noticeable that the butt of most of these waspish epigrams is the Scots *man*. Until recently, women, though no less strong in character, played a subsidiary role in the country's public affairs. It was very much a man's world:

it has taken many centuries for women to be allowed to act as a Clan Chief. And although Scottish law introduced desertion as grounds for divorce in 1573 (364 years before England got around to doing so), it retained a robust, Calvinistic view about what wives ought to endure.

Certainly, the Calvinist tradition is central to the Scots character. While England absorbed the Reformation with a series of cunning compromises, Scotland underwent a revolution, replacing the panoply of Roman Catholicism with an austere Presbyterianism designed to put the ordinary people directly in touch with their God. No person was deemed inherently better than the next – and that included the clergy, who were made directly answerable to their congregations. This democratic tradition, allied with a taste for argument born of theological wrangling, runs deep and has led more than one English politician to brand troublesome Glasgow shipyard workers, for example, as Communists. Some might have been; but most were simply exercising their right to be individualists. It was an attitude that would allow a riveter to regard himself as being every bit as good as the shipyard boss and, whenever necessary, to remind the boss of that fact. Deference? What's that?

SCOTTISH HOME RULE

Over the years the antagonism of Scotland towards England has found a political focus. The 1997 general election was an overwhelming victory for the Labour party: in Scotland not one Conservative MP was returned. It was a devastating rejection of the years of Tory rule and their steadfast opposition to Scottish devolution. The September 1997 referendum in Scotland strongly endorsed the setting up of a Scottish Parliament, by a two-to-one majority. The Parliament, which will deal with a wide range of matters and will have tax-varying powers, will start its work after elections in May 1999.

In many other ways, too, the Scots character is a confusing one. It combines dourness and humour, meanness and generosity, arrogance and tolerance, cantankerousness and chivalry, sentimentality and hard-headedness. One aspect of these contradictions is caught by a *Punch* cartoon showing a hitchhiker trying to entice passing motorists with a sign reading "Glasgow – or else!"

On the positive side, a bad climate and a poor soil forged an immensely practical people. But there was a price to be paid: these disadvantages encouraged frugality and a deep-seated pessimism. "It could be worse" comes easily to the lips of the most underprivileged.

The situation is redeemed by laughter. Scottish humour is subtle and sardonic and, in the hands of someone as verbally inventive as the Glasgow-born comedian Billy Connolly, can leave reality far behind with a series of outrageously surreal non-sequiturs. It has also been used, over the years, to cement many a Scottish stereotype. "My father was an Aberdonian," the veteran comedian Chic Murray would say, "and a more generous man you couldn't wish to meet. I have a gold watch that belonged to my father, he sold it to me on his death bed… so I wrote him a cheque."

Alcohol features prominently in Scottish jokes, as it does in many other aspects of the worst of them could be taken by the Red Army in three days, a day-and-a-half if tactical nuclear weapons were used."

The cult of the kilt

Like the Irish, the Scots have realised that there's money to be made from conforming to a stereotyped image, however bogus it may be. Although few in Scotland ever eat haggis (once described as looking like a castrated bagpipe), it is offered to tourists as the national dish. Heads of ancient Scottish clans, living in houses large enough to generate cashflow problems, have opened their homes to tour groups of affluent Americans.

country's life. Until recently the single aim of Scottish pubs was to enable their clientele to get drunk as fast as possible, a purpose reflected in their decor. "Some of them," wrote the journalist Hugh McIlvanney, "are so bare that anyone who wants to drink in sophisticated surroundings takes his glass into the lavatory." Matters have slowly improved, though some hostelries should still be approached with caution. "There is," wrote McIlvanney, "a relentless inclination to exaggerate the toughness of Glasgow pubs. Experience suggests that the

LEFT: passing the time of day in a pub in Jedburgh.
ABOVE: time for tea in Glasgow.

Others have opened "clan shops" retailing an astonishing variety of tartan artefacts, including Hairy Haggisburger soft toys. Still others have taken to appearing in Japanese TV commercials extolling their "family brand" of whisky. The cult of the kilt – based, someone mused, on the self-deception that male knees are an erogenous zone – is a huge commercial success.

But the image obscures the real Scotland. It's worth lingering long enough to draw back the tartan curtain and get to know one of Europe's most complex peoples. There's no guarantee that the more innocent tourists won't have the wool pulled over their eyes; but, if it's any consolation, it's sure to be best-quality Scottish wool. ❏

...los tuos quesum(us)
dñe deus p(er)petua men
tis et corporis salute gau
dere: et glor(i)osa beate ma
rie semp(er) virginis int(er)
cessione a p(re)senti liba
ri tristicia et et(er)na p(er)fru
i leticia. p(er) dominium

Benedicamus dño.

Deo gr(aci)as.

Hic omnia mihi

na diutorium meu i
tende.

Domine ad adiuuand
me festina.

ia pri   Siaut erate

ent creator spc:

Decisive Dates

Prehistoric times
circa **6000 BC** First signs of human settlement on west coast and islands.
circa **3000 BC** Village established at Skara Brae.
circa **2000 BC** Major burial sites such as Maes Howe and Clava Cairns set up.
circa **1000 BC** First invasion of Celtic tribes.

The Romans
AD 82 Agricola's forces enter Scotland and reach Aberdeenshire.

142 Second Roman invasion reaches Firth of Forth. Major fort established at Trimontium, near Melrose.
150–170 Antonine Wall built from Forth to Clyde.
185 Withdrawal of Roman forces behind Hadrian's Wall.

Early Christians and Kingdoms
397 First Christian Church founded at Whithorn by St Ninian.
400–600 Four "kingdoms" emerge – Dalriada, Pictland, Strathclyde and Bernicia.
563 St Columba lands on Iona and founds monastery.
775–800 Norse forces occupy Hebrides, Orkney and Shetland.

The Birth of Scotland
843 Kenneth MacAlpin becomes first King of Scots.
973 Kenneth II defeats Danish invaders at Luncarty, near Perth.
1018 Malcolm II defeats Northumbrians at Battle of Carham.

The English Influence
1040 Macbeth becomes king by murdering Duncan I.
1057 Macbeth killed at Lumphanan, succeeded by Malcolm Canmore. Anglicisation of church and court started by his queen, Margaret.
1124–1153 Reign of David I. Royal burghs founded, and Border abbeys established.
1138 David defeated by Norman forces at Battle of Northallerton.
1165 William I (the Lion) becomes king.
1174 William defeated at Battle of Alnwick and forced to do homage to English king.
1249 Alexander III becomes king. Start of "Golden Age".

Wars of Succession
1286 Death of Alexander III. Succeeded by infant granddaughter Margaret, but rival claimants to throne include John Balliol and Robert Bruce.
1290 Margaret dies en route to Scotland. Edward I of England declares himself feudal overlord of Scotland, selects Balliol as vassal king.
1291–1296 Edward (the Hammer of the Scots) invades Scotland, wins Battle of Dunbar, takes Stone of Destiny to London.
1297 Rebellion led by William Wallace. English forces defeated at Battle of Stirling Bridge.
1305 English put Wallace to death as a traitor.
1306 Robert the Bruce declares himself King Robert I and is crowned at Scone. Defeated at Methven and Dalry and goes into exile.
1314 Scots forces under Robert the Bruce defeat English at Battle of Bannockburn.
1320 Declaration of Arbroath sent to the Pope.
1333 English defeat Scots at Hamildon Hill.
1346–1357 David II held prisoner in London.

The Early Stewarts
1371 Robert II, first of Stewarts, becomes king.
1406–1542 Reigns of James I–V.
1513 James IV killed at Battle of Flodden.
1542 James V defeated at Battle of Solway Moss. Dies shortly after, succeeded by 6-day-old daughter, Mary Queen of Scots.

1547 Hertford wins Battle of Pinkie. Mary taken to France.
1560 Protestants, led by John Knox, start to destroy religious houses.
1561 Mary returns to Scotland to reclaim throne.
1566 Birth of James VI.
1568 Mary flees to England and is imprisoned.

The Union of Crowns and Parliaments
1603 Elizabeth I dies. James VI becomes James I of England.
1638 National Covenant signed in Edinburgh.
1646 Solemn League and Covenant confirmed.
1650 Cromwell seizes power in England. Scots proclaim Charles II as king in defiance. Cromwell's forces inflict heavy defeat at Dunbar.
1660 Charles II restored as king. Covenanters continued to rebel.
1688 James VII/II deposed by William and Mary. Scots supporters of James (Jacobites) win Battle of Killiecrankie.
1692 Massacre of Glencoe.
1707 Treaty of Union, abolition of separate Scottish parliament.

Jacobite Rebellions and the Clearances
1715 Rebellion led by Earl of Mar fails after abortive battle at Sheriffmuir.
1722–40 Building of "Wade Roads".
1745 Prince Charles Edward Stuart, "Bonnie Prince Charlie", sails to Scotland and raises clans at Glenfinnan. Success at Prestonpans, much of Scotland in Jacobite hands.
1746 Campaign retreats and ends in débâcle at Culloden on 16 April.
1765 James Watt invents steam engine.
1780-on Highland Clearances, people evicted for sheep; "Age of Enlightenment" in literature and the arts.

The Industrial Age
1812 Comet, first passenger-carrying steamship, launched.
1823 Caledonian Canal opened.
1836 Highland potato crop fails.
1843 Disruption of Church of Scotland and formation of the Free Church.
1847 Simpson introduces anaesthetics in childbirth, and chloroform in surgery.

1850-on Massive expansion of heavy industry, particularly around Glasgow.
1852 Victoria and Albert buy Balmoral.
1865 Lister pioneers antiseptics in surgery.
1882 The "Crofters War" including Battle of the Braes on Skye.
1883 Highland Land League formed.
1892 Free Presbyterians ("Wee Frees") split from Free Church.
1901 Death of Queen Victoria.

The Modern Age
1924 Ramsay Macdonald becomes first Labour Prime Minister.

1931–32 Unemployment soars in key industries.
1934 Scottish National Party (SNP) formed.
1964 Forth Road Bridge opened.
1974 Eleven SNP members in Parliament.
1975 Start of North Sea gas and oil exploitation.
1979 Referendum fails to achieve autonomy.
1991 Scottish Enterprise and Highlands and Islands Enterprise companies set up.
1997 Referendum votes in favour of Scottish Parliament with tax-varying powers. Stone of Destiny returned to Scotland.
1998 The Museum of Scotland opens in Edinburgh, soon to be a political capital again.
1999 First general election of the Scottish Parliament is held in May; official opening ceremony on 1 July. ❑

PRECEDING PAGES: *Annunciation to the Shepherds*, from early 14th-century Murthly Book of Hours. **ABOVE LEFT:** Robert the Bruce. **ABOVE RIGHT:** Mary Queen of Scots.

BEGINNINGS

An endless battle for power, early Scottish history was dominated by the continual conflicts of ruthlessly ambitious families

On a bleak, windswept moor three witches crouch round a bubbling cauldron, muttering oaths and prophesying doom. A king is brutally stabbed to death and his killer, consumed by vaulting ambition, takes the throne, only to be murdered himself soon afterwards. "Fair is foul, and foul is fair."

To many people, these images from William Shakespeare's *Macbeth* are their first introduction to early Scottish history. But of course, the Scots will tell you, Shakespeare was English and, as usual, the English got it wrong. There is perhaps some truth to the tale, they admit – Macbeth, who reckoned he had a better hereditary claim to the throne than its occupant, did kill Duncan in 1040 – but thereafter he ruled well for 17 years and kept the country relatively prosperous.

Power games

Where Shakespeare undeniably showed his genius, however, was in managing to heighten the narrative of a history that was already (and remained) melodramatic beyond belief. Scotland's story was for centuries little more than the biographies of ruthlessly ambitious families jostling for power, gaining it and losing it through accidents of royal marriages, unexpected deaths and lack of fertility.

A successful Scottish king needed cunning as well as determination, an ability to judge just how far he could push powerful barons without being toppled from his throne in the process. In a continuous effort to safeguard the future, marriage contracts were routinely made between royal infants and, when premature death brought a succession of kings to the throne as children, the land's leading families fought for advancement by trying to gain control over the young rulers, including occasionally by kidnapping them.

Summarise some of the stories and they seem more histrionic than historical. An attractive

young widow returns from 13 years at the French court to occupy the throne of Scotland, lays claim to the throne of England, conducts a series of passionate affairs, marries her lover a few weeks after he has allegedly murdered her second husband, loses the throne, is incarcerated for 19 years by her cousin, the Queen of

England, and is then, on a pretext, beheaded. No scriptwriter today would dare to invent as outrageous a plot as the true-life story of Mary Queen of Scots.

Nameless people

Our earliest knowledge of Scotland dates back more than 6,000 years, when the cold, wet climate and the barren landscape would seem familiar enough to a time-traveller from the present day. Then the region was inhabited by nameless hunters and fishermen. Later, the mysterious Beaker People from Holland and the Rhineland settled here, as they did in Ireland, leaving as a memorial only a few tantalising

LEFT: Romans building Hadrian's Wall.
ABOVE RIGHT: evidence of the Picts near Inverary.

pots. Were the eerie Standing Stones of Callanish, on the island of Lewis, built by them as a primitive observatory? Nobody can be certain.

Tribal society

Celtic tribes, driven by their enemies to the outer fringes of Europe, settled in Scotland, as they did in Ireland, Cornwall, Wales and Brittany, and mastered iron implements. The blueprint for a tribal society was in place.

It was the Romans who gave it coherence. The desire of Emperor Vespasian in AD 80 to forge northwards from an already subjugated southern Britain towards the Grampian Mountains and the dense forests of central Scotland united the tribes in opposition. To their surprise, the Romans, who called the natives "painted men", encountered fearsome opposition. An early Scots leader, called Calgacus by the Romans, rallied 30,000 men – a remarkable force but unfortunately no match for the Roman war machine. Even so, the Romans respected their enemy's ability enough for the historian Tacitus to feel able to attribute to Calgacus the anti-Roman sentiment: "They make a wilderness and call it peace".

Soon, however, the "barbarians" began to perfect guerrilla tactics. In the year 118, for instance, the Ninth Legion marched north to quell yet another rebellion and was never seen again. Was it really worth all this trouble, the Romans wondered, to subdue such barbarians?

Hadrian's answer, as emperor, was no. He built a fortified wall that stretched for 73 miles (117 km) across the north of England, isolating the savages. A successor, Antoninus, tried to push back the boundaries in 142 by erecting a fortified wall between the Rivers Forth and the Clyde. But it was never an effective exercise. The Roman Empire fell without ever conquering these troublesome natives and Scottish life carried on without the more lasting benefits of Roman civilisation, such as good roads. A com-

plex clan system evolved, consisting of large families bound by blood ties.

Dark Ages

Europe's Dark Ages enveloped the region. What records remain portray raiders riding south to plunder and pillage. True Scots were born in the 6th century when Gaels migrated from the north of Ireland, inaugurating an epoch in which beautifully drawn manuscripts and brilliant metalwork illuminated the cultural darkness.

Like much of Western Europe, Scotland's history at this time was a catalogue of invasions. The most relentless aggressors were the Vikings, who arrived in the 9th century in their

Scandinavian longships to loot the monasteries which had been founded by early Christian missionaries such as St Ninian and St Columba.

Eventually, in 843, the warring Picts – a fierce Celtic race who dominated the southwest – united with the Scots under Kenneth MacAlpin, the astute ruler of the west coast Kingdom of Dalriada. But Edinburgh wasn't brought under the king's influence until 962 and the Angles, a Teutonic people who controlled the south of the country, were not subjugated until

Margaret, a Hungarian-born Christian reformer and strong supporter of English standards. Partly to please her, Malcolm invaded England twice. During the second incursion, he lost his life. This gave William Rufus, the Conqueror's son and successor, an opportunity to involve himself in Scottish affairs by securing the northern throne for Malcolm's eldest son, Edgar, the first of a series of weak kings. A successor, David I, having been brought up in England, gave many estates to his Norman

> **ROYAL STANDARDS**
>
> Some believe it was Queen Margaret who gave the Scots their eternal inferiority complex by forcing them to measure themselves against the English.

1018. Feuding for power was continuous. It was in this period that Macbeth murdered his rival, Duncan, and was killed in turn by Duncan's son.

Norman conquest

The collapse of England to William the Conqueror in 1066 drove many of the English lords northwards, turning the Lowlands of Scotland into an aristocratic refugee camp. Scotland's king, Malcolm, married one of the refugees,

LEFT: Roman panel from Glasgow University's Hunterian Museum.
ABOVE: William Wallace rallies his Scottish forces against the English.

friends. Also, he did nothing to stop English replacing Gaelic and he introduced feudalism into the Lowlands.

But true feudalism never really took root. French knights, accustomed to deference, were surprised to find, when they rode through a field of crops, that the impertinent Scottish peasants would demand compensation. Although the Normans greatly influenced architecture and language, they in no sense conquered the country. Instead, they helped create a social division that was to dominate Scotland's history: the Lowlands were controlled by noblemen who spoke the same Norman French and subscribed to the same values as England's ruling class, while the Highlands remained untamed, under the influence of independent-minded Gaelic speakers, and the islands were loyal, more or less, to Norway.

The Highland clans, indeed, were virtually independent kingdoms,whose chiefs, under the old patriarchal system, had the power of life and death over their people. Feuds between clans were frequent and bloody, provoking one visiting scholar to pronounce: "The Scots are not industrious and the people are poor. They spend all their time in wars and, when there is no war, they fight one another."

Over the next three centuries the border with

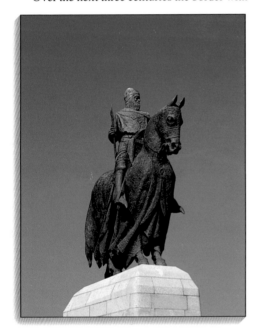

England was to be constantly redefined. The seaport of Berwick-upon-Tweed, now the most northerly town in England, was to change hands 13 times. In the 1160s the Scots turned to French sympathisers for help, concluding what came to be known as the Auld Alliance. In later years the pact would have a profound influence on Scottish life, but on this occasion it was no match for England's might.

After a comparatively peaceful interlude, England's insidious interference provoked a serious backlash in 1297. William Wallace, a violent youth from Elderslie, became an outlaw after a scuffle with English soldiers in which a girl (some think she was his wife) who helped

him escape was killed herself by the Sheriff of Lanark. Wallace returned to kill the Sheriff, but didn't stop there; soon he had raised enough of an army to drive back the English forces, making him for some months master of southern Scotland.

But Wallace wasn't supported by the nobles, who considered him low-born, and, after being defeated at Falkirk by England's Edward I (the "Hammer of the Scots"), he met his expected fate by being hanged, drawn and quartered. His quarters were sent to Newcastle, Berwick, Sterling and Perth.

Bruce's victory

The next challenger, Robert the Bruce, who was descended from the Norman de Brus family, got further as a freedom fighter – as far as the throne itself, in fact, though he didn't sit on it long. During a year's exile on Rathlin Island, off the coast of Ireland, he is said to have been inspired by the persistence of a spider building its web in a cave and he returned to Scotland full of determination and proceeded to win a series of victories. Soon the French recognised him as King of Scotland and the Roman Catholic Church gave him its backing.

England's new king, Edward II, although he had little stomach for Scottish affairs, could not ignore the challenge and, in 1314, the two forces collided at Bannockburn, south of Stirling. Bruce's chances looked slim: he was pitching only 6,000 men against a force of 20,000 English. But he was shrewd enough to hold the high ground, forcing the English into the wet marshes, and he won.

Because the Pope did not recognise the new monarch, Bruce's subjects successfully petitioned Rome, and the Declaration of Arbroath in 1320 confirmed him as King.

Like the Romans, England's Edward III decided that Scotland was more trouble than it was worth and in 1328 granted it independence. He recognised Bruce as king and, cementing the treaty in the customary manner, married his young sister to Bruce's baby son. Peace had been achieved at last between two of the most rancorous of neighbours. It seemed too good to be true – and it was. ❑

ABOVE LEFT: Robert the Bruce's statue in Stirling.
RIGHT: Bruce kills Sir Henry de Bohun in single combat at Bannockburn.

Robert Bruce sends a defiance to Edward III.

BATTLE FOR THE THRONE

For centuries the throne of Scotland was a source of conflict,
inextricably part of the turbulent relationship with England

The outbreak in 1339 of the intermittent Hundred Years' War between England and France kept Edward III's mind off Scotland. He failed, therefore, to appreciate the significance of a pact concluded in 1326 between France and Scotland by Robert the Bruce. Yet the Auld Alliance, as the pact came to be known, was to keep English ambitions at bay for centuries and at one point almost resulted in Scotland becoming a province of France.

Principal beneficiaries of the deal were the kings of the Stewart (or Stuart) family. Taking their name from their function as High Stewarts to the king, they were descended from the Fitzalans, Normans who came to England with William the Conqueror in 1066.

When the Bruce family failed to produce a male heir, the crown passed in 1371 to the Stewarts because Marjorie, Robert the Bruce's daughter, had married Walter Fitzalan. The first of the Stewarts, Robert II, faced a problem that was to plague his successors: he had constantly to look over his shoulder at England, yet he could never ignore another threat to his power – his own dissident barons and warring chieftains.

Youthful monarchs

His son, Robert III, trusted these ambitious men so little that he sent his oldest son, James, to France for safety. But the ship carrying him was waylaid and young James fell into the hands of England's Henry IV. He grew up in the English court and didn't return to Scotland (as James I) until 1422, at the age of 29. His friendliness with the English was soon strained to breaking point, however, and he renewed the Auld Alliance, siding with France's Charles VII and Joan of Arc against the English. But soon James was murdered, stabbed to death before his wife by his uncle, a cousin and another noble.

His son, James II, succeeded at the age of six, setting another Stewart pattern: monarchs who came to the throne as minors, creating what has

been called an infantile paralysis of the power structure. In 1460 James, fighting to recapture Roxburgh from the English, died when one of his own siege guns exploded. James III, another boy king, succeeded. He had time to marry a Danish princess (in the process bringing the Norse islands of Orkney and Shetland into the

realm) before he was locked in Edinburgh Castle by the scheming barons and replaced by his more malleable younger brother. The arrangement didn't last and soon James's son, James IV, was crowned king, aged 15.

This latest James cemented relations with England in 1503 by marrying Margaret Tudor, the 12-year-old daughter of Henry VII, the Welsh warrior who had usurped the English throne 18 years before. The harmony was short-lived: the French talked James into attacking England and he was killed at the battle of Flodden Hill. It was Scotland's worst defeat to the English, wiping out the cream of a generation, and some argue that the country never recovered

---

LEFT: Robert Bruce meets with Edward III.
ABOVE RIGHT: Edward III takes Berwick in 1333.

from the blow. James's heir, predictably, was also called James and was just over a year old. The power-brokers could continue plotting.

Torn between the French connection and the ambitions of England's Henry VIII, who tried to enrol him in his anti-Catholic campaign, the young James V declared his loyalties by marrying two Frenchwomen in succession. Life expectation was short, however, for kings as well as for peasants, and James V died in 1542 just as his second queen, Marie de Guise, gave birth to a daughter. At less than a week old, the infant was proclaimed Mary Queen of Scots.

Ever an opportunist, Henry VIII despatched an invasion force which reduced Edinburgh, apart from its castle, to rubble. It was known as a "Rough Wooing" and left hatred that would last for centuries. The immediate question was: should Scotland ally itself with Catholic France or Protestant England? In the ensuing tug-of-war between the English and the French, the infant Mary was taken to France for safety and, when 15, married the French Dauphin. The Auld Alliance seemed to have taken on a new life and Mary made a will bequeathing Scotland to France if she died childless.

When the King of France died in 1558, Mary, still aged only 16, ascended the throne with her

PREACHERS OF FIRE

The bid for power by a Catholic – Mary – set alarm bells ringing among Protestants. Their faith had been forged in fire, with early preachers such as George Wishart burned at the stake, and it contained little room for compromise. The Protestants' visionary was John Knox, a magnetic speaker and former priest whose aim, inspired by Calvinism, was to drive Catholicism out of Scotland. His followers had pledged themselves by signing the First Covenant to "forsake and renounce the congregation of Satan", and carrying Calvin's doctines to extremes by outlawing the Latin Mass throughout Scotland.

husband. Her ambitions, though, didn't end there: she later declared herself Queen of England as well, basing her claim on the Catholic assumption that England's new queen, Elizabeth I, was illegitimate because her father, the much married Henry VIII, had been a heretic.

Royal drama

When Mary's husband died in 1560, she returned to Scotland, a vivacious, wilful and attractive woman. She married a Catholic, Henry Darnley, who was by contemporary accounts an arrogant, pompous and effeminate idler, and soon she began spending more and more time with her secretary David Rizzio, an

Italian. When Rizzio was stabbed to death in front of her, Darnley was presumed to be responsible, but who could prove it? Mary appeared to turn back to Darnley and, a few months later, gave birth to a son. Immediately afterwards, however, Darnley himself was murdered, his strangled remains found in a building reduced to rubble by an explosion. Mary and her current favourite, James Hepburn, Earl of Bothwell, were presumed responsible – but again, who could prove it?

Bothwell, a Protestant, quickly divorced his wife and, with few fanfares, became Mary's third husband, three months after Darnley's

cousin, Elizabeth I. Her previous claim to the English throne, however, had not been forgotten. Elizabeth offered her the bleak hospitality of various mansions, in which she remained a prisoner for the next 20 years. In 1587 she was convicted, on somewhat flimsy evidence, of plotting Elizabeth's death and was beheaded at Fotheringay Castle.

Southern prospects

Mary's son, by this time secure on the Scottish throne, made little more than a token protest. Because Elizabeth, the Virgin Queen, had no heir, James had his sights set on a far greater

death. Even Mary had gone too far this time. Protestant Scotland forced its Catholic queen, still only 24, to abdicate, locking her in an island castle on Loch Leven. Bothwell fled to Norway, where he died in exile. And so, in 1567, another infant king came to the throne: Mary's son, James VI.

Still fact rivalled fiction. Mary escaped from Loch Leven, tried unsuccessfully to reach France, then threw herself on the mercy of her

prize than Scotland could offer: the throne of England. On 27 March 1603 he learned that the prize was his. On hearing of Elizabeth's death, he set out for London, and was to set foot in Scotland only once more in his life.

Scots have speculated ever since about how differently history would have turned out had James VI of Scotland made Edinburgh rather than London his base when he became James I of England. But he was more in sympathy with the divine right of kings than with the notions of the ultra-democratic Presbyterians, who were demanding a strong say in civil affairs. And, as he wrote, ruling from a distance of 400 miles was so much easier.

FAR LEFT: Robert Herdman's portrait of the execution of Mary Queen of Scots.
ABOVE LEFT: Scottish border raiders.
ABOVE RIGHT: James I of England.

His son Charles succeeded to the throne in 1625, not knowing Scotland at all. Without, therefore, realising the consequences, the absentee king tried to harmonise the forms of church service between the two countries.

Conflict and civil war

The Scots would have none of it: religious riots broke out and one bishop is said to have conducted his service with two loaded pistols placed in front of him. A National Covenant was organised, pledging faith to "the true religion" and affirming the unassailable authority in spiritual matters of the powerful General Assembly

Cavalier supporters of the king. Charles tried to gain the Scots' support by promising a three-year trial for Presbyterianism in England. But his time had run out: he was beheaded on 30 January 1649.

Charles's execution came as a terrible shock north of the border. How dare England kill the king of Scotland without consulting the Scots! Many turned to Charles's 18-year-old son, who had undertaken not to oppose Presbyterianism, and he was proclaimed Charles II in Edinburgh. But Cromwell won a decisive victory at the Battle of Dunbar and turned Scotland into an occupied country, abolishing its separate parliament.

of the Church of Scotland. Armed conflict soon followed: in 1639 the Scots invaded northern England, forcing Charles to negotiate.

Soon the king's luck ran out in England too. Needing money, he unwisely called together his parliament for the first time in 10 years. A power struggle ensued, leading swiftly to civil war. At first the Scottish Covenanters (so named because of their support for the National Covenant of 1638) backed Parliament and the Roundhead forces of Oliver Cromwell; their hope was that a victorious Parliament would introduce compulsory Presbyterianism in English and Irish churches as well as in Scotland. Soon the Roundheads began to outpace the

By the time the monarchy was restored in 1660, Charles II had lost interest in Scotland's religious aspirations and removed much of the Presbyterian church's power. Violent intolerance stalked the land during his reign and the 1680s became known as the Killing Time. The risk to Covenanters increased when, after Charles died of apoplexy in 1685, his brother James, a Catholic, became king. With the rotten judgement that dogged the Stewart line, James II imposed the death penalty for worshipping as a Covenanter. His power base in London soon crumbled, however, and in 1689 he was deposed in favour of his Protestant nephew and son-in-law, William of Orange.

Some Scots, mostly Highlanders, remained true to James. The Jacobites, as they were called, rose under Graham of Claverhouse and almost annihilated William's army in a fierce battle at Killiecrankie in 1689. However, Claverhouse was killed, leaving the Jacobites leaderless; most of them lost heart and returned to the Highlands.

Determined to exert his authority over the Scots, William demanded that every clan leader swear an oath of loyalty to him. Partly because of the bad

ACT OF DISUNION

"We are bought and sold for English gold," the Scots sang following the Treaty of Union of 1707. Like so many Scottish songs, it was a lament.

MacDonald younger than 70 to the sword. The Campbells were only too pleased to carry out their commission and the Massacre of Glencoe in 1692 remains one of the bloodiest dates in Scotland's bloodstained history. The barbarity of the massacre produced a public outcry, not so much because of the number killed but because of the abuse of hospitality.

Queen Anne, the second daughter of James II, succeeded William in 1702. Although she had given birth to 17 children, none had survived and the

weather, partly through a misunderstanding of where the swearing would take place, one chieftain, the head of the Clan MacDonald, took his oath several days after the king's deadline.

Bloody massacre

Here was a chance to make an example of a prominent leader. Members of the Campbell clan, old enemies of the MacDonalds, were ordered to lodge with the MacDonalds at their home in Glencoe, get to know them and then, having won their confidence, put every

Left: Scottish Covenanters meet in Edinburgh.
Above: grief after the Massacre of Glencoe.

English establishment was determined to keep both thrones out of Stewart hands. They turned to Sophie of Hanover, a granddaughter of James VI/James I. If the Scots would agree to accept a Hanoverian line of succession, much needed trade concessions would be granted. There was one other condition: England and Scotland should unite under one parliament.

As so often before, riots broke out in Edinburgh and elsewhere. But the opposition was fragmented and, in 1707, a Treaty of Union incorporated the Scottish parliament into the Westminster parliament to create the United Kingdom. Unknown to the signatories, the foundation of the British Empire was being laid. ❑

THE AGE OF REBELLION

The 18th and 19th centuries witnessed rebellions in Scotland not only against the union, but also in ideas, industry, agriculture and the Church

The ink was hardly dry on the Treaty of Union of 1707 when the Scots began to smart under the new constitutional arrangements. The idea of a union with England had never been popular with the working classes, most of whom saw it (rightly) as a sell-out by the aristocracy to the "Auld Enemy". Scotland's businessmen were outraged by the imposition of hefty, English-style excise duties on many goods and the high-handed Government bureaucracy that went with them. The aristocracy who had supported the Union resented Westminster's peremptory abolition of Scotland's privy council. Even the hardline Cameronians – the fiercest of Protestants – roundly disliked the Union in the early years of the 18th century.

Jacobite insurgency

All of which was compounded by the Jacobitism (support for the Stuarts) which haunted many parts of Scotland, particularly among the Episcopalians of Aberdeenshire, Angus and Perthshire, and among the Catholic clans (such as the MacDonalds) of the Western Highlands.

And, given that one of the main planks of Jacobitism was the repeal of the Union, it was hardly surprising that the Stuart kings cast a long shadow over Scotland in the first half of the 18th century. In fact, within a year of the Treaty of Union being signed, the first Jacobite insurgency was under way, helped by a French regime ever anxious to discomfit the power of the English.

In January 1708 a flotilla of French privateers commanded by Comte Claude de Forbin battered its way through the North Sea gales carrying the 19-year-old James Stuart, the self-styled James VIII and III. After a brief sojourn in the Firth of Forth near the coast of Fife the French privateers were chased round

the top of Scotland and out into the Atlantic by English warships, Many of the French vessels foundered on their way back to France, although James survived to go on plotting. On dry land, the uprising of 1708 was confined to a few East Stirlingshire lairds who marched up and down with a handful of men. They were

quickly rounded up, and in November 1708 five of the ringleaders were tried in Edinburgh for treason. The verdict on all five was "not proven" and they were set free. Shocked by this display of Scottish leniency, the British Parliament passed the Treason Act of 1708, which brought Scotland into line with England, ensuring traitors a long and grisly death.

The next Jacobite uprising, in 1715, was a more serious affair. By then disaffection in Scotland with the Union was widespread, the Hanoverians had not totally secured their grip on Britain, there were loud pro-Stuart mutterings in England, and much of Britain had been stripped of its military.

PRECEDING PAGES: David Morier's portrayal of Culloden, painted in 1746. **LEFT:** Prince Charles Edward Stuart leaving Scotland, from a painting by J.B. MacDonald, and **ABOVE**, in his finery as the Young Chevalier.

An odd outcome

But the insurrection was led by the Earl of Mar, a military incompetent known as "Bobbing John", whose support came mainly from the clans of the Central and Eastern Highlands. When the two sides clashed at Sheriffmuir near Stirling on 13 November, Mar's Jacobite army had a four-to-one advantage over the tiny Hanoverian force commanded by "Red John of the Battles" (as the Duke of Argyll was known). But, instead of pressing his huge advantage,

> ### SPANISH SURRENDER
>
> There is still a niche up in the Kintail mountains called Bealach-n-Spainnteach – The Pass of the Spaniards – recalling the rout suffered by the Spanish in 1719.

Stuarts trying again. In 1719 it was the Spaniards who decided to try to queer the Hanoverian pitch by backing the Jacobites. Again it was a fiasco. In March 1719 a little force of 307 Spanish soldiers sailed into Loch Alsh where they joined up with a few hundred Murrays, Mackenzies and Mackintoshes. This Spanish-Jacobite stage army was easily routed in the steep pass of Glenshiel by a British unit which swooped down from Inverness to pound the Jacobite positions with their

Mar withdrew his Highland army after an inconclusive clash.

The insurrection of 1715 quickly ran out of steam. The Pretender himself did not arrive in Scotland until the end of December and the forces he brought with him were too little, and too late. He did his cause no good by stealing away at night (along with "Bobbing John" and a few others), leaving his followers to the wrath of the Whigs. The Duke of Argyll was sacked as commander of the Government forces for fear he would be too lenient. Dozens of rebels – especially the English – were hanged, drawn and quartered, and hundreds were deported.

Not that the débâcle of 1715 stopped the

mortars. The Highlanders simply vanished into the mist and snow of Kintail, leaving the wretched Spaniards in their gold-on-white uniforms to wander about the sub-arctic landscape before surrendering to the British troops.

The Young Pretender

But it was the insurrection of 1745, "so glorious an enterprise", led by Charles Edward Stuart (Bonnie Prince Charlie), which shook Britain, despite the fact that the Government's grip on the turbulent parts of Scotland had never seemed firmer. There were military depots at Fort William, Fort Augustus and Fort George, and an effective Highland militia (later known as the

Black Watch) had been raised. General Wade had thrown a network of military roads and bridges across the Highlands. Logically Charles, the Young Pretender, should never have been allowed to set foot out of the Highlands.

But having set up a military "infrastructure" in the Highlands, the British Government had neglected it. The Independent Companies (the Black Watch) had been shunted out to the West Indies, there were fewer than 4,000 troops in the whole of Scotland, hardly any cavalry or artillery, and Clan Campbell was no longer an effective fighting force. The result was that Bonnie Prince Charlie and his ragtag army of MacDonalds,

cious little support for his cause in the Lowlands of Scotland. Few Jacobite troops had been raised in Edinburgh, and Glasgow and the southwest were openly hostile. Some men had been drummed up in Manchester, but there was no serious support from the Roman Catholic families of northern England. Charles got as far as Derby and then fled back to Scotland with two powerful Hanoverian armies hot on his heels.

Dashed hopes

After winning a rearguard action at Clifton, near Penrith, and what has been described as a "lucky victory" at Falkirk in January 1746, the

Camerons, Mackintoshes, Robertsons, McGregors, Macphersons and Gordons, plus some lowland cavalry and a stiffening of Franco-Irish mercenaries, was able to walk into Edinburgh and set up a "royal court" in Holyrood Palace.

In September the Young Pretender sallied out of Edinburgh and wrecked General John Copy's panicky Hanoverian army near Prestonpans, and then marched across the border into England. But Stuart's success was an illusion. There was pre-

Jacobite army was cut to pieces by the Duke of Cumberland's artillery on Drummossie Moor, Culloden, near Inverness on 16 April 1746. It was the last great pitched battle on the soil of mainland Britain. It was also the end of the Gaelic clan system, which had survived in the mountains of Scotland long after it had disappeared from Ireland. The days when an upland-chieftain could drum up a "tail" of trained swordsmen for cattle raids into the Lowlands were over.

Following his post-Culloden "flight across the heather", Charles, disguised as a woman servant, was given shelter on the Isle of Skye by Flora MacDonald, thus giving birth to one of

FAR LEFT: Culloden's victor, the Duke of Cumberland.
ABOVE LEFT: Prince Charlie's much romanticised farewell in 1746 to Flora MacDonald.
ABOVE RIGHT: Culloden remembered.

Scotland's abiding romantic tales. He was then plucked off the Scottish coast by a French privateer and taken into exile, drunkenness and despair in France and Italy. A few dozen of the more prominent Jacobites were hauled off to Carlisle and Newcastle where they were tried, and some of them hanged. The estates of the gentry who had "come out" in '45 were confiscated by the Crown. And for some time the Highlands were harried mercilessly by the Duke of Cumberland's troopers (the fiercest of whom were probably Lowland Scots).

In an effort to subdue the Highlands, the government in London passed the Disarming Act of 1746, which not only banned the carrying of claymores, targes, dirks and muskets, but also the wearing of tartans and the playing of bagpipes. It was a nasty piece of legislation, but never much of a success. The British Government also took the opportunity to abolish Scotland's inefficient and often corrupt system of "Courts of Regality" by which the aristocracy (and not just the Highland variety) dispensed justice, collected fines and wielded powers of life and wealth.

Age of enlightenment

It is one of the minor paradoxes of 18th-century European history that, while Scotland was being racked by dynastic convulsions which were 17th-century in origin, the country was transforming itself into one of the most forward-looking societies in the world. Scotland began to wake up in the first half of the 18th century. By about 1740 the intellectual, scientific and mercantile phenomenon which became known as the Scottish Enlightenment was well under way, although it didn't reach its peak until the end of the century.

Whatever created it, the Scottish Enlightenment was an extraordinary explosion of creativity and energy. And while, in retrospect at least, the period was dominated by David Hume the philosopher and Adam Smith the economist, there were many others, such as William Robertson, Adam Ferguson, William Cullen, and the Adam brothers. Through the multifaceted talents of its literati, Scotland in general and Edinburgh in particular became one of the intellectual powerhouses of Western Europe.

But the Enlightenment and all that went with it had some woeful side-effects. The Highland "Clearances" of the late 18th and early 19th century owed much to the "improving" attitudes triggered by the Enlightenment, although the greed of the lairds played its part. The enterprising Sir John Sinclair, for example, pointed out that, while the Highlands were capable of producing from £200,000 to £300,000 worth of black cattle every year, "the same ground will produce twice as much mutton and there is wool into the bargain."

The argument proved irresistible. Sheep – particularly Cheviots – and their Lowland shepherds began to flood into the glens and straths of the Highlands, displacing the Highland "tacksmen" and their families. Thousands were

forced to move to the Lowlands, coastal areas, or in the colonies overseas, taking with them their culture of songs and traditions.

The worst of the Clearances – or at least the most notorious – took place on the huge estates of the Countess of Sutherland and her rich, English-born husband, the Marquis of Stafford. Although Stafford spent huge sums of money building roads, harbours and fish-curing sheds (for very little profit), his estate managers evicted tenants with real ruthlessness. It was a pattern which was repeated all over Highland

Above: a Skye crofter prepares some winter comfort.
Above Right: Glasgow in the 18th century.

Scotland at the beginning of the 19th century, and then again later when people were displaced by the red deer of the "sporting" estates. The overgrown remains of villages all over the Highlands are a painful reminder of this sad chapter in Scottish history.

Radicals and reactionaries

As the industrial economy of Lowland Scotland burgeoned at the end of the 18th century, it sucked in thousands of immigrant workers from all over Scotland and Ireland. The clamour for democracy grew. Some of it was fuelled by the ideas of the American and French revolutions, but much of the unrest was a reaction to Scotland's hopelessly inadequate electoral system. At the end of the 18th century there were only 4,500 voters in the whole of Scotland and only 2,600 voters in the 33 rural countries.

And for almost 40 years Scotland was dominated by the powerful machine politician Henry Dundas, the First Viscount Melville, universally known as "King Harry the Ninth". As Solicitor General, Lord Advocate, Home Secretary, Secretary for War and then First Lord of the Admiralty, Dundas wielded awesome power.

But nothing could stop the spread of libertarian ideas in an increasingly industrialised

INDUSTRIAL GLORY

The Enlightenment was not confined to the salons of Edinburgh. Commerce and industry also thrived. "The same age, which produces great philosophers and politicians, renowned generals and poets, usually abounds with skilled weavers and ship-carpenters," David Hume wrote in 1752.

By 1760 the famous Carron Ironworks in Falkirk was churning out high-grade ordnance for the British military. By 1780 hundreds of tons of goods were being shuttled between Edinburgh and Glasgow along the Forth-Clyde canal. The Turnpike Act of 1751 improved the road system dramatically and created a brisk demand for carriages and stage-coaches. In 1738 Scotland's share of the tobacco trade (based in Glasgow) was 10 percent; by 1769 it was more than 52 percent. There was a huge upsurge of activity in many trades: carpet weaving, upholstery, glass making, china and pottery manufacture, linen, soap, distilling and brewing.

The 18th century changed Scotland from one of the poorest countries in Europe to a state of middling affluence. It has been calculated that between 1700 and 1800 the money generated within Scotland increased by a factor of more than 50, while the population stayed more or less static (at around 1 1/2 million).

workforce. The ideas contained in Tom Paine's *Rights of Man* spread like wildfire in the Scotland of the 1790s. The cobblers, weavers and spinners proved the most vociferous democrats, but there was also unrest among farmworkers, and among seamen and soldiers in the Highland regiments.

Throughout the 1790s a number of radical "one man, one vote" organisations sprang up, such as the Scottish Friends of the People and the United Scotsmen (a quasi-nationalist group which modelled itself on the

KING HARRY THE NINTH

The 19th-century judge Lord Cockburn summed up the relentless grip of Henry Dundas on Scotland: "Who steered upon him was safe; who disregarded his light was wrecked."

noia of the Scottish ruling class lingered on. Establishment panic reached a peak in 1820 when the so-called Scottish Insurrection was brought to an end in the legally-corrupt trial of the weavers James Wilson, John Baird, Andrew Hardie and 21 other workmen. A special (English) Court of Oyer and Terminer was set up in Glasgow to hear the case, and Wilson, Baird and Hardie were sentenced to be hanged, beheaded and quartered. They were spared the latter part of the sentence.

United Irishmen of Wolfe Tone).

But the brooding figure of Dundas was more than a match for the radicals. Every organisation which raised its head was swiftly infiltrated by police spies and *agents provocateurs*. Ringleaders (such as the advocate Thomas Muir) were framed, arrested, tried and deported. Some, such as Robert Watt who led the "Pike Plot" of 1794, were hanged. Meetings were broken up by dragoons, riots were put down by musket-fire, the Scottish universities were racked by witchhunts.

Although Dundas himself was discredited in 1806, after being impeached for embezzlement, and died in 1811, the anti-Radical para-

Reform and disruption

By the 1820s most of Scotland (and indeed Britain) was weary of the political and constitutional corruption under which the country laboured. In 1823 Lord Archibald Hamilton pointed out the electoral absurdity of rural Scotland. "I have the right to vote in five counties in Scotland, in not one of which do I possess an acre of land," he said, "and I have no doubt that if I took the trouble I might have a vote for every county in that kingdom." Hamilton's motion calling for parliamentary reform was defeated by only 35 votes.

But nine years later, in 1832, the Reform Bill finally passed into law, giving Scotland 30 rural constituencies, 23 burgh constituencies and a voting population of 65,000 (compared to a previous 4,500). Even this limited extension of the franchise – to male householders whose property had a rentable value of £10 or more – generated much wailing and gnashing of teeth among Scottish Tories.

No sooner had the controversy over electoral reform subsided than it was replaced by the row between the "moderates" and the "evangelicals" within the Church of Scotland. "Scotland," Lord Palmerston noted at the time, "is aflame about the church question." But this was no genteel falling-out among theologians. It was a brutal and bruising affair which dominated political life in Scotland for 10 years and raised all kinds of constitutional questions.

At the heart of the argument was the Patronage Act of 1712, which gave Scots lairds the same right English squires had to appoint, or "intrude" clergy on local congregations. Ever since it was passed, the Church of Scotland had argued (rightly) that the Patronage Act was a flagrant and illegal violation of the Revolution Settlement of 1690 and the Treaty of Union of 1707, both of which guaranteed the independence of the Church of Scotland.

Free Church

But the pleas fell on deaf ears. The English-dominated parliament could see no fault in a system which enabled Anglicised landowners to appoint like-minded clergymen. Patronage was seen by the Anglo-Scottish establishment as a useful instrument of political control and social progress. The issue came to a head in May 1843 when the evangelicals, led by Dr Thomas Chalmers, marched out of the annual General Assembly of the Church of Scotland in Edinburgh to form the Free Church of Scotland.

Chalmers, theologian, astronomer and brilliant organiser, defended the Free Church against bitter enemies. His final triumph, in 1847, was to persuade the London parliament that it was folly to allow the aristocracy to refuse the Free Church land on which to build churches and schools. A few days after giving evidence, Chalmers died in Edinburgh.

LEFT: a 19th-century poster, now on display in Glasgow's People's Palace.
ABOVE RIGHT: Scottish Presbyterians in the 17th century defying the law to worship.

The rebellion of the evangelicals was brilliantly planned, well funded and took the British establishment completely by surprise. Four hundred teachers left the kirk and, within 10 years of the Disruption, the Free Church had built more than 800 churches, 700 manses, three large theological colleges and 600 schools, and brought about a huge extension of education. After 1847, state aid had to be given to the Free as well as to the established Church schools, and in 1861 the established Church lost its legal powers over Scotland's parish school system. This prepared the ground for the Education Act of 1872, which set up a national system under

the Scottish Educational Department. And, although it ran into some vicious opposition from landowners, especially in the Highlands, the Free Church prevailed.

In fact, it can be argued that the Disruption was the only rebellion in 18th- or 19th-century British history that succeeded. Chalmers and his supporters had challenged both the pervasive influence of the Anglo-Scottish aristocracy and the power of the British Parliament, and they had won. The Patronage Act of 1712 was finally repealed in 1874, and the Free Church re-merged with the Church of Scotland in 1929, the two becoming the United Established Church of Scotland ❏.

THE MAKING OF MODERN SCOTLAND

Despite the economic and social problems of the 20th century, Scotland remains

fiercely confident, particularly in moves towards political independence

During the Victorian and Edwardian eras, Scotland, like most of Europe, became urbanised and industrialised. Steelworks, ironworks, shipyards, coal mines, shale-oil refineries, textile factories, engineering shops, canals and of course railways proliferated all over 19th-century Scotland. The process was concentrated in Scotland's "central belt" (the stretch of low-lying land between Edinburgh and Glasgow), but there were important "out-liers" like Aberdeen, Dundee, Ayrshire and the mill-towns of the Scottish borders. A few smaller industrial ventures found their way deep into the Highlands or onto a few small islands.

It was a process which dragged in its wake profound social, cultural and demographic change. The booming industries brought thousands of work-seeking immigrants flocking into lowland Scotland. Most came from the Highlands and Ireland, and many nursed an ancient distaste for the British establishment which translated itself into left-wing radicalism. Scots of Irish descent are still the main prop of the Labour Party in Scotland. The immigrants were also largely Roman Catholic, which did something to loosen the grip of the Presbyterian churches on Scottish life.

Huge metropolis

Industry transformed the city of Glasgow and the River Clyde. Between 1740 and 1840 Glasgow's population leapt from 17,000 to 200,000 and then doubled to 400,000 by 1870. The small Georgian city became a huge industrial metropolis built on the kind of rectangular grid common in the United States, with industrial princes living in splendour while Highland, Irish, Italian and Jewish immigrants swarmed in the noisome slums.

In many ways 19th-century Glasgow had more in common with Chicago or New York

than with any other city in Britain. Working-class conditions were appalling. Rickets, cholera, smallpox, tuberculosis, diphtheria and alcoholism were rampant. The streets were unclean and distinctly unsafe. Violence was endemic as Highlanders and Irishmen clashed in the stews and whisky dens, while Orangemen

from Ulster were used as violent and murderous strike-breakers. The city hangman was never short of work.

But there was no denying Glasgow's enormous industrial vitality. By the middle of the century the city was peppered with more than 100 textile mills (an industry which by that time employed more than 400,000 Scots). There were ironworks at Tollcross, Coatbridge and Monklands, productive coal mines all over Lanarkshire and the River Clyde was lined with boiler makers, marine-engineering shops, and world-class shipyards. For generations the label "Clyde built" was synonymous with industrial quality.

Nor was industry confined to Glasgow and its

PRECEDING PAGES: the elegant Edinburgh residence of Scotland's Secretary of State.

LEFT: *First Steamboat on the Clyde*, by John Knox.

ABOVE RIGHT: slum dwellers in Glasgow's Gorbals.

environs. The Tayside city of Dundee forged close links with India and became the biggest jute-manufacturing centre in Britain. The Carron Ironworks at Falkirk was Europe's largest producer of artillery by the year 1800; whilst in West Lothian a thriving industry was built up to extract oil from shale. Scotland's east-coast fisheries also flourished, and by the end of the century the town of Wick in Caithness became Europe's biggest herring port.

As well as producing large quantities of books, biscuits and bureaucrats, Edinburgh was a centre of the British brewing industry; at one stage there were more than 40 breweries within the city boundaries. And, in the latter part of the 19th century, the Scotch whisky industry boomed, thanks to the devastation of the French vineyards in the 1880s by phylloxera which almost wrecked the thriving cognac industry.

Rich and poor

By the end of the 19th century, Scotland, with its educated workforce and proximity to European markets, was attracting inward investment. The American-funded North British Rubber Company moved into Edinburgh in 1857. In 1884 the Singer Company built one of the biggest factories in the world at Clydebank to

CASH INCENTIVES

The growth of industry in Scotland generated huge amounts of cash. Edinburgh and Dundee became centres for investment trusts which sunk cash into ventures all over the world, particularly the USA. In 1873 the Dundee jute man Robert Fleming set up the Scottish American Investment Trust to channel money into American cattle ranches, fruit farms, mining companies and railways. The biggest cattle ranch in the USA – Matador Land & Cattle Company – was run from Dundee until 1951. The outlaw Butch Cassidy once worked for a cattle company operated from the fastidious New Town of Edinburgh.

manufacture mass-produced sewing machines. It was the start of a 100-year trend which has done much to undermine the Scottish economy's independence.

Despite the enthusiasm of Queen Victoria and the British gentry for the Highlands, dire poverty stalked upland Scotland. Land reform was desperately needed. Following riots in Skye in 1882 and the formation of the Highland Land League in 1884, Gladstone's Liberal government passed the Crofters (Scotland) Holdings Act of 1886, which gave crofters fair rents, security of tenure and the right to pass their croft on to their families. But it was Lord Salisbury's Conservative government who put the Scottish Secretary in the

British cabinet, and established the Scottish Office in Edinburgh and London in 1886.

By the end of the 19th century the huge majority of the Scottish population was urban, industrialised and concentrated in the towns and cities of the Lowlands. And urban Scotland proved a fertile breeding ground for the British Left. The Scottish Labour Party (SLP) was founded in 1888, although it soon merged with the Independent Labour Party (ILP), which in turn played a big part in the formation of the (British) Labour Party. Britain's first Labour MP, Keir Hardie, was a Scot, as was Ramsay MacDonald, Britain's first Labour prime minister.

percent of the British Army. And when the butcher's bill was added up after the war it was found that more than 20 percent of all the Britons killed were Scots.

In addition to which, the shipyards of the Clyde and the engineering shops of West Central Scotland were producing more tanks, shells, warships, explosives and fieldguns than any comparable part of Britain. That explains why the British Government took such a dim view of the strikes and industrial disputes which hit the Clyde between 1915 and 1919 and led to the area being dubbed "Red Clydeside". When Glasgow workers struck for a 40-hour week in

The Great War

When World War I broke out in 1914 the Scots flocked to the British colours with an extraordinary enthusiasm. Like Ireland, Scotland provided the British Army with a disproportionate number of soldiers. Like the Irish, the Scots suspended their radicalism and trooped into the forces to fight for King and Empire, to the despair of left-wing leaders like Keir Hardie and John Maclean. With less than 10 percent of the British population, the Scots made up almost 15

January 1919, the Secretary of State for Scotland panicked and called in the military.

Glaswegians watched open-mouthed as thousands of armed troops backed by tanks poured onto the Glasgow streets to nip the Red Revolution in the bud. At a huge rally in George Square on 31 January 1919, the police baton-charged the crowd.

The hungry years

The 1920s and 1930s were sour years for Scotland. The "traditional" industries of shipbuilding, steel-making, coal-mining and heavy engineering went into a decline from which they have never recovered. And the whisky industry reeled

LEFT: herring drifters near the port of Peterhead.
ABOVE: Labour Party leader Ramsay MacDonald with his son and daughter in 1929.

Laying Down the Law

One curiosity of the Scottish legal system is Not Proven – "that bastard verdict", as Sir Walter Scott called it. At the end of a criminal trial the verdict can be "guilty" or "not guilty", as in England, or the jury may find the charge "not proven". It's an option that reflects Scots logic and refusal to compromise by assuming a person innocent until proved guilty, though it does confer a stigma on the accused.

The jargon of Scots lawyers is distinctive, too. If you embark on litigation you are a "pursuer". You sue a "defender". "Law Burrows" (nothing to do

with rabbits) is a way of asking the courts to prevent someone harassing you. If you disagree too outspokenly with a judge's decision, you may be accused of "murmuring the judge".

Though few outsiders realise it, the Scots have maintained a distinctive legal system despite three centuries of political union with the rest of the UK. It is unique in being a legal system lacking its own legislature. Since the 1707 Act of Union abolished the Scottish parliament, the UK parliament in London has made laws for the country.

Scottish law is quite different in origin from that of England and those countries (such as the US and many Commonwealth nations) to which the English system has been exported, and is closer to the legal systems of South Africa, Sri Lanka, Louisiana and

Quebec. It was developed from Roman Law and owes much more to continental legal systems than does that of England – thanks partly to the custom of Scottish lawyers, during the 17th and 18th centuries, studying in France, Holland or Germany. Solicitors, the general practitioners of the law, regard themselves as men of affairs, with a wider role than lawyers in some countries have adopted. Advocates, who are based in Parliament House in Edinburgh and to whom a solicitor will turn for expert advice, also refuse to become too narrowly specialised. This is important if they wish to become Sheriffs, as the judges of the local courts are called.

Some practitioners have demonstrated outstanding talents beyond the confines of the law. Sir Walter Scott was, for most of his life, a practising lawyer. In Selkirk, near the palatial house he built at Abbotsford, can be seen the courtroom where he presided as Sheriff. Robert Louis Stevenson qualified as an advocate, the equivalent of the English barrister, though he quickly deserted the law for literature.

Inevitably, English law has had its influence. Much modern legislation, especially commercial law, has tended to be copied from England. The traffic, however, hasn't been all one-way. In Scottish criminal trials, the jury of 15 has always been allowed to reach a majority verdict, a procedure only recently adopted by England. The English have also introduced a prosecution service, independent of the police, similar to that which operates in Scotland. Some in England would also like to import the "110-day rule": this requires a prisoner on remand to be released if his trial doesn't take place within 110 days of his imprisonment. More controversially, Scottish judges have power in criminal cases to create new crimes – a power they use sparingly.

Many in England envy the Scottish system of house purchase. Most of the legal and estate agency work is done by solicitors and seems to be completed far faster than in England. Scottish laws on Sunday trading are more liberal, and divorce was available in Scotland several centuries before it was south of the border.

Along with the kirk, the separateness of the Scottish legal system plays a vital part in establishing a sense of national identity. Many Scots lawyers resent the failure of Westminster to have proper regard to the fact that the law is different in Scotland. Whether it's better is a separate question; the best verdict in this case may be "not proven". ❑

ABOVE LEFT: time for legal exchange between sessions.

from the body-blow of American prohibition.

The new light engineering industries – cars, electrics and machine tools – stayed stubbornly south of the border. Unemployment soared to almost three in 10 of the workforce and Scots boarded the emigrant ships in droves. An estimated 400,000 Scots (10 percent of the population) emigrated between 1921 and 1931. And in 1937 Walter Elliot, Secretary of State for Scotland, described how in Scotland "23 percent of its population live in conditions of gross overcrowding, compared with 4 percent in England".

Most of urban Scotland saw its salvation in the newly-formed Labour Party, which not only

the Scottish literary renaissance of the inter-war years the nationalist movement grew increasingly more political. In 1934 the small (but rightwing) Scottish Party merged with the National Party of Scotland to form the Scottish National Party (SNP).

The world at war

It wasn't until World War II loomed that the Scottish economy began to climb out of the doldrums. And when war broke out in September 1939 the Clydeside shipyards moved into high gear to build warships like the *Duke of York*, *Howe*, *Indefatigible* and *Vanguard*, while the

promised a better life but also a measure of Home Rule. Support for the Labour Party began early. At the General Election of 1922 an electoral pattern was set which has remained (with few exceptions) ever since: England went Conservative even if Scotland voted Labour.

The 1920s and 1930s also saw revival of a kind of left-wing cultural nationalism. which owed a lot to the poetry of Hugh MacDiarmid, the writing of Lewis Grassic Gibbon and the enthusiasms of upper-crust nationalists like Ruaridh Erskine of Marr and R.B. Cunninghame-Graham. From

Above: the Hungry Thirties: Glasgow kids keep smiling through the hard times.

engineering firms began pumping out small arms, bayonets, explosives and ammunition. The Rolls-Royce factory at Hillington near Glasgow produced Merlin engines for the RAF's Spitfires. Clydeside became one of Britain's most important war-time regions.

The point wasn't missed by the Germans. On 13 and 14 March 1941, hundreds of German bombers, operating at the limit of their range, devastated Clydeside. More than 1,000 people were killed (528 in the town of Clydebank) and another 1,500 injured.

War killed more than 58,000 Scots (compared to the 148,000 who had lost their lives in World War I) but had the effect of galvanising the Scottish economy for a couple of decades. And there's no doubt that the Labour Government which came to power in 1945 worked major improvements on Scottish life.

The National Health Service proved an effective instrument against such plagues as infant mortality, tuberculosis, rickets, and scarlet fever. Housing conditions improved in leaps and bounds as the worst of the city slums were pulled down and replaced by roomy (although often badly-built) council houses. Semi-rural new towns like East Kilbride, Glenrothes, Cumbernauld, Irvine and Livingston were established throughout central Scotland.

The postwar period

What went largely unnoticed in the post-war euphoria was that the Labour Government's policy of nationalising the coal mines and the railways was stripping Scotland of much of its decision-making powers, and therefore management jobs. The process continued through the 1960s and 1970s when the steel, shipbuilding and aerospace industries were also "taken into public ownership".

This haemorrhage of economic power and influence has been compounded by Scottish companies being sold to English and foreign predators. In 1988 British Caledonian, originally a Scotland-based airline, was swallowed up by British Airways. To an alarming extent, Scotland's economy now has a "branch factory" status.

English enthusiasm for Labour's experiment flagged and in 1951 Sir Winston Churchill was returned to power. Scotland, of course, continued to vote Labour (although in the general election of 1955 the Conservatives won 36 of Scotland's 71 seats, the only time they have had a majority north of the border). And, while Home Rule for Scotland was off the political agenda, Scottish nationalism refused to go away.

In the late 1940s two-thirds of the Scottish electorate signed a "national covenant" demanding home rule. In 1951 a squad of young nationalists outraged the British establishment by whisking the Stone of Destiny out of Westminster Abbey and hiding it in Scotland. And in 1953 the British establishment outraged Scottish sentiment by insisting on the title of Queen Elizabeth II for the new queen, despite the fact that the Scots had never had a Queen Elizabeth I.

Industrial decline

But while Scotland did reasonably well out of the Conservative-led "New Elizabethan Age" of the 1950s and early 1960s, the old structural faults soon began to reappear. By the late 1950s the well-equipped Japanese and German shipyards were snatching orders from under the noses of the Clyde, the Scottish coalfields were proving woefully inefficient and Scotland's steel works and heavy engineering firms were losing their grip on their markets.

And, although the Conservative Government did fund a new steel mill at Ravenscraig, near Motherwell, and enticed Rootes to set up a car plant at Linwood and the British Motor Corporation to start making trucks at Bathgate, it was all done under duress and all these projects have been abandoned. Scotland's distance from the market-place continued to be a crippling disadvantage. The Midlands and south of England remained the engine-room of the British economy. The drift of Scots to the south continued.

Although the Scots voted heavily for the Labour Party in the general elections of 1964 and 1966, Labour's complacency was jolted in November 1967 when Mrs Winnie Ewing of the SNP snatched the Hamilton by-election from the Labour Party. Although Ewing lost her seat at the 1970 general election, her success marked the start of an upsurge in Scottish nationalism that preoccupied Scottish – and, to some extent, British – politics for a decade.

When Harold Wilson's Labour Government ran out of steam in 1970 it was replaced by the Conservative regime of Edward Heath – although, once again, the Scots voted overwhelmingly Labour. But in the early 1970s Scotland got lucky. The oil companies struck big quantities of oil. All round Scotland engineering firms and land speculators began snapping up sites on which to build platform yards,

ASSEMBLY ROOM

In the 1970s the Royal High School in Edinburgh was purchased and renovated, ready for the new assembly. But after years of indecision it was sold again in 1994.

seats and more than 30 percent of the Scottish vote. It looked as if one more push by the SNP would see the United Kingdom dissolved, and the hard-pressed British economy cut off from the oil revenues it so badly needed.

The Labour government responded to the nationalists' political threat with a constitutional defence. It offered Scotland a directly-elected assembly with substantial (although strictly limited) powers if the Scottish people voted "yes" in a national referendum.

rig repair bases, airports, oil refineries and petrochemical works. Nothing like it had been seen since the industrial revolution.

The SNP was quick to take advantage of the new mood of optimism. Running on a campaign slogan of "It's Scotland's Oil", the SNP won seven seats in the general election of February 1974 and took more than 20 percent of the Scottish vote. In October 1974 they did even better, cutting a swathe through both parties to take 11

LEFT: shipbuilding on the Clyde: now a dying industry.
ABOVE: contrasts of modern Scotland: a Hebridean weaver using a traditional handloom to make Harris tweed; and youths in East Kilbride, soaking up the sun.

At which point Westminster changed the rules. At the instigation of Labour MP George Cunningham, Parliament decided that a simple majority was not good enough, and that devolution would go ahead only if more than 40 percent of the Scottish electorate voted in favour. It was an impossible condition. Predictably the Scots failed to vote yes by a big majority in the referendum of March 1979 (although they *did* vote yes) and the Scotland Bill lapsed. Shortly afterwards, the 11 SNP members joined a vote of censure against the Labour government – which fell by one vote. Margaret Thatcher was voted into power and promptly made it plain that any form of Home Rule for Scotland was out of the question.

The Thatcher years

The Devolution débâcle produced a genuine crisis of confidence among Scotland's political classes. Support for the SNP slumped, the Alliance could do nothing. And the Labour Party, armed with the majority of the Scottish vote, could only watch helplessly as the aluminium smelter at Invergordon, the steel mill at Gartcosh, the car works at Linwood, the pulp mill at Fort William, the truck plant at Bathgate and much of the Scottish coalfield perished in the economic blizzard of the 1980s. Even the energetic Scottish Development Agency could do little to protect the Scottish economy. Unemployment

climbed to more than 300,000, and the electronics industry's much vaunted "Silicon Glen" proved far too small to take up the slack.

So the political triumph of Thatcherism in England found no echoes in Scotland. At the general election of June 1987 the pattern which first emerged in 1922 repeated itself; England voted Tory and Scotland voted Labour. Out of 72 Scottish MPs 50 were Labour and only 10 were Conservative. This raised the argument that the then Scottish Secretary, Malcolm Rifkind, was an English governor-general with "no mandate" to govern Scotland. Rifkind's response was that the 85 percent of the Scottish electorate who voted for "British" parties were voting for the sovereignty of Westminster and therefore had to accept Westminster's rules.

At the end of 1987 the Labour Party tabled yet another Devolution Bill which was promptly thrown out by English MPs to the jeers of the SNP who claimed that Labour's "Feeble Fifty" could do nothing if they were prepared to play the Westminster game.

Into the millennium

In Britain's 1992 general election, by when Mrs Thatcher had been replaced as Tory leader by the more emollient John Major, the Tories did better than forecast north of the border, marginally increasing their vote. One consequence of Labour's defeat, however, was that the party elected a new leader at national level: John Smith, a cautious Edinburgh lawyer. Many saw him as Britain's next prime minister, but he died of a heart attack in 1994.

The commitment to devolution remained, and following Labour's landslide victory in the General Election of May 1997, which left Scotland with no Conservative MPS at all, the Scottish people were asked in a referendum whether they wanted their own parliament. The proposal received a ringing endorsement, a majority of 2-to-1 voting "yes". Proposals for the new parliament to have tax-varying powers were also approved, though by a smaller majority.

The first elections of the Edinburgh-based Scottish Parliament will take place in May 1999 and the Parliament will officially open on 1 July. In parallel to the new system for running domestic affairs, Scotland will continue to send a separate set of MPs to Westminster to vote on UK-wide policies. Scots have now been members of the United Kingdom for nearly 300 years, and Scottish history is deeply enmeshed with that of Britain. Yet a powerful undertow of resentment keeps breaking the surface: the Jacobite insurgencies of 1708, 1715 and 1745; the radical "rebellion" of 1820; the Disruption in the Church of Scotland in 1843; the formation of the SNP in the 1930s; the startling upsurge of nationalism in the 1970s and again in the 1990s. But will it ever surge strongly enough to threaten the Treaty of Union of 1707? It now seems conceivable that it will. ❑

LEFT: campaigning for Scottish devolution.
RIGHT: the Rev. Alan Cameron, who busked for many years outside the Scottish National Gallery.

HIGHLANDERS AND LOWLANDERS

Although the distinctions between Highlanders and Lowlanders are
disappearing, many of the original Gaelic traditions live on

The division between the Highlander and the Lowlander was one of the most ancient and fundamental in Scotland's history. "The people of the coast," said John of Fordun, the Lowland Aberdeenshire chronicler, writing in 1380, "are of domestic and civilised habits, trusty, patient and urbane, decent in their attire, affable and peaceful.... The Highlanders and people of the islands, on the other hand, are a savage and untamed nation, rude and independent, given to rapine, easy-living, of a docile and warm disposition, comely in person but unsightly in dress, hostile to the English people and language and, owing to diversity of speech, even to their own nation, and exceedingly cruel."

The division was based on what Fordun called "the diversity of their speech": the Lowlanders spoke Scots, a version of Middle English, the Highlanders spoke Gaelic. The line between the two languages broadly coincided with the line of the hills. North of the Highland fault running from just above Dumbarton to just above Stonehaven, and west of the plains of Aberdeenshire and the Moray Firth, Gaelic was spoken. Outside that area, Scots was spoken, except in the northern isles of Orkney and Shetland, where a kind of Norse was spoken, and perhaps in a few pockets of the southwest where another form of Gaelic lingered until late in the Middle Ages.

Lingering images

Four hundred years later, things hadn't changed that much. When Patrick Sellar, the Lowland sheep farmer, wrote to his employer, the Countess of Sutherland, about the nature of the people over whom he was appointed as estate manager, John of Fordun would have recognised the tone. Sellar spoke of "the absence of every principle of truth and candour from a population of several hundred thousand souls." He compared these "aborigines of Britain" with the

PRECEDING PAGES: the youth of Scotland demonstrate their loyalty; an Arinacrinachd weaver.
LEFT: bagpipers at Glencoe.
ABOVE RIGHT: starting young at Glenfinnan.

"aborigines of America", the North American Indians: "both live in turf cabins in common with the brutes: both are singular for patience, courage, cunning and address. Both are most virtuous where least in contact with men in civilised State, and both are fast sinking under the baneful effects of ardent spirits."

Then, in the 19th century, a startling turnabout occurred. Many Scots began to adopt as their national symbols the very trappings of the despised Highland minority – the kilt and the tartan, the bagpipe and the bonnet, the eagle's feather and the dried sprig of heather: it blended into a kitsch everyone across the world can recognise. As recently as the late 1980s, when the American broadcasting networks wished to devote a minute of their national news bulletins to the question why Scotland felt unsympathetic to the policies of Britain's then prime minister, Margaret Thatcher, they used 30 seconds setting the scene with men with hairy knees throwing pine trees about at a Highland gathering.

The fact that most Scots only wear a kilt on rare formal occasions and have never attended a Highland games is not very relevant. The adoption of these public symbols has something to do with the campaigns of Sir Walter Scott to romanticise the Highlanders, something to do with the charismatic powers of the Glasgow Police Band, which in Victorian days was largely recruited from Highlanders, and something to do with a music hall that loved a stereotype. The mask stuck.

At the same time, ironically, true Highland society was in a state of collapse. Ever since the 17th century its distinctive character and Gaelic

peasant farms, which paid little rent, in order to accommodate the Lowlander and his sheep, which paid a good deal more. Simultaneously, Gaelic began a catastrophic decline, from being universally the language of the Highland area to being the language, as it is today, only of the Outer Hebrides and a few other communities, mainly on islands, in the extreme west.

Blurred distinctions

So the Highland-Lowland division today has a different meaning from what it had in the past. It is certainly not any longer the most obvious or important division, ethnically and culturally,

culture had been eroded by the steady spread of hostile government power, the march of commercial forces tying Scotland together as one market, and the Lowlandisation of the clan chiefs as they sought wives with better dowries than the mountains could provide. The failure of the Jacobite risings in 1715 and 1745 was important, but the transformation would have come about anyway, for other perfectly mundane reasons.

By 1800 Highland landowners wanted their estates to produce as much cash as possible as quickly as possible, just as landowners did elsewhere in Scotland. In the course of the next 50 years they cleared most of the land surface of

among the Scottish people as a whole. The Lowlanders themselves were never uniform: the folk of Aberdeenshire spoke "Doric", a dialect of their own, very different in vocabulary and intonation from, say, the folk of Lothian or Galloway. In the 19th century this sort of regionalism was greatly compounded and complicated by the immigration of the Irish, about two-thirds of them Catholic and one-third Protestant.

The Catholic Irish, oppressed by poverty and the sectarianism that accompanied their movement, crowded into distinct areas – Glasgow and Dundee among the cities, and the small mining or iron-working towns of Lanarkshire, Lothian and Fife. Today, especially in the west, it is the

Catholic-Protestant division that continues to have most meaning in people's lives. The Catholics are, overall, still a minority in Scotland, but their church now has more attenders on Sundays than any Protestant denomination – even the Church of Scotland itself.

Intermarriage between the two communities has dissolved animosities in the past half-century, but even today politicians deal cautiously with anything that touches, for example, on the right of Scottish Catholics to have their own state-aided schools.

FOOTBALL FAITHFULS

Sports allegiances in Scotland are a subtle blend of the regional and the religious. Celtic, for example, is Glasgow Catholic and Rangers is Glasgow Protestant.

have a name with the prefix "Mac" or theoretically belong to some clan like Grant or Gunn, Murray or Munro; but, apart perhaps from a greater fondness for dressing in tartan and doing Highland reels at party time, there is little that is distinctive about being a Highlander in most communities that lie beyond the geological Highland line.

In the west, however, in the Inner and Outer Hebrides and along the extremities of the mainland coast from Argyll to Sutherland, the ancient significance and

Being a "Lowlander" has less meaning than having a religious affiliation, or coming from Edinburgh rather than Glasgow, or even than backing a particular football team.

Being a "Highlander" has an uncertain and ambiguous meaning over most of the area covered today by Highland and Grampian Region. The citizens of Pitlochry or Inverness don't, for the most part, speak Gaelic, are mostly ordinary lukewarm Protestants, and enjoy a lifestyle and a culture not obviously very different from that of the citizens of Perth or Aberdeen. They may

LEFT: sheep drovers in the 19th century.
ABOVE: assessing the form at the Braemar Gathering.

meaning of being a Highlander is very much alive. Not all these communities necessarily speak Gaelic rather than English, though in the Western Isles the power of the language is much less dimmed than elsewhere.

Crofting communities

All of them are, however, historically "crofting communities": that is, they are the relics of a traditional peasantry who, thanks to a campaign of direct action in the 1880s, won from the British parliament the right to live under the same kind of privileged land-law as their brethren in Ireland. The Crofters Holding Act in 1886 conferred on the crofting inhabitants of these areas security of tenure, the right to hand on their holdings to heirs, and a rent which was fixed not by the whim of the estate manager but by the arbitration of a Land Court sitting in Edinburgh.

Crofting is still largely the economic foundation of these communities. It can best be described as small-scale farming that involves individual use of arable land and some communal use of the grazing on the hill and moor. Very often, crofting is (or was) combined with some other activity, such as fishing or weaving, especially on the islands of Harris and Lewis.

Today, inevitably, it involves regulation and subsidy on a massive scale, and the crofter

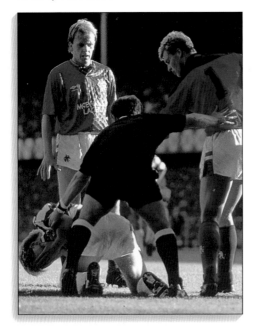

becomes an expert in milking the grants available from the European Community, Scottish Natural Heritage, Highlands and Islands Enterprise, the Department of Agriculture and Fisheries, and anyone else who looks good for a touch. Old animosities are sometimes rekindled when the Lowlander considers the Highlander's expertise in living off the hand-outs of the taxpayer, and the Highlander in return resents the indifference of Edinburgh and London towards the real problems of living in remote communities.

But the Highland way of life in these areas goes beyond the details of economic existence, and can best be understood in Scotland by a

journey to the Outer Hebrides. In Lewis the visitor encounters the Protestant version of a Gaelic culture dominated, especially on Sundays, by grim Calvinist churches known to outsiders as the "Wee Frees". Jesus may have walked on water, but if he had dared walk on the glorious beaches of Harris or Lewis on a Sunday he would have been ostracised. In Barra and South Uist is the Catholic version, implanted by the 17th-century Counter-Reformation and not involving such denial of life's pleasures.

Some people argue that the Highland way of life exists in a still purer form in the Canadian Maritimes, especially in the Catholic Gaelic-speaking communities of Cape Breton Island, who trace their origins directly to the evictions and migrations that followed the 1745 Rebellion and the Clearances of the 19th century.

Into the future

Wherever it survives, irrespective of religious background, the Gaelic tradition often defies the dominant world outside. In some ways, the Gaelic Highlander is indeed aboriginal, as Patrick Sellar said, though he only meant it as an insult. The Highlander is often unmodern in priorities, is materialistic yet with little sense of individual ambition and attaches little importance to clock-watching. Gaelic society is supportive of its members, has an abiding sense of kinship and an unembarrassed love of a song and a story, as it has an unembarrassed love of drink.

With every passing year it appears superficially less likely that its distinctiveness can survive another generation, but its efforts to survive become more, not less, determined as the 21st century approaches. The recent creation of a unified local government authority, the Western Isles Council, which conducts its business in Gaelic, has given a remarkable new confidence and ability to deal with modern political society. It is perhaps unlikely that any Ayatollah will arise in Stornoway, but the Highland way of life is far from finished on the islands.

On the other hand, elsewhere in Scotland, John of Fordun and Patrick Sellar have really had the last word. It is their Anglicised Lowland Scotland that now runs from the Mull of Galloway to John o' Groats. The tartan and the bagpipe ought not to fool the visitor: it does not fool the Scots, though they enjoy the pretence of it all. ❑

ABOVE LEFT: everyday aggro at a football game.

Scots Idioms

There are moments in the lives of all Scots – however educated, however discouraged by school or station from expressing themselves in the vernacular – when they will reach into some race memory of language and produce the only word for the occasion.

The Scots idiom tends to operate at two ends of a spectrum: from abusive to affectionate. So the word for the occasion might well be nyaff. There are few Scots alive who don't know the meaning of the insult nyaff – invariably "wee nyaff" – and there are few Scots alive who don't have difficulty telling you. Like all the best words in the Scots tongue, there is no single English word which serves as translation. The most that can be done for nyaff is to say it describes a person who is irritating rather than infuriating, whose capacity to annoy and inspire contempt is just about in scale with his diminutive size, and the cockiness that goes with it.

The long historical partnership between Scotland and France has certainly left its mark on the Scots tongue. Scottish cooks use "ashets" as ovenware – a word which derives from assiette, meaning plate – while the adjective "douce", meaning gentle and sweet-natured, is a direct import of the French douce, meaning much the same thing. But the most satisfying Scots words – resounding epithets like bauchle (a small, usually old and often misshapen person) and evocative adjectives like shiplit (sickly-looking) and wabbit (weak and fatigued) – belong to that tongue which came under threat in the early 17th century when King James VI moved to London to become James I of England.

Until then, the Lowland Scots (as opposed to Gaelic-speaking Highlanders), whose racial inheritance was part-Celtic and part-Teutonic, spoke their own version of a northern dialect of English, and "Scots" was the language of the nobility, the bourgeoisie and the peasants. But when king and court departed south, educated and aristocratic Scots adopted the English of the "élite", and the Scots tongue received a blow from which it has never recovered.

Yet what could be more expressive than a mother saying of her child, "The bairn's a wee bit wabbit today"? What could be more colourful than the remark that the newspaper vendor on the corner is

"a shilpit wee bauchle"? The words themselves almost speak their meaning, even to non-Scots, and they are beginning to creep back into the vocabulary of the middle-class.

The dialects of Glasgow and Scotland's urban west have been much influenced by the mass infusions of Gaelic and Irish from their immigrant populations from the Highlands and Ireland, but Glasgow's legendary "patter" has an idiom all its own, still evolving and still vitally conscious of every subtle shift in the city's preoccupations. Glasgow slang specialises in abuse which can be affectionate or aggressive. A bampot is a harmless idiot; heidbanger is a dangerous idiot.

Predictably, there is a rich seam of Glasgow vernacular connected with drink. If you are drunk you might be steamin', stotious, wellied, miraculous or paralytic. If you are drinking you might be consuming a wee goldie (whisky) or a nippy sweetie (any form of spirits). And if you are penniless you might have to resort to electric soup, the hazardous mixture of meths and cheap wine drunk by down-and-outs.

If a Glaswegian calls you gallus, it is a compliment. The best translation in contemporary idiom is probably streetwise, although it covers a range of values from cocky and flashy to bold and nonchalant. The word derives from gallows, indicating that you were the kind of person destined to end up on them. In Glasgow that wasn't always a reason for disapproval. ❏

ABOVE RIGHT: sales patter catching buyers' attention at Glasgow's Barras street market.

HOW THE KIRK MOULDS MINDS

The Church of Scotland has had a profound impact on the Scottish character,
encouraging hard work, obedience, and a rigorous independence of mind

When Sunday was still solemnly observed as the Lord's Day, a young minister was asked to preach to George V at at his Highland palace, Balmoral. Nervous at such an honour, the minister enquired: "What would the King like the sermon to be about?" His Majesty replied: "About five minutes."

What he was dreading, of course, was an interminable exhortation to high moral endeavour. Until recent times the Sabbath was a day when profane activity ceased. The intervals between services in the kirk (church) were spent in prayer or with improving books. The Presbyterian ethic is strict and challenging – well-suited to promote survival in a poor country with a harsh climate. Whether the kirk has shaped the Scots or the Scots their kirk, it is impossible to understand Scottish character and attitude without taking into account the austere religious background.

Vain outer show

The Scots worship God, their Maker, in a plain dwelling dominated by a pulpit. There are no idolatrous statues or other Papist frumperies such as stained glass, holy pictures, gorgeous surplices or altar hangings. The clergy are attired in sober black and a sparingly used Communion table replaces the altar. The appeal is to the conscience and to the intellect, with the minister's address based on a text from the Bible, the only source of truth. To avoid "vain repetitions", there's no liturgy, or even such set forms as the Lord's Prayer and the Apostles' Creed. Prayers, sometimes prolonged like the sermon, are *extempore*. The one concession to the senses is the singing of hymns and a psalm.

The reason for this lack of "outer show" is that ritual is thought irrelevant; what matters is the relation of the individual soul to his or her Maker. Hence the emphasis on self-reliance and personal integrity. With honesty a prime virtue,

PRECEDING PAGES: Presbyterian minister.
LEFT: Lorimer's *Ordination of the Elders*.
ABOVE RIGHT: the reformer John Knox.

the Roman Catholic practice of currying divine favour through bribing the saints is despised as devious. Presbyterians bow their heads in prayer, but feel no need to grovel on their knees; they talk to God directly. This directness characterises all other dealings, and strangers may be disconcerted by the forthright expression of opinion, prejudice, liking or disapproval. The belief that all are equal in the eyes of the Lord has produced a people more obedient to the dictates of conscience than to rank or worldly status. The humble shepherd, who roves the mountains in communion with the Almighty, will stomach no affront from his so-called "betters". Even the Lord's anointed are not exempt: though a minister has no qualms about berating sinners from the pulpit, they in turn will take issue with him over errors in his sermon.

Unlike the English, who avoid confrontation, the average Scot has an aggressive zest for argument, preferably "philosophical". At its worst this fosters a contentious pedantry, at its best moral courage and the independence of mind which, from a tiny population, has engendered an astonishing number of innovative thinkers in many diverse fields.

The academic excellence of which the Scots are so proud owes its merit to John Knox, who insisted that every child, however poor, must attend a school supervised by the kirk. By the early 1700s Scotland was almost unique in having universal education.

Knox's concern, however, was more spiritual than scholastic: the newborn babe is not innocent but "ignorant of all godliness", his life thereafter being a thorny and arduous pilgrim-age from moral ignorance at birth towards knowledge of the Lord. With the help of the *tawse* (a strap), children were brought up as slaves to the "work ethic": sober, frugal, compulsively industrious.

Values are positive: duty, discipline, the serious pursuit of worthwhile achievement and a role of benefit to the social good. Hard-headed and purposeful, there's no time to waste on frivolous poetics. Scotland has produced philosophers like David Hume, the economist Adam Smith, Watt, Telford and Macadam, whose roads revolutionised public transport; lawyers, doctors, scientists, engineers and radical politicians in search

INDEPENDENT CHURCH

Rigorously democratic, the Church of Scotland is without bishops or hierarchy. In most other churches, the attenders have no say in the appointment of clergy, who are imposed from above. The Scots minister, however, is chosen by the congregation, whose elders, having searched far and wide for a suitable incumbent, will invite the favourite candidate to test their worth by a trial sermon. Where other churches' cardinals and archbishops hold office for life, the kirk's leader, the Moderator, is elected for one year only.

The kirk is also a symbol of national independence. At its General Assembly the Sassenach (English) Queen or her representative, the Lord High Commissioner, is invited as a courtesy but is not allowed to take part in the debates. These are much publicised by the media, since, as there has been no Scottish Parliament until now, politics and economics have been discussed along with matters clerical, and a report submitted to the Government of the day. The General Assembly, which meets once a year for a week in Edinburgh, is attended by ministers and elders from almost every kirk in the land; its deliberations are keenly observed (sometimes critically) by the general public in the public gallery.

of Utopia – Knox's Godly Commonwealth in secular translation. And, although the General Assembly of 1796 declared that "to spread the Gospel seems highly preposterous, in so far as it anticipates, nay reverses, the order of Nature," yet Scotland would give the world, especially Africa, more Protestant missionaries – such as David Livingstone, John Phillip, Robert Moffat, Mary Slessor – than any other European country.

Balance sheet

With the pressure to achieve so relentless, there's short shrift for the idle. Religious imagery is businesslike: at the Last Day people go to their *reckoning* to settle *accounts* with their Maker; it's not sins or trespasses for which pardon is implored but, "Forgive us our *debts* as we forgive our *debtors*." In a land where it's a struggle to survive, the weakest, who go to the wall, have *earned* their just deserts.

There's nothing meek and mild about the masculine virtues pleasing to God the Father, the Old Testament God of Wrath, who sets the tone for those in command, especially in the family. Some of the most powerful Scottish novels, such as Stevenson's *Weir of Hermiston*, show the terrifying impact of stern fathers on weak or hypersensitive sons.

But with one slip from the "strait and narrow" leading to instant perdition, it's said the Scots have a split personality: Jekyll and Hyde. God's Elect are teetotal, but alcoholism is "the curse of Scotland"; while it's almost unheard of for a kirk member to go to prison, Glaswegians proudly boast the busiest criminal court in Europe. It would seem, therefore, that the unofficial influence of the kirk is defiance of all it stands for.

Its ministers have, at all times, lashed "the filthy sins of adultery and fornication" and the taboo on the flesh is so intense that, even in the nursery, mothers, fearing to "spare the rod and spoil the child", economise on caresses. Yet the poet Robert Burns, a flamboyant boozer and wencher, is a national hero, the toasting of whose "immortal memory" provides an annual excuse for unseemly revels. Visitors to puritan Scotland may be puzzled by the enthusiasm for his blasphemous exaltation of sensual delights.

But perhaps, if paradoxically, Burns' anarchic *joie de vivre* also stems from the teaching of the kirk, to whose first demand, "What is the chief end of man?" the correct response is: "To glorify God and *enjoy* Him forever."

Though the kirk's faithful have declined – today fewer than one in five are regular communicants – its traditions die hard. Fire and brimstone sermons may be a thing of the past and it's only in some of the outer isles that the Sabbath is kept holy. Sunday is a day, as elsewhere, for sport and idle leisure; even Christmas, once by-passed as Papist, is now approved for uniting the family clan. The kirk, however,

remains important both in politics, through the General Assembly, and socially as the principal dispenser of charitable aid to the poor and afflicted in this Vale of Tears.

More significant, though, than its public function is an enduring impact on the moulding of character. Scots are still brought up to be thrifty, upright and hard-working, while those who rebel put an energy into their pleasures that can often seem self-destructive. There's success or failure, no limbo in between. Nothing is done by halves and, however secularised the goal, the spur remains: a punitive drive to scale impossible heights. The jaws of Hell still gape for those found "wanting"	❏.

LEFT: Sunday morning congregation in Stornoway in the Outer Hebrides.
ABOVE RIGHT: solemn thoughts in the park.

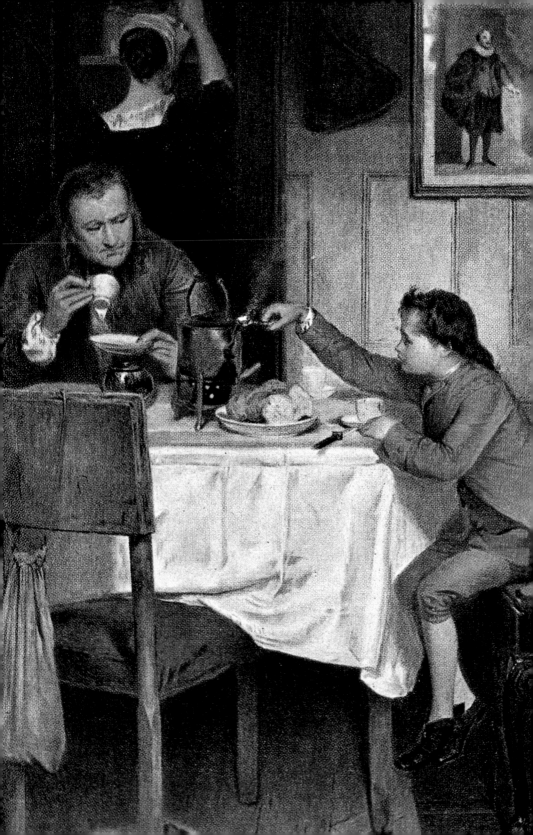

SCOTS GENIUSES

For its size, Scotland has produced a disproportionate number of intellectual geniuses: great thinkers who have changed the face of the modern world

When the English social scientist Havelock Ellis produced his *Study of British Genius* (based on an analysis of the *Dictionary of National Biography*) he came up with the fact that there were far more Scots on his list than there should have been. With only 10 percent of the British population, the Scots had produced 15.4 percent of Britain's geniuses. And when he delved deeper into the "men of Science" category he discovered that the Scots made up almost 20 percent of Britain's eminent scientists and engineers.

Not only that, but the Scots-born geniuses tended to be peculiarly influential. Many of them were great original scientists like Black, Hutton, Kelvin, Ramsay and Clerk Maxwell, whose work ramified in every direction. Others were important philosophers like the sceptic David Hume or the economist Adam Smith, whose words, according to one biographer, have been "proclaimed by the agitator, conned by the statesmen and printed in a thousand statutes".

Great Scots

Scotland, like Ireland, produced a long string of great military men such as Patrick Gordon (Tsar Peter the Great's right-hand man), James Keith, David Leslie and John Paul Jones. There are also great explorers such as David Livingstone, Mungo Park, David Bruce and John Muir, and accomplished financiers like John Law, who founded the National Bank of France, and William Paterson, who set up the Bank of England. Andrew Carnegie, also a Scot, ruthlessly put together one of the biggest industrial empires America has ever seen, sold it when it was at its peak, then gave much of his money away on the fine Presbyterian basis that "the man who dies rich dies disgraced".

Just why a small, obscure country on the edge of Europe should produce such a galaxy of tal-

LEFT: Eureka! A popular version of how James Watt discovered steam power.

ABOVE RIGHT: the possibly apochryphal meeting between Robert Burns and the young Walter Scott.

ent is one of the conundrums of European history. As nothing in Scotland's brutal medieval history hints at the riches to come, most historians have concluded that Scotland was galvanised in the 16th and 17th centuries by the intellectual dynamics of the Protestant Reformation. This is a plausible theory. Not only did

the Reformation produce powerful and challenging figures such as John Knox and his successor Andrew Melville, but it created a church which reformed Scotland's existing universities (Glasgow and St Andrews), set up two new ones (Edinburgh and Aberdeen), and tried to make sure that every parish in Scotland had its own school.

Radical thinkers

When Thomas Carlyle tried to explain the proliferation of genius in 18th- and 19th-century Scotland, he found "Knox and the Reformation acting in the heart's core of every one of these persona and phenomena". This is a large claim, and overlooks the well-run network of primary schools inherited from the Roman Catholic authorities.

But, whatever the reason, 18th-century Scotland produced an astonishing number of talents. As well as David Hume and his friend Adam Smith, Scottish society was studded with able men like Adam Ferguson, who fathered sociology, William Robertson, one of the finest historians of his age, and the teacher Dugald Stewart. There were also gifted eccentrics like the high-court judge Lord James Monboddo, who ran into a barrage of ridicule by daring to suggest (100 years before Darwin) that men and apes

might, somehow, be related. It was a sceptical, questioning, intellectually-charged atmosphere in which talent thrived.

Intellectual freedom

Interestingly, that talent didn't fall foul of established religion: few Scots had a problem squaring their faith with their intellectual curiosity. An extraordinary number of Scotland's ablest and most radical thinkers were "sons of the manse" – that is, born into clergy homes. This meant that, in 1816, when Anglo-Catholics were squabbling over the precise date of the Creation, the Presbyterian intellectual Thomas Chalmers

LITERARY GENIUSES

Scotland has three international class writers in Robert Burns (1759–96), Walter Scott (1771–1832) and Robert Louis Stevenson (1850–94). Stevenson won acclaim with his travelogues, short stories, essays and especially his novels: *Treasure Island* and *Kidnapped* are typical of his entertaining style. To Scott writing was as much a trade as an art, and he produced a long stream of work based on medieval and foreign themes. But it is Burns whose poetry and songs earned him pride of place in every Scottish heart and whose birthday (25 January – Burns Night) is celebrated in rousing style around the world.

could ask: "Why suppose that this little spot (the planet earth) should be the exclusive abode of life and intelligence?"

And nothing thrived more than the science of medicine. In the late 18th and early 19th centuries Edinburgh and Glasgow became two of the most important medical centres in Europe and produced physicians such as William Cullen, John and William Hunter (who revolutionised surgery and gynaecology in London), the three-generation Munro dynasty, Andrew Duncan (who set up the first "humane" lunatic asylums), Robert Liston and James Young Simpson (who discovered the blessings of chloroform). It was a Scot, Alexander Fleming, who, in 1929, discovered the bacteria-killing properties of penicillin, the most effective antibiotic ever devised.

While Scotland has never produced a classical composer of any note, or a painter to compare with Rembrandt or Michelangelo, the reputation of 19th-century portraitists like Raeburn, Wilkie and Ramsay are now being upgraded. And in the Adam family (father William and sons Robert, John and James), Scotland threw up a dynasty of architectural genius which was highly influential. (One of the scandals of modern Scotland is the number of Adam-designed buildings which are collapsing into ruin.)

James "Paraffin" Young, who first extracted oil from shale; Alexander Graham Bell, who invented the telephone; and John Logie Baird, the father of television.

Makers of the modern world

More important in world terms were Scotland's "pure" scientists, such as John Napier who invented logarithms; Joseph Black, who described the formation of carbon dioxide; James Hutton, Roderick Murchison and Charles Lyell, who by their efforts created modern geology; and Lord Kelvin (an Ulster Scot), who devised, among much else, the second law of

However, the number of technologists born in Scotland in truly remarkable: they include James Watt, who improved the steam engine beyond measure; the civil engineer Thomas Telford; R.W. Thomson, who invented both the fountain pen and the pneumatic tyre (which was taken up commercially by John Dunlop); John Macadam, the engineer who gave his name to the metalled road; Charles MacIntosh, who did the same to waterproofed fabric; James Nasmyth, who dreamed up the steam hammer;

LEFT: an 1827 view of the engineer John Macadam.
ABOVE: Alexander Graham Bell, the inventor of the telephone.

thermodynamics and whose name is remembered (like that of Fahrenheit and Celcius) as a unit of temperature.

Then there's the Scotsman who is said to have virtually invented the modern world: James Clerk Maxwell, the 19th-century physicist who uncovered the laws of electrodynamics. Albert Einstein described Clerk Maxwell's work as a "change in the conception of reality" which was the "most fruitful that physics has experienced since the time of Newton". And Max Planck, the German physicist, said Clerk Maxwell was among the small band who are "divinely blest, and radiate an influence far beyond the border of their land" ❑.

THE GREAT TARTAN MONSTER

Tartanry is a big, colourful business in Scotland, displaying

its gaudy wares to willing tourists at every opportunity

When it comes to selling drink, the Mackinnons of Edinburgh (and formerly of Skye) are no slouches. In fact their family company, the Drambuie Liqueur Co. Ltd, is one of the most successful companies in Scotland, and demand for their sweet-tasting liqueur has boomed even at those times when the sales of "conventional" whiskies have been crashing through the floor.

And it has all been done on the coat-tails of that great loser, Bonnie Prince Charlie. Not only does Drambuie claim to be based on a "secret" recipe given to the Mackinnon family by the prince himself, but the Stuart's kilted portrait adorns every bottle. And the conference room in Drambuie's Edinburgh HQ is an exact replica of the 18-century French frigate which sailed the Prince into exile (not to mention drunkenness and despair) in France and Italy.

But, thanks to Bonnie Prince Charlie, the Mackinnons are now turning over more than £23 million a year and paying themselves huge salaries. "The drink itself may be nothing famous," says one Edinburgh expert, "but the marketing has been superb." The Jacobite rising of 1745–46 was a major disaster for the Stuarts, but it was good news for the Mackinnons.

The power of tartan

The success of Drambuie – "the Prince's Dram" – is tartanry in action. The Mackinnon millions are yet another tribute to that *mélange* of chequered cloth, strident music, mawkish song and bad history which has stalked Scotland for generations and refuses to go away. Tartan tea-towels and tartan tea-cosies, tartan pencils and tartan postcards, tartan golf club covers and a wide assortment of comestibles packaged in tartan – all are eagerly purchased.

Tartanry is a vigorous subculture which, somehow, manages to lump together Bonnie

Prince Charlie, John Knox, pipe bands, Queen Victoria, Rob Roy, Harry Lauder, Mary Queen of Scots, Edinburgh Castle and the White Heather Club dancers. It is a cultural phenomenon which has defied every attempt by the Caledonian intelligentsia to understand it or explain it away.

Fun or frightful?

Many resent the fact that this debased and often silly version of Gaeldom has come to represent the culture of Adam Smith, David Hume, Robert Burns and James Clerk Maxwell. Others regard tartanry as a harmless effervescence which has kept alive a sense of difference in the Scottish people that may yet prove politically decisive. Even more think it is wonderful and buy Andy Stewart records.

But it certainly demands elaborate and expensive tribute. A full set of Highland "evening wear" consisting of worsted kilt, Prince Charlie Coatee, silver-mounted sporran, lace jabots and cuffs, ghillie shoes, chequered hose and

---

LEFT: ancient and modern: tartan adapts itself to the punk look.

ABOVE RIGHT: waiting for tourist customers in Bow Street, Edinburgh.

sgian dubh can cost up to £1,000. Even a "day wear" outfit of a kilt in "hunting" tartan, Argyle Jacket, leather sporran and civilian brogues will set the wearer back £350.

Of course, none of this applies to the Highlanders who actually live in the Highlands. As anyone who knows the area will confirm, the day dress of the Highland crofter or shepherd consists of boiler suit, wellington boots and cloth cap. For important evening occasions he takes off his cap.

Tartanry could be regarded as Gaeldom's unwitting revenge on the country which once despised and oppressed it. Right into the 19th century there was nothing fashionable (or even respectable) about Highlanders. They were about as popular in 18th-century Britain as the IRA is now. Their kilts, tartans and bagpipes were hopelessly associated in the public mind with the Jacobite assaults on the Hanoverian ascendancy in 1715, 1719 and 1745. In fact, in 1746 (following the 1745 Rising) the whole caboodle – bagpipes and all – was banned by the British Government "under pain of death" and remained banned until 1782.

But, with the Jacobite menace safely out of the way, the élites of Hanoverian Britain began to wax romantic over the Highland clans. The

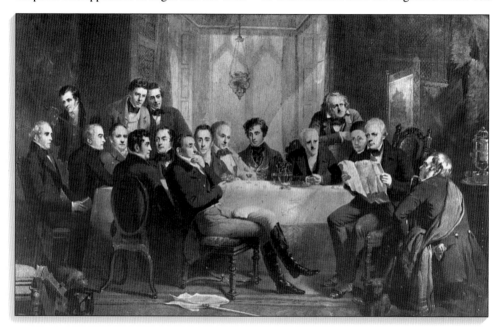

REGIMENTAL COLOURS

The popularity of tartan was helped along by the stirring performances of the Highland regiments in the Crimean War and the Indian Mutiny. In their "Government" tartans, red coats and feathered bonnets, the Highland battalions were an awesome sight. By 1881 the British military were so besotted with tartanry that the War Office ordered all Scotland's Lowland regiments to don tartan trousers and short Highland-style doublets. Venerable Lowland regiments were outraged and protested that their military tradition was both older and a lot more distinguished than that of the Highlanders. But their pleas fell on deaf ears. Only the Scots Guards, as members of the élite Brigade of Guards, were granted the right not to wear tartan on their uniforms.

Today the military victory of tartanry is complete. Every Scottish regiment (including the Scots Guards) has its pipes and drums, all of whom dress in full Victorian-Highland paraphernalia of dress tartan, silver-buttoned doublets, feather bonnets and horsehair sporrans.

Edinburgh Castle is now home of the British Army's school of piping, and the centre of that triumph of Highland-military kitsch, the annual Edinburgh Military Tattoo.

bogus "Ossian" sagas of James Macpherson became the toast of Europe (Napoleon loved them), while Sir Walter Scott's romantic novels became runaway best sellers. And it was Scott who orchestrated the first-ever outburst of tartan fervour: King George IV's state visit to Edinburgh in 1822.

Tartan order

Determined to make the occasion high romance, Scott wheeled into Edinburgh dozens of petty Highland chieftains and their tartan-clad "tails" and gave them pride of place in the processions. The huge 20-stone (127-kg) frame

sheep. "It almost seems as if there was a cruel mockery in giving such prominence to their pretentions," Lockhart wrote.

But there was no stopping the tartan bandwagon. "We are like to be torn to pieces for tartan" wrote an Edinburgh merchant to the weaving firm of William Wilson and Son of Bannockburn in the wake of George IV's visit. "The demand is so great that we cannot supply our customers." Wilson took the hint and installed 40 extra looms.

The tartan business got another boost when a couple of amiable English eccentrics known as the "Sobieski Stuarts" (born Charles and John

of George IV himself was draped in swathes of Royal Stewart tartan over flesh-coloured tights. "Sir Walter Scott has ridiculously made us appear to be a nation of Highlanders," grumbled one Edinburgh citizen at this display of tartan power, "and the bagpipe and the tartan are the order of the day." Scott's own son-in-law, John Lockhart, pointed out that the same gentry strutting around Edinburgh in their Highland finery were the very people who were ousting their own clansfolk to make way for

Allen) popped up, claiming to be the direct descendents of Bonnie Prince Charlie and his wife Louisa of Stolberg. They also claimed to have an "ancient" (in other words fake) manuscript which described hundreds of hitherto unknown tartans.

Royal favour

But the real clincher came in 1858 when Queen Victoria and Prince Albert bought Balmoral Castle as a summer residence and furnished it almost entirely with specially-designed (by Albert) "Balmoral" tartan. After that, the English mania for Highland Scotland knew no bounds. Every Lancashire industrialist and City

LEFT: Sir Walter Scott and friends, who helped create the romantic Highland image.
ABOVE: more modern manifestations of tartanry.

of London financier had to have his shooting lodge in the mountains, while every family name in Scotland was converted into a "clan" complete with its own tartan.

Marauding bands

According to the Royal Scottish Pipe Band Association (RSPBA), there are now more than 400 pipe-bands alive and wailing in the UK alone, with hundreds more all over the world. Every year the bands flock to the one or other of the RSPBA's five championships. The biggest prize is the World Pipe Band Championship, which invariably used to be won by a Scottish

and which, at the last count, had more than 26,000 members prancing and leaping around ballrooms all over the world. This may be understandable in Scot-infested corners of the globe like the United States, Canada and New Zealand, but it isn't so explicable in France, Holland, Sweden, Kenya or Japan. Just why the sensible citizens of Paris, The Hague, Gothenburg, Nairobi and Tokyo should want to trick themselves out in tartan to skip around in strict tempo to tunes like "The Wee Cooper O'Fife", "The Dukes of Perth", "Cadgers in the Canongate" or "Deuks Dang Ower My Daddie" is a deep and abiding mystery.

band, but which in 1987 went to the 75th Fraser Highlanders from Canada and, in 1992 and 1993, to the Field-Marshall Montgomery Band from Northern Ireland. Eighty of the RSPBA's member bands are in Northern Ireland, where the hard-line Protestants are happy to swathe themselves in the tartans of the Jacobite clans, most of whom were Catholic or Episcopalian. On the other side of the Irish fence, the saffron-kilted pipers of Ireland have abandoned their melodic "Brian Boru" pipes for the Great Highland Bagpipe.

Another (somewhat quieter) arm of tartan imperialism is the Royal Scottish Country Dance Society (RSCDS) which is run from Edinburgh

Famous patrons

It may have something to do with Scottish country dancing's royal and aristocratic connections. The Queen herself is patron of the RSCDS and the Royal prefix was granted by her father King George VI just before he died in 1952. Other exalted members include the Earl of Mansfield (who is President of the RSCDS), the Duke of Atholl, Lord Glenconner and Sir Donald Cameron of Lochiel.

But it seems unlikely that the Royal laying on of hands will ever extend to the crowd of kilted warblers, accordion players, comics and fiddlers who make their living entertaining Scotland (and the Scottish diaspora). Usually showbiz tartanry finds its own niche, but occasionally, as in the case of the Bay City Rollers or the fearsome Jesse Rae (half-Highlander, half-Viking), it escapes into the mainstream of pop culture.

Olympic efforts

Yet another manifestation of tartanry is the Highland games circuit. Every year between May and September villages and towns the length of Scotland (plus a few in England) stage a kind of Caledonian olympics in which brawny,

LOUD MUSIC

In contrast to the loud dress sense of some of the Scottish pop world, none of the newer breed of Gaelic-speaking folk-rock bands has ever been seen near a scrap of tartan.

even Braemar cannot compete with the 40,000 or 50,000-strong crowds who flock to watch the big Highland games in the USA. The event at Grandfather Mountain in North Carolina is now the biggest of its kind in the world. American tartanry buffs are very keen on "clan gatherings" in which they get togged up in a kind of "Sword of Zorro" version of Highland dress, and march past their "chief" brandishing their broadswords.

But perhaps the daftest manifestation of competitive tartanry

kilted figures toss the caber, putt the shot and throw the hammer while squads of little girls in velvets and tartans dance their hearts out to the sound of bagpipes.

Andrew Rettie of the Scottish Highland Games Association (which has not yet acquired a "Royal" prefix) estimates there are about 100 such games held in Scotland every year. Most attract crowds of up to 5,000, although the Braemar Gathering (with the Royal Family in attendance), can easily pull in more than 20,000. But

LEFT: tartan helps keep the Royal family warm at the Braemar Gathering.
ABOVE: a sheaf of tartans.

is "haggis-hurling", an event dreamed up in 1977 by an Edinburgh public relations man, Robin Dunseath, as "a bit of an upmarket joke". To Dunseath's utter astonishment the "ancient" sport of haggis-hurling took off and has gone from strength to strength. Dunseath (an Irishman) now despatches his "How To Run a Haggis Hurl" kits all over the globe.

The world record is held by Stewart Pettigrew of Saltcoats, who hurled a 1½-lb (680-gm) "competition" haggis more than 181 ft (55 metres). It has certainly been a golden few decades for the sport's "official" haggis makers, Dalzell and McIntosh of Stockbridge in Edinburgh   ❏.

SCOTLAND'S PAINTERS

*From the Edinburgh Enlightenment to the Glasgow rebels, Scottish
painting retains an exuberance that defies its Calvinistic background*

In spite of its puritanism and thunderings from the kirk against "vain outer show", Scotland is unique among the British provinces in having a distinctive painterly tradition. The art of Protestant northern Europe tends to be tormented and morbid and, given a Calvinist shadow of guilt and sin, one would expect Scottish painting to be gloomily angst-ridden. Instead, as if in defiance of all that the kirk represents, it is extroverted, joyful, flamboyant, robust – much more sensuous (even if less complex) than English art with its inhibiting deference to the rules of good taste.

It is significant that young Scottish artists have mostly by-passed the Sassenach (English) capital to study abroad; those from Edinburgh in Rome, the Glaswegians a century later in pleasure-loving Paris. Growth of the arts in Scotland is linked to the relative importance of its two major cities, and the rivalry between them (culture versus commerce) has resulted in aesthetic dualism: where Edinburgh's painters are rational and decorous, raw but dynamic Glasgow has produced exuberant rebels.

The Enlightenment

Before the 18th century, Scottish art scarcely existed. There was no patronage from the kirk, which forbade idolatrous images, or from the embattled aristocracy. In a country physically laid waste by the Covenanter wars and mentally stifled by religious fanaticism, painters were despised as menial craftsmen.

The return of peace and prosperity, however, gave rise to a remarkable intellectual flowering, the Edinburgh Enlightenment, which lasted, roughly, from 1720 until 1830 and caused the city to be dubbed the "Athens of the North". The rejection of theology for secular thought was accompanied by a new enthusiasm for the world and its appearance, the brothers Adam

evolving a style in architecture and design that was adopted all over Europe and remains to this day the classic model of elegance and grace.

A need arose, meanwhile, for portraits to commemorate the city's celebrated sons. Though the earliest portrait painters, Smibert and Aikman, achieved modest recognition as artists not craftsmen, Allan Ramsay, son of a poet and friend of the philosopher David Hume, expected to be treated as an equal by the intellectual establishment, many of whose members he immortalised with his brush.

Considering the visual austerity of his background – Edinburgh had no galleries, no art school and only a few enlightened collectors – Ramsay's rise to fame is astonishing. Leaving home to study in Italy, he returned to London in 1739 and was an instant success, finally ending up as court painter (in preference to Reynolds) to George III. Despite his classical training, Ramsay cast aside impersonal idealism for "natural portraiture", concentrating on light, space

PRECEDING PAGES: Wilkie's *Pitlessie Fair.*
LEFT: Raeburn's perennially popular Rev. Robert Walker skating on Dunningston Loch.
ABOVE RIGHT: Ramsay's portrait of David Hume.

and atmosphere and the meticulous rendering of tactile detail: ribbons, cuffs, the curl of a wig, the bloom on a young girl's cheek. Above all, he was interested in the character of his sitters, combining formal dignity with intimacy and charm. The refined distinction of his best work, such as the portraits of his two wives, has earned him an honourable position in the history not just of Scottish but of British art.

Scottish arts

Ramsay's achievement was rivalled in the next generation by Sir Henry Raeburn, knighted in 1822 by George IV and made King's Limner

genres, especially landscape. Though Alexander Nasmyth painted an Italianate Scotland, gilded and serene, the choice of local vistas – rather than a classical idyll in the manner of Claude – was startling in its novelty.

Equally novel was David Allan's transfer of the pastoral tradition of nymphs and shepherds into scenes from Scottish rural life. He was followed by David Wilkie, whose *Pitlessie Fair* (painted at 19) was the start of a career which earned him a knighthood and outstanding popularity; his "low-life" comedies like *The Penny Wedding* creating a taste for such subjects that persisted throughout the Victorian era.

(painter) for Scotland. Raeburn also studied in Italy and his *oeuvre*, like Ramsay's, was confined to portraiture with an emphasis on individual character: the fiddler Neil Gow or a homely matron receiving the same attention as a scholar or fashionable beauty. But his style is broader and more painterly, the poses more dramatic: Judge Eldin looking fierce in his study, the Clerks of Penicuik romantically strolling, the Rev. Robert Walker taking a turn on the ice.

Raeburn was the first Scottish painter of national renown to have remained in his native Edinburgh and, in doing so, he established the arts in Scotland and their acceptance by the public. Interested prestige led to ventures in other

Although no one equalled Raeburn or Wilkie, there was a new public interest in the arts, which continued to flourish in Edinburgh during the 19th century. Notable in landscape are David Roberts with his views of the Holy Land and, later, William McTaggart, "the Scottish Impressionist".

The Glasgow Boys

The academic mainstream, however, was confined to historical melodrama, sentimental cottagers and grandiose visions of the Highlands as inspired by Sir Walter Scott. The 1880s saw a new departure when a group of students, nicknamed the Glasgow Boys, united in protest against Edinburgh's stranglehold on the arts. Due to rapid industrial expansion Glasgow had grown from a provincial town into "the second city of the empire" and, in contrast to 18th-century Edinburgh, there were galleries, an art school and lavish collectors among the new rich (one of whom was William Burrell), who were anxious to buy status through cultural patronage.

Initially, though, the Glasgow Boys scandalised their fellow citizens. Rejecting the turgid subjects and treacly varnish of the academic "glue-pots", they abandoned their studios to paint

ART ON SHOW

Confidence in Scottish painting has been boosted by superb municipal collections, notably the Burrell in Glasgow, which has been a major tourist draw ever since it opened in 1983.

disgust to study in Paris – where they were subsequently acclaimed. This success abroad tickled civic pride (what Edinburgh artist could compete?) and the canny burghers, who had once been so hostile, began to pay high prices for their pictures, Sadly, the Glasgow Boys now lost their freshness and became respectable: Lavery a fashionable portrait painter, Guthrie a conservative president of the Royal Scottish Academy, while Hornel retreated into orientalism. Today, there is a revival of interest – and investment.

in the open air, choosing earthy, peasant themes that lacked "message" or moral and gave offence to the genteel. The public, devoted to gain, godliness and grand pianos (whose legs were prudishly veiled) was both affronted and bemused by Crawhall's lyrical cows, the voluptuous cabbages tended by James Guthrie's farm hands, the indecent brilliance of the rhubarb on Macgregor's *Vegetable Stall*.

Influenced by Whistler and the European Realists, most of the Glasgow Boys left Scotland in

LEFT: close scrutiny in Glasgow's art gallery of Sir James Guthrie's *Old Willie, a Village Worthy*.
ABOVE: MacGregor's *Vegetable Stall*.

New experiments

The Glasgow Boys gave younger artists the courage to experiment through their flamboyant handling of paint and colour. Oppressed by the drab Calvinism of Scottish life, rebels of the next generation, led by Peploe, Cadell, Hunter and Fergusson, again fled to Paris where they were intoxicated by the decorative art of Matisse and the Fauves (wild beasts). Discarding conventional realism, they flattened form and perspective into dancing, linear rhythm, with colour an expression of a pagan *joie de vivre*.

As with the Glasgow Boys, fame abroad brought the Scottish Colourists belated success at home. Peploe and Hunter returned to paint a

Scotland brightened by gallic sunshine and the witty Cadell to transform Glasgow housewives into flappers of the Jazz Age.

A gloomier fate, though, awaited the architect and designer Charles Rennie Mackintosh. An originator of *art nouveau*, his distinctive style is typified by a simple geometrical manipulation of space based on combinations of straight line and gentle curves. Glasgow School of Art, his architectural masterpiece, is one of the city's most remarkable buildings and the Glasgow Style he initiated in furniture and the decorative arts is now admired the world over. Yet in his day "Toshie" was dismissed as a

drunken eccentric and was such a failure professionally that he abandoned architecture to paint watercolours in France.

Modern times

From the 1930s landscape has tended to predominate in Scottish painting. In a country where intellectual achievement allied to public service is so highly esteemed, it's curious that the arts in Scotland have mostly been devoted to expressing simple emotion and visual pleasure. In the 1950s, Colquhuon and MacBryde adopted Cubism not for formal reasons but as a means of conveying romantic melancholia.

Since World War II, while modern trends

have been pursued with characteristic vigour, there's been a loss of optimism and sparkle. More poignant than the Modernists is Joan Eardley, who turned her back on artistic fashion to paint urchins in the Glasgow back streets, then, after settling in a remote fishing village in the northeast, somberly elemental landscapes.

John Bellany is unusual in that he has the tormented vision one might expect, but rarely finds, among artists brought up under Calvinism. Overwhelmed, after a visit to Buchenwald, by human wickedness, he gave up modish abstracts to return to figurative art of a tragic, often nightmarish monumentality. Later, after liver failure and confrontation with death, he unleashed intense energy with a prolific output of superb, lyrical autobiographical canvasses.

Glasgow graduates

Another post-war change is that German Expressionism, with its energy and gloom, has replaced the hedonistic influence of the French, especially in recent times when Glasgow School of Art has produced a new group of rebels. Known (unofficially) as the Glasgow Wild Boys, they have also rejected Modernism for gigantic narrative pictures with literary, political or symbolist undertones. The most successful, Adrian Wiszniewski and Stephen Campbell, have been rapturously received in New York.

Wiszniewski, a Pole born in Scotland, has adapted Slavic folk art to express nostalgia for the past, disenchantment with the present. Campbell, combining macho brutalism with whimsy, draws his inspiration from the contrasting writings of P.G. Wodehouse and Bram Stoker (author of *Dracula*). Although affecting social "concern" and apparently doom-laden, the most striking quality of these young painters is anarchic ebullience.

Other brilliant Glasgow graduates include Stephen Conroy, Peter Howson, Mario Rossi, Craig Mulholland and Steven Campbell, who, with the exception of Howson, are all from in and around Glasgow. And Allison Watt, Lesley Banks and Jenny Saville redress the balance for women, though their images of other women are far from conventional: Watt earned notoriety for her painting of the Queen Mother with a teacup on her head. ❑

LEFT: James Guthrie's *Hind's Daughter*.
RIGHT: Joan Eardley's *Street Kids*.

SONG AND DANCE

The folk music revival has had a profound effect in Scotland,
filling the clubs and pubs once more with traditional Celtic sounds

The sound of Scottish music has changed dramatically in the past 25 years – and that's before you take into account the insidious influence of the phenomenally successful Scottish pop groups such as Wet Wet Wet, Big Country and Simple Minds.

Nothing has been more dramatic than the forging of an alliance between two previously alien schools. On the one hand: the inheritor of the bagpipe tradition, regarded until then as a musical law unto themselves. On the other hand: the young adventurers of the folk-music revival, ready to play and sing anything that had its roots embedded somewhere in Celtic culture.

Pipers who joined folk groups were regarded as renegades by the piping fraternity, but for folk musicians, the bagpipe provided much needed instrumental beef in an increasingly noisy market-place.

Piped music

Whether the piping Establishment has benefited is debatable. They are a gritty, stubborn lot, much given to internecine warfare over the etiquette and mystique of piping disciplines which have been handed down like family heirlooms through the generations. Discipline still rules at the sponsored competitions, where pipers from all over the world challenge each other at what in Gaelic is called *pìobaireachd* (pibroch).

Just to confuse the uninitiated, *pìobaireachd* has another title, *ceòl mór* (Great Music). This is a truly classical music, built to complex, grandiloquent proportions and actually playable only after years of study and practice. Those who *can* play it do so by memory, in the manner of the great Indian raga players. The pipe music that most of us are familiar with – stretching from "Mull of Kintyre" to reels, marches, jigs and strathspeys – is referred to by the classicists as *ceòl beag* (Small Music).

***

PRECEDING PAGES: Shetland musicians.
LEFT: accordion players in an Orange parade, Glasgow.
RIGHT: keeping up with the demand for traditional Scottish fiddles.

Great or Small, much of it has survived thanks to patronage rather than household popularity. The earliest royal families in Scotland are credited with having a piper, or several, on their books, and no upwardly mobile landlord of ancient times could afford to be without his piper. But it was in the warring Highland clan

system that the pipes flourished. The blood-tingling quality of the Great Highland Bagpipe, with its three resonant drones, was quickly recognised by the early Scottish regiments, and the military connection remains to this day. Even now, the Scots use the pipes to soften up the English at soccer and rugby internationals.

Despite their role as bearers of the country's national music, the pipes can offer nothing to compare with the phenomenal resurgence of Scots fiddle music, which had thrived only in geographical pockets until the folk music revival got its full head of steam in the 1960s. Today, it's reckoned that there are more fiddlers in Scotland than ever before.

Another traditional instrument that has become increasingly popular is the *clarsach*, or Scots harp, which first appeared in 8th-century Pictish stone carvings. Some of the great *clarsach* music came from Ruaridh Dall Morrison (the Blind Harper) in the 17th century. Much smaller than the modern concert harp, the *clarsach* had become virtually extinct until it was revived in the early 1970s by Alison Kinnaird and other young enthusiasts. Now it finds a place in folk bands and there is a thriving Clarsach Society.

If the fiddle and the *clarsach* have fought their way back into the mainstream of Scottish cul-

ture, they were both a long way behind folksong in doing so. The classic narrative ballads and *pawky bothy* (a Gaelic term meaning "hut") ballads had survived largely in the hands of farm workers and the travelling folk (the tinkers) of Perthshire and the northeast. The advent of the tape recorder has enabled collectors like Hamish Henderson to bring their songs to the ears of the young urban folk revivalists. It was Henderson who discovered Jeannie Robertson, a magnificent traditional singer living in obscurity in Aberdeen. Her influence soon showed itself in the folk clubs that sprang up all over Scotland.

The folk clubs served, too, as spawning

FIDDLERS ON THE HOOF

The fiddle has been part of Scottish music for more than 500 years – King James IV had "fithelaris" on his payroll in the 15th century. The fiddle reached its Golden Age in the 18th century, when Scots musicians sailed to Italy to study and brought back not only the tricks of the classical trade, but also a steady supply of exquisite violins, which were soon copied by enterprising local craftsmen.

At the same time, the dancing craze had begun. Country fiddlers found their robust jigs and reels much in demand at posh balls and parties, and the first major collections of Scots fiddle tunes were published, making the music widely accessible.

By the early 19th century, though, high society had turned its fancy to the new polkas and waltzes that were flooding in from Europe. The rural fiddlers played on regardless, and it was the Aberdeenshire village of Banchory that produced the most famous Scots fiddler of all – James Scott Skinner, born in 1843. Classically trained, and technically virtuosic, the "King of the Strathspey" won international acclaim, and the arrival of recording in the later part of his career helped to spread the message – even as far as fiddle-packed Shetland, which had until then resolutely stuck to its own Norse-tinged style.

grounds for new songwriting, especially of the polemical brand, producing some of the best songs since Robert Burns. Burns is credited with more than 300 songs, many of them set to traditional fiddle tunes, and you can still hear them in all sorts of venues.

Clubs and festivals

Many of the early folk clubs are still in existence – notably those in Edinburgh, Aberdeen, Kirkcaldy, Stirling and St Andrews. Sadly, the type of *ceilidh* that is laid on for tourists tends to be neither traditional nor contemporary but caught in a time-warp of kilt, haggis and musical mediocrity. In the Gaelic, *ceilidh* means a gathering. The Gaelic-speaking community, now mostly confined to the west Highlands and islands, holds its great gathering, the National Mod, in different parts of Scotland every year. There, you can sample some beautiful singing as young and old compete for much-coveted prizes.

Even the folk scene finds competitions stimulating. Since the 1960s there has been a steady growth in the number of folk festivals. From Easter until autumn, there's hardly a weekend when there isn't a folk festival somewhere in Scotland. In cities like Edinburgh and Glasgow, the festivals are among the biggest of their kind in the world; Edinburgh's lasts for 10 days. But there's nothing to beat the smaller traditional folk festivals in rural areas, where the talent tends to be local rather than imported. Among the best events are those at Keith (June), Auchtermuchty (August) and Kirriemuir (September). Orkney (May) is also famous for its annual celebrations of traditional music.

Most folk festivals have their unofficial "fringe"; invariably located in the bars serving the best whisky in town. Many pub sessions can match the finest organised *ceilidh* or competition.

Highland flings

The cunning Irish centuries ago devised a way of dancing in tight cottage corners: they keep their arms rigid at the sides of the body. For the Scots, dancing is reserved for the village hall or the ballroom. Many of the traditional dances, including the famous Highland Fling, call for the raising of the arms to depict the antlers of the red

deer – splendidly symbolic but treacherous at close quarters. Popular formations like the Eightsome Reel and the Dashing White Sergeant also involve much whirling around in large groups.

Like the accordion-pumped music which fires these breath-sucking scenes, Scottish dancing has its more rarified moments. There are country dance societies in various districts, and when the members get together they dance with the kind of practised precision that must have been essential at the earliest Caledonian Balls.

It's fun to go along to a village hop – usually advertised as a *ceilidh* or ceilidh-dance. You don't have to know the steps: the locals will hurl

you in the right directions and there will be time for a beer as the band move from "The Mason's Apron" to their idiosyncratic version of the latest Michael Jackson record.

As it happens, Scottish rock has begun to sit up and notice its Celtic heritage. The pre-eminent folk-rock band is Runrig, all-electronic but hitched musically to ancient Gaelic themes. In songwriting, too, folk music has made its mark in the rock venues. The leading singing songwriters – men such as Eric Bogle, Rab Noakes and the brilliant Dick Gaughan – have found eager new audiences there, and their influence can be clearly heard in the punkish protest music of groups like the Proclaimers. ❏

Above Left: live music is popular in bars.
Above right: scores of young dancers compete in the Highland Gatherings around Scotland every year.

GAMES HIGHLANDERS PLAY

A traditional Highland Gathering, with the skirl of pipes, tartan-clad dancers and muscular athletes, is a wonderfully colourful – and noisy – experience

Highland Gatherings, which are sometimes described as "Oatmeal Olympics", are much more than three-ring circuses. As the Gathering gets going a trio of dancers are on one raised platform; a solitary piper is on another; a 40-piece pipe band has the attention, if not of all eyes, at least of all ears; the "heavies" are tossing some unlikely object about; two men are engaged in some strange form of wrestling; a tug-o'-war is being audibly contested and an 880-yard (800-metre) race is in progress.

Track events are the least important part of these summer games – but don't tell the runners. The venue has been chosen for its scenic beauty rather than its "Tartan" track. At the Skye Games, milers literally become dizzy as they run round and round the track's meagre 130 yards (117 metres).

Pipers and dancers

Everywhere the sound of pipes can be heard. It is not only the piper playing for the dancers; another solitary piper playing a mournful dirge in the individual piper's competition; or the 40-strong pipe band being judged in the arena. Around the arena, behind marquees, under trees, in any place which offers some slight protection to muffle the sound, those still to compete are busy rehearsing under the sharp ear of their leaders and coaches.

The solo pipers are undoubtedly the aristocrats of the Games and the highest honour – and the biggest prize – is awarded the pibroch winner. There are three competitions for solo pipers: pibrochs (classical melodies composed in honour of birthdays, weddings and the like); marches (military music); and strathspeys and reels (dance music). While playing a pibroch the piper marches slowly to and fro, not so much in time to the music, but in sympathy with the melody. On the other hand, when playing dance music, the pipers remain in one position tapping their foot; and, understandably, when playing a

march – for who can resist the skirl of the pipes? – they stride up and down the platform.

Most dancers at Games are female, although, occasionally, a thorn appears among the roses. Seldom are any girls older than 18 and competitions are even held for three-and four-year-olds.

King Malcolm Canmore is credited with

being responsible for one of the more famous dances seen at the Games. In 1054 he slew one of King Macbeth's chieftains and, crossing his own sword and that of the vanquished chieftain, performed a *Gille Calum* (sword dance) before going into battle. The touching of either sword with the feet was an unfavourable omen.

The origin of the Highland fling is also curious. A grandfather was playing the pipes on the moors and his young grandson was dancing to them. Two courting stags were silhouetted against the horizon. The grandfather asked the lad: "Can ye nae raise yer hands like the horns of yon stags?" And so originated the Highland Fling. The dance is performed without travelling

LEFT: hammer throwing at a Highland meeting.
ABOVE RIGHT: tossing the caber.

(that is to say, on one spot) and the reason is that the Scot, like the stag, does not run after his women: he expects them to come to him. A more mundane explanation for the dance being performed on one spot is that it was originally danced on a shield.

In the dance called *Sean Truibhas* – the Gaelic for old trews (trousers) – the performer's distaste for his garb is expressed. This dance originated after Culloden when the wearing of the kilt was proscribed.

One of the original aims of the Games was to select the ablest bodyguards for the king or chieftain, and this is perpetuated in today's heavy events. The objects used in these have evolved from what would be found in any rural community, such as a blacksmith's hammer or even a stone in the riverbed.

Olympic strength

Hurling the hammer and putting the shot are similar, yet different, to these events as practised at the Olympics. At the "Oatmeal Olympics" the hammer has a wooden shaft rather than a chain and the weight of the shot varies. The 56-lb (25-kg) weight is thrown by holding, with one hand, a short chain attached to the weight; the length of weight and chain must not exceed

18 inches (45 cms). Then there is the tossing of the 56-lb (25-kg) weight. In this event it is not distance but height that counts. The competitor stands below and immediately in front of a bar and with his back to it. Then, holding the weight in one hand he swings it between his legs and throws it up and, with luck, over the bar. A correct throw will just miss the thrower on its way down, while a bad throw is liable to cause untold mischief.

The most spectacular event is tossing the caber, a straight, tapered pine-tree trunk shorn of it branches. It weighs about 125 lbs (57 kg) and is about 19 ft (6 metres) long. The diameter at one end is about 9 inches (23 cms) and at the

ROYAL CONNECTIONS

Some claim that Games were first held in 1314 at Ceres in Fife when the Scottish bowmen returned victorious from Bannockburn. Others believe that it all began even earlier when King Malcolm organised a race up a hill called Craig Choinnich. The winner received a *baldric* (warrior's belt) and became Malcolm's foot-messenger. A race up and down Craig Choinnich became a feature of the Braemar Gathering, which is the highlight of the circuit. However, this isn't so much because of the calibre of the competition but because, since the time of Queen Victoria, they are often attended by the Royal Family.

other about 5 inches (13 cms). Two men struggle to carry the caber to a squatting competitor. They place it vertically with the narrow end in his cupped hands. The competitor gingerly rises and, with the foot of the caber resting against his shoulder, and the remainder towering above, starts to run. Finally, at a suitably auspicious moment, the competitor stops dead, lets out an almighty roar, and thrusts his hands upwards. The wide end of the caber hits the ground; now is the moment of truth: will the quivering pole tumble backwards towards the hopeful competitor or will it attain the perpendicular and the turn over completely and fall away from him?

from throwing tree trunks into the river after they have been felled. They would then float to the sawmill. It was important to throw the trunks into the middle of the river or they would snag on the banks.

Colour codes

Colour is the keynote of the Games. All dancers and musicians are dressed in full Highland regalia, as are many of the judges and some spectators. Competitors in the heavy events all wear the kilt. The reds of the Stuarts, the greens of the Gordons and the blues of the Andersons all mingle with the green of the grass and the

But why does an empty-handed, puffing judge trot alongside the competitor? Tossing the caber is judged not on distance but on style. An imaginary clockface is involved, and the athlete is presumed to be standing at the figure 6 when he makes his throw. A perfect throw lands at 12; a somewhat less perfect one at 11 or at 1 and so on. Naturally, the athlete will attempt, after throwing, to swivel his feet so that his throw appears perfect. Hence the puffing judge.

Caber tossing is believed to have evolved

ABOVE LEFT: judges deliberate at the Braemar Games.
ABOVE RIGHT: the tug-o'-war team flexes its porridge-fed muscles.

purple of the heather to produce a muted palette.

Highland Games are very much in vogue and new venues are constantly announced. Currently, more than 100 Gatherings are held during the season, which extends from the end of May until mid-September. In spite of the spectacular appeal of the great Gatherings (Braemar, Cowal, Oban), the visitor might find that the smaller meetings (Ceres, Uist in the Hebrides) are more enjoyable. These have an authentic ambience and competitors in the heavy events are certain to be good and true Scots and not professional intruders from foreign parts. What's more, you may not even have to pay admission! ❑

A FONDNESS FOR FESTIVALS

The Scottish calendar is bursting with local festivals: very different in origin but all offering an excuse to celebrate in spectacular style

Until the middle of this century Puritanical Scotland completely ignored Papish Christmas: offices, shops and factories all functioned as usual on 25 December. The great event on the Scottish calendar was the night of 31 December (Hogmanay) and New Year's Day (which was called *Nollaig Bheag* – Little Christmas – in many parts of the Highlands).

Traditionally, as the bells struck midnight, the crowds gathered around the focal points of towns would join hands and sing "Auld Lang Syne" and then whisky bottles would be passed around before all dispersed to go first-footing. It is important that the first-foot (the first person to cross a threshold in the new year) should be a dark-haired person who brings gifts of coal and salt which ensure that the house won't want for fire or food in the coming year. Also, the first-foot will normally carry a bottle of whisky.

Hot stuff

Fiery New Year processions which will drive out and ward off evil spirits have been held for centuries at Comrie, Burghead and Stonehaven. At the Comrie Flambeaux procession, locals walk through the town carrying burning torches; at Stonehaven, participants swing fireballs attached to a long wire and handle. Some suggest that the swing of fireballs is a mimetic attempt to lure back the sun from the heavens during the dark winter months.

The Burning of the Clavie at Burghead is held on 11 January. (This is when Hogmanay falls according to the Old Style calendar, which was abandoned in 1752 but which still holds sway when deciding the date of many celebrations.) The ceremony begins with the Clavie King lighting a tar-filled barrel which is then carried in procession through the town and from which firebrands are distributed. Finally, the Clavie is placed on the summit of Doorie Hill and left to burn for a time before being rolled down the hill.

LEFT: dressed up for the Galashiels Common Riding.
ABOVE RIGHT: the climax of Lerwick's Up-Helly-Aa Viking festival.

Much more recent in origin is the torchlight procession on Edinburgh's Princes Street on 31 December; this marks the conclusion of a three-day Hogmanay extravaganza which includes carnival and funfair, and indoor and outdoor festivities. However, by far the greatest and most spectacular fire ceremony is Up-Helly-Aa, held

at Lerwick in the remote island of Shetland on the last Tuesday in January. Up-Helly-Aa (compare the old Scots name for Twelfth Night, *Uphaliday*) begins with the posting of "The Bill", a 10-ft (3-metre) high Proclamation at the Market Cross and the displaying of a 30-ft (9-metre) model longship at the seafront.

Come evening, and with the Guizer Jarl magnificently dressed in Viking costume at the steering oar, the longship is dragged to the burning site. Team after team of guizers, each clad in glorious or grotesque garb and all carrying blazing torches, follow the ship. When the burning site is reached the "Galley Song" is sung; the Guizer Jarl leaves the longship; a bugle sounds; and hundreds of blazing torchs are hurled upon and consume the hull. Celebrations continue all through the night.

At Kirkwall, capital of Orkney, those who survived the Hogmanay celebrations gather on New Year's Day at the Mercat Cross for the "Ba' Game". Sides are taken: the Uppies who were born south of the Cathedral and the Doonies, born north of the Cathedral. The two teams attempt to carry a leather ball, about the size of a tennis ball, against all opposition, to their own end of the town. A giant scrum forms. becoming so torrid that steam rises from its centre. A good game lasts for several hours.

Later in the month, Burns Night (25 January) honours the birth of the national poet. In villages and cities throughout the land, Burns clubs and others toast the haggis (*see page 122*).

A different kind of game can be seen at Lanark on 1 March. Then, the church bells peal out and the children of Lanark, armed with home-made weapons of paper balls on strings, race three times around the church, beating each other over the head as they go. After the race, town officials throw handfuls of coins for which the children scramble. Whuppity Scoorie is claimed by some to be a ridding of the town of evil spirits by scourging the precincts of the church. A more

THE RIDING OF THE MARCHES

Throughout the early summer months the clippity clop of horses' hoofs is heard on the cobblestones of Border towns. The Riding of the Marches, introduced in the Middle Ages, is the custom of checking the boundaries of common lands owned by the town. In some cases, the Riding also commemorates local historical events which invariably involved warfare between the English and the Scots in the Middle Ages. The festivities often last for several days and are always stiff with protocol.

The Selkirk Gathering, held in June, is the oldest, the largest and the most emotional of the Ridings. It concludes with the Casting of the Colours, which commemorates Scotland's humiliating defeat at the Battle of Flodden. At the "casting", flags are waved in proscribed patterns while the band plays a soulful melody.

Each town – including Annan, Dumfries, Duns, Galashiels, Jedburgh, Lanark, Langholm and Lauder – has its own variations of the Riding ceremonies; and all have other activities which include balls, concerts, pageants and sporting events. At Peebles the Riding incorporates the Beltane Fair, which is the great Celtic festival of the sun and which marks the beginning of summer.

mundane explanation is that the festival represents the chasing away of winter and the welcoming of spring.

About six weeks later, students at St Andrews University take part in the traditional Kate Kennedy pageant, in which they play the parts of distinguished figures associated with the university or the town. Lady Kate, a niece of the founder of the university, was a great beauty to whom the students are said to have sworn everlasting allegiance. Women are banned from taking part in the procession and the role of Kate is always played by a first-year male student.

Summer festivals

During the summer months, traditional fairs are held throughout the country. Until quite recently, farm employees who wished to change their jobs would seek out new employers at the Feeing Markets, which were held at the end of each term. (The farming year was divided into three contractual terms.) These markets also attracted small stallholders eager to part the labourer from his term's wages. Such a market, enlivened with Highland dancing, country music and other entertainments, is still held in June at Stonehaven.

Later in the month, a similar fair is held at Garmouth. However, the excuse for the Maggie Fair is that it commemorates the landing of the "merry monarch", Charles II, at nearby Kingston, after he had been proclaimed King of Scotland following the execution of his father King Charles I.

The first day of August is Lammas Day, or Lunasdal – the feast of the Sun God, Lugh – and was formerly an extremely popular day for local fairs. Such fairs are still held in August, although not on the first day, at St Andrews and Inverkeithing. Also at this time a bizarre ritual occurs on the day before the South Queensferry Ferry Fair. A man, clad head to toe in white flannel, is covered with an infinite number of burrs until he becomes a moving bush. Bedecked with flowers and carrying two staves, this strange creature makes his way from house to house receiving gifts. One theory for this strange practice equates the Burryman with the scapegoat of antiquity.

ABOVE LEFT: the Galashiels Braw Lads gallop out.
ABOVE RIGHT: Hallowe'en trick-or-treat for a young boy in Berwickshire.

Fleet of foot

In late August, attention switches to the west coast where the ancient burgh of Irvine holds its Marymass Fair, which dates from the 12th century. Horse races, very much a part of this fair, are said to be even older. These races are not only for ponies but also for Clydesdale carthorses which, in spite of their great size, are remarkably fleet of foot. The fair's celebrations, including a pageant whose principal is dressed as Mary Stuart, continue for a week.

"Horses" of a different kind are involved in a mid-August festival on the island of South Ronaldsay in Orkney. The "horses" are young

boys or girls dressed in spectacular costumes. Pulling beautifully wrought miniature ploughs, often family heirlooms, and guided by boy ploughmen, these "horses" turn furrows on a sandy beach. Prizes are awarded for the best turned-out "horses" and for the straightest and most even furrows.

St Andrew's Day (30 November) is the country's national day, but is more or less ignored by most people. It does offer excuses for society types to dress in their finery, attend balls, toast the haggis once again, and imbibe unwise quantities of whisky. And so, inexorably, the festive year rushes headlong towards another Hogmanay. ❏

THE LURE OF THE GREEN TURF

To play on the hallowed ground of Scotland's ancient golf courses

is the ambition of amateur and professional golfers alike

Visit the 19th hole at any of Scotland's 400 golf courses and you're almost certain to hear a heated argument, over a dram or two of whisky, as to where the game of golf originated. The discussion doesn't involve geography but rather topography: the "where" refers to *which* part of Scotland. All know that, in spite of the Dutch boasting of a few old paintings which depict the game, it all began in Scotland centuries ago when a shepherd swinging with his stick at round stones hit one into a rabbit hole. Little did the rustic know the madness he was about to unleash when he murmured to his flock: "I wonder if I can do that again?"

Scottish links

Few courses have the characteristics of the quintessential Scottish course. Such a course, bordering the seashore, is called a links. It is on the links of Muirfield, St Andrews, Troon and Turnberry that the British Open – or "the Open" – is often played.

The word links refers to that stretch of land which connects the beach with more stable inshore land, and a links course is a sandy, undulating terrain which borders the shore. One feature of such a course is its ridges and furrows which result in the ball nestling in an infinite variety of lies. Another feature is the wind which blows off the sea and which can suddenly whip up with enormous ferocity. A hole which, in the morning, was played with a driver and a 9-iron can, after lunch, demand a driver, a long 3-wood and a 6-iron.

Summer days in Scotland are long, and the eager beaver can tee off at 7am and play until 10pm – easily enough time for 54 holes, unless you're prone to slice, hook or pull. But the rough of gorse, broom, heather and whin is insatiable, and a great deal of time can be lost searching for balls.

Most golfers will immediately head for St Andrews. They will be surprised to find that the

LEFT: St Andrews: a magnet for all golfers.
ABOVE RIGHT: teeing off beside the sea.

Old Course has two, rather than the customary four, short holes and has only 11 greens. Yet it is categorically an 18-hole course: seven greens are shared. This explains the enormous size of the greens, on which you can find yourself facing a putt of almost 100 yards (90 metres). Remember it is the homeward-bound player who has the

right of way on these giant double greens.

Don't be too distressed if you fail to obtain a starting time on the Old (two-thirds of starting times are allocated by ballot: contact the starter before 2pm on the day before you wish to play). The New Course is even more difficult, but St Andrews still has four other courses from which to choose.

Ancient as the Royal and Ancient Golf Club of St Andrews is, it must bow the knee to the Honorable Company of Edinburgh Golfers, which was formed in 1774 and which is generally accepted as the oldest golf club in the world. Its present Muirfield course which is at Gullane (pronounced *Gillun*), 13 miles (21 km) east of Edinburgh, is considered to be the ultimate test of golf. The rough here is ferocious and if, on looking around, you fail to see your partner, don't panic and think they have been abducted by the "wee folk": they will merely be out of sight in one of the nearly 200 deep potbunkers which litter the course.

And not to worry if you can't play on Muirfield: the tiny village of Gullane is also the home of the three challenging Gullane courses (simply called 1, 2 and 3) and to Luffness New. The latter is "New" because, by Scotland's standards, it is just that, having been founded as recently as 1894.

Capital courses

Back in the city of Edinburgh are more than a score of courses, two of which are home to very ancient clubs. The Royal Burgess Golfing Society claims to be even older than the Hon. Coy, while the neighbouring Bruntsfield Links Golfing Society is only a few years younger.

On the road from Gullane to Edinburgh you pass through Musselburgh, where golf is known to have been played in 1672 and, most probably, even before that. Was this where Mary Queen of Scots was seen playing a few days after the murder of Lord Darnley, her second husband? Was Mary the world's first golf widow?

CLUB FORMALITIES

At the majority of courses no formal introduction is necessary: as a visitor, you just stroll up, pay your money and play. Some clubs do ask that you be a member of another club. Others require an introduction by a member, although if you are an overseas visitor this formality is usually waived. And the better courses demand a valid handicap certificate, which usually must be below 20 for men and 30 for ladies. Access to the course doesn't mean you will gain entry to the clubhouse – that remains the private domain of a particular club whose members happen to make use of the adjacent course.

Glasgow, never outdone by Edinburgh, has nearly 30 courses. Outstanding among these are Killermont and Haggs Castle. The latter is less than 3 miles (5 km) from the city centre. While golfers thrill over birdies and eagles at Haggs, their non-playing partners can enthuse over the renowned Burrell Collection, which is less than half-a-mile (1 km) away. Even closer to the Burrell is the excellent Pollok course. Further afield at Luss (23 miles/37 km northwest of the city) by the bonnie banks of Loch Lomond is a brand-new course designed by Tom Weiskopf. A second Jack Nicklaus course is a possibility and the Loch Lomond Golf Club may well become the best in Britain.

Troon, 30 miles (48 km) south of Glasgow and frequently the scene of the Open, is the kingpin in a series of nearly 30 courses bordering the Atlantic rollers. Here, without hardly ever stooping to pick up your ball, you can play for almost 30 miles (48 km). Troon itself has five courses.

To the north is Barassie with one, and then Gailes with two courses. South of Troon are three courses at Prestwick – scene of the first Open in 1860 – and Ayr, also with three courses. Fifteen minutes further down the "course" are the exclusive Arran and Ailsa links of Turnberry. There's a much better chance of playing

at Brunston Castle, a few miles to the southeast, where an excellent course – parkland rather than links – opened in 1992.

Over on the east coast is another remarkable conglomerate of courses with St Andrews as its kingpin. About 30 miles to the north, across the Tay Bridge, are the three Carnoustie courses. The Medal course here, formerly scene of many Opens, has been called brutal, evil and monstrous.

Then, 20 miles (32 km) south of St Andrews and strung, like a priceless necklace, along the

ABOVE LEFT: caught in a bunker at Muirfield.
ABOVE: golf can sometimes be a risky business.

north shore of the Firth of Forth, are the Elie, Leven, Lundin Links and Crail courses. The Crail course is claimed by golf-storians to be the seventh oldest in the world.

Other glittering gems are found in the northeast. Here are Balgownie and Murcar, two of Aberdeen's half-a-dozen courses; nearby Cruden Bay; Nairn, which is close to Inverness; and Dornoch, which stands in splendid isolation in the extreme northeast. The Balgownie and Cruden Bay clubs are both 200 years old; the founders of the latter are probably turning in their graves at the new name of their club – the Cruden Bay Golf and Country Club.

Dornoch is, even for a Scottish course, under-played and may be Britain's most under-rated course. Authorities believe that this course, all of whose holes have a view of the sea, would be on the Open rota if it was closer to the main centres of population.

Down at the extreme southwest of the country is Machrihanish, another under-rated, under-played links which is far from the madding crowd. Its turf is so naturally perfect that "every ball is teed, wherever it is". And if the views from here, which include Ireland and the Inner Hebrides, seduce you then you might wish to make your way over the seas to Islay, which is renowned for both its whisky and its Machrie course.

New additions

Scotland, home of golf, also boasts some superb inland courses. Many *aficionados* consider the King's at Gleneagles to be the best inland course in Britain. Certainly nowhere in the world can there be a championship course set in such dramatically beautiful scenery. Recently it was joined by the Monarch, the resort's newest course, which is from the drawing board of Jack Nicklaus and which has the flavour of an American rather than a Scottish course. These are just two of four courses which make up the Gleneagles complex.

If these four aren't enough, a mere 30 miles (48 km) to the north is Blairgowrie with its fabled Rosemount course. Here, among parasol pines, larches, silver birch and evergreens, you'll come upon lost golf balls, partridges, pheasant and otter. And new courses are still being created: near Kelso is the Roxburghe Course, opened in 1997 and designed to Championship standard. ❑

HUNTING, SHOOTING AND FISHING

The natural assets of Scotland are eagerly exploited by wealthy proprietors,
satisfying the continuing demand for upmarket sports

While Scotland may have been blessed with more deer, grouse, salmon and trout than most small European countries, a significant proportion of these assets are controlled by a small number of wealthy estates, whose owners may live a long way from Scotland. This means that "field sports" such as deer stalking, salmon fishing and grouse shooting are touchy political issues, bound up with memories of the Highland Clearances and the ownership and use of the land.

Ownership of large Highland estates varies from local aristocrats who may have been there for centuries to southern financiers, European entrepreneurs and even oil-rich Arabs. While "traditional" estate owners retain a fairly paternalistic approach, some of the newer proprietors arrive with little or no knowledge of the Scottish way of life, and try to recoup their investment any way they can, often at the expense of local interests.

Clash of interests

Rights enjoyed and shared by local people can suddenly vanish. This happened when the then North of Scotland Hydroelectric Board (now Scottish Hydro) sold its fishing rights on the River Conon north of Inverness to a City of London financier for a reputed £1.5 million. He promptly divided the river, into weekly timeshare "beats" which were sold at up to £15,000 per person per week. Not unnaturally, locals who had long fished the river, but who could not afford such prices, were incensed.

There have also been problems in the past with estates covering large areas of prime hillwalking country trying to deny access to walkers and climbers during the shooting seasons. Many walkers regard access as a right, not a privilege, and have been prone to ignore aggressive or intimidating "keep out" notices.

The situation has eased considerably, thanks

to much greater co-operation between the various factions. A national Access Forum, set up by Scottish Natural Heritage, has agreed a "Concordat on Access" which recognises both the needs of the estates and the ambitions of walkers. In several sensitive areas, a "Hillphone" system operates under which walkers

can phone a recorded message which tells them where stalking or grouse shooting is taking place. Such moves recognise the importance of finding ways for the commercial interests of the sporting estates to exist alongside recreations such as hillwalking, since both can make a valuable contribution to the local economy.

Health and safety

The health of Scotland field sports depends heavily on the state of the ecology, so environmental groups and estate owners can have similar concerns. Uneasy bedfellows in the past, they are now working together on such matters as scientific studies into the reasons for the dramatic

---

PRECEDING PAGES: fishing holiday.
LEFT: trophies from hunts in Brodick Castle, Arran.
ABOVE RIGHT: a Highlands gamekeeper.

decline in grouse numbers in many areas. Other common concerns include acid rain and the damage caused by tributyl tin to salmon and sea trout. Over-enthusiastic conifer planting of large areas has, happily, been reined in, though its effects will be felt for some time to come.

Chasing the deer

Stalking the magnificent red deer is one of Scotland's prime attractions for wealthy foreign sportsmen. According to the Deer Commission for Scotland, in 1997 there were more than 330,000 red deer in Scotland, most of them north of the "highland line" between Helensburgh and Stonehaven. Since 1950, numbers have more than doubled, the increase in recent years being partly due to more animals living in woodland – the cover is opening up as forests reach maturity. The annual cull is now set at between 60,000 and 70,000, and this should bring the number down to a more sustainable level.

The vast majority of the shooting is by professional stalkers, foresters or sporting parties under professional guidance. After the stag season ends, hind culling, though not for sport, continues until February. Although the stag stalking season officially runs from 1 July to 20 October, very little shooting is done before mid-

August. For the next two months, shooters from all over Britain, Europe and North America descend on the Highlands in pursuit of a stag. All-terrain vehicles are increasingly used to get them on to the hill, but the final part of the stalk can still be an exhausting belly-crawl through heather or peat until the stalker decides the prey is close enough to get off a clean shot.

Nor does this pleasure come cheap. A week's stalking (six days) can cost up to £2,000 and only the trophy (the head) belongs to the hunter; the venison will be sold by the estate. Accommodation is extra. Rifles can be hired, but most sportsmen bring their own. A decent stalking rifle will cost anything from £500 to £5,000.

EXPENSIVE PURSUITS

The "Glorious Twelfth" is the popular name for 12 August, the day the red grouse season opens. It has been less than glorious in recent years, with a sharp decline in grouse numbers due to predation and disease. There are about 500 grouse moors in Scotland and Northern England, and their management is carefully arranged to provide the best heather conditions for the birds. Like deer stalking, grouse shooting doesn't come cheap. Drive grouse (shot with the aid of teams of beaters) can cost around £100 a brace: even estate-reared pheasants can cost the shooter £40 a brace.

There are around 200,000 roe deer in Scotland and shooting roe deer bucks (males), often from high seats fixed in the trees, is becoming more popular. It is less expensive, costs being roughly between half and two-thirds of those for red deer stag shoot.

Seeking the salmon

The upmarket sport *par excellence* has to be salmon fishing in one of Scotland's great salmon rivers such as the Dee, the Spey, the Tay, the Tweed or the Conon. One survey estimated that it cost the affluent angler over £2,000 to land an Atlantic salmon from a prime stretch of a Scottish river. Certainly, a week's fishing on a good stretch (called a "beat") at the height of the season (July to September) on one of the classier rivers is likely to set the fisherman back between £1,500 and £2,000.

Yet demand is so high that a number of specialist firms, and even some estates, have taken to operating salmon beats on a "timeshare" basis. It works like this. The company buys a decent stretch of a good salmon river for a very large sum of money. The river is then divided into beats, and on each beat a week's fishing is sold "in perpetuity" for up to £30,000 (depending on when the slot occurs in the season and the quality of the fishing). All this is much against the wishes of those, like the Scottish Campaign for Public Angling (SCAPA), who believe that everyone should have the right to fish where they want and that no waters should be closed off to the public.

With so much money at stake, it is little wonder that river proprietors have grown anxious as they have seen salmon stocks decline. In 1967 about 600,000 salmon were taken in Scottish rivers. Thirty years later, that figure has fallen to under 200,000. The drop has been attributed to a number of factors, including net fishing at river mouths, river and sea pollution, and declining fertility in the fish.

The net fishing has almost died out, thanks partly to the efforts of the Atlantic Salmon Conservation Trust, set up in 1986. The Trust rapidly raised several million pounds and acquired the rights to many net fishing operations, then simply closed them down. However, problems still exist. Drift netting still takes place

in the far north Atlantic, off Greenland, Iceland and the Faroe Islands, and poachers are still busy along Scotland's rivers.

While salmon fishing may be the glamour end of the sport, many anglers feel that too much is made of it. They argue that there is much better sport in the brown trout fishing which is available – for far less outlay – on countless Scottish lochs, particularly on the west coast and in the northern Highlands, where the salmon are not abundant. Some remote lochs are still only visited by a few enthusiasts, and 100 fish in a day on two rods from a boat is not just a dream.

Trout are tops

Tourist authorities are beginning to promote this resource through schemes whereby a single ticket will get the angler access to a variety of waters during a holiday. Recent figures indicate that angling is worth over £25 million per year to the Scottish economy, and this figure is bound to grow as the hitherto secret delights of the upland rivers and lochs become better known.

Who knows, you might get lucky and snag one of the ferocious ferox trout found in the west Highlands. They weigh up to 20 lbs (9 kg) and are cannibals, but as one angler said, "a hell of an exciting fish to get on the end of your line". And a great tale to tell afterwards in the pub ❏.

ABOVE LEFT: a catch from the River Don.
ABOVE RIGHT: fishing in the River Spey.

A WEE DRAM

*While many dispute the secret of the unique taste of Scotch whisky,
few deny the pleasures to be had from the "water of life"*

At the end of sophisticated dinner parties in London, guests are invariably offered a choice of brandy or port but seldom a glass of Scotch. Familiarity, perhaps, has produced contempt for the native product – or, the Scots would argue, the English are showing their customary ignorance of all things Scottish.

The prejudice is an ill-founded one because good malt whiskies have a wider range of flavour and aroma than brandy and – an extra bonus – they are less likely to make the over-indulger's head throb the morning after. Snobbery probably accounts for the attitude, too, for Scotland's unique drink has never quite managed to cultivate the exclusive image of cognac.

For one thing, there's a lot more of it on the international market. Scotch is one of Britain's top five export items: even the Vatican, on one recent annual reckoning, bought 18,000 bottles. More than 700 million bottles a year are exported; the major market is the United States, followed by France (which consumes more whisky than cognac), Japan and Spain.

Toddler's tipple

The lowly origins of Scotch may also be partly to blame for its fluctuating fortunes. In the 18th century, it was drunk as freely as the water from which it was made, by peasants and aristocrats alike. A spoonful was given to newborn babies in the Highlands and even respectable gentlewomen might start the day with "a wee dram". The poorest crofter could offer the visitor a drink, thanks to the ubiquity of home-made stills which made millions of bottles of "mountain dew" in the remote glens of the Highlands. Even in Edinburgh, no-one needed to go thirsty: excise officers estimated in 1777 that the city had eight licensed stills and 400 illegal ones.

Yet something as easy to make cannot be made authentically outside Scotland. Many have tried,

PRECEDING PAGES: whisky maturing under the eye of the customs officer.
LEFT: whisky still.
ABOVE RIGHT: tools of the distiller's trade.

and the Japanese have thrown the most modern technology at the problem; but the combination of damp climate and soft water flowing through the peat cannot be replicated elsewhere.

Some historians believe that the art of distilling was brought to Scotland by Christian missionary monks. But it is just as likely that

Highland farmers discovered for themselves how to distil spirits from their surplus barley. The earliest known reference to whisky occurred in 1494, when Scottish Exchequer Rolls record that Friar John Cor purchased a quantity of malt "to make aquavitae".

These days there are two kinds of Scotch whisky: *malt*, made from malted barley only; and *grain*, made from malted barley together with unmalted barley, maize or other cereals. Most popular brands are blends of both types of whisky – typically 60 percent grain to 40 percent malt.

A single malt, the product of one distillery, has become an increasingly popular drink, thanks largely to the aggressive marketing by

William Grant & Sons of their Glenfiddich brand. But sales of single malts still account for only one bottle in 20 sold around the world, and most of the production of single malt distilleries is used to add flavour to a blended whisky.

Making whisky

So automated are Scotland's 100-plus distilleries that visitors, sipping an end-of-tour glass of the product they have watched being manufactured, are left with an image of the beautifully proportioned onion-shaped copper stills and a lingering aroma of malted barley – but not with any clear idea of the process by which

water from a Highland stream is transformed into *usquebaugh*, the water of life.

What happens is this. To make malt whisky, plump and dry barley (which, unlike the water, doesn't have to be local) sits in tanks of water for two or three days. It is then spread out on a concrete floor or placed in large cylindrical drums and allowed to germinate for between eight and 12 days. Next it is dried in a kiln, which ideally should be heated by a peat fire. The dried malt is ground and mixed with hot water in a huge circular vat called a mash tun. A sugary liquid, "wort", is drawn off from the porridge-like result, leaving the remaining solids to be sold as cattle food. The wort is fed into massive vessels containing up to 45,000 litres of liquid, where living yeast is stirred into the mix in order to convert the sugar in the wort into crude alcohol.

After about 48 hours, the "wash" (a clear liquid containing weak alcohol) is transferred to the copper pot stills and heated to the point at which alcohol turns to vapour. This vapour rises up the still to be condensed by a cooling plant into distilled alcohol which is then passed through a second still.

Tricks of the trade

The trick is to know exactly when the whisky has distilled sufficiently. Modern measuring devices offer scientific precision, but the individual judgement of an experienced distiller is hard to beat. Once distilled, the liquid is poured into oak casks which, being porous, allow air to enter. Evaporation takes place, removing the harsher constituents of the new spirit and enabling it to mellow. Legally it can't be sold as

---

TASTE THE DIFFERENCE

Despite the claims of distillers that each whisky blend has a unique taste, the truth is that most people, in a blind tasting, would be hard-pressed to say whether they were drinking Bell's, Teacher's, Dewar's, Johnnie Walker or J&B. Pure malt whiskies, on the other hand, are more readily identifiable. The experienced Scotch drinker can differentiate between Highland malts, Lowland malts, Campeltown malts and Islay malts, and there is certainly no mistaking the bouquet of a malt such as Laphroaig, which is usually described as tasting of iodine or seaweed. So which is best? Whole evenings can be whiled away in Scotland debating

and researching the question with no firm conclusions being reached. It all comes down to individual taste – after all, in the words of Robert Burns: "Freedom and Whisky gang thegither [together]."

However, the one point of agreement is that a good malt whisky should not be drunk with a mixer such as soda or lemonade, which would destroy the subtle flavour. Yet, although it is said there are two things which a Highlander likes naked, connoisseurs may be permitted to add a little water to their single malt. After dinner, malts are best drunk neat, as a liqueur. Blended whisky, in contrast, is refreshing in hot weather when mixed with soda.

whisky until it has spent three years in the cask, and a good malt will stay casked for at least eight years.

It wasn't until the 1820s that distilling began to develop from small family-run concerns into large manufacturing businesses. What accelerated the change was the invention in 1830 by Aeneas Coffey of a patent still. This was faster and cheaper than traditional methods; more importantly it did not need the perfect mix of peat and water, but could produce whisky from a mixture of malted and unmalted barley mashed with other cereals.

But was the resulting grain whisky a real

ing tiny amounts of 30 or 40 malt whiskies with grain whisky, distillers found, could produce a palatable compromise between taste and strength. What's more, an almost infinite variety of combinations was possible, enabling each brand to claim its own unique taste.

Old favourites

In sales terms, Glenfiddich leads the market in single malts, exporting 6 million bottles a year to 185 countries. The Scots themselves tend to favour Glenmorangie, which is matured in old Bourbon casks, charred on the inside, for at least 10 years to produce a smooth spirit with hints

Scotch? Some dismissed it as flavourless surgical spirits; others approved of it as "lighter-bodied". The argument rumbled on until 1905, when one of London's local authorities decided to test in the courts whether pubs could legally sell the patent-still (as opposed to the pot-still) product as "whisky". Even the courts couldn't agree. It was left to a Royal Commission to deliver the verdict that both drinks were equally wholesome and could call themselves whisky.

The industry's future, however, lay in the marriage between malt and grain whiskies. Blend-

of peat smoke and vanilla. The most popular malt in the United States is The Macallan, which is produced on Speyside and matured in 100 percent sherry casks seasoned for two years in Spain with dry oloroso sherry; connoisseurs argue that the 10-year old is a better drink than the more impressive-sounding 18-year old.

The brave should sample Glenfarclas (with over 60 percent alcohol). Those desiring a more diluted sample need only take one of the many distillery tours on the Scotch Whisky Trail. Because whisky "breathes" while maturing in its casks, as much as 4 million gallons (20 million litres) evaporate into the air each year. All you have to do is inhale ❏.

ABOVE LEFT: an Oban bar's whisky selection.
ABOVE: rolling out the barrels on Islay.

PORRIDGE, HAGGIS AND COCK-A-LEEKIE

Cooked breakfasts, high teas and smoked salmon for supper:

traditional Scottish food satisfies the heartiest of appetites

Scotland, as the writer H.V. Morton once remarked, is the best place in the world to take an appetite; and although, on a permanent basis, the local diet has its hazards – many believe it to be the main cause of the country's internationally appalling level of heart attacks and strokes – the seafood at least can hardly fail to be good for the health. Certainly, lobsters, large langoustines and giant Orkney scallops do wonders for the most jaded of appetites.

No doubt Mr Morton's appetite was coaxed also by the Scottish air, which in the Highlands (and even the Lowlands) remains remarkably pure. Indeed, it has traditionally helped to determine the nature of the Scottish kitchen. It is vigorous and sometimes blustery air, calling for the inner warmth and energy produced by porridge (the Scottish equivalent of Italian *polenta*, though grey rather than yellow), by broth and haggis, by baps, butteries, barley bannocks, griddle scones, oatcakes and other examples of local baking; plus numerous nips of whisky and pot after pot of tea.

Scottish roots

The rise of Chinese and Indian restaurants and an increasingly international outlook on food have influenced Scottish taste in recent years. Scottish cookery still has its roots in the soil, however, especially in some of those isolated hotels and restaurants far from the main cities. There, real Scottish cuisine is something the proprietors are genuinely proud of serving, including hearty cooked breakfasts of bacon, egg, black pudding (a type of strong sausage) and perhaps kippers. Elsewhere, Scotland has its own unedifying brand of fast food. "Scotch eggs", for example, are hard-boiled eggs wrapped in sausage meat and then fried; the result is as appetising as a greasy cannonball.

If flour and meat form the basis of English

cookery, meat and fish form the basis of Scottish cuisine, along with bakery, which can sometimes be stodgy, heavy and mass-produced but is often really delectable. Not too long ago in Scotland there were fewer restaurants than tea rooms. Here, people ate not only lunch and

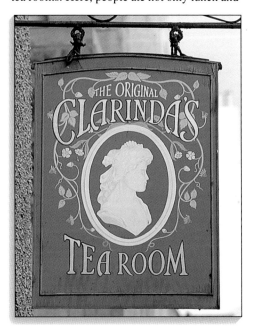

afternoon tea but also "high tea", which usually consisted of fish and chips and an array of scones and cakes.

It is also significant that biscuit-making remains an extensive and popular industry in both Edinburgh and Glasgow and as far north as Kirkwall in Orkney (where the oatcakes are arguably the best in the land). Dundee is renowned for its eponymous cake and for orange marmalade, its gift to the world's breakfast and tea tables – though the theory that the name "marmalade" derives from the words *Marie est malade* (referring to the food given to Mary Queen of Scots when she was ill) must be considered rather far-fetched.

LEFT: fishmongers in Rothesay, on the Isle of Bute.
ABOVE RIGHT: time for afternoon tea and cakes.

Flavourful fish and meat

Kippers, too, are a treat. The best of them are from Loch Fyne or the Achiltibuie smokery in Ross and Cromarty, where their colour emerges properly golden, not dyed repellent red as they are in so many places. Finnan-haddies (otherwise known as haddock) are a tasty alternative, boiled in milk and butter. Salmon and trout, sadly, are just as likely to come from some west-coast or northern fish farm as fresh from the river, but the standard remains high.

If you're buying from a fishmonger, ask for "wild" salmon, more flavourful than the farmed variety. On the other hand, farmed salmon is

generally preferred, to help ensure uniformity, in the production of justifiably renowned smoked salmon.

The beef of the Aberdeen Angus remains the most famous in the world (escaping the worst of the BSE scares). Good Scottish meat, the experts claim, should be hung for at least four weeks or even for eight – unlike supermarket steak, which is not aged at all – and should never be sliced less than 1¹/4 inches (3 cm) thick.

Venison, pheasant, hare and grouse are also established features of the Scottish kitchen. Admittedly, the romance of eating grouse after it has been ritually shot on or around the glorious 12 August should be tempered (if you are honest with yourself) by this bird's depressing fibrous toughness, which makes grouse shooting seem, at least to a gourmet, an unutterable waste of time.

The national dish

As for haggis – though it, too, is hardly a gourmet delight – it does offer a fascinating experience for brave visitors. Scotland's great mystery dish is really only a sheep's stomach stuffed with minced lamb and beef, along with onions, oatmeal and a blend of seasonings and spices. After being boiled, the stomach is sliced open, as spectacularly as possible, and the contents served piping hot.

Butchers today often use a plastic bag instead of a stomach; this has the advantage that it is less likely to burst during the boiling process, resulting in the meat being ruined. But no haggis devotee would contemplate such a substitute.

The tastiest haggis, by popular acclaim, comes from Macsween's of Edinburgh, who also make a vegetarian haggis. (That's progress, as the Orkney poet George Mackay Brown would cynically say.) Small portions of haggis are sometimes served as starter courses in fashionable Scottish restaurants, though the authentic way to eat it is as a main course with chappit tatties (potatoes), bashed neeps (mashed turnips) and a number of nips (Scotch whisky, preferably malt). This is especially so on Burns Night (25 January), when the haggis is ceremonially piped to table, and supper is accompanied by poetry reading, music and Burns's own *Address to the Haggis*; or on St Andrew's Night (30 November), when haggis is again attacked with gusto by loyal Scots the world over.

Colourful cuisine

Many of Scotland's national dishes have names as rugged as Scottish speech. The ubiquitous Scotch broth (made with mutton stock, vegetables, barley, lentils and split peas) is a pale competitor to fare with such names as feather fowlie (a chicken soup), cock-a-leekie (a soup made from chicken and leeks, but authentic only if it also contains prunes), cullen skink (soup made from smoked haddock and potatoes), huggamuggie (Shetland fish haggis, using the fish's stomach), Arbroath smokies (smoked haddock stuffed with butter), crappit heids (haddock heads stuffed with lobster), partan bree (a soup made from giant crab claws, cooked with rice), stovies (potatoes cooked with onion), carageen mould (a Hebridean dessert), cranachan (a mixture of cream, oatmeal, sugar and rum), or hattit kit (an ancient Highland sweet made from buttermilk, milk, cream, sugar and nutmeg).

Though the Scots are said to like far more salt in their soup – and with their fish and vegetables – than the English, they also possess an exceptionally sweet tooth, as some of the above dishes confirm. This is also seen in their penchant for fizzy lemonade and the Glaswegian's

from the Border country make a welcome change from tinted Scottish Cheddar. Crowdie, Scotland's original creamed cottage cheese, has evolved into Caboc from the Highlands; with its original oatmeal coating, it is almost as creamy as France's *crème fraîche*. Pentland and Lothian cheeses are Scotland's answer to camembert and brie.

Cheese before pudding, as a running order, reflects Scotland's Auld Alliance with France, as does the large amount of fine claret to be

favourite thirst-quencher, Irn-Bru, a sparkling concoction said to be "made from girders". And don't miss the chance to sample the enormous variety of puddings and desserts, often served with a generous helping of butterscotch sauce.

Real cheese, at last fighting back against the marketing boards' anonymous mass production, has been making progress in Scotland. Lanark Blue, hand-made from unpasteurised ewe's milk, has been one recent success, worth looking out for in go-ahead restaurants. Unpasteurised (hard) Teviotdale or (soft) Bonchester

found on the wine-lists of good restaurants and hotels and in many homes. But pudding before savoury is also an admirable tradition, for a long time almost defunct but now showing happy signs of revival.

Hot savouries have always tended to have mysterious, sometimes misleading, names. Scotch woodcock, for instance, is no more a bird than Welsh rarebit is a rabbit; a woodcock, in this context, is a portion of anchovies coated with scrambled eggs and served (like most savouries) on small fresh slices of toast. At best, it rounds off a meal most piquantly, as do Loch Fyne toasts, where kipper fillets replace the anchovies.

ABOVE LEFT: on offer: Scotland's most famous dish.
ABOVE: preparing smoked haddock.

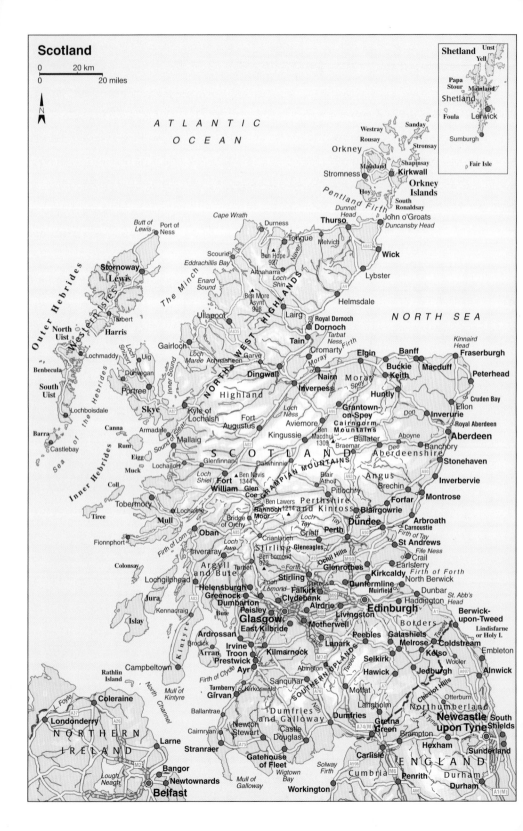

PLACES

A land of dramatic scenery, romantic history and countless outdoor attractions, Scotland is one of Europe's most varied and captivating regions

Scotland has something to suit all tastes. Whether you want the peace of wide, open spaces, or the excitement of dynamic cities, you can find it here. Even the unpredictable weather cannot dull Scotland's charm, as the wildest Highland thunderstorm only enhances the magnificence of the hills.

Edinburgh, a majestic capital city, enchants effortlessly, its castle towering over it on a rugged crag as a daily reminder of its turbulent history. These days, as a "court city" whose court long ago emigrated to London, Edinburgh cultivates culture and rejoices in its appellation of "the Athens of the North". Just 40 miles (64 km) away, Glasgow, by contrast, is Britain's great unknown city, still suffering from an outdated image of industrial grime and urban decay. Yet, having had its heart ripped out by motorways in the 1960s, it remodelled itself to take centre stage as European City of Culture in 1990, and its Burrell Collection museum has, to Edinburgh's chagrin, soared to the top of tourism's league tables.

Outside the two great cities lies an astonishingly varied landscape. To the southwest are the moorlands, lochs and hills of Dumfries and Galloway, haunt of Scotland's national poet Robert Burns; to the southeast, the castles, forests and glens of the Borders, one of Europe's unspoilt areas; to the west, the rugged splendour of the West Highlands, a fragmented wilderness of mountain and moor, heather and stag, and the jumping-off point for Skye and the Western Isles; to the northeast, the farms and fishing villages of Fife and the swing along the North Sea coast through Dundee towards the granite city of Aberdeen, Scotland's oil capital; and, to the north, the elusive monster of Loch Ness, the awesomely empty tracts of the Highlands, and the islands of Orkney and Shetland that are more Norse than Scottish.

Scotland's greatest appeal is to people who appreciate the open air, whether scenery or outdoor pursuits. The attractions range from pleasant rambling across moors and treks along long-distance footpaths to arduous hill walking, hair-raising rock climbs and pony trekking. You can ski down snow-capped mountains, canoe in fast-flowing white water, thrill to some of Europe's best surfing, fish for salmon in crystal-clear streams or play golf in the country that invented the game.

"Scotland's For Me!" chorused a Scottish Tourist Board advertising campaign. Few visitors find any reason to disagree. ❏

PRECEDING PAGES: Blackrock Cottage, Glencoe; the much-photographed Eilean Donan Castle, Wester Ross; Edinburgh Castle from the air.

EDINBURGH

Set among a series of volcanic hills and small lochs, Edinburgh is a stunning confection of late medieval tenements, neo-classical terraces, tidy suburbs, rivers and wooded gardens

Map, page 134–5

Not for nothing was that great parable of the divided self, *Dr Jekyll and Mr Hyde*, written by an Edinburgh man, Robert Louis Stevenson. He may have set the story in London, but he conjured it out of the bizarre life of a respectable Edinburgh tradesman. More than one critic has taken the Jekyll and Hyde story as a handy metaphor for the city of Edinburgh itself: something at once universal yet characteristically Scottish. Where else does a semi-ramshackle late medieval town glower down on such Georgian elegance? What other urban centre contains such huge chunks of sheer wilderness within its boundaries? Does any other city in Europe have so many solid Victorian suburbs surrounded by such bleak housing estates? Stevenson himself was inclined to agree. "Few places, if any," he wrote, "offer a more barbaric display of contrasts to the eye."

Just as Edward Hyde "gave an impression of deformity without any nameable malformation" so the meaner side of Edinburgh tends to lurk unnoticed in the beauty of its topography and the splendour of its architecture. Even the weather seems to play its part. "The weather is raw and boisterous in winter, shifty and ungenial in summer, and downright meteorological purgatory in spring," Stevenson wrote of his home town. But the Jekyll and Hyde metaphor can be stretched too far. For all its sly duality and shifty ways, Edinburgh remains one of Europe's most beautiful and amenable cities.

LEFT: fireworks open the Edinburgh festival.
BELOW: on parade at the Thistle Ceremony.

Living theatre

To the south the city is hemmed in by the Pentland Hills – some of which are almost 2,000 ft (600 metres) high – and to the north by the island-studded waters of the Firth of Forth. In 1878 Stevenson declared himself baffled that "this profusion of eccentricities, this dream in masonry and living rock is not a drop-scene in a theatre, but a city in the world of everyday reality".

Which, of course, it is. At the last count, Edinburgh contained almost 440,000 people rattling around in 100 sq. miles (39 sq. km) on the south bank of the Firth of Forth. While the city's traditional economy of "books, beer and biscuits" has been whittled away by the ravages of recession and change, there is a powerful underpinning of banking, insurance, shipping, the professions (especially the law), the universities, hospitals, and of course government bureaucracies (local and central). By and large, the North Sea oil boom passed Edinburgh by, although some of the city's financiers did well enough by shuffling investment funds around, and for a while Leith Docks was used as an onshore supply base, to coat pipes and to build steel deck modules.

And like every other decent-sized city in the western hemisphere Edinburgh thrives on a rich cultural mix.

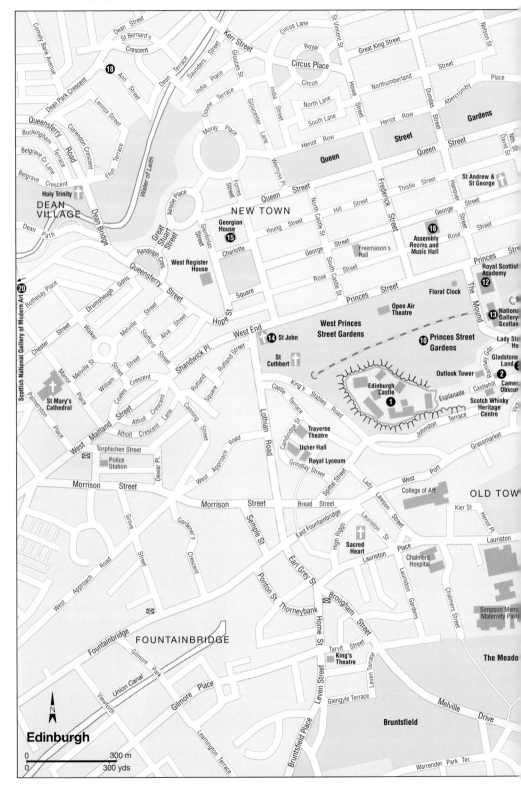

Edinburgh

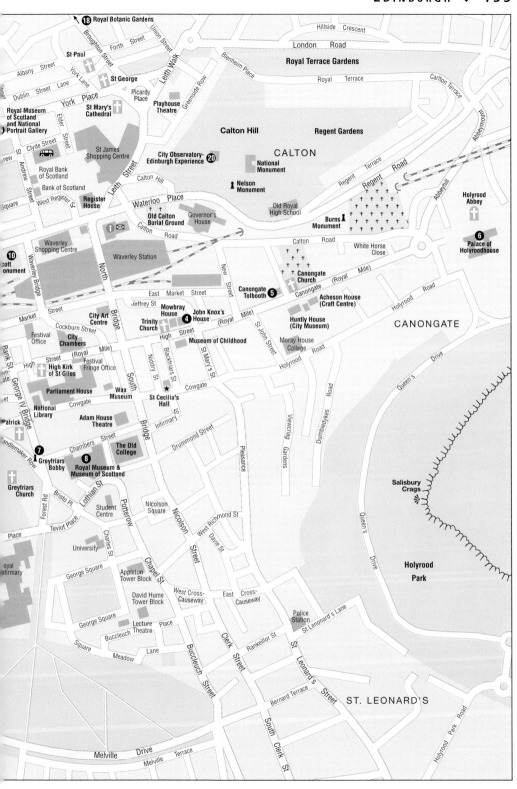

The Scotsman *newspaper, published in Edinburgh, is still arguably the most influential piece of media north of the border, acting as a kind of notice-board of the Scottish establishment.*

The "base" population is overwhelmingly Scots with a large Irish content, but there are also big communities of Poles, Italians, Ukranians, Jews, Pakistanis, Sikhs, Bengalis, Chinese and, of course, English. Within that mix there are echoes of Ulster.

Although Edinburgh has been spared the kind of religious bigotry which bedevils Glasgow, it still has separate schools for Catholic and Protestant children. And every July the city stages one of the biggest "Orange Walks" outside of Northern Ireland.

Capital city

In May 1999 Edinburgh will once again become a capital city with a parliament (initially meeting at the Church of Scotland Assembly Hall, until a purpose-built venue is ready). Following a strong endorsement from the Scottish people in the referendum of September 1997, the devolved parliament signals a significant start to the new millennium. The new Scottish Parliament will be partly elected by proportional representation and it will administer a wide range of matters, but major areas such as defence and foreign policy will still be dealt with by the United Kingdom Parliament at Westminster, London.

Already, Edinburgh wields more power and influence than any British city outside of London. It is the centre of the Scots legal system, home to the Court of Session (the civil court) and the High Court of Justiciary (criminal court) from which there is no appeal to the House of Lords: Edinburgh's decision is final. Edinburgh is also the base of the Church of Scotland (the established church) whose General Assembly every May floods Edinburgh with sober-suited Presbyterian ministers from all over Scotland.

BELOW: a rich mix of cultures.

And the British Government runs its policies in Scotland through the Edinburgh-based **Scottish Office**, whose boss, the Secretary of State for Scotland, is a member of the British cabinet. Anyone seeking to consult the records of Scotland (land titles, company registration, government archives, lists of bankrupts, births, marriages, deaths) must come to Edinburgh.

Map, page 134–5

The early days

No-one is quite sure just how old Edinburgh is, only that people have been living in the area for more than 5,000 years. But it seems certain that the city grew from a tiny community perched on the "plug" of volcanic rock which now supports **Edinburgh Castle**. With steep, easily-defended sides, natural springs of water and excellent vantage points, the castle rock was squabbled over for hundreds of years by generations of Picts, Scots, British (Welsh) and Angles, with the Scots (from Ireland) finally coming out on top. It was not until the 11th century that Edinburgh settled down to be the capital city of Scotland, and a royal residence was built within the walls of Edinburgh Castle.

But Edinburgh proved to be a strategic liability in the medieval wars with the English. It was too close to England. Time after time, English armies crashed across the border laying waste the farmlands of the southeast, and burning Edinburgh itself. It happened in 1174 (when the English held Edinburgh Castle for 12 years), in 1296, in 1313 (during the Wars of Independence), in 1357, in 1573, in 1650 and as late as 1689 when the Duke of Gordon tried, and failed, to hold Edinburgh Castle against the Protestant army of William of Orange.

The hammering of Edinburgh by the English came to an end in 1707 when the Scottish Parliament, many of whose members had been bribed by English

Ready for visitors at Edinburgh Castle: after London, Edinburgh is the most popular tourist destination in Britain.

BELOW: a City Halberdier, called after the halberd (pike) he carries.

The concentration of talent in 18th-century Edinburgh led John Amyat, the King's Chemist, to remark that he could stand at the Mercat Cross and "in a few minutes, take 50 men of genius by the hand".

BELOW: a city by design: Edinburgh's West End.

interests, voted to abandon the sovereignty of Scotland in favour of a union with England. "Now there's an end of an auld sang," the old Earl of Seafield was heard to mutter as he signed the Act. But in fact, power and influence had been haemorrhaging out of Edinburgh ever since the Union of the Crowns in 1603 when the Scottish King James VI (son of Mary Queen of Scots) became the first monarch of Great Britain and Ireland.

Stripped of its Royal Family, courtiers, parliament and civil service, 18th-century Edinburgh should have lapsed into a sleepy provincialism. But the Treaty of Union guaranteed the position of Scots law and the role of the Presbyterian Church of Scotland. With both these powerful institutions still firmly entrenched in Edinburgh, the city was still a place where the powerful and influential met to make important decisions.

The Scottish Enlightenment

In fact, for reasons which are still not clear, 18th-century Scotland became one of Europe's intellectual powerhouses, producing scholars and philosophers like David Hume, Adam Smith and William Robertson, architect-builders like William Adam and his sons Robert and John, engineers like James Watt, Thomas Telford and John Rennie, surgeons like John and William Hunter, and painters like Henry Raeburn and Alan Ramsay.

That explosion of talent became known as the Scottish Enlightenment, and one of its greatest creations was the **New Town** of Edinburgh. Between 1767 and 1840 a whole impeccable new city – bright, spacious, elegant and rational – was created on the land to the north of the **Old Town**. It was very quickly occupied by the aristocracy, gentry and "middling" classes of Edinburgh who left

the Old Town to the poor and to the waves of Irish and Highland immigrants who flooded into Edinburgh from the 1840s on.

Like most British (and European) cities, Edinburgh's population burgeoned in the 19th century, from 90,786 in 1801 to just over 413,000 in 1901. There was no way that the Old Town and the New Town could house that kind of population, and Victorian Edinburgh became ringed by a huge development of handsome stone-built tenements and villas in suburbs such as **Bruntsfield**, **Marchmont**, **the Grange** and **Morningside**, which in turn became ringed about by 20th-century bungalows and speculative housing. And, beginning in the 1930s, the Edinburgh Corporation (and later the Edinburgh District Council) outflanked the lot by throwing up an outer ring of huge council-housing estates.

Although the Old Town has been allowed to deteriorate in a way that is nothing short of disgraceful, it is being revived. Serious efforts have been made to breathe new life into its labyrinth of medieval streets, wynds and closes. As a way of rescuing Edinburgh's many architectural treasures, the city fathers have almost been giving away buildings (along with handsome grants) to private developers. Restored 17th-century tenements and converted 19th-century breweries now cater for those who have discovered the delights of city-centre living.

The Old Town

Even after two centuries of neglect, Edinburgh's Old Town packs more historic buildings into a square mile than just about anywhere in Britain. Stevenson, again, provides the reason. "It [the Old Town] grew, under the law that regulates the growth of walled cities in precarious situation, not in extent, but in height and density. Public buildings were forced, whenever there was room for

Map, page 134–5

BELOW: looking for something new in the Old Town: shopping in Victoria Street.

Pub signs recall Edinburgh's royal history: Mary Queen of Scots.

BELOW: the Royal Mile.

them, into the midst of thoroughfares; thoroughfares were diminished into lanes; houses sprang up storey after storey, neighbour mounting upon neighbour's shoulder, as in some Black Hole in Calcutta, until the population slept 14 to 15 deep in a vertical direction."

In this late-medieval version of Manhattan, the aristocracy, gentry, merchants and commoners of Edinburgh lived cheek by jowl. Often they shared the same "lands" (tenements), the "quality" at the bottom and *hoi polloi* at the top. They rubbed shoulders in dark stairways and closes, and knew one another in a way that was socially impossible in England. Any Lord of Session (high court judge) whose verdict was unpopular could expect to be harangued or even pelted with mud and stones as he made his way home.

Not that life in the Old Town was entirely dominated by mob rule. Until the end of the 18th century the Old Town was the epicentre of fashionable society, a tight little metropolis of elegant drawing rooms, fashionable concert halls, dancing academies, and a bewildering variety of taverns, *howffs* (meeting places), coffee-houses and social clubs. "Nothing was so common in the morning as to meet men of high rank and official dignity reeling home from a close in the High Street where they had spent the night in drinking," wrote Robert Chambers, a lively chronicler.

The heady social life of the Old Town came to an end at the turn of the 19th century when it was progressively abandoned by the rich and the influential, whose houses were inherited by the poor and the feckless. "The Great Flitting" it was called, and crowds used to gather to watch all the fine furniture, crockery and painting being loaded into carts for the journey down the newly-created "earthen mound" (now called **The Mound**) to the New Town.

THE RULE OF THE MOB

Politicians, aristocracy and church leaders came under close scrutiny of the citizens of Edinburgh during the 18th century. When the Scottish parliament voted itself out of existence by approving the treaty of Union with England in 1707, the Edinburgh mob went on the rampage trying to track down the "traitors" who, they felt, had sold Scotland out to the "Auld Enemy" (the English). The Edinburgh mob was a formidable political force. The Porteous Riot of 1737, involving a crowd of 4,000, showed how strong feelings in Scotland could be, and the government in London was sufficiently alarmed that it decided to demolish the Nether Bow Port in order to make it easier for its troops to enter Edinburgh in the event of further rebellions. (It is an episode that is descibed in vivid detail in the opening chapters of Sir Walter Scott's novel, *The Heart of Midlothian*.)

For much of the 18th century the Edinburgh mob was led by a certain "General" Joe Smith, a bow-legged cobbler who believed passionately in the inferiority of women (his wife had to walk several paces behind him) and who could drum up a crowd of thousands within a few minutes. With the mob at his back, Joe Smith could lay down the law to the Magistrates of Edinburgh, and ran a kind of rough justice against thieving landlords and dishonest traders. His career came to an abrupt end in 1780 when, dead drunk, he fell to his death off the top of a stagecoach.

The Royal Mile

The spine of the Old Town is the **Royal Mile**, a wide thoroughfare which runs down from the Castle to the **Palace of Holyroodhouse**, and comprises (from top to bottom) Castlehill, Lawnmarket, the High Street, and the Canongate. This street was described by the author of *Robinson Crusoe*, Daniel Defoe (who lived in Edinburgh at the beginning of the 18th century), as "perhaps the largest, longest, and finest Street for Buildings, and Number of Inhabitants, not in Britain only, but in the world".

The **Castle ❶** (open daily) itself is well worth a visit, if only for the views over the city. Many of the castle buildings are 18th- and 19th-century, although the tiny Norman chapel dedicated to the saintly Queen Margaret dates to the 12th century. Also worth seeking out are the **Scottish National War Memorial**, **Great Hall** (which has a superb hammer-beam roof), and the **Crown Room,** which houses the Regalia (crown jewels) of Scotland, which were lost between 1707 and 1818 when a commission set up by Sir Walter Scott traced them to a locked chest in a locked room in the castle. The Stone of Destiny, returned from London in 1996 after 700 years, is also now housed in the Castle.

Just below the castle esplanade, on **Castlehill**, are an iron fountain which marks the spot where between 1479 and 1722 Edinburgh used to burn its witches; **Ramsay Gardens**, the tenements designed by the 19th-century planning genius Patrick Geddes; and a **Camera Obscura ❷** (open daily) built in the 1850s.

Across the road is the **Scotch Whisky Heritage Centre** (open daily), where visitors can learn about the drink's origin from an audio-visual show and by travelling in a whisky barrel through 300 years of history. The shop sells a good selection of whiskies.

Map, page 134–5

TIP

For an introduction to Edinburgh Castle's colourful past, join one of the excellent guided tours around the Castle.

BELOW: on display.

Next door **Tolbooth Kirk**, where the city's Gaelic speakers used to worship, is being restored.

On the north side of the Lawnmarket is **Gladstone's Land** ❸ (open April–Oct: Mon–Sat and Sun pm), a completely restored six-storey 17th-century tenement now owned by the National Trust for Scotland (NTS), which gives some insight into 17th-century Edinburgh life (dirty, difficult and malodorous). Next door is **Lady Stair's House** (open Mon–Sat; free), now a museum dedicated to Burns, Scott and Stevenson, and **Deacon Brodie's Tavern**, named after William Brodie, the model for the Jekyll and Hyde story.

Further along, on what is now **High Street**, are **Parliament House** (now the law courts); the **High Kirk of St Giles** (often miscalled St Giles Cathedral) (open daily); the **Mercat Cross**, from which kings and queens are proclaimed; the **City Chambers**, which was built as an "exchange" (office block) and was one of the first buildings in the great drive to "improve" Edinburgh in the late 18th century. The lower part of the High Street contains the 15th-century **Moubray House**, which is probably the oldest inhabited building in Edinburgh; **John Knox House** ❹ (open Mon–Sat); and the **Museum of Childhood** (open Mon–Sat; free) with displays of historical toys, dolls and books. Across the road in **Trinity Church** in **Chalmer's Court** enthusiasts can make rubbings of rare Scottish brasses and stone crosses in the **Scottish Stone and Brass Rubbing Centre** (open Mon–Sat; free).

Further east, **Canongate** is particularly rich in 16th- and 17th-century buildings. These include the **Tolbooth** ❺, which houses *The People's Story* (open Mon–Sat; free), an exhibition about ordinary Edinburgh folk from the late 18th century to the present; **Bakehouse Close, Huntly House**, the city's main

Even though it's doubtful that the religious reformer John Knox actually lived in the house that bears his name, it's likely that he preached from its window.

BELOW: the Tolbooth, an ancient entry into Edinburgh.

museum of local history (open Mon–Sat; free); **Moray House**, the most lavish of the aristocracy's town houses; the Dutch-style **Canongate Church**; **White Horse Close** (once a coaching inn) and the 17th-century **Acheson House**. Beyond the Canongate Church is the "**mushroom garden**", a walled garden laid out in the 17th-century manner, and almost completely unknown.

The **Palace of Holyroodhouse** ❻ (open daily with exceptions; tel: (0131) 556 7371) began as an abbey in the 12th century, grew into a Royal Palace in the early 16th century, and much was added in the late 17th century by Sir William Bruce for Charles II, who never set foot in the building. It was here that Mary Queen of Scots witnessed the butchery of her Italian favourite, David Rizzio, in 1558, and here the severed and scattered remains of the Marquis of Montrose were reassembled prior to being given a decent burial in 1661. More recently, Queen Victoria and Prince Albert favoured Holyrood as a stopover on their way to and from Balmoral.

The new **Scottish Parliament** building is under construction at Holyrood, and opposite, a glittering new tourist attraction, **Dynamic Earth** (open Apr–Oct: daily; Nov–Mar: Wed–Sun), opens in May 1999. This will be a family-oriented audio-visual "experience" of the formation and evolution of the planet.

South of the Royal Mile

Close to the Royal Mile, on George IV Bridge, are the **National Library of Scotland** (one of the few copyright libraries in Britain) and the little bronze statue of **Greyfriars Bobby** ❼, the devoted Skye terrier immortalised by Walt Disney. In Chambers Street are two linked national museums: the **Royal Museum** and the new **Museum of Scotland** ❽ (both open Mon–Sat and Sun

Map, page 134–5

When Bobby's master died in 1858 the loyal terrier refused to leave him: he kept watch over the grave in Greyfriars Churchyard every day for 14 years.

BELOW: Holyrood Palace.

pm). The former has a dazzling collection of 19th-century machinery and scientific instruments as well as natural history and other historical displays. The Museum of Scotland was opened by the Queen on St Andrew's Day, 30th November 1998; displays in the striking new building tell the history of Scotland and include national treasures.

On the corner of Chambers Street and the South Bridge lies Robert Adam's **The Old College**, the finest of the university's buildings.

Running roughly parallel with the Royal Mile to the south are the **Grassmarket** – the site of many a riot and public execution – and a long and now rather dismal street called the **Cowgate**, which in the 19th century was crammed with Irish immigrants fleeing the Great Famine. The Irish Catholic nature of the Cowgate is testified to by the huge but inelegant bulk of **St Patrick's Roman Catholic Church**. A more interesting building is **St Cecilia's Hall ❾**, which now belongs to Edinburgh University, but was built by the Edinburgh Musical Society as a concert hall in 1762, modelled on the Opera House at Parma.

A landmark of Europe

"A sort of schizophrenia in stone" is how the novelist Eric Linklater once described **Princes Street**, going on to contrast the "natural grandeur solemnised by memories of human pain and heroism" of the castle rock with the tawdry commercialism of the north side of the street.

If Princes Street is still one of Europe's more elegant boulevards it is no thanks to the architects, developers and retailers of the 20th century. Just about every decent building has been gouged out of the north side of the street and replaced by some undistiguished piece of modern architecture. Yet on the south side

Below: Sir Walter Scott stares down stonily on modern Edinburgh.

Princes Street Gardens ❿ remain as the "broad and deep ravine planted with trees and shrubbery" that so impressed the American writer Nathaniel Willis in 1834. So whether or not Princes Street is barred to cars, as has recently been proposed, its role as one of the glorious landmarks of Europe should be secure for some time to come.

With the exception of the superb **Register House** by Robert Adam at the far northeast end of the street, and a few remaining 19th-century shops (such as Jenners and Debenhams), everything worthwhile is on the south side of the street. The most startling edifice, which may be ascended for splendid views, is the huge and intricate Gothic **monument to Sir Walter Scott** ⓫, erected in 1844 and designed by a self-taught architect called George Meikle Kemp. The unfortunate Kemp drowned in an Edinburgh canal shortly before the monument was completed, and was due to be buried in the vault under the memorial until some petty-minded member of Scott's entourage persuaded the Court of Session to divert the funeral. Another blow for Edward Hyde.

Much more typical of Edinburgh are the two neo-classical art galleries at the junction of Princes Street and The Mound. Now known as the **Royal Scottish Academy** ⓬ (open Mon–Sat and Sun pm) and the **National Gallery of Scotland** ⓭ (open Mon–Sat and Sun pm; free), both buildings were designed by William Playfair between 1822 and 1845. The space around the galleries has long been Edinburgh's version of London's Hyde Park Corner, and is heavily used by preachers, polemicists and bagpipers.

Exhibitions at the Royal Scottish Academy come and go, but the National Gallery of Scotland houses the biggest permanent collection of Old Masters outside London. There are paintings by Raphael, Rubens, El Greco, Titian, Goya,

Map, page 134–5

At the foot of The Mound is the world's oldest Floral Clock. Laid out annually with more than 20,000 plants, it has electrically driven hands.

BELOW: lunchtime refreshment.

A WEE DRAM

The *Good Pub Guide* lists Edinburgh, with more than 700 pubs for fewer than 500,000 people, as the best place in Britain for boozers. Yet it is an extraordinary fact of Edinburgh life that there is not one pub the whole length of Princes Street. A few plushy clubs, certainly, but no pubs. But Rose Street, a narrow and once infamous thoroughfare that runs just behind it, has more than its share. The more diverting Rose Street hostelries are the Kenilworth (which has a lovely ceramic-clad interior), Scotts, Paddy's and the Abbotsford. A favourite Edinburgh sport has been to try to get from one end of Rose Street to the other, downing half a pint in every pub and still remain standing.

In Rose Street you will also find a *howff* (meeting place) called Milnes Bar, which was once the haunt of 20th-century Edinburgh literati – writers like Hugh MacDiarmid and Norman MacCaig and jazz musicians like Sandy Brown. Live music is heard in many Edinburgh pubs today, particularly during the annual Edinburgh Jazz Festival. And the main International Festival transforms the pubs of Edinburgh, which are granted extended licences to cope with the increased custom in these summer weeks. Not that drinkers here usually have a problem: ever since the relaxation of licensing regulations in 1976 genteel Edinburgh has long been one of the easiest places in Britain in which to buy a drink, with bars open well into the "wee sma' hours".

Vermeer and a clutch of superb Rembrandts. Gaugin, Cézanne, Renoir, Degas, Monet, Van Gogh and Turner are well represented, and the gallery's Scottish collection is unrivalled. There are important paintings by Raeburn, Ramsay, Wilkie and the astonishing (and underrated) James Drummond.

At the southwest end of Princes Street is a brace of fine churches: **St John's** (Episcopalian) and **St Cuthbert's** (Church of Scotland). St John's supports a lively congregation which is forever decking the building out with paintings in support of various Third World causes and animal rights. The church, a Gothic revival building designed by William Burn in 1816, has a fine ceiling which John Ruskin thought "simply beautiful".

The New Town

What makes Edinburgh a truly world-class city, able to stand shoulder to shoulder with Prague, Amsterdam or Vienna, is the great neo-classical New Town, built in an explosion of creativity between 1767 and 1840. The New Town is the product of the Scottish Enlightenment. And no-one has really been able to explain how, in the words of the historian Arthur Youngson, "a small, crowded, almost medieval town, the capital of a comparatively poor country, expanded in a short space of time, without foreign advice or foreign assistance, so as to become one of the enduringly beautiful cities of western Europe".

It all began in 1752 with a pamphlet entitled *Proposals for carrying on certain Public Works in the City of Edinburgh*. It was published anonymously, but was engineered by Edinburgh's all-powerful Lord Provost (Lord Mayor), George Drummond. Drummond was determined that Edinburgh should be a credit to the Hanoverian-ruled United Kingdom which he had helped create, and should

TIP

To see Scotland at its most colourful, call in at the Scottish Tartans Museum in Princes Street (open Mon–Sat).

BELOW: fanlight in Queen Street.

rid itself of its reputation for overcrowding, squalor, turbulence and Jacobitism.

To some extent the New Town is a political statement in stone. It is Scotland's tribute to the Hanoverian ascendancy. Many of the street names reflect the fact, as witnessed in their names: **Hanover Street**, **Cumberland Street**, **George Street**, **Queen Street**, **Frederick Street**.

The speed with which the New Town was built is still astonishing, particularly given the sheer quality of the building. Built mainly in calciferous sandstone from Craigleith Quarry to a prize-winning layout by a 23-year-old architect/planner called James Craig, most of the more important New Town buildings were in place before the end of the century: **Register House** (1778), the North side of **Charlotte Square** (1791), the **Assembly Rooms and Music Hall** (1787), **St Andrew's Church** (1785), most of **George Street**, **Castle Street**, **Frederick Street** and **Princes Street**.

The stinking Nor' Loch (north loch) under the castle rock was speedily drained to make way for the "pleasure gardens" of Princes Street. By the 1790s the New Town was the height of fashion, and the gentry of Edinburgh were abandoning their roots in the Old Town for the Georgian elegance on the other side of the newly-built North Bridge. Some idea of how they lived can be glimpsed in the **Georgian House** ⓭ (open April–Oct: Mon–Sat and Sun pm) at 7 Charlotte Square (on the block designed by Robert Adam). The house has been lovingly restored by the National Trust for Scotland. It is crammed with the furniture, crockery, glassware, silver and paintings of the period, and even the floorboards have been dryscrubbed in the original manner. The basement kitchen is a masterpiece of late 18th-century domestic technology.

Also in Charlotte Square is **West Register House** (part of the Scottish Record

Map,
page
134–5

Register House was built especially to store public records: its thick, stone walls guard against the risk of fire.

BELOW: the Georgian House in Charlotte Square.

The Money Men of Charlotte Square

One of the more remarkable facts about Edinburgh is that it is the biggest financial centre in Europe apart from the City of London. "Of course it's very difficult to measure these things," says Professor Jack Shaw of Scottish Financial Enterprises (the Edinburgh financiers' mouthpiece). "But Edinburgh handles more fund money than anyone outside of London. We calculate that it amounts to around £50 billion. And that's a lot of money."

Naturally, this huge community of bankers, investment-fund managers, stockbrokers, corporate lawyers, accountants and insurance executives has to be "serviced". Which means nice business for Edinburgh's glossier advertising agencies, public relations firms, design studios and photographers – not to mention restaurants, wine bars and auction houses like Sotheby's, Philips and Christie's.

Just as "the City" is shorthand for London's vast financial community, so Edinburgh's is known as "Charlotte Square". But the financial district it inhabits extends far beyond the elegant boundaries of the square itself. It now takes in much of George Street, St Andrew Square, Queen Street, Melville Street and various other large chunks of the New Town.

Edinburgh's star role in the financial world can be traced back to the enthusiasm of the Scots for making and then keeping money. The Scots have always been among the modern world's best and canniest bankers. Which is why the Scottish clearing banks have a statutory right (dating from 1845) to print their own distinctive banknotes. This is a right the Scottish banks relish, particularly as the English banks were stripped of it following a string of bank failures in the 19th century, and the Scots are remarkably attached to their Edinburgh-based banks.

Probably the biggest fish in Edinburgh's financial pond are the giant Scottish insurance companies, which handle funds in the region of £30 billion. The most important by far is the Standard Life Assurance Company, which has offices all over Britain, Ireland and Canada and is now Europe's biggest "mutual fund". Like most of the Edinburgh insurance companies, the Standard Life is a vintage operation (1825). Some are even older, with names that have a satisfyingly old-fashioned ring, like the Scottish Widows Fund and Life Assurance Society or the Scottish Provident Institution for Mutual Life Assurance.

Although Charlotte Square took much stick for being slow to get in on the booming unit trust business (a complaint it fast put right), there is no shortage of old-fashioned "investment trusts". It was with money from these trusts that much of the American West was built. In the 19th century, Charlotte Square was heavily into cattle ranching, fruit farming and railways in the USA.

Nowadays it prefers to sink its "bawbees" into the high-tech wizardry of Silicon Valley or East Texas oil wells. And while Edinburgh as a whole benefited little from North Sea oil, parts of Charlotte Square did very nicely, thank you.

LEFT: talking business outside the Finance Office.

Office) which was built by Robert Reid in 1811 and began life as St George's Church. A few hundred yards along George Street are the **Assembly Rooms and Music Hall** (1787) ⓰, once the focus of social life in the New Town, and still a top venue during the festival. Across the road is the **Church of St Andrew and St George** (1785), whose oval-shaped interior witnessed the "Great Disruption" of 1843. The Church of Scotland was split down the middle when the "evangelicals", led by Thomas Chalmers, walked out in disgust at the complacency of the church "moderates" who were content to have their ministers foisted on them by the gentry (as was the custom in England). Chalmers and his colleagues went on to form the Free Church of Scotland, which proclaimed a sterner but more democratic form of Presbyterianism.

Parallel to George Street lies **Queen Street**, whose only public building of any interest is an eccentric Doge's Palace housing the **Scottish National Portrait Gallery** ⓱ (open Mon–Sat and Sun pm; free) and the **Royal Museum of Scotland (Antiquities)** (open Mon–Sat and Sun pm; free). The portrait gallery is well stocked with pictures of generations of Scots worthies, while the museum contains many an intriguing artefact. The Pictish and Gaelic cross stones and carvings are extraordinary. The children's favourite seems to be "the maiden", the guillotine that stood in the Old Town and was used to execute malefactors.

Although St Andrew Square at the west end of George Street has been knocked about a bit, it is still recognisable, with the most noteworthy building in the square being the head office of the Royal Bank of Scotland. Originally built in 1774 as the Town House of Sir Laurence Dundas, it was remodelled in the 1850s when it acquired a quite astonishing domed ceiling with glazed star-shaped coffers. The 150-ft-high (45-metre) monument in the centre of St Andrew

Map, page 134–5

TIP

During the weeks of the Festival in August many of Edinburgh's attractions have longer opening hours.

BELOW: two's company in St Andrew Square.

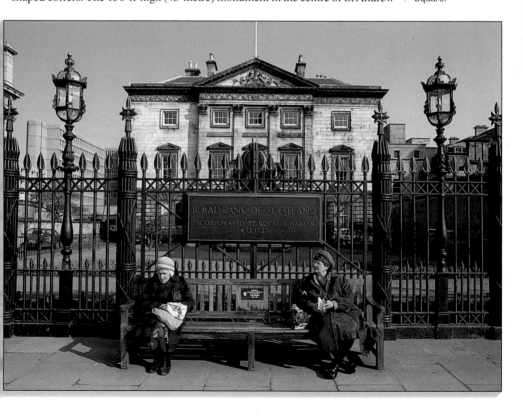

Ann Street was the creation of the painter Henry Raeburn, who named it after his wife. It was described by the English poet Sir John Betjeman as "the most attractive street in Britain".

Square is to Henry Dundas, 1st Viscount Melville, who was branded "King Harry the Ninth" for his autocratic (and probably corrupt) way of running Scotland.

To the north of the Charlotte Square/St Andrew Square axis lies a huge acreage of Georgian elegance which is probably unrivalled in Europe. Most of it is private housing and offices. Particularly worth seeing are **Heriot Row, Northumberland Street**, **Royal Circus**, **Ainslie Place**, **Moray Place** and **Drummond Place**. **Ann Street** near the Water of Leith is beautiful but atypical, with its gardens and two- and three-storey buildings. Nearby **Danube Street** used to house Edinburgh's most notorious whore-house, run by the flamboyant Dora Noyes (the house has reverted to middle-class decency).

The **Stockbridge** area on the northern edge of the New Town is an engaging bazaar of antique shops, curiosity dealers, picture framers and second-hand bookstores, with a sprinkling of decent restaurants and noisy pubs. The **Royal Botanic Garden** (open daily; free)**,** half a mile (0.8 km) north of Stockbridge, is 70 acres (28 hectares) of woodland, green sward, exotic trees, heather garden, rockeries, rhododendron walks and exotic planthouses.

Also in this area, on Belford Road, is the **Scottish National Gallery of Modern Art** (open Mon–Sat and Sun pm; free), with a fine permanent collection of 20th-century art, including works by Matisse and Picasso, Magritte and Hockney. From spring 1999 the display space will be extended to the Dean Gallery, in another fine 19th-century building across the road; Dada and Surrealist works and temporary exhibitions will be shown here.

Pleasure seekers

Edward Hyde lurks in the New Town, too. The designers of the New Town provided it with a plethora of handsome "pleasure gardens" which range in size from small patches of grass and shrubbery to the three **Queen Street Gardens** which cover more than 11 acres (4.5 hectares). All three are closed to the public and accessible only to the "keyholders" who live nearby. One of the drearier summer sights is to see puzzled tourists shaking the gates, at a loss to understand why they are barred from ambling round the greenery.

Between 1815 and 1840 another version of the New Town grew beyond the east end of Princes Street and Waterloo Place. **Regent Terrace**, **Royal Terrace**, **Blenheim Terrace** and **Leopold Place** were its main thoroughfares.

This eastward expansion also littered the slopes of **Calton Hill** with impressive public buildings, which probably earned Edinburgh the title "Athens of the North" (although a comparison between the two cities had been made in 1762 by the antiquarian James Stuart). On the hill are monuments to Dugald Stewart, the 18th/19th-century philosopher, and Horatio Nelson, whose memorial in the shape of a telescope may be ascended for great views, and the old **City Observatory** , now home to *The Edinburgh Experience* show (open Apr–Oct: daily; Apr–June and Oct closed Mon–Fri am).

The oddest of the early 19th-century edifices on the Calton Hill is known as "Scotland's Disgrace". It is a war memorial to the Scots killed in the Napoleonic wars modelled on the Parthenon in Athens. The foundation stone was laid with a great flourish during George IV's visit to Edinburgh in 1822, but the money ran out after 12 columns were erected so the monument remains incomplete.

Beyond Calton Hill, on Regent Road, are the former **Royal High School** (called "the noblest monument of the Scottish Greek Revival"), the **Robert Burns Monument**, modelled on the Choragic Monument of Lysicrates in Athens, and the **Old Calton Burial Ground**, with 18th- and 19th-century memorials (including one honouring David Hume), in the lee of the empty, semi-derelict **Governor's House** of the Old Calton Jail.

Maritime Edinburgh

Although more ships now sail in and out of the Firth of Forth than use the Firth of Clyde, maritime Edinburgh has taken a terrible beating over the past 20 years. Edinburgh's port of **Leith** ㉒ was, until recently, one of the hardest-working harbours on the east coast of Britain (the city's coastline on the Firth of Forth is studded with former fishing villages: **Granton, Newhaven**, **Portobello**, **Fisherrow**, and further east, **Cockenzie**, **Port Seton** and **Prestonpans**). Ships from Leith exported coal, salt fish, paper, leather and good strong ale, and returned with (among much else) grain, timber, wine, foreign foods and Italian marble. The destinations were Hamburg, Bremen, Amsterdam, Antwerp, Copenhagen and occasionally North America and Australia.

Right up to the mid 1960s at least four fleets of deep-sea trawlers plied out of Leith and the nearby harbour of **Granton**, and the half-Scottish, half-Norwegian firm of Christian Salvesen was still catching thousands of whales every year into the 1950s (which is why there is a Leith Harbour in South Georgia).

Map, page 154

BELOW: street art defies Scotland's rainy climate.

The rules drawn up by the Honourable Company of Edinburgh Golfers at Leith Links in 1774 still form the basis of golf today.

The 2-mile (3-km) stretch of shore between Leith and Granton was once littered with shipyards, ship repair yards and drydocks. The streets of Leith itself were full of shipping agents, marine insurance firms, grain merchants, ships' chandlers, plus a burgeoning "service sector" of dockside pubs, clubs, flophouses, bookies and whores.

But most of it is gone. The trade has shifted to the container ports on the east coast of England. The maritime heart has gone out of Leith, and therefore Edinburgh. A few cruise liners still make an occasional appearance, and every now and again an oil industry supply boat comes through the harbour mouth.

There have been attempts to turn Leith round. Scottish Enterprise and the local authorities have been spending millions restoring the exteriors of some of Leith's handsome commercial buildings, such as the old **Customs House**, the **Corn Exchange**, the **Assembly Building**, and **Trinity House** in the Kirkgate. At the same time private developers have been converting old warehouses, office buildings, lodging houses and at least one veteran cooperage into high-priced flats and houses. Leith is now home to a new Scottish Office building. Here also, in Bangor Road, is **Scotland's Clan Tartan Centre** (open daily; free) where tartanry holds sway and where, with the assistance of computers, you can learn that you too are a clan member. Recently come to Leith docks is the decommissioned **Royal Yacht Britannia** (visitor centre and yacht open daily; tel: (0131) 555 5566).

Leith now hosts a cluster of fashionable restaurants (with vaguely maritime names like "Skippers"), at least one art gallery, and one of the dock-gate buildings has been converted into the successful *Waterfront Wine Bar*. A pub which used to be known (for obvious reasons) as *The Jungle* and where the police

feared to tread, is now an up-market watering-hole called *The King's Wark*.

But the ancient port is worth a visit, if only for its powerful sense of what it used to be. And many of the buildings on **Bernard Street**, **Commercial Street**, **Constitution Street** and **The Shore** are handsome and interesting. Leith has an intriguing constitutional history, first part of Edinburgh, then a separate burgh, and then swallowed up by Edinburgh again (in 1920). Halfway up the street known as **Leith Walk** is a pub called the *Boundary Bar* through which the municipal border between Edinburgh and Leith used to run. As the two towns then had different drinking hours, customers could extend their happiness by moving from one end of the bar to the other when the time came.

Newhaven

If ever a village had been killed by conservation it must be the little port of **Newhaven ㉓**, a mile west of Leith. Into the 1960s this was a brisk community, with a High Street and a Main Street lined with shops and little businesses through which tram-cars and later buses used to trundle. But now that the picturesque houses have been "restored" there is hardly a shop left in the place, the once-crowded Main Street is a ghostly dead end, and Newhaven harbour is occupied by a few pleasure yachts. The Ancient Society of Free Fishermen, the trade guild founded in 1572, still exists but lists few fishermen among its members.

All of which is a great pity. Newhaven is one of Edinburgh's more interesting corners. The village was founded in the late 15th century by James IV to build the *Great Michael*, then the biggest warship on earth and destined to be the flagship of a new Scottish navy. But like many such grandiose schemes – particularly the grandiose schemes hatched in Scotland – the *Great Michael* was

Map, page 154

> **TIP**
>
> Enjoy fish and chips at their best at the famous Harry Ramsden restaurant on Newhaven's harbourside.

BELOW: echoes of Leith's maritime tradition.

never a success. After the ruin of the Scots army (and the death of James IV) at Flodden in 1513, the great ship which was the pride of Newhaven was sold to the French, who left her to rot in Brest harbour.

The villages

Like most other cities sprawling outwards, Edinburgh has enveloped a number of villages. The most striking of them is probably **Dean Village ㉔**, a few minutes' walk from the West End of Princes Street. Now one of Edinburgh's more fashionable corners, Dean Village is at least 800 years old, and straddles the Water of Leith at a point which was once the main crossing on the way to Queensferry. The Incorporation of Baxters (bakers) of Edinburgh once operated 11 watermills and two flour granaries here. Its most striking building is **Well Court**, an unusual courtyard of flats built in the 1880s as housing for the poor by John Findlay, proprietor of *The Scotsman*. Dean Village is linked by a riverside walk to the shops and pubs of Stockbridge.

Other villages which have been swallowed by the city include **Corstorphine** in the west of the city, where Edinburgh keeps its famous **Zoological Garden ㉕** (open daily; tel: (0131) 334 9171), housing in the world's largest penguin enclosure a fine collection of flightless birds from the Antarctic. There is also **Colinton ㉖** in the south, which features an 18th-century parish church and a "dell" beside the Water of Leith, and **Cramond ㉗** on the Firth of Forth, which used to sport an ironworks and which was the site of a Roman military camp.

More interesting is **Duddingston ㉘**, tucked under the eastern flank of Arthur's Seat, beside a small loch which is also a bird sanctuary. Duddingston claims that its main pub, *The Sheep's Heid*, is the oldest licensed premises in

The walk from Dean to Stockbridge takes you past St Bernard's Well, whose natural spring inspired the creation in the18th century of a Roman temple with a statue of Hygeia, the Greek goddess of health.

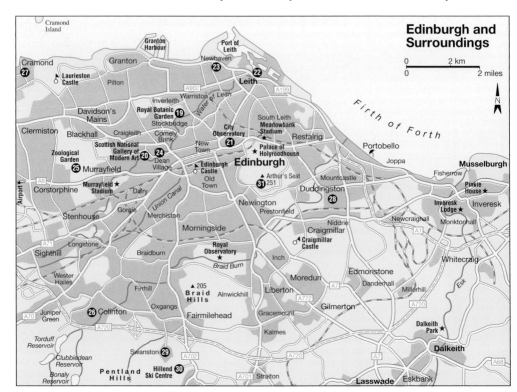

Edinburgh and Surroundings

0   2 km
0   2 miles

N

Firth of Forth

Scotland. It also has a fine Norman-style church and a 17th-century house which was used by Bonnie Prince Charlie in 1745.

On the northern slopes of the Pentland Hills lies **Swanston ㉙**, a small huddle of white-painted cottages, near where the Stevenson family used to rent Swanston Cottage as a summer residence for the sickly RLS. For some odd reason, the gardens of Swanston are decorated with statuary and ornamental stonework taken from the High Kirk of St Giles when it was being "improved" in the 19th century.

The hills of Edinburgh

If there is such a creature as the Urban Mountaineer, then Edinburgh must be his or her paradise. Like Rome, the city is built on and around seven hills, none of them very high but all of them offering good stiff walks and spectacular views of the city. They are, in order of altitude, Arthur's Seat (823 ft/251 metres), Braid Hill (675 ft/205 metres), West Craiglockhart Hill (575 ft/173 metres), Blackford Hill (539 ft/162 metres), Corstorphine Hill (531 ft/159 metres), Castle Hill (435 ft/131 metres) and Calton Hill (328 ft/98 metres).

In addition, Edinburgh is bounded to the south by the Pentland Hills, a range of amiable mini-mountains which almost (but not quite) climb to 2,000 ft (600 metres), and which are well used by Edinburgh hill walkers, fell runners, mountain bicyclists, rock scramblers and the British Army. Here, too, is the **Hillend Ski Centre ㉚** (open daily; tel: (0131) 445 4433), once the largest artificial ski slope in Europe and still an impressive challenge. Non-skiers can take the lift and then a short walk to Caerketton Hill for magnificent panoramic views of Edinburgh, the Firth of Forth and the hills of Fife and Stirlingshire.

Map, page 154

TIP

The penguin parade at Edinburgh Zoo takes place every day in the summer between March and October at 2pm.

BELOW: on parade at Edinburgh zoo.

Dorothy Wordsworth (sister of the poet William) wrote in 1803 how she found Arthur's Seat "as wild and solitary as any in the heart of the Highland mountains".

Of the "city-centre" hills, Calton Hill at the east end of Princes Street probably offers the best view of Edinburgh. But it is **Arthur's Seat** , that craggy old volcano in the Queen's Park, which must count as the most startling piece of urban mountainscape. It is one of the many places in Britain named after the shadowy (and possibly apocryphal) King Arthur. But, surprisingly enough, Edinburgh has a better claim to Arthur than most other regions. The area around Edinburgh was one of the British (Welsh) kingdoms before it was overrun by the Angles and the Scots.

On the flanks of Arthur's Seat, the feeling of *rus in urbe* can be downright eerie. And its 823 ft (251 metres) high bulk provides some steep climbing, rough scrambling and fascinating geology on **Salisbury Crags**. But one of the choicest experiences Edinburgh has to offer is to watch the sun go down over the mountains of the west from the top of Arthur's Seat.

The outer darkness

Although Edinburgh may not have an "inner city" problem, it certainly has had its "outer city" difficulties. It is ringed to the east, south and west with sprawling council-housing estates, places like **Craigmillar** and **Niddrie**, **Oxgangs** and **Gilmerton**, **Pilton**, **Muirhouse** and **Wester Hailes**. Most of the people who live here were "decanted" there from the High Street, the Cowgate and Leith, and many would eagerly go back if only they could find an affordable house. But respectable Edinburgh has long since learned to contemplate the other Edinburgh with the equanimity of Henry Jekyll seeing the face of Edward Hyde in the mirror for the first time. "I was conscious of no repugnance," Dr Jekyll says, "rather of a leap of welcome. This, too, was myself." ❏

BELOW: colourscape created for the Edinburgh Festival.

The World's Biggest Arts Festival

When the Edinburgh International Festival explodes into life every August, the city, as the *Washington Post* once pointed out, becomes "simply the best place on Earth". Certainly the display of cultural pyrotechnics is awesome. Every concert-hall, basement-theatre and church hall in the centre of Edinburgh overflows with dance groups, theatre companies, string quartets, puppeteers, opera companies and orchestras. And for three weeks the streets of Edinburgh are awash with fire-eaters, jugglers, bagpipers, clowns, warblers, satirists and theatrical hopefuls of every shape, size and colour.

All of which is a distant cry from the dead and dreary days after World War II when the idea of the festival was hatched by Sir John Falconer, then Lord Provost of Edinburgh, Harry Harvey Wood of the British Council, and Rudolf Bing, the festival's first artistic director. The notion was, said the novelist Eric Linklater, "the triumph of elegance over drab submission to the penalties of emerging victorious from a modern war".

Today 180,000 people buy tickets for the main events, a figure which doesn't include the 80,000 or so who troop into the (free) art shows or the thousands who pack the "esplanade" of Edinburgh Castle every night to relish the stunning (if occasionally somewhat sinister) glamour of the Edinburgh Military Tattoo. Not that it has been all plain sailing: there has been much wrangling with the Scottish Arts Council over money, and bickering with the Edinburgh District Council over the "elitism" of the Edinburgh Festival Society, the festival's ruling body.

During the 1980s artistic director Frank Dunlop sounded off regularly about upstart arts festivals trying to "poach" Edinburgh's hard-won commercial sponsors. In fact, in spite of relatively small loans, the Edinburgh Festival is now doing very nicely out of big business, and box office takings are running at over £1 million. This sounds a lot; but, as Dunlop said, "no major festival in the world has to make do with as little money as Edinburgh does. Salzburg gets 10 times as much public money."

Edinburgh's "other" festival, the Festival Fringe (which also began in 1947), has become a behemoth – so big, in fact, that it is in real danger of outgrowing the city. In 1997 the 640 companies on the Festival Fringe staged more than 15,600 performances of 1,423 shows in 186 venues all over the city. Over the years it's been a nursery for new talent: Maggie Smith, Tom Stoppard, Rowan Atkinson, Billy Connolly and Emma Thompson all made their entrance into the business on the Festival Fringe.

Nor is that all. On the fringe of the Fringe (as it were) there is also a Television Festival (full of heavyweight discussions about the Role Of The Media), a Film Festival (which gets many a good movie long before London), a Book Festival (held in Charlotte Square), and a Jazz Festival (staged in just about every pub in the city centre).

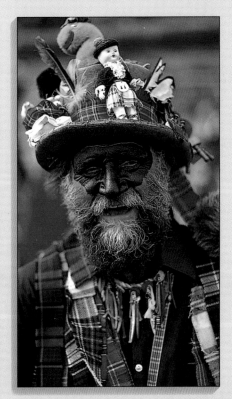

RIGHT: face at the Festival Fringe.

OLD AND NEW TOWN ARCHITECTURE

Declared a UNESCO World Heritage Site in 1995, the centre of Edinburgh is a fascinating juxtaposition of medieval confusion and classical harmony

Architecturally, Edinburgh's Old and New Towns are utterly disparate. In the Old, everything is higgledy-piggledy; in the New – now more than 200 years old – order and harmony prevail.

The Old Town lies to the south of Princes Street Gardens. Its backbone is the Royal Mile, described by the writer Daniel Defoe in the 1720s as "perhaps the largest, longest and finest street of buildings and number of inhabitants in the world". Then it was lined with tall, narrow tenements, some with as many as 14 storeys, where aristocracy, merchants and lowly clerks all rubbed shoulders in friendly familiarity in dark stairways and through which ran a confusing maze of wynds (alleys), courts and closes.

A NEW ORDER

In 1766 James Craig, an unknown 23-year-old, won a competition for the design of the New Town. His submission was a "gridiron" consisting of two elegant squares – Charlotte and St Andrew – linked by three wide, straight, parallel streets: Princes, George and Queen. Robert and John Adam, Sir William Chambers and John Henderson, premier architects of the day, all contributed plans for glorious Georgian buildings. During the first part of the 19th century the New Town was extended by the addition of an extraordinary grouping of squares, circuses, terraces, crescents and parks, all maintaining the neoclassical idiom and permitting the New Town to boast the largest area of Georgian architecture in all Europe.

▷ **STATELY ELEGANCE**
New Town architecture reached its apotheosis with Robert Adam's superb design for Charlotte Square. The north frontage – the most magnificent – houses Bute House, official residence of the Secretary of State for Scotland, and the Georgian House. On the west side is West Register House with its green dome. The statue in the centre of the Square is of Prince Albert, consort to Queen Victoria.

JOHN KNOX HOUSE

STEPPING INSIDE THE PAST

Two of the finest examples of Edinburgh's Old and New Towns have been restored to their former glory and are open to visitors, thanks to the National Trust for Scotland (NTS), a charity founded in 1931 to promote the conservation of landscape and of historic buildings.

The Georgian House in Charlotte Square (*above and below*) evokes elegant living in the New Town: it has been beautifully furnished to show how a wealthy family lived in the 18th century. Gladstone's Land on the Old Town's Royal Mile is a skilful restoration of a merchant's house. The six floors behind its narrow frontage were once occupied by five families: an example of a 17th-century Edinburgh skyscraper. The arcaded ground floor has been restored to its original function as a shopping booth.

◁ HOME DECORATION

A picturesque late 15th-century building, John Knox's house is a splendid example of overhanging wooden upper floors with crow-stepped gables. Its outside stairway and fanciful decorations provide an idea of how the Royal Mile once looked

△ REST IN PEACE

Greyfriars churchyard is a haven for the living as well as the dead, with magnificent 17th-century monuments and tombstones.

◁ BUILT TO DESIGN

Every last detail in 12-sided Moray Place was included in its design; this is New Town at its grandest, including Tuscan porticos and a central garden.

▷ DEFENDERS OF THE FAITH

A simple stone monument in the Old Town's Grassmarket recalls the occasion in 1638 when "For the Protestant Faith on this spot many Martyrs and Covenanters died".

GLASGOW

A city of noble character, handsome buildings and invincible spirit, Glasgow accommodates no neutrality: it is either loved or loathed by native Scots and admired or avoided by visitors

Map, pages 164–5

Glasgow is a city for connoisseurs. It always has been, from the days when one of its earliest tourists, the 18th-century writer Daniel Defoe, described it as "the cleanest and beautifullest and best built city in Britain", to its recent, silver-tongued, brass-necked promotion of itself as the city that's "miles better". Yet there are few places in Europe that have been more publicly misunderstood and misrepresented than this monstrous, magnificent citadel to the worst and the best of commerce and capitalism, to the price and the prizes of Empire and the Industrial Revolution. And few cities can have inspired more furious conflicts of opinion of its worth, or ignited so much controversy.

Invincible spirit

Yet even in the darkest days of its reputation, when Glasgow slums and Glasgow violence were the touchstone for every sociologist's worst urban nightmares, it was still a city for connoisseurs. It appealed to those who were not insensitive to the desperate consequences of its 19th-century population explosion, when the combination of cotton, coal, steel and the River Clyde transformed Glasgow from elegant little merchant city to industrial behemoth; and who were not blind to the dire effect of 20th-century economics which, from World War I onwards, have presided over the decline of its shipbuilding and heavy industries; but who were nevertheless able to uncover, behind its grime and grisliness, a city of nobility and invincible spirit.

PRECEDING PAGES: regenerated Glasgow. **LEFT:** old-style Glasgow pub. **BELOW:** new-style coffee lounge.

Its enthusiasts have always recognised Glasgow's qualities, and even at the height of its notoriety they have been able to give Glasgow its place in the pantheon of great Western cities. Today, it is fashionable to describe Glasgow as European in character, for the remarkable diversity of its architecture and a certain levity of heart, or to compare it with North America for its gridiron street system and wisecracking street wisdom.

But these resonances have long been appreciated by experienced travellers. In 1929, at a time when social conditions were at their worst, the romantic but perceptive travel writer H.V. Morton found "a transatlantic alertness about Glasgow which no city in England possesses" and – the converse of orthodox opinion – was able to see that "Edinburgh is Scottish and Glasgow is cosmopolitan". And in 1960 the "British place-taster" Ian Nairn discovered with a sense of shock that "Glasgow was without doubt the friendliest of Britain's big cities", noting that "any Glasgow walk is inflected by a multitude of human contacts – in shops, under umbrellas (there *is* a good deal of rain in Glasgow), even from policemen – and each of them seems to be a person-to-person recognition, not the mutual hate of cogs in a machine who know their plight but cannot escape it."

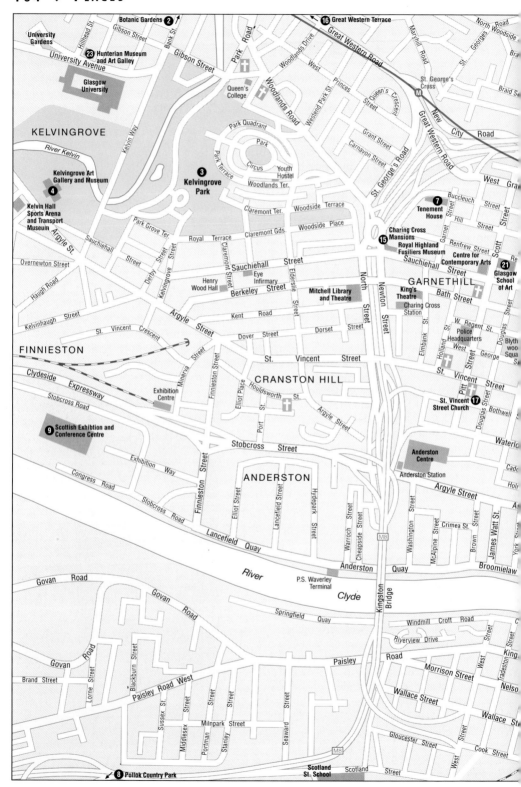

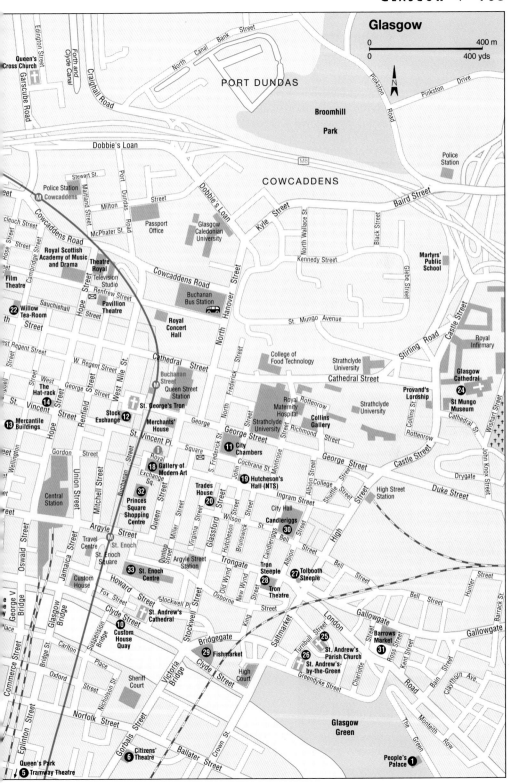

Glasgow

| 0 | 400 m |
| 0 | 400 yds |

PORT DUNDAS

Broomhill Park

COWCADDENS

Police Station

Police Station
Cowcaddens

Passport Office

Glasgow Caledonian University

Royal Scottish Academy of Music and Drama

Theatre Royal

Television Studio

Film Theatre

Pavillion Theatre

22 Willow Tea-Room

Royal Concert Hall

Buchanan Bus Station

College of Food Technology

Martyrs' Public School

Royal Infirmary

Glasgow Cathedral

24

St Mungo Museum

Buchanan Street Queen Street Station

St George's Tron

The Hat-rack

14

12 Stock Exchange

Merchants' House

Strathclyde University

Royal Rottenrow Maternity Hospital

Collins Gallery

Strathclyde University

Provand's Lordship

13 Mercantile Buildings

11 City Chambers

18 Gallery of Modern Art

Royal Exchange Sq.

19 Hutcheson's Hall (NTS)

20 Trades House

City Hall

Central Station

32 Princes Square Shopping Centre

30 Candleriggs

High Street Station

St. Enoch

Travel Centre

33 St. Enoch Centre

St. Enoch Square

Argyle Street Station

27 Tolbooth Steeple

Tron Steeple

28 Tron Theatre

Custom House

St. Andrew's Cathedral

10 Custom House Quay

29 Fishmarket

25

26 St. Andrew's-by-the-Green

St. Andrew's Parish Church

31 Barrows Market

Sheriff Court

High Court

Glasgow Green

Citizens' Theatre

6

People's Palace 1

Queen's Park
5 Tramway Theatre

Culture city

Glasgow today is visibly, spectacularly, a city in transformation. It ha
allowed its "hard, subversive, proletarian tradition" to lead it into brick w
of confrontation with central government. The result? A city which has r
sively re-arranged its own environment; which sees its future in the ser
industries, in business conferences, exhibitions and indeed in tourism; w
has already achieved some startling coups on its self-engineered road to bec
ing "Europe's first post-industrial city"; and which has probably never b
more exciting to visit since, at the apogee of its Victorian vigour, it held
International Exhibition of Science and Art more than 100 years ago.

Glaswegians allow themselves a sly smile over their elevation to the first r
of Europe's cultural centres, and have taken to calling their home town "C
ture City". But the smile becomes a little bitter for those who live in those dis
areas of the city as yet untouched by the magic of stone-cleaning, floodligh
or even modest rehabilitation. Defenders of the new Glasgow argue that t
turn will come; that you can't attract investment and employment to a city, v
better conditions for everyone, unless first you shine up its confidence on
inside and polish up its image on the outside.

Like all four Scottish cities, Glasgow is defined by hill and water. Its subu
advance up the slopes of the vast bowl which contains it, and the pinnacles, t
ers and spires of its universities, colleges and cathedral occupy their own s
mits within the bowl. It is, therefore, a place of sudden, sweeping vistas, v
always a hint of ocean or mountain just around the corner. Look north from
heights of **Queen's Park** and you will see the cloudy humps of the Cam
Fells and the precipitous banks of Loch Lomond. Look west from **Gilmore**

Opened in 1983, the Burrell Gallery became the icon of the Glasgow renaissance.

BELOW: high-rise in 20th-century Glasgow.

FISTS OF IRON

The Glaswegian comedian Billy Connolly said of Glasgow "There's a lightness about the town, without heavy industry. It's as if they've discovered how to work the sun-roof, or something." Yet Glaswegians themselves will admit that their positive qualities have a negative side. Even today, matiness can turn to menace in certain dismal pubs where too much whisky is chased by too much
(The working man's tipple here has traditionally been "a wee
and hauf" – a measure of whisky pursued by a half pint of t
often replaced today by a lethal mixture of vodka and ch
wine.) Religious bigotry, the obverse of honest faith, still ex
finding its most aggressive focus in the sub-culture of footb

And Glasgow's legendary humour, made intelligible eve
the English through the success of comedians like Billy Conn
but available free on every street corner, is the humour of
ghetto. It has been nurtured on hard times. It is dry, scept
irreverent and often black. It's the humour of self-defence
wit of people who know if they don't laugh they will cry. The G
gow writer Cliff Hanley compares it to American-Jewish hun
in its fast pace, but places it in "the hard, subversive proleta
tradition of the city".

to the great spangled mouth of the Clyde and you will sense the sea fretting at its fragmented littoral and the islands and resorts which used to bring thousands of Glaswegians "doon the watter" for their annual Fair Fortnight.

The antiquity of this July holiday – Glasgow Fair became a fixture in the local calendar in 1190 – gives some idea of the long-term stability of the town on the Clyde. But for centuries Glasgow had little prominence or significance in the history of Scotland. Although by the 12th century it was both market town and cathedral city (with a patron saint, St Mungo) and flourished quietly throughout the Middle Ages, it was largely by-passed by the bitter internecine conflicts of pre-Reformation Scotland and the running battles with England. Most of Scotland's trade, too, was conducted with the Low Countries from the East Coast ports. But it had a university, now five centuries old, and a distinguished centre of medical and engineering studies, and it had the Clyde. When trade opened up with the Americas, Glasgow's fortune was made.

Instant city

The tobacco trade with Virginia and Maryland brought the city new prosperity and prompted it to expand westwards from the medieval centre of the High Street. (Little of medieval Glasgow remains.) In the late 18th century the urbanisation of the city accelerated with an influx of immigrants, mainly from the West Highlands, to work in the cotton mills with their new machines introduced by merchants who were forced to desert the tobacco trade. The Industrial Revolution had begun, and from then on Glasgow's destiny – grim and glorious – was fixed.

The deepening of the Clyde up to the Broomielaw, near the heart of the city, in the 1780s and the coming of the steam engine in the 19th century consolidated

Map, pages 164–5

Today, the names of the streets of 18th-century Glasgow – like Virginia Street, and Jamaica Street – tell something of the story which turned a small town into the handsome fief of tobacco barons.

BELOW: motorways cut a swathe through the city.

A tribute to the working people of Glasgow, the decoration on the facade of the People's Palace includes allegorical figures representing the textile industry, shipbuilding and engineering.

BELOW: down by the River Kelvin, near the university.

a process of such rapid expansion that Glasgow has been called an "instant city". In the 50 years between 1781 and 1831 the population of the city quintupled, and was soon to be further swelled by thousands of Irish immigrants crossing the Irish Sea to escape famine and seek work. The Victorians completed Glasgow's industrial history and built most of its most self-important buildings as well as the congested domestic fortifications which were to become infamous as slum tenements. Since World War II, its population has fallen below the million mark to fewer than 700,000, the result of policies designed to decant citizens into "new towns". New policies are now encouraging the repopulation of the inner city.

The dear green place

There's some dispute about the origins of the name Glasgow. Scholars say it derives from the language of the British Celts, but variously interpret the genesis of its two syllables to mean anything from "dear stream" to "greyhound" (which some say was a nickname of St Mungo). But there's no dispute about the version which has been adopted by the city, which was the title of a novel about Glasgow and which has now worked its way into its tourist literature and marketing lore: Glasgow means "dear green place". What else? It has, after all, over 70 parks – "more green space per head of population than any other city in Europe," as the tour bus drivers tell you.

The most unexpected, idiosyncratic and oldest of its parks – in fact, the oldest public park in Britain – is **Glasgow Green**, once the common grazing ground of the medieval town and acquired by the burgh in 1662. To this day Glasgow women have the right to dry their washing on Glasgow Green, and its Arcadian sward is still spiked with clothes poles for their use, although there are few takers.

Municipal Clydesdale horses, used for carting duties in the park, still avail them-selves of the grazing, and the general eccentricity of the place is compounded by the bizarre proximity of Templeton's Carpet Factory, designed in 1889 by William Leiper, who aspired to replicate the Doge's Palace in Venice. (The factory is now a business centre.)

Here, too, you will find the **People's Palace ❶** (open daily; free), built at the turn of the century as a cultural centre for the East End community, for whom its red sandstone munificence was indeed palatial. It's now a museum dedicated to the social and industrial life of the 19th-century city.

The most distinguished of the remaining 69-odd parks include the **Botanic Gardens ❷**, in the heart of Glasgow's stately West End, with another palace – the **Kibble Palace** – the most enchanting of its large two hothouses. It was built as a conservatory for the Clyde Coast home of a Glasgow businessman, John Kibble, and shipped to its present site in 1873. The architect has never been identified, although legend promotes Sir Joseph Paxton, who designed the Crys-tal Palace in London.

Kelvingrove Park ❸, in the city's West End, was laid out in the 1850s and was the venue of Glasgow's principal Victorian and Edwardian international exhibitions, although that function is now performed by the new Scottish Exhi-bition and Conference Centre. It is a spectacular park, traversed by the River Kelvin and dominated on one side by the Gothic pile of **Glasgow University** (this seat of learning was unseated from its original college in the High Street and rehoused on Gilmorehill in 1870) and by the elegant Victorian precipice of **Park Circus** on the other side.

The **Kelvingrove Art Gallery and Museum ❹** (open daily; free) includes a

Map,
pages
164–5

TIP

Next door to the People's Palace is the huge conservatory known as the Winter Gardens, which now house the cosiest and most verdant cafeteria in town.

BELOW: traditions live on at Glasgow University.

Culture Comes in from the Cold

Glasgow's elevation to the position of European City of Culture 1990 (a title bestowed by the Ministers of Culture of the 12 member states of the European Community) was received with a mixture of astonishment and amusement in Edinburgh, which had long perceived itself as guardian of Scotland's most civilised values.

But, ever so quietly, Glasgow had been stealing the initiative. Edinburgh had been trying to make up its mind for nearly 30 years about building an opera house, but Glasgow went ahead and converted one of its general-purpose theatres, the Theatre Royal, into a home for the Scottish Opera. The city is also the home of four major orchestras, the acclaimed Scottish Ballet and the Royal Scottish Academy of Music and Drama.

Besides its traditional theatres – the King's and the Pavilion – the city boasts the cavernous

Tramway Theatre **❺**, the former home of the City's tramcars in which Peter Brook staged his ambitious *Mahabharata*. Studio theatres include the Tron, founded in 1979; the Mitchell Theatre, housed in an extension of the distinguished Mitchell Library; and two small theatres in the multi-media complex of the dynamic Centre for Contemporary Arts on Sauchiehall Street. However, Glasgow's most distinctive stage is the innovative **Citizens' Theatre ❻**.

Each year, or so it seems, Glasgow adds a new festival to its calendar. Mayfest, a general celebration of the arts, has been followed by international jazz, folk music and early music festivals, each held during successive months of the summer to keep the visitors coming. But the turning point in Glasgow's progress towards cultural respectability in the wider world came with the opening, in 1983, of the new building in Pollok Country Park, which houses the Burrell Collection. Its inventive design attracts people with only a slight interest in the eclectic taste of Sir William Burrell, the Glasgow shipowner who bequeathed his collections to the city in 1944.

It claims to be Scotland's most popular tourist attraction, and its popularity has tended to overshadow Glasgow's other distinguished art galleries and museums: Kelvingrove, at the Western end of Argyle Street, which has a strong representation of 17th-century Dutch paintings and 19th-century French paintings as well as many fine examples of the work of the late 19th-century Glasgow Boys; the university's Hunterian Museum and Art Gallery, and the St Mungo Museum of Religious Life and Art. In addition, the restored McLellan Galleries mount half a dozen major exhibitions a year in the largest temporary exhibition space outside London.

Other museums of special interest are the Museum of Transport, which contains the UK's largest range of vehicles and an unsurpassed collection of model ships; Haggs Castle, a period museum with a focus on children's educational activities, on the South Side; and the charming, miniature repository of social history, the **Tenement House ❼** (open Mar–Oct: daily pm) a two-room-and-kitchen flat in a 1892 tenement in Garnethill, wonderfully preserved in its original state.

LEFT: a night at the opera.

major collection of European paintings and extensive displays on the natural history, archaeology and ethnology of the area. Its magnificent organ is regularly used for recitals. Nearby is the intriguing **Museum of Transport** (open daily; free) with cars, lorries, buses and the much-loved Glasgow trams on display.

Pollok Country Park ❽ on the city's South Side (those who live south of the Clyde consider themselves a separate race of Glaswegian) has a well-worn path beaten to the door of the **Burrell Collection** (open daily; free), where there are over 8,000 exhibits from artifacts of ancient civilisations to Impressionist paintings. The park is also the home of the 18th-century **Pollok House** (open May–Sept: daily; free). It, too, is an art gallery with works by El Greco, Murillo, Goya and William Blake. From the windows of Pollok House visitors can see a prize-winning herd of Highland cattle and Pollok Golf Course.

Yet more greenery can be found among the sylvan glades of **Queen's Park**, also on the South Side, and in **Victoria Park**, near the north mouth of the Clyde Tunnel, which has a glasshouse containing several large fossil trees of some 350 million years' antiquity. Back across the river is **Bellahouston Park**, a magnet for the city's active sports people.

Old and new by the Clyde

At Stobcross Quay, site of the **Scottish Exhibition and Conference Centre ❾** on the north bank, you can marvel at the industrial colossus of the **Finnieston Cran** (crane), preserved to remind us of the heavy locomotives once hefted on board ships which carried them all over the world.

Stobcross Quay is also a terminus of the **Clyde Walkway**, Glasgow's first attempt to direct its great river towards the new industries of leisure and tourism. You can walk from the quay through the centre of the city past Glasgow Green to the suburb of **Cambuslang**, but somehow the journey isn't as cheerful as it should be, still lacking the kind of vigorous commercial, social and domestic life which has turned other derelict waterfronts into major attractions.

The central section is the most interesting, taking in the city's more distinguished bridges and many of the buildings associated with its maritime life. (The architectural historians Gomme and Walker identify only two bridges, the pedestrian Suspension Bridge and the Victoria Bridge, as worthy of notice, dismissing the others as "a sorry lot".) The Victoria Bridge was built in 1854 to replace the 14th-century Old Glasgow Bridge, and the graceful Suspension Bridge was completed in 1871 and designed by Alexander Kirkland, who later became Commissioner of Public Buildings in Chicago.

Custom House Quay ❿, which looks across to the delicate, newly restored Georgian façades of Carlton Place on the south bank, has opulent sandstone landscaping, a bandstand and a pub.

In contrast, there's much still to be done to the **Broomielaw**, which is rich in sailing history. To the west of George V Bridge and Central Station's railway bridge, it was once the departure point for regular services to Ireland, North America and the west coast towns of Scotland. From here, up to 50 passenger steamers a day would depart for Port Glasgow,

Map, pages 164–5

During the construction of the Kelvingrove Art Gallery and Museum the location of the main road was altered, so visitors now enter from the "rear".

BELOW: viewing the Burrell Collection.

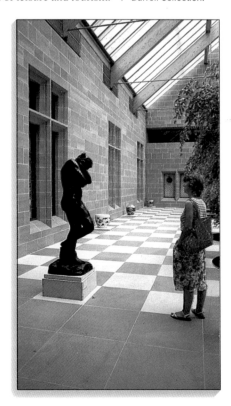

Glasgow District Subway, opened in 1896, was one of the earliest underground train systems in Britain and the only one in the country that is called, American-style, "the Subway".

Greenock, Gourock, Helensburgh and the islands in the Firth; these were the forerunners of today's suburban trains. When moorings were not available, steamers would tie up across the river at Bridge Quay, now called **Clyde Place Quay**. The result was often "a regatta of demented chimney-pots".

There is new life stirring, however, on the vast deserted wharfs of the Clyde. On the south bank, near Govan, up-market apartments have been built at the old **Princes Dock**, and the massive Rotunda at the north of the old Clyde Tunnel, designed for pedestrians and horses and carts (a new road tunnel was built in the early 1960s) has been restored as a restaurant complex.

Rough sentimentalism

"Rough, careless, vulnerable and sentimental." That's how the writer Edwin Morgan described Glaswegians, and they are certainly qualities which Glaswegians have brought to their environment. The city has been both brutal and nostalgic about its own fabric, destroying and lamenting with equal vigour. When the city fathers built an urban motorway in the 1960s they liberated Glasgow for the motorist but cut great swathes through its domestic and commercial heart, and were only just prevented from extending the Inner Ring Road, which would have demolished in the process much of the Merchant City.

But the disappearance of the last tramcars in the 1960s has been regretted ever since and today there is nostalgic talk of retrieving them; while Glaswegians have taken a long time to accept their updated underground transport system and to grow to love the "Clockwork Orange" – the violently coloured new rolling stock which replaced the original carriages in the 1970s.

But to Morgan's list of adjectives might have been added "pretentious" and

BELOW: enjoying spare time by the River Clyde.

DEATH ON THE CLYDE

The old adage that "the Clyde made Glasgow and Glasgow made the Clyde" can no longer be taken as a true description of the relationship today. In his book *In Search of Scotland*, H.V. Morton describes the launching of a ship on the Clyde in a passage which brings tears to the eyes: "Men may love her as men love ships…. She will become wise with the experience of the sea. But no shareholder will ever share her intimacy as we who saw her so marvellously naked and so young slip smoothly from the hands that made her into the dark welcome of the Clyde". That was written in 1929 – at a time when the Clyde's shipbuilding industry was on the precipice of the Great Depression from which it never recovered.

Soon another writer, the novelist George Blake, was calling the empty yards and silent cranes "the high, tragic pageant of the Clyde", and today that pageant is nothing more than a side-show. Not even the boost of demand during World War II, nor replacement orders in the 1950s, not even the work on supply vessels and oil platforms for the oil industry in the 1970s, could rebuild the vigour of the Clyde. Today Glasgow no longer depends on the river for its economic survival, though developments like the Clyde Walkway show a new future for the river in the leisure industry.

"aspirational", two sides of the architectural coin which represents Glasgow's legacy of magnificent Victorian buildings. They aren't hard to find: the dense gridiron of streets around George Square and westwards invites the neck to crane at any number of soaring façades, many bearing the art of the sculptor and all signifying some chapter of the 19th-century history.

Victorian splendour

George Square is the heart of modern Glasgow. Like most Scottish squares, it contains a motley collection of statues, commemorating 11 people who seem to have been chosen by lottery. The 80-ft (24-metre) column in its centre is mounted by the novelist Sir Walter Scott, gazing southwards, so they say, to the land where he made all his money. But the square is more effectively dominated by the grandiose **City Chambers** , designed by William Young and opened in 1888. The marble-clad interior is even more opulent and self-important than the exterior. The *pièce de résistance* is the huge banqueting hall, 110 ft (33 metres) long, 48 ft (14 metres) wide and 52 ft (16 metres) high; it has a glorious arched ceiling, leaded glass windows and paintings depicting scenes from the city's history. The south wall is covered by three large murals, works of the Glasgow Boys (*see pages 86-87*).

George Square's other monuments to Victorian prosperity are the former Head Post Office on the south side (now the main **Tourist Information Centre**) and the noble **Merchants' House** on the northwest corner (now the home of Glasgow Chamber of Commerce). Its crowning glory is the gold ship on its dome, drawing the eye ever upwards – a replica of the ship on the original Merchants' House.

Just off Buchanan Street is **Nelson Mandela Place** (its name having been

TIP

Guided tours are conducted around the City Chambers every weekday at 10.30am and 2.30pm.

BELOW: all lit up in George Square.

*Sir John Betjeman,
an architectural
enthusiast as well
as the Poet Laureate,
described Glasgow
as the "greatest
Victorian city in
Europe".*

BELOW: old-style in
the West End.

changed from St George's Place in tribute to the South African political leader). Here you will find **Glasgow Stock Exchange ⑫**, designed in the 1870s by John Burnet, whose reputation was to be eclipsed by his celebrated son J.J. Burnet; and the **Royal Faculty of Procurators** (1854), which is rich in decorative stonework and influenced by Italian Renaissance style.

Nearby are examples of the work of another distinguished Glasgow architect, the younger James Salmon, who designed the **Mercantile Buildings ⑬** (1897–98) in Bothwell Street and the curious **Hat-rack ⑭** in St Vincent Street, named for the extreme narrowness and the projecting cornices of its tall façade. Further west, J.J. Burnet's extraordinary **Charing Cross Mansions ⑮** of 1891, with grandiloquent intimations of French Renaissance style, was spared the surgery of motorway development which destroyed many 19th-century buildings around Charing Cross.

On the other side of one of these motorways are the first buildings of the **Park Conservation Area**. These buildings have resulted in the statement that Glasgow is the "finest piece of architectural planning of the mid-19th century". Stroll upwards through this area to a belvedere above **Kelvingrove Park** and marvel at the glorious vistas. The belvedere is backed by **Park Quadrant** and **Park Terrace**, which are probably the most magnificent of all the terraces in the Park Conservation Area.

Still in the west end, in Great Western Road, you will find **Great Western Terrace ⑯**, one of the best examples of the work of Glasgow's most famous Victorian architect, Alexander "Greek" Thomson, called "Greek" for the passion of his classicism.

Back towards the city centre in St Vincent Street is Thomson's prominent

St Vincent Street Church . It is fronted by an Ionic portico, with sides more Egyptian than Greek and a tower that wouldn't have been out of place in India during the Raj. Here the streets rise towards **Blythswood Square**, once a haunt of prostitutes but now, with its surroundings, providing a graceful mixture of late Georgian and early Victorian domestic architecture.

Art and architecture

A recent addition to Buchanan Street is the **Glasgow Royal Concert Hall**, a major investment by the city which regularly attracts top artists and orchestras. Behind **St Vincent Place** is **Royal Exchange Square**, which is pretty well consumed by the city's new **Gallery of Modern Art** ⓲ (open daily; free). The glorious building in which it is housed began life as the 18th-century mansion of a tobacco lord, has since been a bank, the Royal Exchange, and more recently a public library and extensive archive. In 1832, to the design of David Hamilton, it was extended to include the portico and the cupola.

Among the city centre's most distinguished Georgian buildings are, in Ingram Street, **Hutcheson's Hall** ⓳ (open Mon–Sat; free), also designed by David Hamilton and now housing National Trust for Scotland offices with a Trust visitor centre and shop; and, in nearby Glassford Street, **Trades House** ⓴ which, despite alterations, has retained the façade designed by the great Robert Adam.

But any excursion around Glasgow's architectural treasures must include the work of the city's most innovative genius, Charles Rennie Mackintosh, who overturned the Victorians in a series of brilliant designs between 1893 and 1911. Mackintosh's influence on 20th-century architecture, along with his leading contribution to *art nouveau* in interiors, furniture and textile design, has long

No. 7 Blythswood Square was where Madeleine Smith poisoned her French lover in 1858. She later moved to London, entertained George Bernard Shaw and married a pupil of the designer William Morris.

BELOW: Great Western Terrace in winter.

Mackintosh's startling design for the School of Art was inexpensive to build, thanks to its lack of ornamentation.

been acknowledged and celebrated throughout Europe, although all his finest work was done in and around Glasgow.

His sometimes austere, sometimes sensuous style, much influenced by natural forms and an inspired use of space and light, can be seen in several important buildings: his greatest achievement, the **Glasgow School of Art** ㉑ (designed in 1896) in Renfrew Street; **Scotland Street School**, on the South Side, opened in 1904 and now a Museum of Education (open Mon–Sat and Sun pm); and the **Martyrs' Public School**, perched above a sliproad to the M8 motorway near Glasgow Cathedral, and now housing Glasgow Museum's Conservation Department.

In Sauchiehall Street the façade of his **Willow Tea-Room** ㉒ (1903) remains, and a room on the first floor has been turned over to tea-time again; with reproduction Mackintosh furniture. But more stunning examples of his interior designs can be seen at the **Mackintosh House** at the University of Glasgow's **Hunterian Art Gallery** ㉓ (open Mon–Sat; free) on Gilmorehill. There, rooms from the architect's own house have been reconstructed and exquisitely furnished with original pieces of his furniture, water-colours and designs. Also worth a visit are the **House for an Art Lover** (open daily) in Bellhouston Park – erected long after his death, but to his exact specifications – and the **Queen's Cross Church** (open Mon–Fri and Sun pm) in Garscube Road.

Old and new

There's not much left in Glasgow which is old by British standards. The oldest building is **Glasgow Cathedral** ㉔ (open Mon–Sat and Sun pm; free), most of which was completed in the 13th century, though parts were built a century earlier by Bishop Jocelyn. It was completed by the first Bishop of Glasgow, Robert Blacader (1483–1508). The only pre-Reformation dwelling house is **Provand's Lordship** (open daily; free) built in 1471 as part of a refuge for poor people and extended in 1670. It now contains a museum of medieval material and, less logically, hosts an early 20th-century sweet shop.

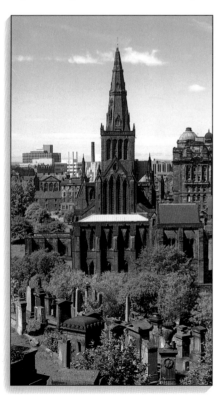

Both old buildings stand on **Cathedral Street**, at the top of the High Street – the cathedral on a site which has been a place of Christian worship since it was blessed for burial in AD 397 by St Ninian, the earliest missionary recorded in Scottish history. A severe but satisfying example of early Gothic, it contains the tomb of St Mungo. Behind the cathedral, overseeing the city from the advantage of height, are more tombs – the intimidating Victorian sepulchres of the **Western Necropolis**. This cemetery is supervised by a statute of John Knox, the 16th-century reformer, and among the ranks of Glaswegian notables buried there is one William Miller, "the laureate of the nursery". He wrote the popular bedtime jingle, "Wee Willie Winkie".

A brand-new cream-coloured Scottish baronial building in front of the cathedral is home to the **St Mungo Museum of Religious Life and Art** (open daily; free), with its Japanese Zen garden. Don't miss the comments on the visitors' board.

The two oldest churches in Glasgow, other than the cathedral, are **St Andrew's Parish Church** ㉕, which contains some spectacular plaster-work, and the episcopal **St Andrew's-by-the-Green** , once known as the Whistlin' Kirk because of its early organ. Both were built in the mid-18th century and both can be found to the northwest of Glasgow Green, in the Merchant City.

There you will also find two remnants of the 17th century, the **Tolbooth Steeple** and the **Tron Steeple**. The Tolbooth Steeple, at Glasgow Cross (where the Mercat Cross is a 20th-century replica of a vanished one) is a pretty substantial remnant of the old jail and courthouses, being seven storeys high with a crown tower. The Tron Steeple was once attached to the Tron Church, at the Trongate, and dates back to the late 16th and early 17th centuries. The original church was burnt down in the 18th century and the replacement now accommodates the lively Tron Theatre.

Those truly dedicated to the pursuit of antiquity, however, could always proceed to the refined northwest suburb of **Bearsden**, where once rough Romans roamed. Bearsden lies on the line of the Antonine Wall, built during the 2nd century, and chunks of the Roman occupation remain to be seen.

Market forces

Heavy industry has come and gone, but Glasgow still flourishes as a city of independent enterprise – of hawkers, stallholders, street traders and marketeers. Even the dignified buildings of its old, more respectable markets – fish, fruit and cheese – have survived in a city which has often been careless with its past, and have now become part of the rediscovery of the Merchant City area, which stretches from the **High Street** and the **Saltmarket** in the east to **Union Street** and **Jamaica Street** in the west. It contains most of the city's remaining pre-Victorian

Map, pages 164–5

TIP

Tours around the Glasgow School of Art start at 11am and 2pm, Monday to Friday, and at 10.30am on Saturday.

BELOW LEFT: a Mackintosh room in the Hunterian Art Gallery. **BELOW RIGHT:** inside Glasgow's School of Art.

Map, page 164–5

Tobias Smollett, writing in 1771, had no doubts about Glasgow's standing as a commercial centre: "one of the most flourishing in Great Britain... it is a perfect bee-hive in point of industry".

BELOW: the Barrows: Scotland's largest flea market.
RIGHT: modern shopping in the St Enoch Centre.

buildings. The old **Fishmarket** in Clyde Street is in fact Victorian, but it accommodates a perpendicular remnant of the 17th-century Merchants' House which was demolished in 1817. This slender steeple was built in the Dutch style in 1659.

In **Candleriggs** , slightly to the north, the old Fruitmarket now houses a more traditional style of weekend market selling fresh produce and inexpensive clothes, but Glasgow's market celebrity still belongs to the **Barrows** , in the Gallowgate to the east, where both repartee and bargains were once reputed to rival those of Paris's Flea Market and London's Petticoat Lane. Founding queen of "the Barras" was a certain Mrs McIver, who started her career with one barrow, bought several more to hire out on the piece of ground she rented in the Gallowgate and was claimed to have retired a millionaire.

More local colour and open-air tat, useful or useless, can be found in **Paddy's Market**, in the lanes between Clyde Street and the Bridgegate, many of the stalls occupying the arches of an old railway bridge. This market has its genesis in Ireland's "Hungry Forties", when the great potato famines of the 1840s sent hundreds of thousands of destitute Irish people to Glasgow (and elsewhere) to find a toehold or to starve.

Commercial interests

The West Highlands of Scotland were almost as badly affected by the potato famines and they, too, looked to Glasgow for salvation. Comic tradition has it that they also looked to **Argyle Street** for shelter. This famous shopping street is traversed by the railway bridge to Central Station. The bridge has always been called the Heilanman's Umbrella. The slander is that Highlanders stood under it when it rained rather than buy umbrellas; but the truth is that it has long been a favourite rendezvous of Glasgow's Highland community.

Argyle Street, **Sauchiehall Street** and the more upmarket **Buchanan Street** are Glasgow's great shopping thoroughfares, although an area round **Byres Road**, in the West End, has recently become a centre for interesting bric-a-brac and boutiques. **West Regent Street** has a Victorian Village (a collection of small antique shops in old business premises) and the old Tobacco Market in **Virginia Street**, where once the American shipments were auctioned, now houses the Virginia Antique and Crafts Galleries.

Glaswegians have always spent freely, even flashily, belying the slur on the open-handedness of Scots, and the city's commercial interests still seem to believe that the appetite for shopping is insatiable. An open loading area just off Buchanan Street has been converted with great imagination into the **Princes Square shopping mall** , which is worth visiting even for those who don't wish to shop or eat.

The site of the demolished St Enoch Railway Station and hotel (one of Glasgow's major acts of vandalism) is now occupied by **St Enoch Centre** , a spectacular £62 million glass-covered complex of 50 shop units, a fast-food "court", ice rink and multi-storey car park.

"Edinburgh is the capital," as the old joke goes, "but Glasgow *has* the capital." And it flaunts it ❑.

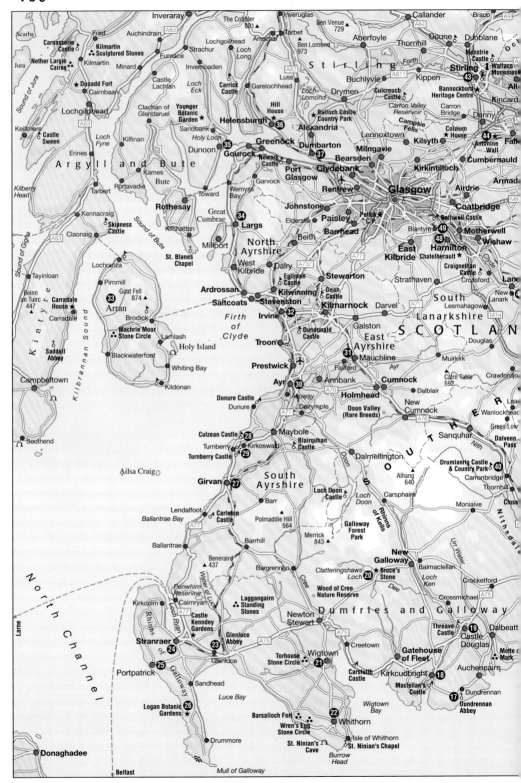

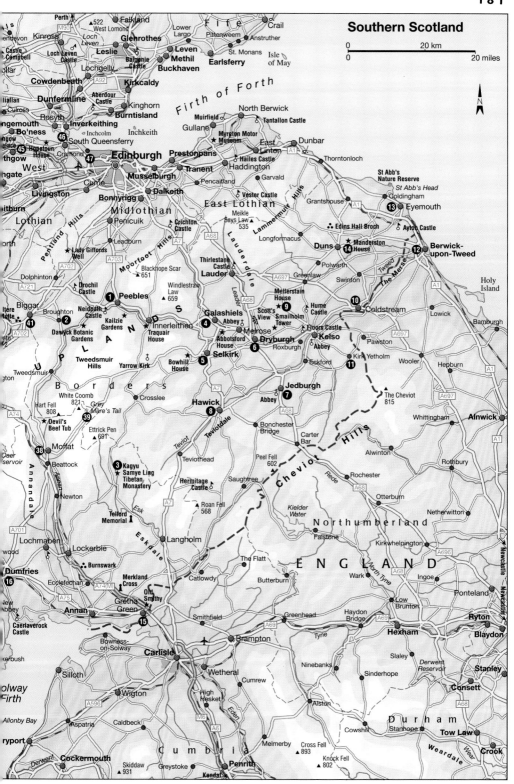

0   20 km
0   20 miles

N

Fife

Perth · 522 · West Lomond · Falkland · Crail
M90
Kinross · Loch Leven · Glenrothes · Lower Largo · Pittenweem · Anstruther
Castle Campbell · Loch Leven Castle · Leslie · Leven · St. Monans · Isle of May
ollar · Lochgelly · Balgonie Castle · Methil · Earlsferry
Cowdenbeath · A92 · Kirkcaldy · Buckhaven
liallan · Dunfermline · Aberdour Castle
Culross · Kinghorn
ngemouth · Rosyth · Inverkeithing · Burntisland
Bo'ness · Inchcolm · Inchkeith
hgow · Hopetoun House · South Queensferry
lace · Cramond · **46** · **45** · North Berwick · Tantallon Castle
thgow · **47** · **Edinburgh** · Prestonpans · Muirfield · Gullane · East Linton · Dunbar
West · Myreton Motor Museum · Hailes Castle · Thorntonloch
gate · Musselburgh · Tranent · Haddington · A1
ngate · Currie · Pencaitland · Garvald · St Abb's Nature Reserve · St Abb's Head
Livingston · Dalkeith · Bonnyrigg · Vester Castle · Grantshouse · Coldingham
itburn · Midlothian · East Lothian · A1 · **13** · Eyemouth
Lothian · Penicuik · Meikle Says Law 535 · Lammermuir Hills · Edins Hall Broch · Ayton Castle
orth · Crichton Castle · Longformacus · Manderston House · **12** · Berwick-upon-Tweed
Pentland Hills · Leadburn · A7 · A68 · Duns · **14** · Holy Island
Lady Giffords Well · Thirlestane Castle · Polwarth · The Merse
Dolphinton · A703 · Blackhope Scar 651 · Lauder · A697 · Greenlaw · Swinton · A1
A702 · Drochil Castle · Windlestraw Law 659 · Leader · **10** · Coldstream · Lowick · Bamburgh
Biggar · **1** · Peebles · Mellerstain House · **9** · Hume Castle · **11** · Pawston · Wooler
41 · Broughton · **2** · Neidpath Castle · Kailzie Gardens · Galashiels · **4** · Scott's View · Smailholm Tower · Floors Castle · Kirk Yetholm · Hepburn
otte · Dawyck Botanic Gardens · Innerleithen · Abbey · Melrose · **6** · Dryburgh · Roxburgh · **Kelso** · Eckford
Tweedsmuir · Traquair House · Abbotsford House · **5** · **Selkirk** · Abbey · **11** · Alnwick
Tweedsmuir Hills · Bowhill House · Yarrow Kirk · A7 · A697 · A1
U P L A N D S · B o r d e r s · Jedburgh · **7** · Whittingham
Tweedsmuir · White Coomb 821 · Grey Mare's Tail · Crosslee · Hawick · **8** · Abbey · Bonchester Bridge · The Cheviot 815 · Rothbury
gton · Hart Fell 808 · **39** · Devil's Beef Tub · Ettrick Pen 691 · Teviotdale · Carter Bar · Cheviot Hills · Netherwitton
A74 · Moffat · **38** · Beattock · Teviothead · Peel Fell 602 · Alwinton
Daer servoir · Newton · **3** · Kagyu Samye Ling Tibetan Monastery · Teviot · Saughtree · Rochester · Otterburn
Lochmaben · Hermitage Castle · Roan Fell 568 · Kielder Water · N o r t h u m b e r l a n d
wood · Lockerbie · Telford Memorial · Esk · Falstone · Kirkwhelpington · A696
A701 · Burnswark · Langholm · The Flatt · E N G L A N D · Wark · Ingoe · Ponteland
Dumfries · **16** · Ecclefechan · A74(M) · Merkland Cross · Catlowdy · Butterburn · North Tyne · A68 · Low Brunton · Newcastle
Jew · Annan · Gretha Green · Old Smithy · Smithfield · Greenhead · Haydon Bridge · **Hexham** · **Ryton** · Blaydon
bbey · **15** · Bowness-on-Solway · A69 · Tyne · A69
Caerlaverock Castle · Carlisle · Brampton · Slaley · Derwent Reservoir · **Stanley**
kerbush · Wetheral · Ninebanks · Sinderhope · **Consett**
olway Firth · Silloth · Cumrew · Alston · D u r h a m · Tow Law
Allonby Bay · Wigton · High Hesket · A68 · **Crook**
ryport · Aspatria · Caldbeck · A6 · Cowshill · Stanhope · Weardale · Wear
Derwent · Melmerby · Cross Fell 893 · Weardale
C u m b r i a · **Cockermouth** · Skiddaw 931 · Greystoke · **Penrith** · Knock Fell 802 · Kendal

THE BORDERS

*Castles, ruined abbeys, baronial mansions and
evidence of past turbulent struggles against the English give the
green hills of the Borders a romance all of their own*

Map,
pages
180–1

There's an assumption that, compared with all those northerly lochs and glens, rushing rivers and barren moors, the Borders has only borderline appeal. In reality the region is much more magnificent than the name suggests. The Borders (administratively, it includes the four "shires" of Peebles and Berwick in the north and Selkirk and Roxburgh in the south) comprises one of Europe's last unspoilt areas.

Quiet beginnings

Directly south of Edinburgh, **Peebles** ❶ owes much of its charm to its Tweedside location. Here the river already runs wide and fast. Peebles' central thoroughfare is equally wide but much more sedate. The town was never renowned for its hustle and bustle: an 18th-century aristocrat coined an ungenerous simile: "As quiet as the grave – or Peebles". Each June things liven up considerably with the week-long Beltane festival, but during the rest of the year Peebles is still a quiet introduction to the Borders.

The **Cross Kirk** was erected in 1261 after the discovery of a large cross on this site. The remains include a large 15th-century tower and foundations of cloister and monastic buildings. St Andrew's Collegiate Church, the forerunner to the Cross Kirk, sits in a cemetery on the Glasgow road. Here, too, only a tower remains; the remainder was burnt by the English at the time of the sacking of the four great Border abbeys. At the bottom of Peebles High Street, the Gothic outline of Peebles Parish Church adds to the town's air of sobriety.

The **Chambers Institute**, Peebles' civic centre and museum, was a gift to the place from William Chambers, a native of the place and the founding publisher of Chambers Encyclopedia.

Following the Tweed

Just a few minutes out of Peebles (west on the A72), perched high on a rocky bluff overlooking the Tweed, **Neidpath Castle** (open Easter–Sept: Mon–Sat and Sun pm; tel: (01721) 720333), a well-preserved example of the many medieval Tower Houses in the region, offers more excitement. Wordsworth visited in 1803 and wrote a famous poem lamenting the desolation caused in 1795 when the absentee landowner, the 4th Duke of Queensberry, cut down all the trees for money to support his extravagant London lifestyle.

Wordsworth would have been happier had he journeyed 8 miles (13 km) southwest of Peebles on the B712 to **Dawyck Botanic Gardens** (open Mar–Oct: daily; tel: (01721) 760254), an outstation of Edinburgh's Royal Botanic Garden containing a fine collection of mature specimen trees, many over 100 years old.

PRECEDING PAGES:
beauty in the
Borders.
LEFT: a shepherd
near Moffat.
BELOW: crossing the
Tweed into Peebles.

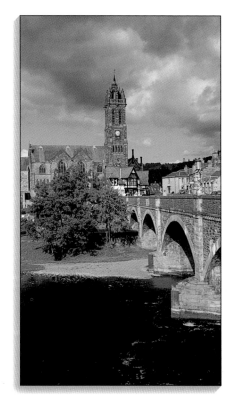

The novelist John Buchan never forgot his roots. He took his title of Baron of Tweedsmuir from his home parish and wrote of Broughton, the village where he grew up, that he "liked it better than any place in the world".

Continue on the B712 to **Broughton** , the site of **Broughton Place**, an imposing castillian house that looks as if it was built centuries ago: it was in fact designed this century. Inside, Broughton Gallery has a fine collection of work by British artists and craftsmen for sale. John Buchan, author of the best-selling *The Thirty Nine Steps*, grew up in this village. Just south of the village, the **John Buchan Centre** (open Easter and May–mid-Oct: daily pm; tel: (01899) 221050) is a small museum that paints a detailed picture of a man who led a varied life which eventually saw him become Governor General of Canada.

Buchan also liked the **Crook Inn**, just outside **Tweedsmuir**, 15 miles (24 km) south of Broughton. One of the oldest Border inns, it has strong literary associations. Robert Burns was inspired to write his poem "*Willie Wastle's Wife*" in the kitchen (now the bar). Sir Walter Scott used to visit here, as did his lesser known contemporary James Hogg, the poet known locally as "The Ettrick Shepherd".

Step southwards outside the Borders towards Eskdalemuir, and you'll be greeted by a real surprise: the **Kagyu Samye Ling Tibetan Monastery** ❸ (open daily; tel: (01387) 373232). This Tibetan Buddhist centre was founded in 1967 for study, retreat and meditation and incorporates Samye Temple, an authentic Tibetan Buddhist monastery in the centre's grounds. Visitors, regardless of faith, can join free tours around the centre's facilities.

East of Peebles on the A72 is **Traquair House** (open Easter week, May and Sept: daily pm; June– Aug: daily; grounds open May–Sept: daily; tel: (01896) 830323), still owned by the family that acted as hosts when Mary Queen of Scots stayed there with her husband Darnley in 1566. Its history goes much further back; parts of it date from the 12th century. The wide avenue leading away from

BELOW: Sir Walter Scott towers over Selkirk.

BORDER COUNTRY

The River Tweed has inspired romantic Borders ballads for hundreds of years and was held by the novelist Sir Walter Scott to be the most precious river in the world. Its source is just a few miles south of the village of Tweedsmuir, and the river cuts right through three of the most important Border towns: Peebles, Melrose and Kelso. Here, too, you will find rugged moorland and craggy terrain, reminiscent of the Scottish Highlands. The two highest points in the Borders, Broad Law and Dollar Law, rise to more than 2,750 ft (840 metres) and 2,680 ft (820 metres) respectively.

Draw a line between Hawick and Broughton and then stay south of it and you'll see the best the Border has to offer. A popular route is the side-road out of Tweedsmuir up to the Talla and Megget Reservoirs. Steep slopes and rock-strewn hillsides provide a stunning panorama as you twist and turn down to the A708, where, to the south, is another favourite spot: St Mary's Loch, the only loch in the Borders region. If you are fit, you should foresake the car and follow the Southern Uplands Way, which runs alongside the loch and north across the moors to Traquair House, or south to the valley of Ettrick Water.

the house to the large gates by the main road has been disused for more than two centuries. After Bonnie Prince Charlie visited in 1745, the 5th Earl of Traquair closed the Bear Gates after him and swore they would not open until a Stuart king had been restored to the throne.

On the road west back to Peebles, **Kailzie Gardens** (open daily; tel: (01721) 720007) adds to the beauty of the Tweed Valley with its formal walled garden, greenhouses and woodland walks.

Heart of the Borders

Though it has little to tempt today's visitor, **Galashiels** ❹ has played a pivotal role in the Borders economy as a weaving town for more than 700 years. The Scottish College of Textiles, founded in 1909, has helped to cement the reputation of the tartans, tweeds, woollens and other knitted materials sold in the mills here. Although the industry across the region has gone into decline, there are numerous working mills open to the public: **Lochcarron of Scotland** in Huddersfield Street (open Mon–Sat and Sun pm; Oct–May closed Sun; tel: (01896) 752091), which holds conducted tours and features a textiles museum.

It's not only Galashiels that lets you sample the Borders' textiles. Tourism has fashioned the Borders Woollen Trail, which includes eight other towns involved in this industry. One of them, **Selkirk** ❺, became a textile centre in the 19th century when the growing demand for tweed could no longer be met by the mills of Galashiels. Other than shopping there are several interesting places to visit, including the 18th-century **Halliwell's House Museum** (open Easter–Oct: Mon–Sat and Sun pm; tel: (01750) 20096), a former old ironmongers which now tells the story of Selkirk in entertaining detail. Nearby is **Sir Walter Scott's**

**Map,
pages
180–1**

TIP

Traditional ale, which is regularly brewed in the 18th-century alehouse of Traquair House, can be purchased by thirsty visitors.

BELOW LEFT: on parade at Traquair House.
BELOW RIGHT: peace at Samye Ling Monastery.

Sir Walter Scott wrote all the Waverley novels at Abbotsford House, but only admitted to being the author late in life, feeling that it wasn't "decorous" of a Clerk of Session to be seen writing novels.

BELOW: Dryburgh Abbey: a brooding reminder of bloody history.

Courtroom (open Easter–Oct: Mon–Sat; June and Aug also Sun pm; tel: (01750) 20096) where the great writer dispensed judgement during his 35 years as sheriff here. Down by the Ettrick Water is Selkirk Glass (open daily; tel: (01750) 20954).

Don't leave the locality without visiting **Bowhill House and Country Park** (house open July: daily pm; country park open May–Aug: daily pm except Fri; tel: (01750) 22204). Dating from 1812, Bowhill is the home of the Scotts of Buccleuch and Queensberry, once one of the largest landowners of all the Border clans. More than 300 years of discerning art collecting has amassed works by Canaletto, Guardi, Leonardo, Reynolds and Gainsborough.

If the Borders have a sort of visitors' Mecca, then **Abbotsford House** (open late March–Oct: Mon–Sat and Sun pm; tel: (01896) 752043), home of Sir Walter Scott from 1811 to 1832, undoubtedly lays claim to that title. Scott spent £50,000 and the rest of his life turning a small farm into an estate that could do justice to his position as a Border laird.

Scott was buried at **Dryburgh ❻**, one of the four great 12th-century abbeys in the Borders (open Mon–Sat and Sun pm; tel: (01835) 822381). While the ruins at Jedburgh, Kelso and Melrose lie near the edge of their respective towns, Dryburgh, founded by Hugh de Morville for monks from Alnwick in Northumberland, is tucked away in an idyllic location among trees by the edge of the Tweed.

Dryburgh's setting is no match for **Scott's View** on the B6356, which offers a sweeping view of the unmistakeable triple peaks of the **Eildon Hills** (reputed to be the legendary sleeping place of King Arthur and his knights) and a wide stretch of the Tweed Valley. Scott came here many times to enjoy the panorama.

The town of **Melrose,** between Dryburgh and Galashiels, escaped much of

the industralisation that affected Selkirk, Hawick and Galashiels. **Melrose Abbey** (open daily; tel: (01896) 822562) seals the town's pedigree. It even accounts for the beginning of Sir Walter Scott's rise to fame, for it was eloquently described in *The Lay of the Last Minstrel*, the great narrative poem of 1805 that made him famous. The abbey was founded in 1136 by King David I, who helped to found all four of the great Border abbeys, and was the first Cistercian monastery in Scotland. Tragically it lay in the path of repeated English invasions long before Henry VIII made his presence felt in the 16th century. An attack in 1322 by Edward II prompted Robert Bruce to fund its restoration. Also in Melrose is Scotland's only **Teddy Bear Museum** (open daily) where enthusiasts can commission their own bears to be made.

North of Melrose, on the outskirts of **Lauder**, is **Thirlestane Castle** (open Easter week, May, June and Sept: pm Mon, Wed, Thur and Sun; July and Aug: daily except Sat; tel: (01578) 722430), once the seat of the Earls of Lauderdale. One of Scotland's oldest and finest castles, it was built on a 12th-century foundation and today houses an impressive collection of furniture and paintings as well as some renowned 17th-century plaster ceilings.

Roman reminders

Historically, **Jedburgh ❼** is the most important of the Border towns. It was also strategically important; as the first community across the border it frequently received the full brunt of invading English armies. Earlier invaders came from even more distant lands than the English. Two miles north of Jedburgh it is possible to follow the course of Dere Street, the road the Romans built in southern Scotland more than 1,900 years ago.

Map, pages 180–1

The heart of Robert the Bruce was said to be buried near the high altar of Melrose Abbey, but subsequent excavations have failed to locate any trace of it.

BELOW: playtime in the shadow of Jedburgh Abbey.

Contrary to popular belief, the word "tweed" does not come from the river; in fact, it was originally a misprint – by an English publisher – for tweels, the Border name for woollen fabrics.

BELOW: the Duke of Roxburghe at home in Floors Castle.

The most ancient surviving building, **Jedburgh Abbey** (open Mon–Sat and Sun pm; tel: (01835) 863925), was founded in 1138 by Augustinian canons from northern France. Stonework in the abbey's museum dates from the first millennium AD and proves that the site had much older religious significance. Malcolm IV was crowned here and Alexander III married his second wife in the abbey in 1285. Their wedding feast was held at nearby Jedburgh Castle, which occupied a site in Castlegate. It was demolished in 1409 to keep it out of English hands. In 1823 the **Castle Gaol** (open Easter–Oct: Mon–Sat and Sun pm; tel: (01835) 863254) was built on the old castle's foundations; its museum of social history is well worth a visit.

Near the High Street, display panels and artefacts in **Mary Queen of Scots' House** (open Easter–Nov: daily; tel: (01835) 863331) tell a short but crucial chapter in Scotland's history. It was in this house in late 1566 that Queen Mary spent several weeks recovering from serious illness after her renowned dash on horseback to Hermitage Castle to see her injured lover James Hepburn, Earl of Bothwell. Her ride resulted in scandal that was made all the worse by the murder of her husband Darnley in the following February. From there on, her downfall was steady. Years later, during her 19 years of imprisonment, Mary regretted that her life hadn't ended in the Borders: "Would that I had died in Jedburgh".

If you decide to retrace Mary's footsteps to Hermitage Castle, you're likely to pass through **Hawick ❽** (pronounced *Hoik*). The Borders' textile industry is all around you here. World-famous brand names are emblazoned boldly above factory gates, while at the **Hawick Museum** in **Wilton Lodge Park** (open Mon–Fri, Sat and Sun pm; Oct–Mar: closed Mon–Fri am and Sat; tel: (01450) 373457) a fascinating collection of exhibits picks up older sartorial threads.

Still retaining its central cobbled streets leading into a spacious square, **Kelso** is one of the most picturesque of the Border towns. Just over 100 yards from the town's centre is **Kelso Abbey** (open daily; free), once the largest and richest of the Borders abbeys. It suffered the same fate as its counterparts at Melrose, Jedburgh and Dryburgh and is today the least complete of all of them.

It's ironic that, while the English destroyed Kelso's abbey, the Scottish were responsible for the much greater devastation of the town of **Roxburgh** and its castle. Roxburgh had grown up on the south bank of the Tweed around the mighty fortress of Marchmount. An important link in the chain of border fortifications, Marchmount controlled the gateway to the north. In the 14th century the English took Roxburgh and its castle and used it as a base for further incursions into Scottish territory. In 1460 James II of Scotland attacked Marchmount but was killed by a bursting cannon. His widow urged the Scottish troops forward.

On achieving victory they destroyed Roxburgh's castle (to make sure it stayed out of enemy hands for good) with a thoroughness that the English would have found hard to match. Today, on a mound between the Teviot and the Tweed just west of Kelso (the plain village of Roxburgh a few miles on is no direct relation of the ancient town), only fragments of Marchmount's walls survive.

Floors Castle is the largest inhabited castle in Scotland.

Art and architecture

On the north bank of the Tweed, Kelso thrived, however. **Floors Castle** (open Easter–Oct: daily; tel: (01573) 223333) was designed by Robert Adam and built between 1721 and 1726. It owes its present flamboyant appearance to William Playfair, who remodelled and extended the castle between 1837 and 1845. An outstanding collection of German, Italian and French furniture, Chinese and Dresden porcelain, paintings by Picasso, Matisse and Augustus John, and a 15th-century Brussels tapestry are some of the many glittering prizes that give Floors an air of palatial elegance.

Smailholm Tower (open Apr–Sept: Mon–Sat and Sun pm; tel: (01573) 460365) stands gaunt and foreboding 6 miles (10 km) northwest of Kelso (B6404). Walter Scott made a deal with the owner of this superb 16th-century peel tower: in exchange for saving it, Scott would write a ballad – *The Eve of St John* – about it. Today, the stern-faced fortress is a museum of costume figures and tapestries relating to Scott's *Minstrelsy of the Borders*.

Northwest from Kelso on the A8069 is **Mellerstain House ❾** (open May–Sept: Sun–Fri pm; tel: (01573) 410225), one of Scotland's finest Georgian mansions and the 18th-century product of the combined genius of William Adam and his son Robert. Externally it has the dignity, symmetry and well-matched proportions characteristic of this period. Inside there's furniture by Chippendale, Sheraton and Hepplewhite as well as paintings by Gainsborough, Constable, Veronese and Van Dyck, and some exquisite examples of moulded plaster ceilings, doorheads, mantelpieces and light-fittings.

As if all this weren't enough to impress, formal Italian gardens were laid out in 1909 to create a series of gently sloping terraces and the house became a popular venue for fashionable dances.

BELOW: the ruins of Kelso Abbey.

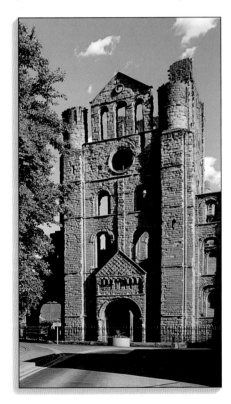

Border crossings

East of Kelso the Tweed marks the natural boundary between England and Scotland. **Coldstream** , one of the last towns on this river before Berwick, has little to offer the visitor other than history. The town's name was taken by the famous regiment of Coldstream Guards that was formed by General Monck in 1659 before he marched south to support the restoration of the Stuart monarchy. The regiment today loans material to the **Coldstream Museum** (open Easter–Oct: Mon–Sat and Sun pm; tel: (01890) 882630), set up in a house that was Monck's headquarters.

Nearly 150 years earlier, in 1513, James IV of Scotland crossed the Tweed at Coldstream to attack the English with a much larger force. Though Henry VIII was at that time fighting in France (James IV's invasion was a diversion intended to aid the French) an English army was sent north to meet the threat. The encounter, which took place near the English village of Branxton but was known as the Battle of Flodden, was a military disaster for Scotland: the king, his son, and as many as 46 nobles and 9,000 men were slain.

Happier endings are to be had at **Kirk Yetholm** ⓫, just a mile (1.6 km) from the English border. Overlooking the village green, the Border Hotel bills itself as the "End of the Pennine Way". A few miles away **Linton Kirk**, said to be the oldest building in continuous use for Christian worship in the area, sits proudly on a hummock of sand in a picturesque valley. Here the slopes rise steeply to join the Cheviots – a ridge of hills that forms another natural ingredient in the border between Scotland and England.

When it comes to identifying precise borderlines, **Berwick-upon-Tweed** ⓬ can be forgiven for feeling a little confused. Boundaries around here lack a sense

BELOW: Mellerstain: one of Scotland's most glorious Georgian houses.

of fair play: Berwick is not part of Berwickshire. And although the town takes its name from a river that has its source in the Scottish Borders, Berwick-upon-Tweed is not part of Scotland. It's in Northumberland, England. It wasn't always like that. Berwick made its way into Scotland many times previously. The town changed hands no fewer than 13 times between 1147 and 1482 (when it was finally taken for England by Richard, Duke of Gloucester – later Richard III).

Historically Berwick is very much a part of the Borders. The town's castle, built in the late 12th century by Henry II, once towered high above the Tweed. Much of it was demolished in 1847 to make space for the station, which bears an appropriate inscription by Robert Stephenson: "The Final Act Of Union". Berwick's Town Wall, built on the orders of Edward I, has fared better and is one of the most complete of its kind in Britain.

Situated in Scotland, along the coast just north of Berwick, **Eyemouth** ⓭ is a small, working fishing town whose **Museum** (open Apr–Sept: Mon–Sat and Sun pm; Oct: closed Sun; tel: (01890) 750678) vividly outlines Eyemouth's long tradition as a fishing port. The museum's centrepiece is the Eyemouth Tapestry, made by local people in 1981 to commemorate the Great Disaster of 1881 when 189 local fishermen were drowned, all within sight of land, during a storm.

A few miles north, **Coldingham's Medieval Priory** and **St Abbs' Head Nature Reserve** (open daily; free; tel: (01890) 771443) are two further justifications for making this detour off the A1 to Edinburgh. You could head inland and take another route to Edinburgh: the A6105/A697. If you do, make a point of stopping at **Manderston House** ⓮ (open mid May–Sept: Thur and Sun pm; tel: (01361) 883450), just outside Duns, to enjoy what has been dubbed "the finest Edwardian country house in Scotland". ❏

Map, pages 180–1

Each of the 36 bells in the servants' quarters of Manderston House has a different tone: the cacophony must have been deafening when the servants were summoned to clean the silver staircase, the only one in the world.

BELOW: the old bridge over the River Tweed in Berwick.

HISTORIC CASTLES AND ABBEYS

An Englishman's home may be his castle but for centuries and, in some instances even today, a Scotsman's castle has been his home

Dotted throughout the Scottish landscape are more than 2,000 castles, many in ruins but others in splendid condition. The latter, still occupied, do not fulfil the primary definition of "castle" – a fortified building – but rather meet the secondary definition: a magnificent house, such as Fyvie *(above)*.

Either way, all are not merely part of Scottish history: they are its essence. Many carry grim and grisly tales. Thus, Hugh Macdonald was imprisoned in the bowels of Duntulum Castle and fed generous portions of salted beef, but he was denied anything – even whisky – to drink.

In 1746 Blair Castle was, on the occasion of the Jacobite uprising, the last castle in the British isles to be fired upon in anger. Today, the Duke of Atholl, the owner of Blair Castle, is the only British subject permitted to maintain a private army, the Atholl Highlanders. Prior to the siege, Bonnie Prince Charlie slept here (visitors might be excused for believing there are few castles in Scotland where the Bonnie Prince and Mary, Queen of Scots did not sleep).

You, too, can sleep in Scottish castles. Culzean, Skibo and Inverlochy are but a trio where accommodation is available. And, for those eager to become a laird, don the kilt and own a castle, several are invariably on the market.

◁ **STRONGHOLD**
In 1314 Robert the Bruce reaffirmed Scottish supremacy won at Bannockburn by reclaiming Stirling Castle from the English.

△ **RELIGIOUS RELICS**
The ruins of St Andrews Cathedral give some idea of the grandeur of ecclesiastical building: this was once the greatest church in Scotland.

◁ GUARDING THE GLEN

Urquhart Castle was built to guard the Great Glen. It played an important role in the Wars of Independence, being taken by Edward 1 and later held by Robert the Bruce. During the Jacobite troubles part of the castle was blown up to prevent it falling into "rebel" hands. Today, its walls are a strategic spot from which to sight the Loch Ness Monster.

▽ ROYAL RESIDENCE

Stirling Castle, once called "the key to Scotland" because of its strategic position between the Lowlands and Highlands, witnessed many bloody battles between the Scots and English. Later, it became a favourite residence of Stuart monarchs. Nowadays it is also the home of the regimental museum of the Argyll and Sutherland Highlanders.

◁ BARONIAL SPLENDOUR

Dunrobin, the largest pile in the Highlands, is seat of the Dukes of Sutherland who once owned more land than anyone in Europe. Originally a fortified square keep, it was transformed into a castle and then in the 19th century into a French château with Scottish baronial overtones. The gardens are magnificent.

SCOTTISH BORDER ABBEYS

Scotland, especially the Borders, is full of abbeys that now lie ruined but were once powerful institutions with impressive buildings. During the reign of David I (1124–53), who revitalized and transformed the Scottish church, more than 20 religious houses were founded. Outstanding among these is a quartet of Border abbeys – Dryburgh (Premonstratensian), Jedburgh (Augustinian), Kelso (Tironensian) and Melrose (Cistercian). All have evocative ruins, though perhaps it is Jedburgh (*above*) with tower and remarkable rose window still intact, which is Scotland's classic abbey.

It was not the Reformation (1560) that caused damage to these abbeys but rather the selfishness of pre-Reformation clergy, raids in the 14th–16th centuries by both English and Scots, the ravages of weather and activities of 19th-century restorers. The concern of the Reformation, spearheaded by firebrand John Knox, was to preserve, not to destroy, the churches they needed.

Monasteries continued to exist as landed corporations after the Reformation. Why upset a system that suited so many interests? After all, the Pope, at the King's request, had provided priories and abbeys for five of James V's bastards while they were still infants.

THE SOUTHWEST

*The Southwest is a gentle country, with a dense concentration
of literary associations and a colourful history whose sometimes
brutal nature belies the comeliness of the land*

Map,
pages
180–1

I n the landscape and seascapes of Southwest Scotland, in the pretty villages of
Dumfries and Galloway and the hill farms of south Lanarkshire, in the industrial townships of Ayrshire and the ports and holiday resorts of the Clyde coast,
you will find something of the rest of Scotland. All that is missing, perhaps, is the
inspiring grandeur of the West Highlands. The **Galloway Hills** are lonely, lovely
places in their own right, but none rises to more than 2,800 ft (850 metres).

Yet travellers from England often bypass the Solway with its pastoral hinterland in their scamper up the A74 to points north and the Highlands, hesitating
only at a name which is legendary for rather trivial reasons. **Gretna Green** ⑮,
just over the Border (until the boundary between England and Scotland was
agreed in 1552, this area was known simply as the Debatable Land), became
celebrated for celebrating marriages. It was the first available community where
eloping couples from England could take advantage of Scotland's different marriage laws. Many a makeshift ceremony was performed at the **Old Smithy**,
which is now a visitor centre (open daily; tel: (01461) 338441), and many a
romantic bride still chooses to be married at Gretna Green today.

The Burns legend

A few miles farther north is **Ecclefechan**, where the
pretty white **Arched House** in which the man of letters
Thomas Carlyle was born in 1795, is now a modest literary shrine (open May–Sept: Mon–Fri pm; tel: (01576)
300666). But the Southwest is more inescapably identified with the poet Robert Burns, whose life and legend remains one of the main props of Scottish tourism.

The urban centres of the Burns industry are Dumfries
and Ayr. **Dumfries** ⑯ is also "the Queen of the South",
an ancient and important Border town whose character
survives the unsightly housing estates and factories on
its periphery, and which is within easy reach of the
haunting, history-rich Solway coast. Burns, the farmer-
poet, took over Ellisland Farm some 6 miles (10 km)
outside the town in 1788, built the farmhouse and tried
to introduce new farming methods. His venture col-
lapsed and he moved to Dumfries to become an excise-
man, but **Ellisland** (open Oct–Mar: Mon–Sat), where
he wrote *Tam o'Shanter* and *Auld Lang Syne,* is now a
museum – as is **Burns House** in Mill Vennel (now
Burns Street), Dumfries, where he died in 1796 (open
Apr–Sept: Mon–Sat and Sun pm; Oct–Mar: closed Sun
and Mon; free; tel: (01387) 255297). His first home in
the town was a three-room flat in the Wee Vennel (now
Bank Street), which Burns re-christened Stinking Vennel, but it isn't open to the public.

To bring it all together, visit the stone mill on the
River Nith. This is home to the **Robert Burns Centre**

PRECEDING PAGES:
interior of Culzean
Castle.
LEFT: the castle's
exterior.
BELOW: Tam o'
Shanter rides on.

TIP

End your tour of Burns
country with a drink
at the Globe Inn in
Dumfries, where you
can sit in the poet's
favourite chair.

(open Apr–Sept: Mon–Sat and Sun pm; Oct–Mar: Tues–Sat; tel: (01387) 264808), the major feature of the Scottish Tourist Board's Burns Heritage Trail.

The handsome waterfront of the **River Nith**, with its 15th-century bridge, and the red sandstone dignity of nearby **St Michael's Church**, in whose churchyard Burns is buried, give Dumfries its distinctive character. Its environs have just as much to offer. On opposing banks of the Nith estuary, where it debouches into the Solway, are **Caerlaverock Castle** (open Mon–Sat and Sun pm; tel: (0131) 668 8800), the **Wildfowl and Wetlands Trust Reserve** (open daily; tel: (01387) 770200) – a winter haunt of wildfowl – and **Sweetheart Abbey**.

The castle is strikingly well-preserved, dates back to the 13th century and was the seat of the Maxwell family, later Earls of Nithsdale – one of the most powerful local dynasties. It was besieged by Edward I during the Wars of Independence and in 1640 fell to a 13-week siege mounted by the Covenanters.

The graceful ruin of Sweetheart Abbey (open Apr–Sept: Mon–Sat and Sun pm; Oct–Mar: closed Thur pm and Fri; tel: (0131) 668 8800), in the pretty village of New Abbey, is a monument to the marital devotion of the noble Devorgilla Balliol, who not only founded this Cistercian abbey in 1273 but founded Balliol College, Oxford, in memory of her husband. She also carried his heart around her until her own death in 1290, when she and the heart were buried together in front of the high altar.

The shallow estuary of the Solway is noted for the speed of its tidal race and the treachery of its sands, but the hazardous areas are well signposted and if you follow the coastal roads from River Nith to **Loch Ryan** you will find an amiable succession of villages, yachting harbours, attractive small towns and good beaches, not to mention many secret coves and snug, deserted little bays.

BELOW: Sculptures by Rodin (left) and Henry Moore (right) gaze from Shaw-head towards nearby Dumfries.

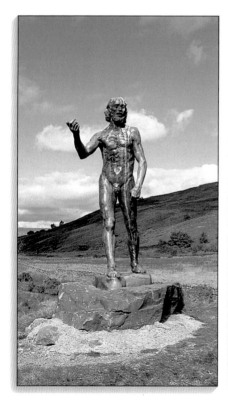

Ancient Galloway

This is the ancient territory of Galloway, whose people once fraternised with Norse raiders and whose lords preserved a degree of independence from the Scottish crown until the 13th century. Many of Scotland's great names and great causes have seen action among these hills and bays. At **Dundrennan Abbey** ⓱ (open Apr–Sept: Mon–Wed, Sat, Fri am and Sun pm; Oct–Mar: Sat and Sun; tel: (0131) 668 8800), 7 miles (11 km) southeast of Kirkcudbright on the A711, Mary Queen of Scots is believed to have spent her last night in Scotland, on 15 May 1568, sheltering in this 12th-century Cistercian house on her final, fatal flight from the Battle of Langside to her long imprisonment in England.

Kirkcudbright ⓲ (pronounced *Kir-koo-bree*), at the mouth of the River Dee, has the reputation of being the most attractive of the Solway towns, with a colourful waterfront (much appreciated and colonised by artists) and an elegant Georgian town centre. Little remains of the Kirkcudbright which took its name from the vanished Kirk of Cuthbert (which once played host to the saint's bones), but it has a **Market Cross** of 1610 and a **Tolbooth** from the same period. **Broughton House** (open Easter–Oct: daily pm; tel: (01557) 330437) in Kirkcudbright has a major gallery of paintings by the Glasgow Boys and an exhibition of the life of E.A. Hornel, who lived there.

Ten miles (16 km) northeast from Kirkcudbright is another neat and dignified little town, **Castle Douglas** ⓳, which stands on the small loch of Carlingwark, where you will find one of the most formidable tower strongholds in Scotland. **Threave Castle** (open Apr–Sept: Mon–Sat and Sun pm; tel: (0131) 668 8800) was built towards the end of the 14th century by the wonderfully named Archibald the Grim, third Earl of Douglas. It was the last Douglas castle

Map, pages 180–1

The Tolbooth at Kirkcudbright once entertained John Paul Jones, who was imprisoned for the manslaughter of his ship's carpenter. Jones restored his reputation in later life by laying the foundations of the American navy.

BELOW: keeping the telephones in working order in the rural southwest.

to surrender to James II during the conflict between the king and the maverick Border family. It also has associations with the Covenanters, who seized it in 1640 and vandalised the interior. **Threave Gardens** (open daily; tel: (01556) 502575) has superb flower, plant and tree displays all year.

Villages of Galloway

In Galloway you will find villages unusually pretty for a country which isn't famous for the aesthetics of its small communities. Their characteristic feature is whitewashed walls with black-bordered doors and windows – as if they have taken their colour scheme from the black and white Belted Galloway cattle.

Castle Douglas serves as market centre to a large tract of Galloway's rich hinterland, giving it some of the best food shops in Scotland – particularly butchers.

Many of the most pleasant villages – **New Galloway**, **Balmaclellan**, **Crossmichael** – are in the region of long, skinny **Loch Ken**, which feeds the River Dee; while to the west, shrouding the hills to the very shoulders of the isolated **Rhinns of Kells**, a tableland of hills around 2,600 ft (800 metres), is the massive Galloway Forest Park, 150,000 acres (60,000 hectares) criss-crossed by Forestry Commission trails and the South Upland Way.

Amongst the trees you can find **Clatteringshaws Loch** ⑳, 12 miles (19 km) north of Newton Stewart (a "planned town" built in the late 17th century by a son of the Earl of Galloway) on the A712, which is the site of the **Clatteringshaws Forest Wildlife Centre** (open Apr–Sept: daily; tel: (01644) 420285) and a fascinating introduction to the range of the area's natural history.

BELOW: The old church in Portpatrick.

Nearby, **Bruce's Stone** represents the site of the Battle of Rapploch Moss, a minor affair of 1307 but one in which the energetic Robert the Bruce routed the English. There are, in fact, two Bruce's Stones in **Galloway Forest Park**, which creeps within reach of the coast at Turnberry, where he may have been born. The second stone – reached only if one backtracks from Newton Stewart and then travels northwest for 10 miles (16 km) on the A714 before taking an unmarked road to the west – is poised on a bluff above Loch Trool and recalls those hefted down the hill by the hero in another successful wrangle with the English. About 4 miles (6.5 km) away is a sombre landmark: the **Memorial Tomb** of six Covenanters murdered at prayer. It is a simple stone which records their names and the names of their killers.

Saints and stones

Back on the coast, the A75 between benign **Gatehouse of Fleet** and **Creetown**, which hugs the sea below the comely outriders of the distinctive hill **Cairnsmore of Fleet**, was said by Thomas Carlyle to be the most beautiful road in Scotland.It has good views across **Wigtown Bay** to the flat green shelf which was the cradle of Scottish Christianity. The **Creetown Gem Museum** (open Mar–Nov: daily; Dec–Feb: Sat and Sun; tel: (01671) 820357) has a wide range of precious stones on display.

On the other side of the bay is the pleasant town of **Wigtown** ㉑, whose **Martyrs' Monument** is one of the most eloquent testaments to the Covenanters, who were heroically supported in the Southwest; the site of the stake where in 1685 two women, one elderly and one young, were left to drown on the estuary flats.

On the promontory south of Wigtown, the coast becomes harsher and the villages bleaker, as if it indeed required the gentling influence of Christianity. **Whithorn ㉒** is the birthplace of Christianity in Scotland, and at the **Whithorn Visitor Centre** (open Apr–Oct: daily; tel: (01988) 500508) in the centre of the town the first known Christian church in Britain, built by St Ninian around the year 400, was uncovered. Next to the Centre is the **Priory** where Mary Queen of Scots once stayed. Here you will find the Latinus Stone of 450, the earliest Christian memorial in Scotland, as well as a significant collection of early Christian crosses and stones.

Four miles (6 km) away is the misnamed **Isle of Whithorn**, a delightful town built around a busy yachting harbour and with more St Ninian connections: there is the ruined **St Ninian's Chapel**, which dates from 1300 and may have been used by overseas pilgrims, and along the coast is **St Ninian's Cave**, said to have been used by the saint as an oratory.

A little inland from the undistinguished shoreline of Luce Bay, playground of the Ministry of Defence, are some relics of the Iron Age and Bronze Age, including **Torhouse Stone Circle**, a ring of 19 boulders standing on a low mound. The most impressive sight in this corner, however, is **Glenluce Abbey ㉓** (open Apr–Sept: Mon–Sat and Sun pm; Oct–Mar weekends; tel: (0131) 668 8800), a handsome vaulted ruin of the 12th century.

From Glenluce the traveller crosses the "handle" of that hammer of land called the **Rhinns of Galloway**, the southwest extremity of Scotland terminating in the 200-ft (60-metre) high cliffs of the Mull of Galloway, from which Ireland seems within touching distance. At the head of the deep cleft of **Loch Ryan** is the port of **Stranraer ㉔**, market centre for the rich agricultural area, modest holiday resort and Scotland's main seaway to Northern Ireland. The Rhinns' other main resort is **Portpatrick ㉕**, and among the somewhat limited attractions of

Map, pages 180–1

TIP

Portpatrick is the start of the Southern Upland Way, a coast-to-coast route across Southern Scotland which runs for 212 miles (340 km) to Cockburnspath on the Berwickshire coast.

BELOW: Cattle auction at Newton Stewart, a busy market town in Wigtownshire.

The Ploughman Poet

Few poets could hope to have their birthday celebrated in the most unexpected parts of the world 200 years after their death. Yet the observance of Burns Night, on 25 January, goes from strength to strength. It marks the birth in 1759 of Scotland's national poet, Robert Burns, one of seven children born to a poor Ayrshire farmer. It was an unpromising beginning, yet today Burns's verses are familiar in every English-speaking country and are especially popular in Russia, where Burns Night is toasted in vodka. Millions who have never heard of Burns have joined hands and sung his words to the tune of that international anthem of good intentions, *Auld Lang Syne* (dialect for "old long ago"):

Should auld acquaintance be forgot,
And never brought to mind?
Should auld acquaintance be forgot,
And days o' auld lang syne?

This was one of many traditional Scottish songs which he collected and rewrote, in addition to his original poetry. He could and did write easily in 18th-century English as well as in traditional Scots dialect (which, even in those days, had to be accompanied by a glossary). His subjects ranged from love songs (*Oh, my luve's like a red, red rose*) and sympathy for a startled fieldmouse (*Wee, sleekit, cowrin', tim'rous beastie*) to a stirring sense of Scottishness (*Scots, wha hae wi' Wallace bled*) and a simple celebration of the common people (*A man's a man for a' that*).

The key to Burns's high standing in Scotland is that, like Sir Walter Scott, he promoted the idea of Scottish nationhood at a time when it was in danger of being obliterated by the English. His acceptance abroad, especially in Russia, stems from his championing of the rights of ordinary people and his satirical attack on double standards in church and state.

An attractive and gregarious youth, Burns had a long series of amorous entanglements and, once famous, took full advantage of his acceptance into Edinburgh's high society. Finally, he married Jean Armour, from his own village, and settled on a poor farm at Ellisland, near Dumfries. No more able than his father to make a decent living from farming, he moved to Dumfries in 1791 to work as an Excise Officer. It was a secure job, and riding 200 miles (320 km) a week on horseback around the countryside on his duties gave him time and inspiration to compose prolifically. His affairs continued: the niece of a Dumfries innkeeper became pregnant, but died during childbirth. Four years later, in 1796, Burns too was dead, of rheumatic heart disease. He was 37.

The 612 copies of his first edition of 34 poems sold in Kilmarnock in 1786 for three shillings (15p); today each will fetch £10,000. Almost 100,000 people in over 20 countries belong to Burns clubs, and the poet's popularity embraces the unlikeliest locations. The story is told, for example, of a black gentleman who rose to propose a toast at a Burns Night supper in Fiji. "You may be surprised to learn that Scottish blood flows in my veins," he declared. "But it is true. One of my ancestors ate a Presbyterian missionary." ❑

LEFT: Burns, pictured at Alloway.

this remote peninsula are two horticultural ones; the sub-tropical plants of **Logan Botanic Garden** ㉖ (open mid-Mar–Oct: daily: tel: (01776) 860231) and the great monkey puzzle trees of **Castle Kennedy Gardens**, near Stranraer (open Apr–Sept: daily; tel: (01776) 702024).

Stranraer's trunk roads are the A75, infamous for the volume of heavy traffic disembarking from the ferries from Ireland, which strikes east to Dumfries and points south and blights Thomas Carlyle's "loveliest stretch" between Creetown and Gatehouse of Fleet; and the A77, which conducts you north past the cliffs of **Ballantrae** (*not* the Ballantrae of R.L. Stevenson's novel) to the mixed pleasures of Ayrshire and, ultimately, the edge of the Glasgow conurbation.

En route is the pleasant resort of **Girvan** ㉗, first of a series of resorts interspersed with ports and industrial towns, which stretches to the mouth of the Clyde. About 10 miles (16 km) offshore is a chunky granite monolith over 1,000 ft (300 metres) high – the uninhabited island of **Ailsa Craig**, sometimes called Paddy's Milestone for its central position between Belfast and Glasgow.

Here, too, you begin to see more clearly the mountains of Arran and the lower line of the Kintyre peninsula, while at **Turnberry**, a mecca for golfers and site of some fragments of castle which promotes itself as the birthplace of Robert the Bruce, there is a choice of roads to Ayr.

Approaching Ayr

The coast road (A719) invites you to one of the non-Burnsian showpieces of Ayrshire – **Culzean Castle** ㉘ (castle open Apr–Oct: daily; country park daily all year; tel: (01655) 760274), magnificently designed by Robert Adam and built between 1772 and 1792 for the Kennedy family. Now owned by the National

Map, pages 180–1

Transatlantic visitors are entertained at Culzean Castle by the Eisenhower Presentation, which recalls the flat given to the General for his private use.

BELOW: Burns characters at Souter Johnnie's Cottage.

According to Burns, Ayr was unsurpassed "for honest men and bonnie lasses".

Trust for Scotland, it has a country park of 560 acres (226 hectares) – the first in Scotland. A few miles beyond Culzean the road entertains drivers at the **Electric Brae**, where an optical illusion suggests you are going downhill rather than up.

The inland road (A77) takes you through the village of **Kirkoswald** ㉙, where Burns went to school, and the first of the cluster of Burns shrines and museums: **Souter Johnnie's Cottage** (open Easter–Oct: daily; tel: (01655) 760274), once the home of the cobbler who was the original of Souter Johnnie in *Tam o' Shanter*. The B7024 then conducts you to the Mecca of Burns pilgrims, the village of **Alloway**, where he was born. Here, amid visitor and "interpretation" centres, you can visit in quick succession: **Burns Cottage** (open June–Aug: daily; Apr, May, Sept, Oct: closed Sun am; rest of year closed Sun; tel: (01292) 441215), **Alloway Kirk** (where his father is buried and which features critically in *Tam o' Shanter*), the pretentious **Burns Monument** (a neo-Classical temple) and the 13th-century **Brig o' Doon**, whose single span permitted Tam o' Shanter to escape from the witches.

You are now on the doorstep of **Ayr** ㉚, a bustling resort associated not only with Burns but also the warrior-patriot William Wallace, who is thought to have been born in **Elderslie**, near Paisley, and who was once imprisoned in Ayr.

Inland from Ayr, to the west and north, is another clutch of Burns associations: the village of **Mauchline** ㉛, where he married Jean Armour and where their cottage is now yet another museum (open Easter–Oct: Mon–Sat and Sun pm; tel: (01290) 550045); and **Poosie Nansie's Tavern**, the ale-house (still a pub) which inspired part of his cantata *The Jolly Beggars*. Nearby at **Failford** is Highland Mary's Monument, which allegedly marks the spot where Burns said farewell to the doomed Mary Campbell, who died before they could marry; while the sprawling town of **Kilmarnock** also claims intimacy with Burns, who published the first edition of his poems there in 1786. A hundred years later the town built him a monument containing yet more Burns material.

BELOW: Brodick Castle on Arran.

Coasts and islands

The A77 from Kilmarnock – that road which began life in Stranraer – takes you straight to the heart of Glasgow. But, if you are island or Highland bound, you should return to the coast. Between the industrial port and new town of **Irvine** ㉜ – which is the home of the **Scottish Maritime Museum** (open Apr–Oct: daily; tel: (01294) 278283) and whose **Magnum Centre** claims to be Scotland's largest leisure centre – and the shipbuilding town of **Greenock** are various ferry points for the Clyde islands and the Cowal peninsula. South of Irvine are two golfing resorts, **Troon** and **Prestwick**.

Ardrossan serves the island of **Arran** ㉝, the ferries disembarking passengers and cars at **Brodick**, the capital. Arran is popular with walkers and climbers (the sharp profile of the Arran ridge, which reaches 2,866 ft/ 874 metres at the elegant summit of Goatfell, provides some challenging scrambles). Even most unenthusiastic pedestrians will find the 2 miles (3 km) walk from Brodick's attractive harbour to **Brodick Castle** congenial and effortless. The castle (open Easter–Oct: daily; gardens open daily all year; tel: (01770) 302202), parts of which date from the 14th century, is the ancient seat of the dukes of Hamilton. It contains various paintings and *objets d'art* from the collections of the dukes.

Arran's other main villages are **Lochranza**, **Blackwaterfoot**, **Whiting Bay** and **Lamlash**, where a precipitous offshore island spans the mouth of Lamlash Bay. **Holy Island** owes its name to St Molaise, who lived and meditated in a cave on its west coast. It is now a Buddhist retreat.

The other Clyde islands regularly served by ferry are **Bute**, with its attractive, ancient capital **Rothesay** and the huge Victorian Gothic palace of **Mount Stuart** (open May–Sept: Fri–Mon and Wed; tel: (01700) 503877), and **Great Cumbrae**, with the family resort of **Millport**. The amiable little island of Great Cumbrae is reached from **Largs** ❸, the most handsome of the Clyde resorts and the scene, in 1263, of a battle which conclusively repelled persistent Viking attempts to invade Scotland when the forces of Alexander III defeated those of Haakon, King of Norway. The **Vikingar** centre (open daily: tel: (01475) 689777) dramatically traces the history of the Vikings in Scotland. The ferry crossing to Bute is from **Wemyss Bay**, between Largs and Gourock – from where you can also board a ferry for Dunoon and the Cowal peninsula.

Escaping the city

For many people in west central Scotland, the **Cowal peninsula** represents Highland escapism. It has a new population of second home-owners from the Glasgow conurbation, which makes it busy during weekends and holidays, despite the time it takes to negotiate its long fissures of sea-lochs (**Loch Fyne** to the west and **Loch Long** to the east, with several others in between). **Dunoon** ❸ is its capital, another ancient township turned holiday resort with another 13th-

Map, pages 180–1

The woodland garden of Brodick Castle is justly claimed to be one of the finest rhododendron gardens in Britain.

BELOW: Lochranza, one of the villages on Arran.

THE ISLAND OF BUTE

Bute is a comely and undemanding island with no great heights to scale but provides its own spectacle at the narrow Kyles of Bute, where the northern end of the island almost closes the gap with the Cowal peninsula. Bute's capital of Rothesay was once the premier destination for day trippers on the Clyde paddle steamers which took Glaswegians "doon the water" from the heart of their city. Rothesay is a Royal burgh which gives the title of Duke to the Prince of Wales, and the ruin of its unusual castle with four round towers dates back to the early 13th century, when it was stormed by the Norsemen soon to be routed at Largs.

The beaches and beautiful scenery on Bute still make it a popular resort for visitors: the elegant promenade and Winter Gardens in Rothesay are especially busy in summer, despite the rapid rise of package holidays to the Mediterranean and further afield. Bute's continued appeal lies partly in its mild climate and also its relative tranquillity: the main tourist areas are the two bays on the east of the island and it's easy to leave the crowds behind and escape into the green hills. Canada Hill is worth the climb for a good view of the island.

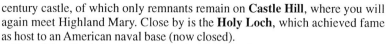

century castle, of which only remnants remain on **Castle Hill**, where you will again meet Highland Mary. Close by is the **Holy Loch**, which achieved fame as host to an American naval base (now closed).

East of Gare Loch (not to be confused with Gairloch in the northwest), the Clyde begins to be compressed between the once-great shipbuilding banks of **Clydeside**, with the first of its resort towns on the north bank at **Helensburgh 36**, now a stately dormitory for Glasgow. Those smitten with "Mackintoshismus" will wish to visit here the **Hill House** (open Easter–Oct pm; restricted at peak times; tel: (01436) 673900), Charles Rennie Mackintosh's finest domestic commission.

Industrial **Dumbarton 37** is even closer to the city and its name confirms it has been there since the days of the Britons. Its spectacular lump of rock was their fort, and supports a 13th-century castle which has close connections with – inevitably – Mary Queen of Scots.

The Grey Mare's Tail waterfall near Moffat drops 200 ft (60 metres) from a hanging valley.

BELOW: Largs, a popular resort for Glasgow holiday makers.

Hidden treasures

The eastern edge of Southwest Scotland is dominated by the AM74, the frenzied highway which is Glasgow's access to the Borders and England. It carves through some of the shapeliest hills in Scotland, with some lovely, lonely places and unexpected treasures tucked away in their folds.

The briefest of detours will bring you to **Moffat 38**, an elegant little town which was once a minor spa and has the broadest main street in Scotland. Northwest of Moffat is **Devil's Beef Tub**, a vast, steep, natural vat in the hills where Border raiders used to hide stolen cattle. Northeast of Moffat on the A708 is the spectacular **Grey Mare's Tail 39** waterfall. Further north is **Tibbie Sheil's Inn**, the meeting place of the renowned writer James Hogg (the "Ettrick Shepherd") and friends.

On either side of the A74, a few miles driving on suddenly silent roads will take you to the highest villages in Scotland: **Leadhills** and **Wanlockhead**. Once centres of lead, gold and silver mining, an idea of their past can be seen at the **Wanlockhead Museum of Lead Mining** (open Apr–Oct: Mon–Sat pm; plus Sun July–Aug; tel: (01659) 74387). Here too are Drumlanrig Castle, the historic market town of Lanark and the lush orchards and dramatic falls of the River Clyde.

Drumlanrig Castle and Country Park 40 (open May–Aug: Fri–Wed; tel: (01848) 330248) is reached by descending the precipitous **Dalveen Pass**, a natural stairway between the uplands of South Lanarkshire and the rolling pastures and exquisite broadleaf woodland of Dumfriesshire. It is a palace of pink sandstone fashioned in late 17th-century Renaissance style on the site of an earlier Douglas stronghold and near a Roman fort. Its rich collection of French furniture and Dutch paintings (Holbein and Rembrandt are represented) includes interesting relics of Prince Charles Edward Stuart.

The A74's tributary to **Lanark** skirts **Tinto Hill**, the highest peak in Lanarkshire, much-climbed and much-loved by Lanarkshire schoolchildren who traditionally carry stones to add to its enormous cairn.

Biggar 41 is a lively and rewarding little town, with an active museum life focusing on local history as if in defiance of the greater celebrity of its big neighbour,

Lanark. The high, handsome old Royal burgh was already important in the 10th century, when a parliament was held there, but is more closely identified with William Wallace. It is said that he hid in a cave in the Cartland Craigs, just below the town, after killing an English soldier in a brawl. When he heard that his wife had been murdered he attacked the English garrison with a band of friends, who became his first army of resistance against the invaders.

Lanark was also a Convenanting centre and is still a place of great character, much of it due to its weekly livestock market and the steep fall of the Clyde below the town at **New Lanark** ⓧ, Scotland's most impressive memorial to the Industrial Revolution, which has been honoured as a World Heritage Site. Here, between 1821 and 1824, a cotton spinning village became the scene of the pioneering social and educational experiment of Robert Owen. The old, handsome buildings have been brought back to life and feature an imaginative **Visitor Centre** (open daily; tel: (01555) 661345) and working models.

Nearby, the cataracts of the **Falls of Clyde Nature Reserve** are the preface to one of the river's prettiest passages, its last Arcadian fling among the orchards and market gardens of Kirkfieldbank and Hazlebank and Rosebank before it reaches the industrial heartland of North Lanarkshire.

Near one of those pastoral villages, **Crossford**, is one of Scotland's best-preserved medieval castles. **Craignethan Castle** (open Apr–Sept: Mon–Sat and Sun pm; Mar and Oct: Mon, Wed, Sat, Thurs am and Sun pm; tel: (01555) 860364), was built between the 15th and 16th centuries on a site above a wooded pass 2 miles (3.2 km) from the Clyde, and was a stronghold of the Hamiltons, friends of Mary Queen of Scots. It has well authenticated claims to be the original Tillietudlem in Sir Walter Scott's *Old Mortality*. ❑

The first Duke of Queensberry, for whom Drumlanrig Castle was built, was so horrified by its cost that he spent only one night in it.

BELOW: New Lanark: memories of old industries.

FORTH AND CLYDE

*Standing strategically as the gateway to the Highlands, the
ancient town of Stirling is a focal point for any visit to central
Scotland and the waterways of the Forth and Clyde*

Map,
pages
180–1

For centuries, Stirling's Old Bridge has given access to the north across the
lowest bridging point of the River Forth, while the 250-ft (75-metre) volcanic plug which supports its castle was the natural fortress which made
Stirling ⓭ significant from the 12th century onwards. The **Castle** (open daily)
– every bit as impressive as Edinburgh Castle – was long the favourite residence of the Stuart monarchy, and the palace, built by James V around a central courtyard, is one of Scotland's renaissance glories. Close to it is the **Royal
Burgh of Stirling Visitor Centre** (open daily: tel:(01786) 479901), which
vividly describes the long history of the castle and town.

Heroes of the past

The achievements of both Wallace and Bruce are conspicuously recalled in the
environs of Stirling. On the rock of **Abbey Craig**, above the site where Wallace
camped, is the ostentatious **Wallace Monument** (open daily; tel: (01786)
472140), home of the hero's two-handed sword. From its elevation at the top of
246 spiral steps, you can see the leaping ramparts of the **Ochil Hills**, while to
the southeast the Forth spreads across its flat plain to the spectacular flare-stacks
of **Grangemouth**.

    The site of the Battle of Bannockburn, a few miles
south of Stirling, has been more or less consumed by a
housing estate. No one is precisely sure where the battle was fought, but the rotunda beside the heroic bronze
equestrian statue of Bruce is said to mark his command
post. The **Bannockburn Heritage Centre** (open
Mar–Dec: daily; tel: (01786) 812664) gives an audio-
visual account of the matter. Also close to Stirling is the
Alloa Tower (open Easter and May–Sept: daily pm; tel:
(01259) 211701) the superbly restored former home of
the Earls of Mar, built in the late 15th century with dungeon, medieval timber roof and an impressive rooftop
parapet walk with fine views.

    Stirling is almost equidistant from Edinburgh and
Glasgow. If you take the M9 to Edinburgh, you stay
roughly parallel to the broadening course of the Forth.
There are rewarding diversions to be made on this route.
Near the industrial town of Falkirk are four good sec-
tions of the **Roman Antonine Wall** ⓮, a turf rampart on
a stone base which the Emperor Antoninus Pius caused
to be built between the firths of Clyde and Forth around
AD 140; while the motorway itself has opened up a dis-
tracting view of the loch and **palace of Linlithgow** ⓯
(open Mon–Sat and Sun pm; tel: (0131) 688 8800), the
well-preserved ruins of Scotland's most magnificent
palace. The birthplace of Mary Queen of Scots, Linlithgow's chapel and great hall are late 15th century, while
its courtyard has an elaborate 16th-century fountain.

PRECEDING PAGES:
men at work in
New Lanark.
LEFT: the Forth
Railway Bridge.
BELOW: the Wallace
Monument, Stirling.

Adjacent to the palace of Linlithgow is the Church of St Michael, Scotland's largest pre-Reformation parish church; the abstract golden crown was mounted on its tower in 1964.

BELOW: Robert the Bruce standing guard at Stirling Castle.

From the M9, you can also visit the village of **South Queensferry** ⓐ on the southern bank of one of the Forth's oldest crossings, where river becomes estuary. Until the **Forth Road Bridge** was built, ferries had plied between South and North Queensferry for 900 years. Today, South Queensferry huddles between and beneath the giant bridges which provide such a spectacular contrast in engineering design – the massive humped girders of the 1890 rail bridge and the delicate, graceful span of the suspension bridge, opened in 1964.

At South Queensferry, you can take a boat excursion to the island of **Inchcolm** in the Firth and visit the 12th-century ruined abbey (open Mar–Sept: Mon–Sat and Sun pm; tel: (0131) 668 8800), well-preserved monastic buildings and gardens. Cross the Forth Road Bridge or take the train to North Queensferry to visit the **Deep Sea World** (open daily; tel: (01383) 411411) for a diver'seye-view of myriad fish in Europe's largest aquarium.

Near South Queensferry are **Hopetoun House** (open Easter–Sept: daily; tel: (0131) 331 2451), home of the Earls of Hopetoun, magnificently situated in parkland beside the Forth and splendidly extended and rebuilt by William Adam and his son John between 1721 and 1754; and **Dalmeny House** (open July–Aug: Mon, Tues and Sun pm; tel: (0131) 331 1888), home of the Earls of Rosebery and a fine collection of paintings.

The Forth and Clyde

You can walk beside the Forth through the wooded Rosebery estate to the **River Almond**, where a little rowing-boat ferry transports you across this minor tributary to the red pantiles and white crowstep gables of **Cramond** ⓑ. Still very much its own 18th-century village, Cramond has a harbour which was used by

STIRLING CASTLE

The impressive bulk of Stirling Castle was a formidable challenge to any invaders. It had its most active moments during Scotland's Wars of Independence: surrendered to the English in 1296, it was recaptured by the warrior-patriot William Wallace after the Battle of Stirling Bridge (not today's stone bridge, built around 1400, but a wooden structure). It became the last stronghold in Scotland to hold out against Edward I, the "Hammer of the Scots". Eventually, it went back to the English for 10 years, until Robert the Bruce retook it in 1314 after the Battle of Bannockburn, which decisively secured Scotland's independence.

The Stewarts favoured Stirling Castle as a Royal residence, James II and V were born in it, Mary Queen of Scots was crowned there at the age of nine months, and its splendid collection of buildings reflects its history as palace and fortress. Perhaps the most striking feature is the exterior façade, with ornate stonework which was largely cut by French craftsmen. The Great Hall, or Parliament House (so-called because before 1707 this was one of the seats of the Scottish Parliament), also has exquisite carving and tracery, which has recently been carefully reconstructed. A programme of major restoration has also included the kitchens of the Castle, which now recreate the preparations for a sumptious Renaissance banquet given by Mary, Queen of Scots for the baptism of her son, the future James VI.

the Romans. Its **Roman Fort**, whose foundations have been exposed, was built around AD 142, and may have been used by Septimius Severus.

Scotland's pre-eminent river, the **Clyde**, undergoes more personality changes than any other in its progress to the western seaboard. The limpid little stream, which has its source 80 miles (130 km) southeast of Glasgow, moves prettily through the orchards and market gardens of Clydesdale before watering the industries of North Lanarkshire and welcoming the ships and shipyards of Glasgow. The lower reaches of its valley have been colonised by the city's satellites, and by a clutter of hill towns: Wishaw, Motherwell and Hamilton.

Once drab coal and steel towns, they are attempting to recover their dignity and vitality: witness the creation of **Strathclyde Country Park**, a huge recreational area which includes a 200-acre (80-hectare) loch, formed by diverting the Clyde, and part of the old estate of the Dukes of Hamilton. Of the three towns, **Hamilton** ❹ has the longest history, with associations with Mary Queen of Scots, Cromwell and the Covenanters, who were defeated by Monmouth at nearby Bothwell Bridge in 1679. Immediately south of Hamilton is the recently restored **Chatelherault** (open daily; tel: (01698) 426213), a glorious hunting lodge and kennels built in 1732 for the Duke of Hamilton by William Adam.

Bothwell Castle (open Mon–Sat and Sun pm; Oct– Mar: closed Thur pm and Fri; tel: (01698) 816894), a red ruin above the Clyde and perhaps the finest 13th-century castle in Scotland, was repeatedly fought over by the Scots and English. Memories of more recent adventures can be found in the adjacent community of **Blantyre** ❹, birthplace of the explorer and missionary David Livingstone, whose early life and work in Africa is commemorated at the **David Livingstone Centre** (open Mon–Sat and Sun pm; tel: (01698) 823140).   ❏

Map, pages 180–1

Most of the original 18th-century furniture and wall-coverings can still be seen at Hopetoun House.

BELOW: Bothwell Castle: Scotland's finest 13th-century stronghold.

THE WEST COAST

*Mountain and moor, heather and stag, castle and loch – and
a magical seaboard of isolated villages and small ports – are all
to be found on the glorious west coast of Scotland*

Map,
page 220

From the long finger of Kintyre to the deep fissure of Loch Broom, the west coast is that part of Scotland which most perfectly conforms to its romantic image. Nowhere else in Scotland (outside Caithness and Sutherland) is a physical sense of travelling more thrillingly experienced; and few other areas provide such opportunities for solitude and repose, as well as the slightly awesome impression that this dramatic landscape is not to be trifled with.

It all begins gently enough at the Clyde estuary, where the deep penetration of the sea at **Loch Fyne** has created Scotland's longest peninsula, which is 54 miles (87 km) from Crinan to the Mull of Kintyre and never wider than 10 miles (16 km). This mighty arm is nearly bisected by West Loch Tarbert into the two regions of Knapdale and Kintyre, and its isolated character makes it almost as remote as any of the islands.

Here there are rolling hills rather than mountains, rough moors and forests in Knapdale, grassy tops in Kintyre and a coast which is most interesting on its west side, with a close view of the island of Jura from **Kilberry Head ❶** (where you can also view a fine collection of medieval sculptured stones). **Tarbert ❷** is an agreeable little port very popular with yachties. On its south side is the heritage centre of **An Tairbeart** (open daily; tel: (01880) 820190), which provides a full history of this fascinating area.

Further south is **Tayinloan ❸**, from where you can take the 20-minute ferry ride across to the tiny island of Gigha, noted for the fine **Achamore Gardens**, and south again is the vast beach of **Machrihanish ❹**. Few have kind words for the Kintyre "metropolis" of **Campbeltown**. However, from here it is only a short drive to the tip of the peninsula, the **Mull of Kintyre** itself (now an RSPB bird reserve). The Northern Ireland coast is only 12 miles (19km) away, and legend has it that St Columba first set foot in Scotland at **Keil ❺**, near the holiday village of Southend. You can see his "footprints" imprinted on a flat rock near a ruined chapel.

Scenic drama

From the great lighthouse on the Mull, first built in 1788 and remodelled by Robert Stevenson, grandfather of Robert Louis, there is nowhere else to go. You can retreat back up the secondary road (B842) of Kintyre's east coast, which has its own scenic drama in the sandy sweep of **Carradale Bay** and the view across the water to the mountains of Arran, reached by car ferry from Claonaig. The hump behind Carradale is **Beinn an Tuirc**, Kintyre's highest hill (1,490 ft/447 metres). The name means Mountain of the Boar, from a fearsome specimen said to have been killed by an ancestor of the Campbells. You can take in the ruined walls and sculptured tombstones of **Saddell Abbey**, a 12th-century

PRECEDING PAGES:
Rannoch Moor.
LEFT: Glenfinnan
railway station.
BELOW: steam
excursions run regularly in summer.

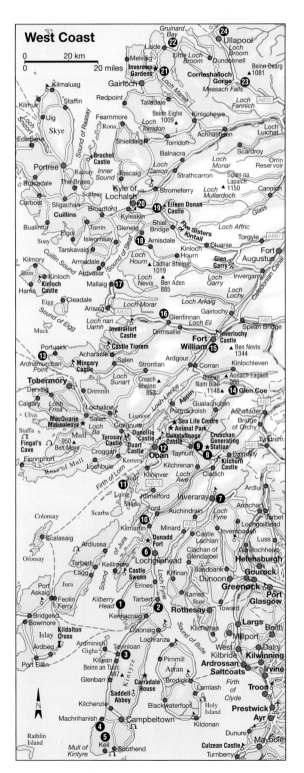

Cistercian house, and the 13th-century **Skipness Castle and Chapel** (open Mon–Sat and Sun pm).

From **Lochgilphead** ⑥, where the 9-mile (15 km) Crinan Canal crosses the neck of the peninsula and connects Loch Fyne to the Atlantic Ocean, you have a choice of two main routes to the handsome port and resort of Oban. The longer route, up Loch Fyne by Inveraray to Loch Awe (A83 and then A819) is probably the more dramatic, although the shorter route (A816) keeps you close to the coast and its vistas of those low-lying islands, which are the floating outriders of the mountains of Jura and Mull.

Past communities

Both routes are punctuated by places of interest. The most celebrated castle in the area is **Inveraray** ⑦ (open Jul–Aug, daily; May, June, Sept and Oct: closed Fri and Sun am; tel: (01499) 302203), the seat of the chiefs of Clan Campbell, the Dukes of Argyll, for centuries. The present building – Gothic-revival, famous for its magnificent interiors and art collection – was started in 1743, when the third Duke also decided to rebuild the village of Inveraray. The result is a dignified community with much of the orderly elegance of the 18th century. By means of wax figures, commentary and imaginative displays, **Inveraray Jail** (open daily; tel: (01499) 302381) brings to life an 1820 courtroom trial and life in the cells in the 19th century.

Two very different museums call for a visit. In the castle complex is the **Combined Operations Museum** (open Apr–mid-Oct: daily; tel: (01499) 500218), which recalls the passing of a quarter of a million Allied troops through this little Highland village during World War II, when Inveraray was a British Combined Operations base. Some 5 miles (8 km) south is **Auchindrain Museum of Country Life** (open May–Sept: daily; Apr: Sun–Fri; tel: (01499) 500235), whose dwellings and barns of the 18th and 19th centuries were once a communal-tenancy Highland farm, paying rent to the Duke.

see map
opposite

Between the two is the **Argyll Wildlife Park** (open Apr–Oct: daily; tel (01499) 302264), an extensive area of woodland, grassland and ponds featuring a wide variety of mammals and birdlife, and a popular place with children.

Loch Awe, where the road takes you past the fallen house of the Breadalbane dynasty – the romantic ruin of **Kilchurn Castle** (open daily) on a promontory on the water – is the longest freshwater loch in Scotland. At its northwest extremity, where it squeezes past the mighty mountain of Ben Cruachan and drains into Loch Etive through the dark slit of the Pass of Brander, it's as awesome as its name promises. Almost a mile inside Ben Cruachan is the **Cruachan pumped storage generating station ❽**, an artificial cavern you can view on a bus trip from the lochside visitor centre (open Apr–Nov: daily; tel: (01866) 822673).

The road continues through **Taynuilt ❾**, a village of more than passing interest. One of the earliest monuments to Nelson was erected here when locals dragged an ancient standing stone into the village and carved an inscription on it. It can still be seen, near the church. The main attraction, however, is the **Bonawe Iron Furnace** (open Apr–Oct Mon–Sat and Sun pm; tel (01866) 822432). Founded in 1753 by a North of England partnership, it is the most complete charcoal-fuelled ironworks in Britain. A little nearer to Oban, the road passes by the Connel Bridge, under which are the foaming **Falls of Lora**.

Coastal sights

If you take the A816 from Lochgilphead to Oban by the coast, you will pass one of the ancient capitals of Dalriada, the kingdom of the early Scots. The striking eminence of **Dunadd Fort** (*circa* AD500–800) sets the mood for a spectacular group of prehistoric sites around the village of **Kilmartin ❿**; standing stones,

The Pass of Brander is so steep and narrow that legend claims it was once held against an army by an old woman wielding a scythe.

BELOW: Glen Tarbert: almost as remote as one of the Western Isles.

burial cairns and cists are all accessible. Start with the collection of sculptured stones in the churchyard. As you drive north, the coast becomes more riven, while the natural harbours of the sea lochs and the protective islands of **Shuna**, **Luing** (noted for its beef) and **Seil** attract the yachting fraternity.

Here too is **Arduaine Garden**, a 20-acre (8-hectare) promontory owned by the National Trust for Scotland and renowned for superb rhododendrons, azaleas, magnolias and herbaceous perennials (open daily; tel: (01852) 200366).

Seil and its neighbours were supported by a vigorous slate industry until a great storm in 1881 flooded the quarries deep below sea level and efforts to pump them out failed. You can see vivid evidence of those days at **Easdale Island Folk Museum** (open Apr–Oct: daily; tel: (01852) 300370). It is a short ferry crossing from Seil, which itself comes so close to the mainland that it's reached by the single stone arch of the 1791 Clachan Bridge, the "bridge over the Atlantic".

Tourist capital

Every facility for visitors can be found in **Oban** , whose only beach, **Ganavan Sands**, is 2 miles (3 km) north of the town. Whisky-making is explained at **Oban Distillery** (open April–Oct: Mon–Sat; Nov–Mar: Mon–Fri; tel: (01631) 572004) and there are castles to be visited: the scant fragment of **Dunollie** on its precipitous rock and, at Connel, the fine 13th-century fortress of **Dunstaffnage** (open daily; Oct–Mar: closed Sun am, Thur pm and Fri; tel: (0131) 668 8800). Three miles (5 km) east of Oban is the **Rare Breeds Farm Park** (open Easter–Oct: daily; tel: (01631) 770608) with all sorts of exotic animals and birds.

Oban is a great place for island-hopping. **Mull** is just a 40-minute ferry ride away, as is the long fertile island of **Lismore**, whose name means "great garden".

BELOW: Oban, dominated by the folly of McCaig's Tower.

SEAWAY TO THE HEBRIDES

Ringed by wooded hills and clasped within the sheltered bay, Oban has the finest harbour on the Highland seaboard. Here even a landlocked traveller feels the pull of the islands: there are regular ferries to Mull, Barra, South Uist and Colonsay, as well as the nearby islands of Kerrera and Lismore. Oban is the focal point for tourists throughout the whole of Argyll, but also serves as the shopping centre for the rural population of the region, so it's likely to be busy all year round. In August there's the added attraction of the Argyllshire Highland Gathering, with displays of traditional dancing and folk music.

Hotels and boarding houses abound – a far cry from 1773 when Dr Johnson had to content himself with a "tolerable inn". However, modern tourism hasn't been so kind to the dignity of its high street; it lost the delightful Victorian buildings of its railway station in an act of institutionalised vandalism. But the town still has atmosphere – mostly centred on the busy harbour. Pulpit Hill is Oban's best viewpoint – and there is also the extraordinary folly of McCaig's Tower. John Stuart McCaig was an Oban banker who financed this strange enterprise on a hill above the town centre to give work to the unemployed and provide himself with a memorial. The tower was raised between 1890 and 1900 but McCaig's grand plan was never completed. What remains looks like an austere Scottish Colosseum.

In Oban Bay is pretty little **Kerrera**, reached by a small foot ferry. A walk round the island takes you past the dramatic ruin of **Gylen Castle** at its southern tip, commanding a spectacular view of sea, coastline and islands.

North from Oban, the A828 crosses the Connel Bridge to reach the lovely lands of Benderloch and Appin. Here is the delightfully sited **Sea Life Centre** (open daily; tel: (01631) 720386) with walk-through aquarium, touch tanks and a seal pond. At **Barcaldine** is found the **Black Castle** (open May–Sept: daily; tel: (01631) 720598) with secret stairs, bottle dungeon and resident ghost.

Continuing north leads you through **Appin**, a name which evokes romantic tragedy. In a historical incident made famous by Robert Louis Stevenson in *Kidnapped*, James Stewart of the Glens was wrongly hanged for the murder of Colin Campbell, the "Red Fox" and government land agent, in yet another of the internecine feuds which followed the Jacobite Rising of 1745. Further north still, at **Corran**, you can cross **Loch Linnhe** on a five-minute ferry ride to **Ardgour** and the tortuous drive to isolated **Ardnamurchan Point** ⑬, the most westerly point of the Scottish mainland.

Mountain grandeur

Once across the Ballachulish Bridge, the full grandeur of the West Highlands lies before you. To the east is the sublime mountain scenery of perhaps the most famous glen in Scotland, though for the wrong reason: **Glen Coe** ⑭, where in a savage winter dawn in February 1692, 40 members of the Clan Donald were slaughtered by government soldiers to whom they had given shelter and hospitality. The power of the landscape here does not diminish and even the unimaginative must feel a shiver of the spine as they follow the A82 between the dark

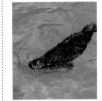

Map, page 220

The Sea Life Centre near Barcaldine includes all kinds of marine life, from small crustaceans to seals and even sharks.

BELOW: Glen Coe: even the unimaginative feel their spine tingle.

"Yesterday we went up Ben Nevis," wrote the poet John Keats in 1818. *"I am heartily glad it is done – it is almost like a fly crawling up a wainscot."*

BELOW: the Glenfinnan Viaduct, still carrying trains from Glasgow to Mallaig.

buttresses of **Buachaille Etive Mor, Bidean nam Bian** and the **Aonach Eagach**. These mountains are notorious: they are among Britain's supreme mountaineering challenges, and nearly every winter they claim lives. The National Trust for Scotland owns most of Glen Coe and exhibitions at its **Glencoe Visitor Centre** (open Apr–Oct: daily; tel: (01855) 811307) near the foot of the glen tell its story. An attraction of a very different kind is **Highland Mysteryworld**, a multi-media historical presentation including an Astromyth theatre (open daily; tel: (01855) 811660).

Big Ben

Some 15 miles (24 km) north of Ballachulish on the A82 is **Fort William ⑮**. The Fort itself was demolished, not by the Jacobites but by the railway. A secret portrait of Bonnie Prince Charlie, and his bed, are among the Jacobite relics in the **West Highland Museum** (open Mon–Sat; tel (01397) 702169). Despite its fine position between the mountains and Loch Linnhe, this straggling town has little to commend it beyond its proximity to **Ben Nevis** and glorious Glen Nevis. Britain's highest mountain (4,406 ft/1,340 metres) looks a deceptively inoffensive lump from below, where you can't see its savage north face. But the volatile nature of the Scottish climate should never be underestimated when setting out on any hill walk: the "Ben" is a long, tough day, and you can get advice from the visitor centre at its foot in Glen Nevis.

From Fort William, turn west on A830, taking the "road to the Isles" to **Mallaig**, another ferry port for the Hebrides (particularly the "Small Isles" of Canna, Rum, Eigg and Muck). At **Corpach** you will find **Treasures of the Earth** (open daily; tel: (01397) 772283), an intriguing geology-based exhibition of gem-

stones and rare minerals. The road continues past Loch Eil to **Glenfinnan**. The area has a dense concentration of associations with Bonnie Prince Charlie, running as it does between the clan territories of Moidart and Morar, whose chief, MacDonald of Clanranald, raised the clans in support of the prince along with Cameron of Lochiel.

Map, page 220

In August 1745 Charles raised the white and crimson Stuart banner at **Glenfinnan**  to the cheers of 5,000 men who had rallied behind the charismatic young prince's impetuous adventure, which was to cost the Highlands dear. A monument was raised on the spot in 1815; the National Trust for Scotland's **Glenfinnan Visitor Centre** (open Easter–Oct: daily; tel: (01397) 722250) tells the story well.

The prince had landed from his French brig at **Loch nan Uamh**, a few miles further west. Just over a year later, after the disaster of Culloden, he left from the same place, having fled pursuing government troops for months around the Highlands and Islands: despite a price of £30,000 on his head – a fortune for the time – he was never once betrayed. A memorial cairn on the shore of Loch nan Uamh marks his final exit from Scotland.

Contrary to popular belief, the figure at the top of the Glenfinnan monument is simply a Highlander, not Prince Charlie.

From **Arisaig** the road passes between the silver sands of **Morar** and the deep **Loch Morar** (said to be the home of another water monster) and comes to an end at **Mallaig** 🄒, an important landing place for white fish and shellfish. **Mallaig Marine World** at the harbour (open daily; Nov–Feb: closed Sun; tel: (01687) 462292) will tell you more. You can take a car ferry across the Sound of Sleat to **Armadale** on Skye or enjoy a cruise which hugs the great, roadless mountain wilderness of **Knoydart** with its two long sea lochs, **Hourn** and **Nevis** – said to be the lochs of Heaven and Hell.

BELOW: Mallaig fishermen hauling in their nets.

*A short diversion
from Kyle of
Lochalsh takes you
to the popular
holiday village of
Plockton, where,
because of its shel-
tered position, palm
trees flourish.*

BELOW: looking out
across Loch Maree.

Peak district

The alternative from Fort William is to continue on the A82 and at **Invergarry** turn west on A87 to climb past a spectacular roadside viewpoint looking down Glen Garry and then drop to the head of Glen Shiel with the famous peaks of the **Five Sisters of Kintail** soaring above on your right. At Shiel Bridge, a minor road turns left over the Mam Ratagan pass to reach **Glenelg** ⓲, worth a visit not only for its beauty but also for **Dun Telve** and **Dun Troddan**, two superb brochs – circular towers with double walls which still stand over 30 ft (9 metres) high. Here, too, are the remains of **Bernera Barracks**, quartered by Hanoverian troops during the 18th century.

Go back to Shiel Bridge and continue on A87 along lovely Loch Duich to reach **Eilean Donan Castle** ⓳ (open Easter–Sept: daily; tel: (01599) 555202), a restored Mackenzie stronghold on an islet reached by a causeway and probably the most photographed castle in Scotland. The road runs on to **Kyle of Lochalsh** and the bridge across to Skye.

Sublime scenery

From **Kyle of Lochalsh** ⓴, mainland travellers continue north by lovely **Loch Carron**, leaving Inverness-shire for the tremendous mountain massifs of **Wester Ross**. Here, on the isolated peninsula of **Applecross** or among the mighty peaks of **Torridon** with their views to the Cuillin of Skye and the distant, drifting shapes of the Outer Hebrides, is some of Europe's most spectacular scenery – with exhilarating driving yielding to richer rewards for those prepared to use their feet.

More gentle pursuits – amid equally wild and empty scenery – can be found at the village of **Poolewe**, where the road through Gairloch passes between

Loch Ewe and **Loch Maree**, possible the most sublime inland loch in Scotland, sentiments echoed by Queen Victoria on a visit here in 1877. The loch's particular features are the old Scots pines which line its shores and the impressive presence of **Slioch**, the "mountain of the spear", on its eastern shore.

Inverewe Gardens ㉑ (open daily; visitor centre open Easter–Oct: daily; tel: (01445) 781200) provide a sumptuous international collection of sub-tropical plants, growing – thanks to the mild climate created by the North Atlantic Drift – on the same latitude as Siberia. The gardens were begun in 1862 by Osgood Mackenzie (working on what was just a bare headland), further developed by his daughter Mrs Mairi Sawyer, and given to the National Trust for Scotland in 1952.

A few miles further north is the glittering 4-mile (6 km) scoop of **Gruinard Bay** ㉒, with its coves of pink sand from the red Torridon sandstone, nearly 800 million years old. The road then takes you round **Little Loch Broom**, below the powerful shoulders of **An Teallach** ("The Forge", 3,483 ft/1,062 metres), highest of these mighty peaks and a mountain which, said W.H. Murray, made "most Munros of the south and central Highlands seem tame by comparison". (A Munro is a Scottish mountain of over 3,000 feet, named for the man who collated them. There are 284 in all.)

You are now within easy reach of **Loch Broom** itself, and the substantial fishing port and tourist centre of **Ullapool** (*see page 294*). On your way, stop at the **Measach Falls** ㉓, 10 miles (16 km) before **Ullapool** ㉔, to admire the 120-ft (35-metre) drop into the spectacular **Corrieshalloch Gorge**, crossed by a swaying suspension bridge. ❑

Map, page 220

TIP

From Glenelg you can cross the water of Loch Duich to Kylerhea in Skye, as Dr Johnson and Boswell did, although the little car ferry runs only in summer. Alternatively, use the Skye Bridge at Kyle of Lochalsh.

BELOW: enjoying the sun in Inverewe Gardens.

SKYE

Map, page 232

Arguably the most magnificent of the dozens of Scottish islands, Skye is a romantic, misty isle of dramatic sea lochs, rocky peaks and breathtaking views

So deep are the incisions made by the sea lochs along the coast of Skye that, although the island is about 50 miles (80 km) long and 30 miles (50 km) wide, no part is more than 5 miles (8 km) from the sea. The population, unlike that of most Scottish islands, is on the increase – mainly due to immigrants, many of whom are from south of the border.

Dominating the "Misty Island" are the jagged **Cuillins**, on a sharp winter's day providing as thrilling a landscape as any in Nepal or New Zealand. Strangely, this greatest concentration of peaks in Britain, are referred to as "hills" rather than mountains; although they attain a height of not much more than 3,000 ft (900 metres), they spring dramatically from sea level.

Most visitors now reach Skye by driving over the road bridge which spans the **Kyleakin Narrows** between Kyle of Lochalsh and **Kyleakin ❶**. Alternative car-ferry routes are from Glenelg to Kylerhea and from Mallaig to Armadale. The former, a ferry accommodating a mere handful of cars, runs only during the summer – never on a Sunday – while the latter becomes a passenger ferry only in the winter.

PRECEDING PAGES: looking toward the Hebrides.
LEFT: Skye scape.
BELOW: taking the boat to Skye.

Garden of Skye

Overlooking Kyleakin harbour are the scanty ruins of **Castle Moil**, once a stronghold of the Mackinnons and a look-out post and fortress against raids by Norsemen. Six miles (10 km) out of Kyleakin, turn south on the A851 and, after 17 miles (27 km), arrive at **Armadale ❷** and its ruined castle. This was formerly the home of the MacDonalds, who were once one of Scotland's most powerful clans and Lord of the Isles. The **Clan Donald Trust**, formed in the 1970s, which has members throughout the world, has turned one wing of the ruined castle into a museum with audio-visual presentations (open Apr–early Nov: daily; gardens open daily; tel: (01471) 844305). The old stables house an excellent restaurant, a good bookshop and a giftshop and have luxurious self-catering accommodation. There's a ranger service and guided walks through the grounds with their mature trees and rhododendrons. Further exploration of this area called **Sleat** (pronounced *Slate*) reveals why it bears the sobriquet "Garden of Skye".

Return to the A850 and immediately reach **Broadford**, from where a diversion southwest on the B8083 leads, after 14 miles (22 km), to the scattered village of **Elgol ❸**. It was from here on 4 July 1746 that the Young Pretender, after being given a banquet by the Mackinnons in what is now called **Prince Charles's Cave**, finally bade farewell to the Hebrides. The view of the **Black Cuillins** from here is one of the most splendid views in all Britain.

In summer, motor-boats sail from Elgol across wide **Loch Scavaig**, past schools of seals, to land passengers on the rocks from where they can scramble upwards to **Loch Coruisk** in the very heart of the Cuillins. The scene was much painted by Turner and other romantics and written about by Sir Walter Scott.

Croft and castle

Backtrack once more to the A850 and, after 7 miles (11 km) with the Red Cuillins to the left – they are much more rounded, much less dramatic than the Black Cuillins – you arrive at Luib and the **Luib Croft Museum** (open Apr–Oct: daily; tel: (01471) 822427), the first of the Skye folk museums. Of particular interest is the collection of newspaper cuttings from the end of the 19th century which deal with crofters' grievances. Skye was the scene of some of the most intense fight-backs by crofters threatened with eviction during the Clearances. The Battle of the Braes (1882) was the last such "battle" fought in Britain.

The road continues through **Sligachan ❹**, a base for serious climbers of the Black Cuillins, and then descends into **Portree ❺**, the island's capital, an attractive town built round a natural harbour and with neat and brightly painted houses rising steeply from the water. In 1773, when they visited Portree, Dr Johnson and James Boswell dined in the Royal Hotel, then called McNab's hostelry, believing it was "the only inn on the island". A quarter of a century before that, Prince Charlie bade farewell to Flora MacDonald at MacNab's. Just south of Portree is the **Aros Experience** (open daily; tel: (01478) 613649), where a multimedia presentation tells the story of the island from 1700 to the present day. There are also attractive woodland walks.

Magnificent rock scenery and breathtaking views can be enjoyed by driving

Many British mountaineers who have challenged Everest and other great peaks of the world did part of their serious training on the Cuillin hills.

BELOW: Skye's romantic landscape.

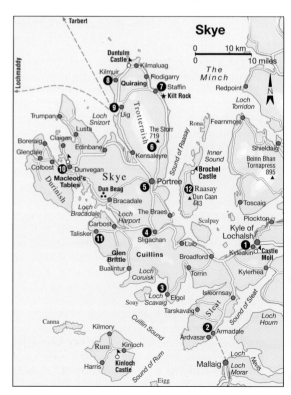

north from Portree on the **Trotternish Peninsula**. Seven miles (11 km) out along the A855 is **The Storr ❻**, a 2,360-ft (719-metre) height which is shaped like a crown and offers a stiff two-hour climb; to its east is the **Old Man of Storr**, an isolated150-ft (45-metre) pinnacle of rock. Further north is **Kilt Rock**, a sea cliff which owes its name to columnar basalt strata overlying horizontal ones beneath, the result bearing only the most fanciful relationship to a kilt.

A further 2 miles (4 km) leads to **Staffin ❼**, immediately beyond which is **The Quiraing**, so broken up with massive rock faces that it looks like a range in miniature rather than a single mountain. The various rock features of the Quiraing – the castellated crags of **The Prison**, the slender unclimbed 100-ft (30-metre) **Needle** and **The Table**, a meadow as large as a football field – can be appreciated only on foot and can be reached readily by a path from a glorious minor road which cuts across the peninsula from Staffin to Uig.

see map opposite

However, to take this road rather than to loop around the tip of the Trotternish Peninsula is to forego some historic encounters. The annexe of the **Flodigarry Hotel** was Flora MacDonald's first home after her marriage in 1750 to Captain Allan MacDonald. Adjacent to the cottage is **Kilmuir churchyard ❽** (open Apr–Oct: daily; gardens open daily), where Flora lies buried, wrapped in a sheet from the bed in which the fugitive prince had slept. On a clear day there are fine views from here of the Outer Hebrides, from where Charlie and Flora fled to Skye.

Then, at the northwest tip of the peninsula, is the ruined **Duntulm Castle**, an ancient MacDonald stronghold commanding the sea route to the Outer Hebrides. South of the castle is the **Skye Museum of Island Life** (open Apr–Oct: Mon–Sat; tel: (01470) 552279) whose seven thatched cottages show how the crofters lived. And so, after a few miles, to **Uig ❾** from where ferries depart

A Celtic cross marks the spot where Flora MacDonald is buried in Kilmuir.

BELOW: the way we were: the Skye Museum of Island Life.

for Lochmaddy on North Uist and Tarbert on Harris. The road south from Uig returns to Portree but rather than turning left at the junction with the A850 turn right and travel westwards, across the base of the Trotternish peninsula, to arrive after 19 miles (30 km) at Dunvegan.

Just before Dunvegan, look south to **Macleod's Tables,** which dominate the **Duirinish Peninsula**. Their flatness is attributed to the inhospitality shown Columba when he preached to the local chief: in shame the mountains shed their caps so that the saint might have a flat bed on which to lie.

Legendary past

No other castle in Scotland boasts so long a record of continuous occupation by one family as **Dunvegan ❿** (castle and gardens open daily; tel: (01470) 521206), which has been home to the MacLeods for the past 700 years. Set on a rocky platform overlooking Loch Dunvegan, its stuccoed exterior lacks the splendour of at least a dozen other Scottish castles. Its interior, however, is another matter, with a wealth of paintings and memorabilia, including a painting of Dr Johnson by Sir Joshua Reynolds and a lock of Bonnie Prince Charlie's hair. Best known, though, is the "Fairy Flag", a torn and faded fragment of yellow silk spotted with red. Some say a fairy mother laid it over her half-mortal child when she had to return to her own people: others, more prosaic, that it was woven on the island of Rhodes in the 7th century and that a MacLeod captured it from a Saracen chief during the Crusades. Whatever its origins, the Fairy Flag is said to have three magic properties: when raised in battle it ensures a MacLeod victory; when spread over the MacLeod marriage bed it guarantees a child; and when unfurled at Dunvegan it charms the herring in the loch. The flag should

BELOW: Dunvegan Castle.

be flown sparingly: its powerful properties will be exhausted when used three times. So far, it has twice been invoked.

Three miles (5 km) before Dunvegan, take the secondary B886 and travel northwards for 8 miles (13 km) to **Trumpan** where, in 1597, the "Fairy Flag" was unfurled. A raiding party of MacDonalds from the island of Uist landed and set fire to a church packed with worshipping MacLeods. The alarm was raised: the MacDonalds were unable to escape as a falling tide had left their longboats high and dry: they were decimated. The bodies of friend and foe alike were laid out on the sands below the sea wall, which was then toppled to cover the corpses.

Primitive justice once practised on Skye is seen in the **Trumpan churchyard** in the shape of a standing stone pierced by a circular hole. The accused would be blindfolded and, if he could put his finger unerringly through the Trial Stone, was deemed innocent.

Local flavour

A few miles west of Dunvegan are Colbost, then Glendale and Boreraig. The **Colbost Croft Museum** (open daily; tel: (01470) 521296) is very atmospheric, with a peat fire of the floor of the "black house" waiting to cook a stew and a boxbed uncomfortable enough to be genuine. Behind the house an illicit whisky still is sadly no longer in use, but the fully restored 200-year-old watermill at **Glendale** is fully operational. A cairn at **Boreraig** marks the site of the piping school of the MacCrimmons, for 300 years the hereditary pipers to the MacLeods. The school is now in ruins but opposite is a piping centre (open Easter–mid-Oct: daily; tel: (01470) 511316) which records the feats of the Mac-Crimmon family, exhibits innumerable bagpipes and gives piping classes.

Heading south from Dunvegan, the A863 follows the shores of **Loch Bracadale**, one of the most magnificent fjords of the west coast, with the black basalt wall of **Talisker Head** away to the south. At **Dun Beag**, near Bracadale, is a well-preserved broch. A left turn onto the B885 before reaching **Talisker ⓫** leads back to **Portree**. Alternatively, remain on the A863 and either continue to Portree via Sligachan or, on reaching the head of **Loch Harport**, go right on B8009, and immediately cut back left into wooded **Glen Brittle** and more glorious views of the Black Cuillins. Remaining on the B8009 would lead to **Carbost** and the **Talisker Distillery** (open Mon–Fri, plus Sat July–Sept; closed am Nov–Mar; tel: (01478) 640314) where you can see how the whisky is made and sample it for yourself.

The claim has been made that the sole purpose of Skye is to protect the small lush island of **Raasay ⓬**, just to the east. In the 18th century the English burned all Raasay's houses and boats because the laird had sheltered Bonnie Prince Charlie after Culloden. Today the island has population of 150. **Dun Caan**, an extinct volcano, dominates the centre of the island.

Visitors can see the ruined **Brochel Castle**, home of the MacLeods of Skye and the grounds of Raasay House. When the exuberant Boswell stayed with Dr Johnson at Raasay House, now an outdoor pursuits centre, he danced a jig on top of the 1,456-ft (443-metre) high **Dun Caan** ridge. ❑

Map, page 232

With a distinctive peaty flavour all of its own, the whisky from the Talisker Distillery has been described by one expert as having "all the uncertainties of the Skye weather".

BELOW: sunny day at Sligachan.

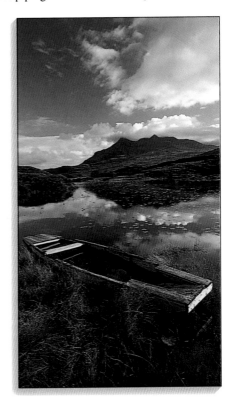

A CROFTER'S RUGGED LIFE

The 17,000 crofts in the Scottish Highlands keep people on the land, but they function more as a traditional way of living than as a source of income

The word "croft" derives from the Gaelic *croit*, meaning a small area of land. Often described as "a piece of land fenced around with regulations", the croft is both much cherished and highly frustrating. Its emotive power comes from its origins. In the aftermath of the Highland Clearances of the 19th century, groups of local men banded together to protect their families from being swept overseas to make way for sheep. At the time they were entirely at the whim of often absentee landowners.

By standing their ground despite all the odds – particularly at the so-called Battle of the Braes, in Skye – these men earned widespread public support. They were rewarded in 1886 by an Act of Parliament which gave them security of tenure. It also regulated the rents they had to pay, and gave them a right to compensation for any improvements made to their properties. The croft had officially come into being.

CROFTING TOWNSHIPS TODAY

A croft is usually a combination of a house and a handful of barren, boggy acres for the crofter to cultivate or graze livestock. The crofting community – commonly called a township – acts together in such activities as fencing, dipping or hiring a bull. Very few crofters rely solely on their smallholding for an income. But without the family croft, many would move away from the area altogether, thus depopulating the more remote rural areas.

Only 3,200 crofts are owner-occupied. The rest are tenanted, although the rental they pay to their landlord is minimal, and will barely have increased in the last 50 years. Grants to encourage crofting can amount to up to 85 percent of the cost of constructing agricultural buildings, and there are also loans available for new housing.

In two recent developments – in Assynt and the island of Eigg – crofters have banded together to become landowners themselves. To do so, they've raised millions of pounds with appeals through the Internet and the support of charities wanting to preserve traditional land use.

△ **A VARIED LIVING**
Crofting is often more a way of life than a viable means of living. A modern crofter has to have several occupations and maybe even a couple of part-time jobs to make ends meet and support a family. The average crofting income is just £8,000 a year.

△ **FURNACE WORKSHOP**
Every crofting township used to have a blacksmith. Even today, crofters have to be self-sufficient and able to mend practically everything.

◁ **A FAMILY AFFAIR**
When tenants get too old to work the croft themselves, they have the right to assign the croft to the next generation. Some 65 percent do just that.

A TRADITION THAT TIES UP THE LAND

The most common criticisms of crofting are that it ties up land in segments which are too small to ever be economically viable; that most crofters are too old to cope; and that too many crofts are left to run down by absentee tenants who have gone off in search of other, more rewarding ways of life.

These are all problems faced daily by the Crofter's Commission, the government body which was set up to oversee crofting affairs. Certainly, as far as agricultural production is concerned, crofting is a very small player. In fact, estimates suggest that some two-thirds of crofts are not actively farmed at all. However, crofting has lately been re-defined to include any economic activity, so it can also cover such enterprises as running a Bed & Breakfast establishment.

The number of run-down crofts and older crofters is a sad fact of life today; younger Highlanders will inevitably move away to the cities in search of a career, only returning to the croft in later years. But any alternative agricultural projects have been shown to provide little in the way of employment, and they would radically alter the landscape.

Crofting has proven an effective stewardship of the land as it is. Without it, whole communities would simply pack up and leave.

△ THE ELECTRONIC CROFT
Problems of remoteness are gradually being overcome by new technology. With the advent of computer networking and satellite communication, increasing numbers of crofters, particularly on the islands, are replacing the tweed loom in the shed with a keyboard in the living room.

△ NOT JUST A MAN'S WORLD
Despite the physical labour, some women are attracted to the crofting life, particularly as new housing replaces the poor conditions of the past.

◁ ALL MOD CONS
New self-built bungalow properties make life in the Highlands more appealing, with central heating and picture windows.

THE INNER HEBRIDES

The Inner Hebrides have a variety of pleasures to explore: the attractive landscape of Mull, the restored abbey on Iona, and a host of smaller islands, some inhabited only by wildlife

Map, page 242

Visitors come to the volcanic island of **Mull** ❶ for the contrasting scenery, wooded and soft to bleak and bare; for fishing in the lochs; and for walking. Some scorn Mull's green prettiness, dismissing it as Surrey with a tartan fringe. They might think again if they strolled on a wet day past Loch Scridain through the boggy desolation of the **Ross of Mull** or walked to the top of Mull's highest mountain, **Ben More**, a respectable 3,169 ft (950 metres).

The island is shaped like a gigantic teddy bear, but don't be deceived by its size, only 25 by 26 miles (40 by 41 km). A drive on the mainly single-track roads, running mostly round the perimeter, is made even slower by Scotland's most feckless and fearless sheep, which regard roads simply as grassless fields.

Natural charm

Mull's trump card is **Tobermory**, the prettiest port in Western Scotland, tucked in a wooded protected bay whose waters are almost invariably unruffled. Yet, in 1588, an explosion reverberated across the bay and the waters gurgled as the Spanish galleon *Florida* sank to the bottom. The exact spot, just 100 yards (90 metres) straight out from the pier, is well defined. And here, it is believed, a vast treasure of gold awaits salvage. Not that innumerable attempts have not been made, unsuccessfully, to retrieve it.

The tall, brightly painted houses curving round the harbour go back to the late 18th century when the British Fisheries Society planned a herring port. But the fish were fickle, and today Tobermory's sparkling harbour bobs with pretty pleasure yachts. Be sure to stop in at the small chocolate factory and shop, where the speciality is chocolate made with whisky.

The other towns, **Craignure** in the east where the Oban ferry docks; **Salen**, in the narrow neck of the island; and **Dervaig** in the northwest, are neat serviceable little places. Drive through Glen More, the ancient royal funeral route to Iona which bisects Mull from east to west, for some of the best scenery on the island. Also in Dervaig is the most enjoyable **Mull Little Theatre**, which, with 43 seats, is the smallest professional theatre in Britain.

Then, on the west of the island, you will find **Calgary**, the silver-sand beach where, after the Clearances, despairing emigrant ships set sail for the New World. The beach held happy memories for one émigré: Colonel McLeod of the North West Mounted Police named a new fort in Alberta after it.

Further proof, if it be needed, that Scotland's two main exports are whisky and brains can be found just south of Calgary at **Loch Ba** near Salen. The **MacQuarie Mausoleum** houses the remains of Major-General Lachlan MacQuarie, the first Governor-General of

PRECEDING PAGES: Tobermory on Mull. **LEFT:** Iona Abbey. **BELOW:** local inhabitant on Iona.

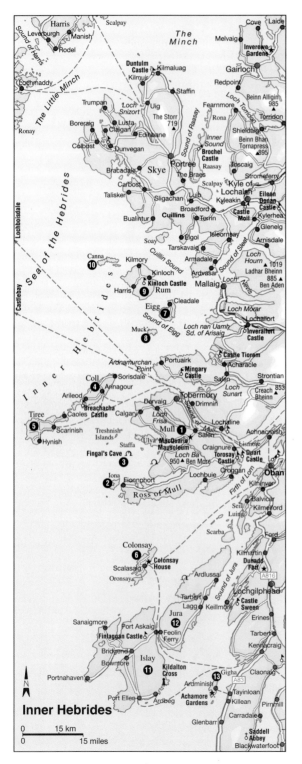

Inner Hebrides

New South Wales, who is sometimes called the "Father of Australia".

To understand what the 19th-century Clearances meant to all Hebrideans and to grasp the harshness of a crofting life, see the tableaux, with sound commentary, at the **Old Byre Heritage Centre** (open Easter–Oct: daily; tel: (01688) 400229) at Dervaig. They help explain the islanders' fatalistic attitude to life. Some charitable outsiders think this attitude stems from the trauma of the Clearances, which still trouble the collective consciousness. But cynical mainlanders say the islanders are simply idle. Islanders – when you find them, for many service jobs, particularly those which are connected with tourism, seem to be run by incomers – say they work as hard as anyone. Crofting and fishing, they argue, just aren't understood by urbanised outsiders.

Two castles are open to the public, both on the east. **Torosay** (open mid-Apr–Oct: daily; gardens open daily; tel: (01680) 812421), with 19th-century Scottish baronial turrets and crenellations, is near Craignure and is reached from there on a 1¹/₂-mile (2-km) steam miniature railway. The castle is still lived in by the Guthrie-James family. It's full of family memorabilia and is a friendly, non-imposing house. On wet days (frequent), you can leaf through old books in the drawing room. There's shapely Italian statuary in the 11 acres (4.5 hectares) of terraced grounds, fine clematis climbing on old brick walls and a sweet-smelling rock garden.

The 13th-century **Duart Castle** (open May–mid-Oct: daily; tel: (01680) 812 309), on a dramatic headland overlooking the Sound of Mull, was the MacLeans' stronghold. Mull belonged to the clan until it was forfeited when the MacLeans supported young Prince Charles Edward, who was defeated at Culloden in 1746. The castle was deserted for almost 200 years, then restored by Sir Fitzroy MacLean early in the 20th century. The tearoom on the castle grounds is a good place to stop for a slice of homemade cake.

Mull is the jumping-off point for several islands: Iona, Staffa, the Treshnish Isles, Coll and Tiree.

You feel a bit like a pilgrim as you board the serviceable little 10-minute shuttle to **Iona ❷**. Cars and big coaches on day trips from the mainland line the ferry road at **Fionnphort** on Mull's southwest tip, for visitors must cross to the Holy Island on foot. The main destination of visitors is the restored abbey (always open; free; tel: (0141) 445 4561) but the general store near the ferry has added bicycle hire to its varied services, so in theory there's time to see **Coracle Cove** where Columba landed in AD 563. From the abbey it is just 100 yards (90 metres) to the cemetery of **Reilig Oran** *(see below)*.

Fingal's Cave on **Staffa ❸** is a big attraction; supposedly it inspired Mendelssohn to compose his overture. The experience of going into the cave, if the weather is good enough for landing, is well worth the 90-minute boat journey. The primeval crashing of the sea, the towering height of the cave and the complete lack of colour in the sombre rocks make a powerful impression. Even if the little 47-ft (14-metre) partially covered passenger launch can't land, it's worth making the journey just to see the curious hexagonal basalt rocks with the gaping black hole of the cave. Birdwatchers, too, have plenty to enjoy.

Beyond Staffa are the uninhabited **Treshnish Islands** – a haven for puffins, kittiwakes, razorbills, shags, fulmars, gannets and guillemots.

The ferry from Oban for Coll and Tiree calls at Tobermory for additional passengers. There's the usual rivalry between these sister islands, most distant of the Inner Hebrides. People from Tiree can't understand why anyone wants to get off the ferry at Coll. The people of Coll maintain that the inhabitants of Tiree are permanently bent by the island's ceaseless wind.

Map, page 242

Sir Fitzroy MacLean of Duart Castle was a Hussar in the Light Brigade in the Crimea in 1854: his mementoes are displayed in the Grand Banqueting Room.

BELOW: the cloisters of the abbey of St Iona.

HOLY PILGRIMAGE

Curiosity and a search for some intangible spiritual comfort draw well over half a million people from all over the world each year to the tiny 3-mile (5-km) island of Iona. Here Saint Columba and 12 companions landed from Ireland in the 6th century to set up the mission that turned Iona into the Christian centre of Europe. In 1773 Dr Samuel Johnson was impressed with the piety of Iona. The abbey, which had been suppressed at the Reformation, was still in ruins and there were not many visitors then. In the 1930s the low, sturdy building was restored by the Iona Community and visitors have increased ever since. Some of the best restoration is to be seen in the tiny cloister, especially the birds and plants on the slender replacement sandstone columns, which were meticulously copied from the one remaining medieval original.

Until the 11th century the Reilig Oran – or royal cemetery – was the burial place of Scottish kings and there are said to be 48 Scottish rulers buried here, including Duncan, who was murdered by Macbeth in 1040. Here lie also the bodies of eight Norwegian, four Irish and two French kings. The cemetery is also the last resting place of John Smith, who was leader of Britian's Labour Party from 1992 until his untimely death in 1994.

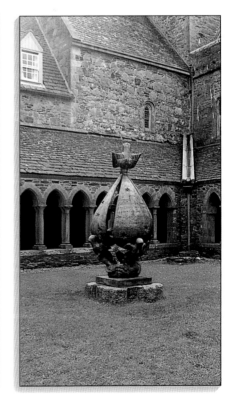

Dr Johnson was well aware of the bleaker side of the Hebrides: "Of these islands it must be confessed, that they have not many allurements, but to the mere lover of naked nature".

Purists, or those against progress, feel **Coll ❹** is too civilised. A young cyclist, camping near the glorious west coast beaches, complained that the island's only hotel had gone suburban when it installed a sauna; while a 75-year-old resident of **Arinagour**, the island's only village, where most of the population of 150 live, spoke with astonishment of the local café's advanced ideas – recently revitalised and repainted, it had emerged as a bistro.

Young families go to Coll for the simple holiday, pottering on uncrowded beaches. Much of the coast can be reached only on foot – although bicycles can be hired. This isn't an island for antiquities, and the restored medieval castle of **Breachacha** is only sometimes open to the public.

A later, 18th-century castle is where Samuel Johnson and James Boswell spent most of their time when stranded on Coll for 10 days during their Highland Tour. Johnson commented on the island's garden flowers but neither he nor Boswell attempted to climb – neither was energetic – the giant dunes (100 ft/30 metres) separating the nearby sandy beaches of Feall Bay and Crossapool Bay.

The Gaelic name for **Tiree ❺**, *Tir fo Thuinn*, means "land below the waves". It's a good description of this flat, sunny island whose two hills are only 400 ft high (120 metres). One of the islands' most eccentric visitors was Ada Goodrich Freer, who claimed telepathic gifts and an ability to receive messages through sea shells. She spent three weeks on Tiree in 1894 investigating Highland second sight. She spoke no Gaelic and was finally defeated, not by the language, but by the monotonous diet of tea, eggs, bread and jam provided by the Temperance hotel.

Nowadays international windsurfers, who call Tiree the Hawaii of the North, are attracted to the island by the great Atlantic rollers that break on the long, curving silver beaches.

BELOW: fascinating rock formations on Staffa.

Some people find **Colonsay ❻**, 40 miles (64 km) southwest of Oban, too bland. But for others it is an antidote to the prettiness of Mull and the glowering Cuillins of Skye. It has its antiquities: seven standing stones and six forts, as well as excellent wildlife: birds, otters and seals. It also has good white beaches and isn't over-mountainous. Visitors are few as there are no organised day-trips and, because the ferry calls only three times a week, accommodation has to be found either at the one hotel or with families providing bed and breakfast.

The island, 8 miles (12 km) long and 3 miles (4 km) wide, has a population of 120 and is one of the largest British islands still in private hands. It is warmed by the North Atlantic Drift, and the gardens of **Colonsay House** have a variety of exotic plants.

At low tide it's possible to walk across muddy sands to tiny **Oronsay**, off the southern tip of Colonsay; alternatively there are boat trips. Oronsay is about 2 miles (3 km) square and has a population of six. Its fine 14th-century priory is the biggest medieval monastic ruin in the islands, after Iona.

Island-hopping

The small islands of Eigg, Muck, Rum and Canna can be reached from Mallaig on the Sleat peninsula, the end of the "Road to the Isles". There's not a great deal to do on the islands. Mostly people go for the wildlife, for a bit of esoteric island-hopping or for superb walking, particularly on Rum.

The islands are all different and, if you just want to see them without landing, take the little boat that makes the five- to seven-hour round-trip six times a week in the summer, less often in winter. It's a service for islanders rather than a pleasure boat for visitors, and carries provisions, mail, newspapers and other essentials.

Map,
page 242

It's said that the wild goats on Colonsay are descended from survivors of the Spanish Armada ships wrecked in 1588.

BELOW: the calm before the storm at Tiree.

Only those planning to stay are allowed to disembark. However, in summer, boarding the *MV Shearwater* at Arisaig, 8 miles (13 km) before Mallaig, allows you to stop for several hours at either Eigg or Rum.

Eigg ❼ has had a chequered history in recent years. Owned first by Yorkshire businessman Keith Schellenberg and then by an eccentric German artist called Marum, it has now been bought by the Isle of Eigg Heritage Trust, a partnership between the islanders and the Scottish Wildlife Trust with a large contribution from public subscriptions. The famous rock prow known as The Scurr can be climbed for magnificent views.

Muck ❽ is the smallest of the four islands, only 2 miles (3 km) long, and has neither transport nor shops. Visitors must bring provisions and be landed by tender. Eighty breeds of birds nest on Muck.

There's an incongruous Greek temple on the rugged island of **Rum** ❾: the mausoleum of Sir George Bullough, the island's rich Edwardian proprietor. His castellated **Kinloch Castle** was used as a convalescent home during the Boer War just after it was built, and was for a time a hotel. The island is owned by Scottish Natural Heritage. There is fine bird watching and hill walking.

Graffiti adorn the rocks near the landing stage at **Canna** ❿; they are at least 100 years old and record the names of visiting boats. The harbour's safe haven is one of the few deepwater harbours in the Hebrides. This sheltered island, most westerly of the four, is owned by the National Trust for Scotland and is particularly interesting to botanists. No holiday accommodation exists.

Islay ⓫ is the place to go if you enjoy malt whisky. There are over half a dozen distilleries on this attractive little island, some with tours. Islay, where Clan Donald started, was once the home of the Lord of the Isles. A fascinating

Map, page 242

insight into its medieval history is to be found at the archaelogical site of **Finlaggan** (open Apr–Oct: daily; tel: (01496) 840644). Islay also has some good beaches on the indented north coast.

Also on this side of the island is one of the best Celtic crosses in Scotland: the 9th-century **Kildalton Cross** stands in the churchyard of a ruined, atmospheric little chapel. **Port Askaig**, where the ferry from the Kintyre peninsula docks, is a pretty little place with a hotel, once a 16th-century inn on the old drovers' road a few steps away from the ferry.

Peace and quiet

Jura ⑫, Islay's next-door neighbour, is so close you can nip over for a quick inspection after dinner. Three shapely mountains, the Paps of Jura, 2,500 ft (750 metres) high, provide a striking skyline. Although palms and rhododendrons grow on the sheltered east side, it's a wild island inhabited by sheep and red deer and is much favoured by sportsmen, birdwatchers and climbers. It was to the island of Jura that George Orwell came in 1947, seeking seclusion while working on his novel *1984*.

Gigha ⑬ has one of the nicest hotels in the islands – bright, Scandinavian and beautifully neat and simple. No need to take a car on the 3-mile (5-km) crossing from **Tayinloan** to this small green island popular with yachting people: no walk is more than 3 miles from the attractive ferry terminal at **Ardminish** with its sparkling white cottages.

The formal attraction on Gigha is **Achamore Gardens** (open daily; tel: (01583) 505254). Seals, barking amiably, cruise in the waters off the little- used north pier. ❏

TIP

Free tastings are on offer when you visit the distilleries of Laphroig and Lagavulin at Port Ellen on Islay.

BELOW: can a scarecrow also scare seagulls?

THE OUTER HEBRIDES

The dramatic islands of the Outer Hebrides are relentlesssly pounded by the cold Atlantic: visitors are either thrilled by their wild bleakness or find their remoteness disconcerting

Map,
page 252

The Outer Hebrides, 40 miles (64 km) west of the mainland, are known locally as the Long Islands. They stretch in a narrow 130-mile (208-km) arc from the Butt of Lewis in the north to Barra Head in the south. Each island regards itself as the fairest in the chain. The people live mainly by crofting and fishing, with commercial fish farming – crabs and mussels as well as the usual salmon and trout – growing fast.

There are enormous flat peat bogs on Lewis and North Uist and the islanders cut turf to burn rather than to export to the garden centres of England. The men cut it during the summer and stack it *in situ*; when it has dried the women and children cart it home and stack it against the house for winter fires. A traditional blessing on Lewis is: "Long may you live, with smoke from your house".

PRECEDING PAGES:
Hercules Irvine,
crofter.
LEFT: a corner of the
Outer Hebrides.
BELOW: the port of
Tarbert.

Fierce loyalty

These climatically hostile Western Isles of few trees and stark scenery are the Gaidhealtachd, the land of the Gael. When their Gaelic-speaking inhabitants change to English, as they politely do when visitors are present, they have virtually no accent and are among the easiest Scots for visitors to understand. They were fiercely loyal to Bonnie Prince Charlie. When, after the Battle of Culloden in 1746, the young man, with a £30,000 price on his head, dodged round the Outer Hebrides pursued by Government forces, no-one betrayed him.

Harris and the larger **Lewis** are really one island. Lewis is mostly flat. Harris rises into high, rocky mountains culminating in North Harris in the peak of Clisham (2,622 ft/799 metres).

Turn north from the ferry terminal at **Tarbert ❶** for Lewis; south for Harris. Tarbert is technically in Harris, a land of bare hills and fierce peaks. Ferries from Lochmaddy on North Uist and Uig on Skye dock in this sheltered port tucked into the hillside. There are a few shops, the Harris Hotel, a tourist office and sheds selling Harris tweed.

A drive around South Harris (40 miles/64 km) is rewarding. As you head south on the A859 down the west coast, you pass many glorious beaches – **Luskentyre, Scarista** – before reaching **Leverburgh**, with the remains of the buildings erected by the industrialist Lord Leverhulme (of Sunlight soap fame) for a projected fishing port. The road ends at **Rodel ❷** with the 16th-century **St Clement's Church**, one of the best examples of ecclesiastical architecture in the Hebrides.

The single track road up the east coast offers superb seascapes and views across the Minch to Skye and tiny crofts from where you hear – as you do throughout the Long Islands – the click-clack of crofters' looms producing tweed.

Outer Hebrides

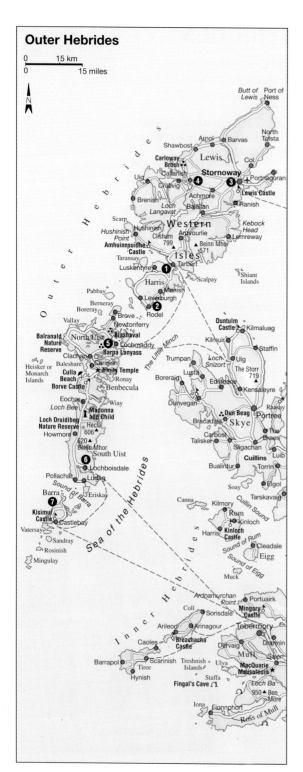

Leave Tarbert for the north on the A859 and after 4 miles (6 km) turn onto the B887, which clings to the shore of **West Loch Tarbert**. The 16-mile (26-km) drive from Tarbert to golden **Hushinish Point** is dramatic, particularly in the evening as the sun catches the peaks of Beinn Dhubh on Harris across the water.

The road goes straight through the well-maintained grounds of **Amhuinnsuidhe Castle** (pronounced *Avin-suey*), so close to the house you can almost see inside. This pale turretted castle, now a fishing lodge, was built in 1868 and James Barrie began his novel *Mary Rose* here. A stone's throw from the lodge, a salmon river runs into the sea.

From Hushinish, ferries cross to the small island of **Scarp**. In the 1930s a new postal service was announced here. A special stamp was issued; the first rocket was fired, but unfortunately it exploded, destroying mail and project.

Back-track to the A859 which twists and turns past lochs and through mountains to arrive after 35 miles (56 km) at **Stornoway ❸**, the capital of Lewis and the only large town in the Western Isles. Most activity in this solid town of 6,000 inhabitants is at the harbour, where seals can nearly always be seen. They give Stornoway its nickname of Portrona (Port of Seals). Here too thousands of silver fish, which will be turned into fertiliser, can be seen sucked by giant vacuum hoses from boats' decks into waiting lorries. This is also where the ferry from Ullapool, on the mainland, docks.

The best view of **Lews Castle** is from the harbour. Lord Leverhulme bought the castle in 1918. In 1920 he purchased Harris, becoming Britain's largest landowner. His visions were admirable: to turn the islanders into a viable community not dependent on crofting but making its living from the sea. He failed only because of timing: today, fishing dominates the island's economy.

To explore Lewis's many antiquities, leave Stornoway on the A859 and, after a couple of miles, bear right onto the A858. **Callanish ❹** and its magnificent standing stones is 16 miles (26 km) from Stornoway. The 13 ritual stones, some 12 ft (3 metres) high, are set in a circle like Stonehenge. The **Callanish Visitor Centre** (open Mon–Sat; tel: (01851) 621422) is close by.

Keeping to the A858, you soon reach the upstanding remains of the 2,000-year old **Carloway Broch**; then the folk museum at **Shawbost** (open Apr–Nov: Mon–Sat) and then **Arnol** with its **Black House Museum** (open Mon–Sat; Oct–Mar: closed Fri; tel: (01851) 710395), which shows how the people of Lewis used to live. A different world unfolds if, just before Callanish, you take the B8011: it leads to **Uig** and its wondrous beaches.

The Uist archipelago

Lochmaddy ❺, where the ferry from Uig in Skye docks, is the only village on **North Uist**, and you're almost through it before you realise it's there. But to show its status it has a hotel and a bank.

The Uist archipelago of low bright islands dominated by the glittering sea is 50 miles long and only 8 miles at its widest (80 by 13 km) and is so peppered with lochs that on the map the east coast round Benbecula looks like a sieve.

Rather than setting south on the A865, which runs for 45 miles (72 km) and which, because of causeway and bridge, virtually makes North Uist, Benbecula and South Uist one island, travel around North Uist counter-clockwise on the A865. On a 45-mile (72-km) trip, you will pass superb beaches and antiquarian treasures.

Three miles (5 km) from Lochmaddy are the standing stones of **Blashaval.** Three miles further on, a turn-off on the right (B893) leads to **Newtonferry** and the short ferry trip to the island of **Berneray**, where Prince Charles occasion-

see map opposite

Nobody knows why the Callanish stones are there. Once known as Nu Fir Breige – the false men – they have been claimed as a Viking parliament, a landing base for UFOs and a site for predicting eclipses.

BELOW: the Callanish standing stones.

FINDING YOUR WAY

The official tourist map of the Outer Hebrides is essential for the Uists. Even though only one main road links the three islands of North Uist, Benbecula and South Uist, most signposts are in Gaelic; the map gives them in English too. The Lochmaddy tourist office has a free sheet of English/Gaelic names put out by the Western Isles Islands Council. To help preserve one of Europe's oldest languages, the Council has put up Gaelic-only place names and signposts in the Outer Hebrides. In English-speaking Benbecula and in Stornoway on Lewis, the signs are also in English. Gaelic is a living language on these islands: local people often speak Gaelic among themselves and in the schools the children are taught in both English and Gaelic. And Church services – on both the Protestant islands in the north and the Catholic islands in the south – are also usually held in Gaelic.

There are other problems to waylay the unsuspecting visitor: locals warn that roads in North Uist may be different from the map because the constant movement of the bog makes them change direction. Certainly at times the causeway road feels as springy as a dance floor.

TIP

Over 180 species of bird have been seen at the Balranald sanctuary: contact the supervisor for information.

ally recharges his batteries. Back on Uist, in the middle of the north shore, is the rocky islet of **Eilean-an-Tighe**, the oldest pottery "factory" in Western Europe: it produced quality items in Stone Age times.

Still on the north coast is the superb beach of **Vallay** (actually an island reached on foot: beware tides). Round on the west coast, green and whiter than in the east, is **Baleshare,** another island with a great beach joined to Uist by a causeway. Before reaching here, you pass the **Balranald Nature Reserve**, which was created to protect the breeding habitat of the red-necked phalarope.

At **Clachan** the A865 turns south while the A867 runs east to return to Lochmaddy. Five miles (8 km) along the latter is **Barpa Lanyass**, a 5,000-year-old squashed beehive tomb. Nearby is the **Pobull Fhinn** standing stone circle. Backtrack to the A865; just before the causeway is **Carinish**, where Scotland's last battle with swords and bows and arrows took place. Close by is the ruined 12th-century **Trinity Temple**.

Cross the North Ford by the 5-mile (8-km) causeway to reach tiny **Benbecula**, whose eastern part is so pitted with lochs that most people live on the west coast. The traveller now has the choice of proceeding due south for 5 miles (8 km) to the southern tip of Benbecula or turning right onto the B892, which makes a 10-mile (16-km) loop around the west of the island before rejoining the A865.

The loop road first passes the small airport (flights to Glasgow, Barra, Stornoway) and a Royal Artillery base before reaching **Culla Beach** – the best of many great beaches – and the ruins of **Borve Castle** with 10-foot (3-metre) thick walls. The castle, one of the most important medieval ruins in the Outer Hebrides, was built in the 14th century and was the home of the MacDonalds of Clanranald, who once ruled Benbecula.

BELOW: sheep shearers at work on South Uist.

The South Ford, separating Benbecula and **South Uist**, is crossed by a half-mile long single-track bridge. Immediately on entering South Uist turn right and drive for a mile (1.6 km) along the loch-lined road to **Eochar** and the shell-covered school bus in Flora Johnstone's garden. Flora so enjoyed sticking on shells that, in the 1960s, she then started on her cottage walls. Beyond this is **Loch Bee** with its hundreds of mute swans.

Map, page 252

Beach beauty
Return to the main road (A865), which runs down the west of the island for 22 miles (35 km) before terminating at Pollachar at the southwest tip. All the time, to the west, are seascapes with yet more splendid beaches and, to the east, mountains and peat bogs dominated by **Beinn Mhor** (2,034 feet/620 metres) and **Hecla** (1,988 feet/606 metres). These names, Celtic and Norse, reveal the dual main stream in the island's population.

First encountered to the east, after 4 miles (6 km), atop **Rueval Hill**, "hill of miracles", is the modern pencil-like statue of **Madonna and Child**, which was paid for by world-wide donations. Just beyond this, still to the east, is the **Loch Druidibeg Nature Reserve** with its corncrakes and greylag geese.

Next, to the west, is **Howmore**. Little here indicates that this was the ancient ecclesiastical centre of the island: now, protected white-washed cottages, one a youth hostel, stand in flowery meadows. Continue beyond Howmore to reach a superb beach. Another 6 miles (10 km) to the south and, on the right, before the turn-off to **Milton**, is a bronze cairn and plaque honouring the birthplace of Flora MacDonald. Two miles (3 km) further south, the A865 turns left to run for 4 miles (6 km) to tiny **Lochboisdale ❻**, the main village in the south of the island and the terminal for the Oban ferry.

Flights to Barra have to work to a flexible timetable: the runway disappears twice a day under the incoming tide.

BELOW: coming out of her shell: Flora Johnstone of Eochar, South Uist.

At **Pollachar** is a 3,000-year-old standing stone surrounded by wild orchids and clover from where you can gaze across to Eriskay and Barra. From **Ludag**, a mile to the east, a car ferry (subject to tides) crosses the 1 1/2-mile (3-km) stretch of water to **Eriskay**.

The island, famous because of the hauntingly beautiful "Eriskay Love Lilt", is disappointing: just an unimpressive hump. For a fishing island only 2 by 3 miles (3 by 5 km) with a population of around 200, it has had much fame. Bonnie Prince Charlie landed on the long silver beach on the west side on 23 July 1745. Two hundred years later the *Politician*, a cargo ship carrying 24,000 cases of whisky, sank in the Eriskay Sound. Compton Mackenzie's *Whisky Galore* (known in America as *Tight Little Island*) was a hilarious re-telling of the redistribution of the cargo.

Fishing dominates **Barra ❼**, as it always has. In the 1880s, choice Barra cockles were eaten in London. By the 1920s Barra herring were so important that girls came from as far away as Yarmouth in England to work 17 hours a day in **Castlebay**, the capital, gutting the silver darlings. In the past 20 years, lobster fishing has become important, with about 40 boats operating.

The **Barra Heritage Centre** (open Easter–Sept: daily; tel: (01871) 810413) tells the island's story. Also worth visiting is **Kisimul Castle** off Castleby, the traditional home of the MacNeils of Barra. ❑

CENTRAL SCOTLAND

Map, page 260

Perth, Scotland's one-time capital, is a superb centre for exploring the central highlands – the lochs of the Trossachs, the ancient city of St Andrews, and romantic castles nestling in the hills

Georgian terraces and imposing civic buildings line the riverside in the genteel city of **Perth ❶**, but principal streets are uncompromisingly Victorian. No dullness, though. "All things bright and beautiful" on the bells of the handsome 15th-century **St John's Kirk** heralds the hour strike in a 36-bell belfry – a contrast to the iconoclastic rantings and ravings when John Knox preached here in the mid-16th century.

Behind the imposing portico and dome of the **Museum and Art Gallery** (open Mon–Sat; free; tel:(01738) 632488) is drama in Sir David Young Cameron's landscape *Shadows of Glencoe*, in the stuffed but still snarling wildcat, its bushy tail black-tipped, and in Perth's link with space, the Strathmore Meteorite of 1917. More art can be enjoyed in the round-house of the old waterworks, now the delightful **Fergusson Gallery** devoted to the life and works of the Perthshire painter J. D. Fergusson, one of the Scottish colourists (open Mon–Sat; free; tel:(01738) 441944). *The Fair Maid of Perth*, Sir Walter Scott's virginal heroine, lived in **Fair Maid's House**, the setting for his novel of the time of the battle of Clans on the meadow of the North Inch nearby. The house is now a contemporary crafts shop.

Those with aesthetic tastes or presents to buy are also catered for at **Caithness Glass** at Inveralmond (open daily; free; tel:(01738) 637373), where the mysteries of glass-blowing are revealed. If you want exercise you can walk round the **Bell's Cherrybank Gardens** (open Apr–Oct: daily; tel:(01738) 627330) or go for something more energetic at **Bell's Sports Centre**, both on Glasgow Road. History and tradition take the stage in the **Perth Theatre**, the longest established theatre in Scotland.

Beyond the city

Splendid views over the city and River Tay can be enjoyed from the top of **Kinnoull Hill** on the outskirts of the city, while **Branklyn Garden** has been described as "the finest two acres of private garden in the country" (open Mar–Oct: daily; tel:(01738) 625535).

Perth is ringed with castles, some still family homes, but many are romantic ruins like **Huntingtower**, 3 miles (4 km) west (open Mar–Oct: Mon–Sat and Sun pm; Mar and Oct: closed Thur pm and Fri; tel:(01738) 627231). An intriguing rooftop walk gives glimpses of hidden stairs and dark voids that must have struck terror into James I during his year's imprisonment here.

Scone Palace (open Easter–Oct: daily; tel:(01738) 552300), 2 miles (3 km) north of Perth, was Scotland's Camelot and home to the much travelled Stone on which 40 kings of Scotland were crowned. Brought here in the 9th century and taken to London in 1296 by Edward I, it was stolen in 1950 from beneath the Coronation Chair

PRECEDING PAGES: taking a dip in Loch Lomond.
LEFT: Scone Palace.
BELOW: a race on the river Tay.

A guided tour of Falkland Palace includes an explanation of Royal Tennis, the game of kings (quite unlike modern tennis) that has been played on the court here ever since 1539.

in Westminster Abbey and recovered from Arbroath. It is now in Edinburgh Castle. The Earl of Mansfield's home offers such diverse charms as six generations of family photographs, Highland cattle, ornamental fowls and giant trees as well as a treasure house of period furniture, elegant porcelain and paintings.

A lake for all seasons, **Loch Leven ❷** is heaven for trout anglers and the chosen wintering ground for wild geese and other waterfowl. On an island and reached by ferry from the lochside is ruined **Loch Leven Castle** (open Apr–Sept: Mon–Sat and Sun pm; tel:(0131) 668 8800), once prison to the notorious Wolf of Badenoch and Mary Queen of Scots.

Falkland Palace ❸ (open Easter–Oct: Mon–Sat and Sun pm; tel:(01337) 857397), sitting cosily in the main street of its old Royal Burgh, was the favourite retreat of the Stuart kings. Stone lintels that top many doors carry the incised initials of the couples the houses were built for in the 1600s, the date and a heart. Loving care is evident everywhere in the many laundered green spaces and carefully conserved weavers' houses.

Castle Campbell ❹ (open Mon–Sat and Sun pm; Oct–Mar: closed Thur pm and Fri; tel:(0131) 668 8800) is rather impressively situated at the head of Dollar Glen, southwest of Perth. **Menstrie Castle** (open May–Sept; Sat and Sun pm; free), near Stirling, the birthplace of Sir William Alexander, James VI's lieutenant, links Scotland with Nova Scotia.

The Kingdom of Fife

The M90 motorway that links Perth to Edinburgh does more than bypass Fife, thrust out into the North Sea between the Firth of Forth and the Tay. It bypasses an area rich in history, architecture and scenery. The kingdom's harbours nudge

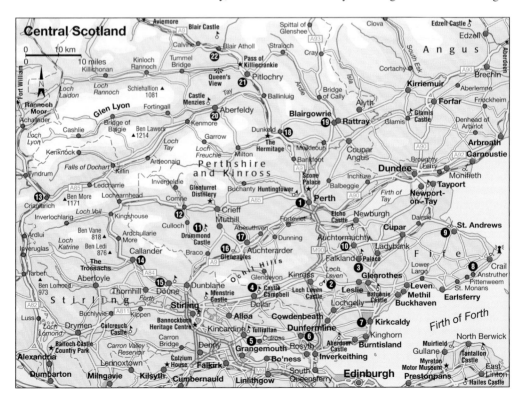

one another on a coast tilted towards Scandinavia, buildings reflecting the thriving trade it had in the 17th century with the Baltic and the Low Countries.

Culross ❺, where the Firth of Forth narrows, is a unique survival: a 17th- and 18th-century town that looks like a film set, and often is. Then it was a smoky, industrial town with coal mines and salt pans, manufacturing griddles and baking plates for oatcakes. Sir George Bruce, who took over where the mining monks left off in 1575, went on to such success that James VI made Culross a Royal Burgh. Today, the town's wealth of old buildings, with crow-stepped gables and red pantiled roofs, make it one of Scotland's finest showplaces. The **Town House**'s clock tower dominates the waterfront and the **Mercat Cross**, the tiny market place and oldest house (1577).

Wynds, or pathways, lead past the **Palace** (open Apr–Sept: daily; tel:(01383) 880359), which is probably the finest gentleman's house of its period in Scotland, the "**Study**", with a 17th-century Norwegian painted ceiling, and **Snuff Cottage** (1673). Past the house with the Evil Eyes are the church, the ruined abbey and the magnificent Abbey House.

Although **Dunfermline** ❻ was for 600 years capital of Scotland, burial place of kings, with a fine church and abbey (open Mon–Sat and Sun pm; Oct–Mar: closed Thur pm and Fri; tel:(01383) 739026), it owes its international fame to its humblest son, Andrew Carnegie. The great philanthropist opened the first of 3,000 free libraries here in 1881. The tiny cottage where he was born (open Mon–Sat and Sun pm; Nov–Mar: closed am; tel:(01383) 724302) contrasts vividly with **Pittencrieff**, the mansion he left to the town on his death (open May–Oct: Wed–Mon; tel:(01383) 722975). The cut-out words "King Robert the Bruce" on the church tower advertise his burial here in 1329.

see map opposite

An inscription on Snuff Cottage reads "Wha wad ha thocht it". "Noses wad ha bought it" is the second line, which is on a house in Edinburgh owned by the same snuff merchant.

BELOW: the gardens at Falkland Palace, a favourite retreat of the Stuarts.

TIP

Near Crail you can visit Scotland's Secret Bunker (open daily), which would have been the government headquarters for Scotland in the event of nuclear war.

At Leven, behind the esplanade and the parked oil rigs, are marvellous shell gardens. Begun in 1914, walls, walks, menagerie and aviary are patterned with shells, broken china and Staffordshire figures.

Kirkcaldy's association with coal and floor coverings may not appeal, but the Lang Town, as it is often called, made important contributions to architecture, economics and literature. Robert Adam and Adam Smith were born here and the **Kircaldy Museum** (open daily; free; tel:(01592) 412860) has superb collections of paintings by Scottish colourists and of the distinctive Wemyss Ware pottery.

Lower Largo, its tiny harbour and inn stage-set beneath a viaduct, gave birth in 1676 to Alexander Selkirk, Daniel Defoe's "Robinson Crusoe".

The original "Fifie" fishing boats were built at **St Monans**, but the shipyard now builds only pleasure craft. A path leads from the harbour to the 14th-century church, its feet on the rocky shore.

Pittenweem bustles with the business of fish. Nearby, **Anstruther** ⓧ, with the **Scottish Fisheries Museum** (open Mon–Sat and Sun pm; tel:(01333) 310628), and **Crail** end the run of picturesque harbours before Fife Ness is reached. The oldest Royal Burgh in East Neuk, Crail's crow-stepped gables and red-tiled roofs ensure that artists outnumber fishermen.

There is a nice contrast in leaving the simplicities of Crail for the concentration of learning, religious importance and historical significance that is **St Andrews** ⓧ. Best known as the home of golf, it has six courses to offer players and a collection of memorabilia on display at the **British Golf Museum** (open daily; Nov–Mar: closed Tues and Wed; tel:(01334) 478880) immediately opposite the "Old" starters' hut.

BELOW: gutting fish in Crail harbour.

ANCIENT AND ROYAL

The Scots are so obsessed with golf that it is said that Mary Queen of Scots went off to play when her husband had just been assassinated. Wherever you are in Scotland there will be a golf course nearby. There are over 400 courses to choose from and even tiny Highland villages have their own 9-hole courses. The game was developed as far back as the 16th century on the coastal courses known as "links" and you can still play on some of the world's oldest courses along the east coast of Scotland – though for a cheaper round it's advisable to avoid the Championship courses.

At St Andrews, golf qualifies as "Ancient" as well as "Royal": its Old Course was laid out in the 15th century and the Royal and Ancient Golf Club formed in 1754. There are no fewer than six courses here. The Old Course is flanked by the New on the seaward and by the Eden on the inland side. Tucked between the New and the white-caps of the North Sea is the shorter Jubilee course. Then, in 1993, two more courses were squeezed in: the Strathtyrum is an 18-hole course of modest length, while the Balgrove is a 9-hole beginners' layout. (*See also pages 105-107.*)

Map, page 260

The damage to the cathedral following John Knox's impassioned sermons started neglect that reduced it to ruins. **St Rule** nearby survives as a tower and **St Andrews Castle** (open daily; tel:(01334) 477196) fared little better, though it has a wonderful dungeon that children find irresistible. Elsewhere, the **West Port** spans a main street and steeples abound, but not for climbing, as Dr Johnson found. At the **Sea Life Centre** (open daily: tel:(01334) 474786) all kinds of marine life can be seen settings that resemble their natural surroundings. The **University**, whose buildings line North Street, is the oldest in Scotland.

Off the road back to Perth is **Hill of Tarvit** (open Easter and May–Sept: daily pm; Oct: Sat and Sun pm; tel:(01334) 653127), a superb mansion house remodelled by Sir Robert Lorimer with magnificent garden and grounds (open daily all year). Further on, **Auchtermuchty** ❿ has surviving thatched cottages once used by weavers. The tea shop keeps the key to the Pictish, chimney-like church tower. At the base of the tower is an incised Pictish stone.

Lochs, rivers and mountains

Westward from Perth, roads follow rivers in the ascent to the lochs and watershed of the Grampians. At **Crieff** good taste demands visits to **Glenturret**, the oldest distillery in Scotland (open Mon–Sat and Sun pm; tel:(01764) 656565), and glass, pottery and textile workshops. What romance attaches to the **Drummond Arms** as the scene of Prince Charles Edward's council of war in 1746 is a little dimmed by its having been rebuilt since. Five miles (8 km) southeast of Crieff is the oldest public library in Scotland, the **Innerpeffray Library** (open Feb–Nov: Mon–Sat and Sun pm; closed Thur; tel:(01764) 652819), which was founded in 1680. Also near Crieff, **Drummond Castle** ⓫ opens only its gardens (open

Innerpeffray Library has a Treacle Bible, so called because "Is there no balm in Gilead?" is translated into "Is there no treacle in Gilead?"

BELOW: students at St Andrews Castle.

The cathedral and town of Dunkeld were fought over and the Highlanders defeated in 1689. Only the choir of the cathedral was restored and the main building is still roofless.

BELOW: climbing up the Black Watch Monument near Aberfeldy.

Easter and May–Oct: daily pm; tel:(01764) 681257) and surprisingly they are Italian – statues, trees and shrubs.

Comrie's  situation on the River Earn where two glens meet makes it an attractive walking centre. The town is on the Highland Boundary Fault and is known as "Scotland's Earthquake Centre" because of the frequency of the tremors felt here. From Comrie the road passes Loch Earn with magnificent mountain scenery until **Lochearnhead** is reached. Beyond here the high peaks have it – **Ben More**, **Ben Lui** and **Ben Bhuidhe** – until the lochs reach in like fingers from the coast of the Western Isles.

Crianlarich ⑬ is a popular centre with climbers and walkers. For those on wheels, **Ardlui** is a beautiful introduction to **Loch Lomond**. The largest body of water in Britain, full of fish and islands, it is best known through the song which one of Prince Charles Edward's followers wrote on the eve of his execution. At the south end of the Loch is the **Balloch Castle Country Park** (castle open Easter–Oct: daily; garden open daily all year; tel: (01389) 758216).

The road back to **Aberfoyle** traverses the Queen Elizabeth forest park and leads to the splendid wooded scenery of the **Trossachs**, best viewed on foot or from the summer steamer on **Loch Katrine**. Scott's *Lady of the Lake* and *Rob Roy* attracted flocks of Victorian visitors. **Callander** ⑭ found fame as the "Tannochbrae" of the BBC TV series *Dr Finlay's Casebook*. The **Trossachs and Rob Roy Visitor Centre** (open daily; Jan–Feb: closed Mon–Fri; tel:(01877) 330342), in an old kirk, tells you all about this glorified cattle thief.

Doune's 15th-century castle ⑮ (open Mon–Sat and Sun pm; Oct–Mar: closed Thur pm and Fri; tel:(0131) 668 8800) is remarkably complete with two great towers and hall between. Close to Doune is **Dunblane**; the west front of its 13th-century cathedral was described by the Victorian writer Ruskin as a perfect example of Scotland's church architecture. Eleven miles (18 km) east of Dunblane, the moorland courses of **Gleneagles** ⑯ are a golfer's paradise.

Auchterarder's ⑰ situation to the north of the Ochil Hills is a convenient point at which to hit the Mill Trail. Thanks to good grazing and soft water, Scotland's world-famous tweeds, tartans and knitwear have been produced here in the Hillfoots villages since the 16th century. From the Heritage Centre in Auchterarder, with the only surviving steam textile engine and Tillicoultry's handsome Clock Mill powered by waterwheel, to the most modern mills in Alloa and Sauchie, the trail links modern technology with the cottage production of the past.

Moving north

From Perth, the road north bypasses **Bankfoot's** raspberry canes and motor museum. At **Dunkeld** ⑱, cross Telford's fine bridge over the Tay's rocky bed for the charm and character of this old ecclesiastical capital of Scotland. A delightful museum in the cathedral's **Chapter House** introduces Niel Gow, the celebrated fiddler.

Romantics will feel at home at **The Hermitage**, a mile (0.8 km) west of the town. Built in 1758, this is the centrepiece of a woodland trail beside the River Braan, a folly poised over a waterfall. Wordsworth wrote a verse about it and Mendelssohn sketched it.

At the foot of the Highlands is **Blairgowrie ⑲**. Matter-of-fact, it reserves its charm for anglers and lovers of raspberries and strawberries. At **Meikleour** the road to Perth is bordered by a beech hedge, over 100 ft (30 metres) high and 1,980 ft (600 metres) long and planted in 1746.

Aberfeldy ⑳, easily reached from Dunkeld, is noted for the fine Wade bridge across the Tay, built in 1733. Here the world-renowned Black Watch Regiment became part of the British Army in 1740. A beautiful walk is through the **Birks of Aberfeldy** to the Moness Falls. To the west of Aberfeldy is **Castle Menzies** (open Apr–Oct: Mon–Sat and Sun pm; tel:(01887) 820982), a good example of a 16th-century Z-plan tower house. Beyond is glorious **Glen Lyon**, the longest and one of the most beautiful glens in Scotland, with the thatched-cottage village of **Fortingall**. Nearby, **Loch Tay**, a centre for salmon fisheries, has **Ben Lawers** 3,984 ft (1,214 metres) above it and the beginnings of the River Tay at its foot.

Seek out **Pitlochry ㉑** for spectacle. The Festival Theatre, famous as the "Theatre in the Hills" and magnificently situated overlooking the River Tummel, is an attraction in itself. But it's upstaged by the dam at the hydroelectric power station where in spring and summer thousands of migrating salmon can be seen through windows in a fish ladder.

The Queen's View, 8 miles (13 km) northwest of Pitlochry, a viewpoint named after Queen Victoria's 1866 visits, is a truly royal vista up Loch Tummel, dominated by the cone-shaped Schiehallion (3,547 ft/ 1,081 metres).

Beyond the **Pass of Killiecrankie** where Soldier's Leap recalls the battle of 1689, is **Blair Atholl ㉒**, key to the Central Highlands. Scottish at its most baronial, Blair Castle (open Apr–Oct: daily; tel:(01796) 481207) owes much to Victorian restoration. ❏

Map, page 260

Blair Castle is home to the Duke of Atholl, the only person in Britain permitted to have a private army.

BELOW: reliving medieval times in a pageant at Arbroath.

THE EAST COAST

*The coast and countryside between the Firth of Tay and the sandy
Moray Firth is a region of rare and subtle loveliness: here the scale
is human and the the history dense*

Map,
pages
270–1

Scotland's east coast and its hinterland are often neglected by indolent
tourists, but reward industrious ones. This is, after all, probably the most
industrious (but not industrial) region of the country. Its ports and coastal
villages have given Scotland its fishing industry. Its agriculture, from the rich
croplands of Angus to the famous beef farms of Aberdeenshire – the largest
stretch of uninterrupted farmland in Britain – has been hard won and hard
worked. "Our ancestors imposed their will on Buchan," says the writer John R.
Allan of that flinty outcrop buffeted by the North Sea, "…an idea imposed on
nature at great expense of labour and endurance, of weariness and suffering."

It is, therefore, the east coast of Scotland which most physically and visibly
exemplifies that which is most dogged and determined (and perhaps dour) in
the Scottish character; and that which best knows how to exploit its assets. The
northeast port of Peterhead, for example, already Europe's busiest fishing harbour, turned itself into a major berth for North Sea oil supply vessels; while the
gentle, wooded valley of the River Spey is not only the centre of malt whisky
production but with its "Whisky Trail" has made tourist capital out of its celebrated local industry.

Along this coast you can learn to live without the majestic wilderness and
Gothic melodrama of the West Highlands and their
archipelago – although you will find echoes of their
atmosphere in the Grampian glens of Angus and the outriders of the Cairngorms which reach into Aberdeenshire – and explore the versatility of our dealings with
the land and the sea.

PRECEDING PAGES:
Aberdeen anglers.
LEFT: making Port-
soy marble.
BELOW: harvesting
the barley: the area
is rich in croplands.

Tale of two cities

The east coast cities are **Dundee** and **Aberdeen**. They
are of comparable size (about 200,000), separated only
by 70 miles (110 km), yet they couldn't be more different. Dundee has been the sad exception to the general
rule of east coast energy and enterprise. Despite a vigorous industrial past rooted in textiles, shipbuilding and
the jute industry Dundee, until recently, has long had
the feel of a city down on its luck; whereas Aberdeen,
the Granite City, is as solid and unyielding as its nickname, a town of such accustomed prosperity and self-
confidence that it assumed its new title of oil capital of
Europe as though doing the multinationals a favour.

Topographically, **Dundee ❶** promises more than it
fulfills. It has a magnificent position on the Tay estuary.
It is dominated by an extinct volcano called the Law, and
it has been fancifully called the Naples of the North.
From the south side of the estuary, from the spectacular
approaches of its road and rail bridges, you might be persuaded that its setting merits the comparison. There are
other points of similarity. Like Naples, Dundee has had

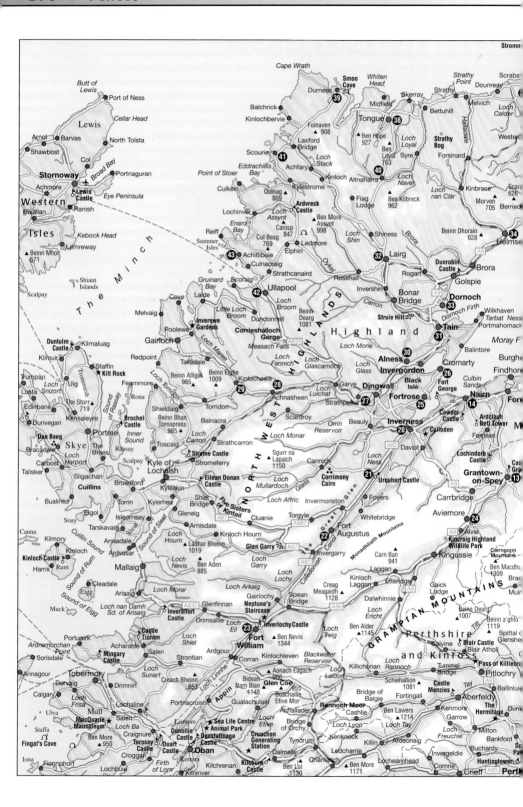

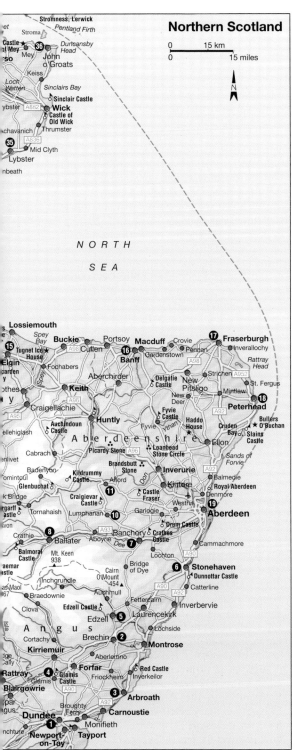

Northern Scotland

0   15 km
0   15 miles

N

NORTH

SEA

its share of slums and deprivation; like Naples, it is a port with a long maritime history (it was once the centre of the Scottish wine trade, and a leading importer of French claret). Unlike Naples, it has dealt its own history a mortal blow by destroying its past in a series of insensitive and sometimes shady developments. (In the 1970s the city's local authority was plagued by a succession of corruption scandals.)

"Perhaps no town in Scotland has been oftener sacked, pillaged and destroyed than Dundee," wrote an 18th-century historian, commenting on the fact that since the 11th century Dundee had the habit of picking the losing side in the various internecine and international conflicts which plagued Scotland. The city's own fathers – and the **University of Dundee** – completed the process in the 20th century. A distinguished Scottish newspaper editor refused to set foot in Dundee after its graceful 17th-century town house was demolished to make way for the building of the **Caird Hall** (concerts and civic events) in the 1930s.

Building on the past

Little is left of antiquity for the history-conscious tourist: the 15th-century **Old Steeple**; the venerable **Howff graveyard**, which occupies land given to the city by Mary Queen of Scots; the **East Port**, remnant of Dundee's fortified wall. But showing new initiative – and in the spirit of enterprise which is revitalising its economy through sunrise industries – Dundee is now capitalising on its maritime past.

The major attraction is **Discovery Point** (open daily; tel: (01382) 201245), which tells the story of Antarctic discovery. Captain Scott's ship *Discovery*, built in Dundee, is moored here. In Victoria Dock is HMS *Unicorn* (open Apr–Oct: daily; Jan–Mar: Mon–Fri; tel: (01382) 200900), the oldest British warship still afloat and one of only four frigates left in the world. Dundee had a high reputation for building clippers and whalers 100 years ago and sent its own fleet of whalers north to the Arctic. Their story is recalled at the **Broughty Castle Museum** (open

Mon–Sat; free; tel: (01382) 436916) in the attractive seaside suburb of Broughty Ferry. Another reminder of past glories is to be found at the Verdant Works (open Mar–Nov: daily; tel: (01382) 225282), which is a major new industrial heritage centre celebrating Dundee's textile industry, and in particular the city's long association with jute.

The city's hinterland is reason alone for visiting Dundee. The county of Angus is an eloquent fusion of hill, glen, farmland, beaches and cliffs, and its towns and villages reach back into the dawn of Scottish history. The twin Caterthun hills near **Brechin** ❷ (which has a 12th-century cathedral and one of the only two Celtic round towers remaining on the Scottish mainland) are ringed with concentric Iron-Age ramparts. There are Pictish sculptured stones in the churchyard of **Aberlemno**, off the A90, while the former Royal Burgh of **Arbroath** ❸, a fishing port and holiday resort moving into light industry, was once a Pictish settlement.

Arbroath Abbey (open Mon–Sat and Sun pm; tel: (01241) 878756), now a handsome ruin, dates back to 1178 and was the scene, in 1320, of a key event in the troubled history of Scotland: the signing of the Declaration of Arbroath. There, the Scottish nobles reaffirmed their determination to resist the persistent invasions of the English and to preserve the liberty and independence of their country. (The most noble and dignified sentiments of the Declaration are chiselled into the base of the enormous bronze statue of Sir William Wallace, the Scottish patriot, in Aberdeen's Union Terrace.)

Arbroath's red cliffs and harbour at the Fit o' the Toon (foot of the town) remain atmospheric, and you will find there the local cottage industry of smoking haddock to produce the celebrated Smokies. The **Signal Tower** complex, built in 1813 to serve the families of the keepers of the lonely Bellrock Lighthouse, now houses a museum (open Mon–Sat and Sun pm; Sept–June: closed Sun; free; tel: (01241) 875598) telling the story of the lighthouse and its keepers.

Royal setting

Between Arbroath and Dundee is the resort of **Carnoustie**, which has a famous golf course and a lot of sand, while 13 miles (22 km) to the north is the elegant town of **Montrose**, built at the mouth of a vast tidal basin, which is the winter home of pink-footed Arctic geese and pink-cheeked ornithologists. Inland, the country town of **Forfar** (where King Malcolm Canmore held his first parliament in 1057) is a striking point for the gloriously underused and somehow secretive glens of Angus and lies close to what must be considered the county's star attraction: **Glamis Castle** ❹ (open Easter–Oct: daily; tel: (01307) 840393), the exquisite fairy-tale home of the Earls of Strathmore and Kinghorne. It was claimed by Shakespeare for the legendary setting of *Macbeth*. ("Hail Macbeth, Thane of Glamis!")

A group of 17th-century cottages in the village of Glamis have now been turned by the National Trust for Scotland into the **Angus Folk Museum** (open May–Sept: daily; Oct: Sat and Sun; tel: (01307) 840288), indicating the nature of domestic and agricultural life over the past 200 years.

A visit to Glamis can be combined with a visit to **Kirriemuir,** birthplace of the writer J.M. Barrie and the "Thrums" of his novels. The house in which the author of *Peter Pan* was born is now maintained as a museum by the National Trust for Scotland (open Easter and May–Sept: Mon–Sat and Sun pm; Oct: Sat and Sun; tel: (01575) 572646) and you can see there Barrie's very first theatre.

Kirriemuir is also the gateway to **Glen Prosen** and **Glen Clova**, from where the committed walker can penetrate deep into the heart of the Grampians to **Glen Doll** and pick up the old drove roads over to Deeside. These ancient routes were used by armies, rebels and whisky smugglers, as well as cattle drovers and look deceptively easy and appealing walks on the Ordnance Survey map. But the Grampians can be as treacherous as any Scottish hills; the drove roads have claimed the lives of walkers, caught in blizzards, in the past.

To the southwest is **Glen Isla** and to the north **Glen Lethnot** (route of a "whisky road" formerly used by smugglers to outwit Revenue men). Here too is the graceful, meandering **Glen Esk**, which is reached through the pretty village of **Edzell ❺** where **Edzell Castle** (open Mon–Sat, Sun pm; Oct–Mar: closed Thur pm and Fri; tel: (01356) 648631), the ancestral home of the Lindsay family, has a magnificent walled renaissance garden or "pleasance".

The challenge of the northeast

Edzell lies on the Angus boundary with the county of Kincardine, and here the countryside begins to alter subtly. It lies, too, on the western edge of the **Howe of the Mearns**, which means something special to lovers of Scots literature. This is the howe, or vale, which nurtured Lewis Grassic Gibbon, whose brilliant trilogy *A Scots Quair* gave the 20th-century Scottish novel and the Scots

Map, pages 270–1

TIP

The Scottish Wildlife Trust has a splendid new Visitor Centre (open daily) on the south side of the tidal basin at Montrose, from which many birds can be viewed and identified.

BELOW: Glamis Castle: interior grandeur and exterior splendour.

BELOW: Dunnottar Castle: Covenanters were once left there to rot.

language its most distinctive voice: *Sunset Song, Cloud Howe, Grey Granite*. The **Grassic Gibbon Centre** at Arbuthnot (open Apr–Oct: daily; tel: (01561) 361668) tells his life story. His lilting, limpid prose sings in your ears as you cross these rolling fields of rich red earth and granite boulders to a coast that becomes ever more riven and rugged as you near **Stonehaven ❻** and the big skies, luminous light, spare landscape and chilly challenge of the northeast.

"The Highland Fault meets the sea at Stonehaven, and when you cross it you say goodbye to ease and amplitude," writes John R. Allan, the northeast's most eloquent advocate. "By the stony fields and diffident trees you may guess you have come to a soil very roughly ground through the mills of God." The A92 to Aberdeen now by-passes Stonehaven, but this solid, dignified if plain little fishing port-turned-seaside resort is worth a visit for the drama of its cliffs and **Dunnottar Castle** (open daily; Nov–Mar: closed Sat and Sun; tel: (01569) 762173) standing on its own giant rock south of the town. In the dungeons of these spectral ruins Covenanters were left to rot and the Scottish Regalia – the "Honours of Scotland" – were concealed in the 17th century from Cromwell's Roundheads.

From Stonehaven to Aberdeen is a clear, high, exhilarating run of 15 miles (24 km) along the cliffs. But why not let the Granite City and the coast be the climax to your northeast tour and take, instead, the A957 to the lower Dee valley? Called the Slug Road from the Gaelic for a narrow passage, it deposits you near the little town of **Banchory ❼**, where you can watch salmon leaping at the **Bridge of Feugh** and visit the late 16th-century tower house of **Crathes** (open Easter–Oct: daily; tel: (01330) 844525) and its renowned gardens. This perfect castle is still furnished with period pieces and wall hangings as it was when the family seat of the Burnetts.

Royal haunts

The **Dee valley** is justly celebrated for its expansive beauty and the pellucid, peat-brown grace of its river, and at the handsome village of **Aboyne**, between Banchory and Ballater, you begin to tread on the rougher hem of the Eastern Highlands. Deeside's Royal associations make it the tourist honeypot of Aberdeenshire. **Ballater ❽** is where the family pops down to the shops (look for the "By Appointment" signs) while staying at **Balmoral** (open May–July: daily; Apr: closed Sun; tel: (01339) 742334). Since 1855 Balmoral has been a royal residence, though in midsummer the Queen shares her gardens with the public and her prayers with her subjects at nearby **Crathie** church. Eight miles (13 km) west of Balmoral on the A93 is the village of **Braemar ❾**, much loved by Queen Victoria, and best enjoyed in September when the Highland Gathering brings people from all over the world. Fairy-tale **Braemar Castle**'s surprising charm and intimacy stem from being lived in (open Easter–Oct: Sat–Thur; tel: (01339) 741219).

From Banchory you can strike over to Donside (the valley of Aberdeen's second, lesser known river), taking the A980 through the village of **Lumphanan ❿**, alleged to be the burial place of the doomed King Macbeth whose history has so often been confused with Shakespeare's fiction. But **Macbeth's Cairn** doesn't mark the grave of the king. Not only is it a prehistoric cairn, but it has now been established that Macbeth, like so many of the early Scottish kings, was buried on Iona. You can see at Lumphanan, however, one of Scotland's earliest medieval earthworks, the **Peel Ring of Lumphanan.**

Near the explosively-named village of Echt is **Castle Fraser** (open Easter, May, June, Sept: daily pm; July and Aug: daily; Oct: Sat and Sun pm; tel: (01330) 833463). Completed in 1636, it has been the home of the Fraser chiefs ever since. Extensive walks can be taken in the grounds.

Donside's metropolis is the little country town of **Alford ⓫**, now promoting itself as a tourist centre. It can offer the **Alford Valley Railway**, a narrow-gauge passenger steam railway which runs during the summer months; **Grampian Transport Museum** (open Apr–Oct: daily; tel: (01975) 562292) and nearby **Kildrummy Castle** (open Apr–Sept: Mon–Sat and Sun pm; tel: (01975) 571331) a romantic and extensive 13th-century ruin which featured prominently in the Jacobite Rebellion of 1715 and which now slumbers exotically in a Japanese water garden.

Older history can be found at the **Archaeolink** at Oyne (open Apr–Oct daily; tel: (01464) 851500) a "prehistory park" which takes you on a journey back in time.

Journey through the hills

Both Dee and Don have their sources in the foothills of the **Cairngorms**, that lonely, savage massif which dominates the Eastern Highlands. There is no direct route through its lofty bulk, but from Deeside and Donside you can pick up the road which circles round it and give yourself a thrilling journey.

At the hamlet of **Cock Bridge**, 32 miles (52 km) west of Alford, beside the austere, curtain-walled **castle of**

Highlight of the Donside summer is the Lonach Highland Gathering, traditional games of a kind more authentic than the glitzy gathering at Braemar.

BELOW: Balmoral Castle, the Queen's holiday home.

You can view Strath-spey in comfort and style from the Strath-spey Railway: the steam train runs through the valley during the summer months.

BELOW: blooms in the properous heartland of Aberdeenshire.

Corgarff (open Mon–Sat and Sun pm; Oct–Mar closed Mon–Fri; tel: (01975) 651460), the A939 becomes the **Lecht Road**, which rises precipitously to some 2,000 ft (600 metres) before careering giddily down into the village of Tomintoul. In winter, the Lecht is almost always the first main road in Scotland to be blocked with snow, encouraging an optimistic ski development at its summit. A mile or so to the north of that summit, look out for the **Well of the Lecht**. Above a small natural spring, a white stone plaque, dated 1745, records that five companies of the 33rd Regiment built the road from here to the Spey.

Tomintoul ⑫, at 1,600 ft (500 metres), is one of the highest villages in Scotland and a pickup point for the "Whisky Trail" which, if you have the energy and the interest, can take you meandering (or perhaps reeling) through eight famous malt whisky distilleries in and around the Spey Valley. The **Glenlivet Distillery** (open Mar–Oct: daily; tel: (01542) 783220) was the first in Scotland to be licensed. From Glenlivet you can also enjoy the extensive walks and cycleway network on the Crown Estate.

Strathspey – *strath* means valley – is one of the loveliest valleys in Scotland, as much celebrated for the excellence of its angling as for its malt whisky industry. When you descend from the dark uplands of the Lecht passage through Tomintoul to the handsome granite town of **Grantown-on-Spey** ⑬, you see a land gradually tamed and gentled by natural woodland, open pastures and the clear, comely waters of the River Spey itself.

Grantown, like so many of the small towns and large villages in this area, was an 18th-century "new town", planned and built by its local laird. It makes a good centre for exploring Strathspey and it's also within easy reach of the Moray Firth, and the leading resort and former spa town of Nairn. The route from

Grantown (the A939) takes you past the island castle of **Lochindorb** – once the lair of the Wolf of Badenoch – Alexander Stewart, the notorious outlawed son of Robert II, who sacked the town of Forres and destroyed Elgin Cathedral.

Nairn ⓮, when the sun shines – and the Moray Firth claims to have the biggest share of sunshine on the Scottish mainland – is a splendid place, even elegant, with fine hotels and golf courses, glorious beaches and big blue vistas to the distant hills on the north side of the firth. It is also at the heart of this amiable region's most picturesque and interesting attractions. On its doorstep is **Cawdor Castle** (open May–Oct: daily; tel: (01667) 404615), 14th-century home of the Thanes of Cawdor (more Macbeth associations); eastwards up the coast are the ghostly **Culbin Sands**; and on the Ardersier peninsula to the west is the awesome and still occupied **Fort George** (open Mon–Sat and Sun pm; tel: (01667) 462777) – one of the outstanding artillery fortifications of Europe – built to control and intimidate the Highlands after the 1745 Rebellion.

Blasted heath

The most poignant and atmospheric reminder of Charles Edward Stuart's costly adventure, however, is **Culloden Moor**, which lies between Nairn and Inverness. Culloden was the last battle fought on Britain's mainland and here in April 1746 the Jacobite cause was finally lost to internal conflicts and the superior forces of the Hanoverian Army. Now owned by the National Trust for Scotland, it is a melancholy, blasted place – in effect, a war graveyard where the Highlanders buried their dead in communal graves marked by rough stones bearing the names of each clan. The visitor centre (open Feb–Dec: daily; tel: (01463) 790607) tells the gruesome story of how in only 40 minutes the Prince's army

Map, pages 270–1

In a great sandstorm of 1695 the Culbin Sands finally overwhelmed the village of Culbin, which now lies buried beneath them.

BELOW: looking for a bargain at Turriff Show.

Aberdeenshire is said to have more castles, both standing and ruined, than any other county in Britain.

BELOW: rough seas can confine fishing boats to port for between three weeks and three months a year.

lost 1,200 men to the King's 310. "Butcher" Cumberland's Redcoats performed with such enthusiasm that they slaughtered some of the bystanders who had come out from Inverness to watch.

The coast and countryside to the east of Nairn is worth attention – a combination of fishing villages like **Burghead** and **Findhorn** (now famous for the Findhorn Foundation, an international "alternative" community whose life and work, based on meditation and spiritual practice, have turned the sand dunes into flourishing vegetable gardens). And there are pleasing, dignified inland towns built of golden sandstone like **Forres**, **Elgin** ⓑ and **Fochabers** the ancient capital of Moray. Elgin's graceful cathedral dates back to 1224 (it was rebuilt after its destruction by the Wolf of Badenoch in 1390) and, although now partially ruined, is undergoing restoration. With its medieval street plan still well preserved, Elgin must be counted one of the loveliest towns in Scotland.

Monks clad in coarse white habits add a medieval touch to the giant **Pluscarden Abbey** (open daily; tel: (01343) 890257), hidden in a sheltered valley 5 miles (8 km) southwest of Elgin. The abbey, founded in 1230, fell into disrepair until, in 1948, an order of converted Benedictines started to rebuild it.

Decision time

The **River Spey** debouches at Spey Bay, which is the site of the **Tugnet Ice House** (open May–Sept: daily; tel: (01309) 673701), built in 1830 to store ice for packing salmon and now housing an exhibition dedicated to the salmon fishing industry and wildlife of the Spey estuary. The Spey marks something of a boundary between the fertile, wooded country and sandy coast of the Moray Firth and that plainer, harsher land which pushes out into the North Sea.

Here the motoring tourist, with Aberdeen in sight, is faced with a choice. You can either cut the coastal corner by driving straight through the prosperous heartland of Aberdeenshire by way of **Keith, Huntly, Inverurie** and yet more Aberdeenshire castles (Huntly, Fyvie and Castle Fraser, to name but three); or you can hug the forbidding littoral of Banffshire and Buchan and see for yourself John R. Allan's "stony fields and diffident trees", the workmanlike ports of **Buckie, Fraserburgh** and **Peterhead**, and that whole chain of rough-hewn fishing villages and harbours which has harnessed this truculent coast into something productive. Here you will find gusty, spectacular seascapes, rich bird life and the enduring fascination of working harbours, fish markets and museums dedicated to the maritime history. One of these, in Fraserburgh, is **Scotland's Lighthouse Museum** (open daily; tel: (01346) 511022), which tells the story of the lights and keepers who manned them.

Banff **⑯** itself is a town of some elegant substance with a Georgian centre, while the 16th-century merchants' houses around **Portsoy** harbour have been agreeably restored. This village is also distinguished for the production and working of Portsoy marble, and a pottery and marble workshop are installed in one of the harbour buildings, while there is beauty and drama to be found in **Cullen** with its striking 19th-century railway viaducts and its sweep of sand.

Between Macduff and **Fraserburgh ⑰**, where the coast begins to take a right-angle bend, tortuous minor roads link the precipitous villages of **Gardenstown, Crovie** and **Pennan**, stuck like limpets to the cliffs, and south of **Peterhead ⑱** the sea boils into the **Bullers O'Buchan**, a high circular basin of rocky cliff which in spring and summer is home to untold thousands of seabirds.

Close by are the gaunt clifftop ruins of **Slains Castle**, said to have ignited

Map, pages 270–1

TIP

For a fascinating route along what was the Herring Coast – recalling the more prosperous days of the British fishing industry – follow the Fishing Heritage Trail.

BELOW: Macduff: the safest haven for fishing boats on the Moray Firth.

The Impact of Big Oil

The days when it was assumed that the North Sea's "black gold" would cure all Scotland's social and industrial ailments have long gone. The huge oil revenues (£7.5 billion a year) have disappeared into the maw of the British Treasury, and precious little has come back across the border. As one Scottish nationalist put it: "Scotland must be the only country on Earth to discover oil and become worse off".

Which is not quite true. Scotland may have no access to the revenues, but it has acquired a mature, technologically advanced industry which employs many thousands of people and underwrites a great many other jobs all over the country. The offshore oil industry almost (but not quite) makes up for the thousands of jobs lost in traditional heavy industries like coal, shipbuilding, engineering and steel.

Crude oil is now flowing from 49 oilfields off the east coast of Scotland. The fields range in size from established giants like Forties, Brent and Ninian to barely economic mini-fields like Arbroath and Ivanhoe-Rob Roy. Many are in the deep, stormy waters of the East Shetland Basin, while others lie under the shallower seas east of Edinburgh. The North Sea was producing, at its peak, nearly 120 million tonnes of oil a year, but by the early 1990s only 100 million tonnes a year was flowing.

The early days between 1972 and 1979, however, were astonishing. Every week new schemes were announced for supply bases, refineries and petrochemical works. Scotland was galvanised. The Scottish National Party (SNP) startled Britain by getting 11 members elected to parliament in 1974 on the crude but effective slogan "It's Scotland's Oil".

Heady days, but they didn't last. When the price of oil slumped in 1985–86 from $40 to less than $10 a barrel, recession struck the east coast, and job losses have continued ever since. But reports of the demise of Aberdeen have been greatly exaggerated. The old Granite City remains the oil capital of Europe, the town where every oil company, exploration firm, oil-tool manufacturer and diving company has a foothold.

The oil comes ashore in Scotland at three points: on the island of Flotta in Orkney, at St Fergus north of Aberdeen, and at Sullom Voe in Shetland. Sullom Voe is the biggest of the three terminals, with a "throughput" of 1.2 million barrels of oil a day from the oilfields of the East Shetland Basin. The tiny Shetland Island Council argued with the oil giants over the rent for Sullom Voe. The council asked for £100 million a year; the companies initially offered £300,000.

In the early days industrial Scotland had high hopes of "downstream" developments such as oil refineries and petrochemical plants. But not many came about, and those that were built employed very few people. It's a sign of the times that the Cromarty Firth and the Firth of Forth are now heavily used to "stack" redundant drilling rigs and pipe-laying barges. And companies have been scouting the east coast for a site to break up unwanted drilling rigs and platforms into scrap. ❑

Left: North Sea oil rig.

the imagination of Bram Stoker and inspired his novel Dracula. It is certainly true that Stoker spent holidays at the golfing resort of Cruden Bay, where the craggy shore begins to yield to sand until, at the village of Newburgh and the mouth of the River Ythan, you find the dramatic dune system of the **Sands of Forvie** nature reserve. South from here, an uninterrupted stretch of dune and marram grass reaches all the way to Aberdeen.

Granite city

Of all Britain's cities, **Aberdeen** 🔟 is the most isolated. It comes as a shock to drive through miles of empty countryside from the south and, breasting a hill, find revealed below you the great grey settlement clasped between the arms of Dee and Don, as if it were the simple, organic extension of rock and heath and shore instead of a complex human artifice. On the sea's horizon you might see a semi-submersible oil rig on the move; in the harbour, trawlers jostle with supply vessels; and there are raw new ribbon developments of housing and warehousing to the north and south of the city. But otherwise Aberdeen, in its splendid self-sufficiency and glorious solitude, remains curiously untouched by the coming of the oil industry.

Aberdeen is largely indifferent to the mixed reception it receives from outsiders. Its infuriating complacency, however, has been its strength, and will almost certainly be its salvation when the North Sea oil wells run dry and the city refocuses on its own considerable resources of sea, land and light industry.

Much of historic Aberdeen remains, although most of its imposing city centre dates only from the 19th century, with the building of **Union Street**, its main thoroughfare, in the early 1800s and the rebuilding of **Marischal College**, part

Map, pages 270–1

Writing in 1929, H.V. Morton was uncompromising in his description of Aberdeen: "... a city of granite palaces, inhabited by people as definite as their building material. Even their prejudices are of the same hard character."

BELOW: the graceful crown tower of King's College.

STONY FAÇADE

The city of Aberdeen inspires strong emotions. You are either convinced that its own conceit of itself is well deserved – the city's Book of Remembrance contains the sentiment, "Aberdeen to Heaven – nae a great step" – or you find its exposed interface with the North Sea and its granite austerity wintry of aspect and chilly of soul. Even those who affect to dislike it do so with ambivalence. The northeast's most famous writer, Lewis Grassic Gibbon, wrote: "It has a flinty shine when new – a grey glimmer like a morning North Sea, a cold steeliness that chills the heart... Even with weathering it acquires no gracious softness, it is merely starkly grim and uncompromising.... One detests Aberdeen with the detestation of a thwarted lover. It is the one haunting and exasperatingly lovable city in Scotland."

To counteract its critics, the city's tourist board has tried hard to change the image of Aberdeen from Granite City to Rose City, lavishing attention on every flower bed in the city. Its efforts were rewarded by winning the "Britain in Bloom" award 10 times – though now the city is debarred from entering to give other places a sporting chance.

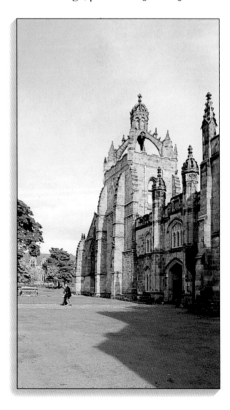

Marischal College is the second largest granite building in the world – the largest is the Escorial in Madrid.

of the ancient University of Aberdeen, in 1891. The façade of Marischal College, which stands just off Union Street in Broad Street, is an extraordinary fretwork of pinnacles and gilt flags in which the unyielding substance of white granite is made to seem delicate.

Union Street's die-straight mile (1.6 km) from Holborn Junction skirts the arboreal churchyard of St Nicholas, Aberdeen's "mither kirk", and terminates in the **Castlegate**, which is virtually the same square which has occupied that space since the 13th century. Its centrepiece is the 17th-century **Mercat Cross**, with its sculptured portrait gallery of the Stuart monarchs.

The cross is the focus of Aberdeen's long history as major market town and import-export centre. For centuries fishwives from **Fittie**, the fishing village at the foot of the Dee, and farmers from the expansive hinterland brought their produce to sell round the cross, while more exotic products from Europe and the New World were hefted up the hill from the harbour by porters from the Shore Porters' Society, Britain's oldest company. (Founded in 1498, Shore Porters now concentrate on furniture removals.)

Historic sights

Aberdeen's oldest quarter and civic origins, however, lie to the northwest of the city centre on the banks of the River Don, whose narrow, sandy estuary was never developed as harbour and port in the manner of its larger twin, the Dee. Although Aberdeen was already a busy port when it was granted a royal charter in the 12th century by King William the Lion, its earliest settlement was to be found clustered around **St Machar's Cathedral** in Old Aberdeen, once an independent burgh.

BELOW: local colour in Fittie village.

The cathedral, founded in the 6th century, is one of the oldest granite buildings in the city (although it has a red sandstone arch which is a remnant of an earlier building) and the cobbled streets and lamplit academic houses surrounding it are atmospheric and peaceful. Here, too, is Aberdeen's first university, **King's College** (founded in 1495 by Bishop Elphinstone).

Aberdeen's history has often been self-protective; the city gave the Duke of Cumberland, later to become infamous as "Butcher" Cumberland, a civic reception as he led his Hanoverian army north to confront Prince Charles Edward Stuart's Jacobites at Culloden. But it is to its credit that it offered protection to Robert the Bruce during Scotland's Wars of Independence in the 14th century. In return, Bruce gave the "Freedom Lands" to the city (which still bring it an income) and ordered the completion of the **Brig o' Balgownie**, whose building had been interrupted by the wars.

Present attractions

The vigorous **art gallery** on Schoolhill (open Mon–Sat and Sun pm; free) has an impressive collection of European paintings mainly from the 18th to the 20th century, as well as works by a number of contemporary Scottish artists and a sculpture court. For anyone with a military bent, the **Gordon Highlanders Museum** (open Apr–Oct: Tues–Sat and Sun pm) is a must. This unique collection tells the story of one of the most celebrated fighting units in the British Army. There is also a fine new **Maritime Museum** (open daily; free) that recalls Aberdeen's long and fascinating relationship with the sea.

A lively theatre, a succession of festivals and games – you could go on listing the more obvious attractions of Aberdeen. Today, besides all its other activities, Aberdeen confidently promotes itself as a holiday resort, and indeed it is one of the few cities to be recommended for a family holiday. Children of all ages make a beeline for **Satrosphere** in Justice Mill Lane (open Mon–Sat and Sun pm; Nov–Mar closed Tues), a "hands-on" interactive science and technology centre.

And between the mouths of the two rivers the sands are authentically golden, though don't expect to sunbathe often or comfortably on them: the northeast gets a major share of Scotland's sunshine, but Aberdeen's beach is open-backed and exposed to every bitter breeze from the North Sea. Its parks, however, are glorious, wonderfully well kept and celebrated, like many of the other open spaces, for their roses. The **Cruickshank Botanic Garden** (open Mon–Sat) in the University area also has a splendid variety of plants from many parts of the world.

Futher afield, **Hazelhead**, on the city's western perimeter, **Duthie Park**, with extensive winter gardens, and **Seaton Park** on the River Don are probably the most superior open spaces, but all have above-average play areas and special attractions for children during the summer. There is also a well-run permanent funfair at the beach, and a few miles inland at Maryculter in the Dee Valley one of the country's most attractive small "theme parks": **Storybook Glen** (open daily; Nov–Feb: closed Mon–Fri) with lifesize and giant tableaux of many favourite childhood characters. ❏

Map, pages 270–1

Brig o' Balgownie, near St Machar's Cathedral, is the oldest Gothic bridge in Scotland.

BELOW: At home in Storybook Glen.

THE NORTHERN HIGHLANDS

*Favourite haunt of royalty – past and present – the Highlands
is a place of many colours: faded industrial glory, wild northern
coastline, and the beauty of glen and mountain*

Map,
pages
270–1

Nowhere in Britain is the bloodied hand of the past so heavily laid as it is in the Highlands. The pages of its history read like a film script – and have often served as one. There are starring roles for Bonnie Prince Charlie, Flora MacDonald, Mary Queen of Scots, Rob Roy, the Wolf of Badenoch and Macbeth, with a supporting cast of clansmen and crofters, miners and fisher folk, businessmen and sportsmen.

The cameras could find no better point at which to start turning than **Inverness** ⑳, the natural "capital" of the Highlands. It is assured of that title by its easily fortified situation on the River Ness where the roads through the glens converge. Shakespeare sadly maligned the man who was its king for 17 years, Macbeth. His castle has disappeared, but from **Castlehill** a successor dominates the city: a pink cardboard cut-out, like a Victorian doll's house, that makes Flora Mac-Donald in bronze shield her eyes and her dog lift a paw.

In the nearby **Museum** (open Mon–Sat; free; tel: (01463) 237114), the death mask of Flora's Bonnie Prince shares cases with Mr Punch in his "red Garibaldi coat", and Duncan Morrison's puppet figure that once delighted local children. Traditions are strongly represented in silversmithing, taxidermy, bagpipes and fid-dles, and even a 7th-century Pictish stone depicting a wolf. Preserved in front of the **Town House**, on busy High Street, uphill from the river, is the **Clach-na-Cuddain**, a stone on which women rested their tubs of washing. **Abertarff House**, on Church Street, rescued from years of neglect by the National Trust for Scotland, is now its Highland Office, with a chim-neypiece marriage lintel of 1691 in the gift shop.

Here be monsters

From an area of Inverness rich in industrial archaeology the **Caledonian Canal** climbs through six locks like a flight of stairs to the "Hill of Yew Trees", **Tomnahurich**. This Highland waterway, which joins the North Sea and the Atlantic Ocean through the Great Glen, was pre-dicted by a local seer a century before it was built: "Full-rigged ships will be seen sailing at the back of Tomnahurich." Now you can set sail here in summer for a trip on **Loch Ness** and enjoy "a wee dram in the lin-gering twilight". The dram may assist you in spotting the Monster, the lake's supposed ancient occupant.

Another way to find "Nessie" is to board the Taurus, a five-person submarine for a one-hour voyage to the depths of Loch Ness, Britain's deepest body of fresh water. The submarine's base is just north of **Urquhart Castle** ㉑ (open daily), a picturesque ruin on the loch's edge (15 miles/24 km south of Inverness on the A82) which bears the scars of having been fought over for two centuries. Across the water, at Foyers, Britain's first hydroelectric scheme feeds power into the National Grid.

PRECEDING PAGES:
Suilven, Scotland's
Matterhorn.
LEFT: fishing at all
hours in Inverness.
BELOW: Flora Mac-
Donald, Inverness.

At **Fort Augustus** ㉒ (29 miles/48 km further south), the canal descends in another flight of locks near the **Clansmen Centre** (open Easter–Oct: daily; tel: (01320) 366444), which illustrates the glen's history from Pictish to modern times. The garrison, set up after the 1715 Jacobite Rising, later became a Bene-dictine abbey.

Turn right at **Invergarry** onto the A87 for the beauty of glen and mountain on the road to Kyle of Lochalsh and Skye. Or, continuing south on the A82, stop at the "Well of the Heads" monument, which records the murder of a 17th-cen-tury chieftain's two sons and, as reprisal, the deaths of seven brothers, whose heads were washed in the well, then presented to the chief.

The A82 now crosses to the east bank of **Loch Lochy**. Six miles (10 km) before Fort William is **Nevis Range**, where gondolas whisk you in 12 minutes to 2,150 ft (645 metres), giving stunning views of Scotland's highest mountains. On the outskirts of **Fort William** ㉓ (*see page 224*), take the A830 and you'll immediately reach "Neptune's Staircase", where eight locks lead the Caledon-ian Canal into the sea and from where there are grand views of Ben Nevis.

Outdoor attractions

From Inverness you can also head southeast towards **Aviemore** ㉔ and the mag-nificent scenery of the Cairngorms. Aviemore barely existed before the railway came here on its way to Inverness in the 1880s, but since the creation of the Aviemore Centre in the 1960s it has become a popular destination for outdoor enthusiasts. Nearby, at Carrbridge, is the **Landmark Centre** (open daily; tel: (01479) 841613). The attractions at this heritage park include theme displays, a treetop trail through the forest, an adventure playground and horse logging.

BELOW: Loch Ness: inspiration for mon-ster fantasies.

Six miles (10 km) southwest of Aviemore at Kincraig is the **Highland Wildlife Park** (open daily; tel: (01540) 651270), an outpost of the Royal Zoological Society of Scotland. Here once indigenous animals, including boar and bison, run free. Part of the park is drive-through, part walk-through. Further south is the **Highland Folk Museum** at **Kingussie** (open daily; Nov–Mar: closed Sat and Sun; tel: (01540) 661307). The museum has displays on Highland life, architecture, crafts and farming, and a peat fire fills a replica of an Isle of Lewis stone house with pungent smoke.

Map, pages 270–1

Moving north

Back at the northern end of the Great Glen the A9 crosses the neck of the **Black Isle**, which is neither island nor black but forest and fertile farmland, and is bisected by roads serving the oil centres on the north shore of the Cromarty Firth.

Two plaques can be found at **Fortrose ㉕**, on the east shore. One marks where Scotland's last witch was burnt in 1722; the other where the Brahan Seer was burnt in an oil barrel in the 17th century but not before he had foretold the building of the Caledonian Canal, the demise of crofting and much more. Also in Fortrose are the magnificent ruins of a 14th-century cathedral. Nearby, at Rosemarkie, is **Groam House Museum** (open Mon–Sat and Sun pm; Oct–Apr: closed Mon–Fri; tel: (01381) 620961), a Pictish interpretive centre with a superb collection of sculptured stones, audio-visual displays and rubbings.

Cromarty ㉖, at the extreme tip of the Isle, lost face as a Royal Burgh through declining fortunes as a sea port and trading community, but has earned rightful popularity as a place where visitors can literally step back into history in the unspoilt old town. Taped tours point out some of the most beautiful late 18th-

Real-life Highland folk recall days gone by at the Highland Folk Museum .

BELOW: cross-country skiing near Loch Morlich.

OUTDOOR PURSUITS

It's doubtful if the Clan Grant, whose war cry was "Stand Fast Craigellachie", could have resisted the forces at work in Aviemore, below their rallying place. The quiet Speyside halt has been transformed into a year-round resort by the opening of roads into the Cairngorms and chairlifts for the skiers. Brewers built the Aviemore Centre in the 1960s and soon hotels, restaurants, a theatre, ice rink and go-cart tracks followed. Shops along the main street cater for the mass of visitors, selling outdoor equiment for skiing and mountaineering. In summer, Aviemore goes German for a Beer Fest with oompah music, sauerkraut, bratwurst, and foaming tankards. The Highlands answers with nail hammering, haggis throwing, barrel hurling and the Games.

The beginnings of Aviemore's expansion date back to the 1880s when the railway arrived here on its way to Inverness. Once an important junction, Aviemore had a branch line to Grantown-on-Spey and Forres. Today, Aviemore is still a central base from which to explore the spectacular moutains and moors: a relaxing way to enjoy the scenery can be had by wining and dining on a Highland Railway steam train which runs in the summer months en route from Aviemore to Boat of Garten.

TIP

If you want a taste of the Strathpeffer waters, call in at the town's Water Sampling Pavilion.

century buildings in Britain: the **Courthouse**, now a prize-winning museum (open Easter–Oct: daily; Nov–Easter: closed am; tel: (01381) 600418); the thatched cottage where early geologist Hugh Miller, Cromarty's most famous scholarly son, lived (open May–Sept: Mon–Sat and Sun pm; tel: (01381) 600245); and the **East Kirk**, with its three wooden lofts.

A road leads to **South Sutor**, one of two precipitous headlands, guarding the narrow entrance to the Firth of Cromarty, where numerous oil rigs are moored. Around the rigs swim the North Sea's only resident group of bottlenose dolphins, plus innumerable grey and common seals.

Though Scots had long known the local sulphur and chalybeate springs at **Strathpeffer ㉗**, it took a doctor who had himself benefited to give substance to "miracle" recoveries and incidentally recognise their profitable potential. Dr Morrison opened his pump room around 1820 and the new railway brought thousands to fill the hotels and, if they felt inclined, enjoy "low-pressure subthermal reclining manipulation douche". A couple of wars intervened and the spa declined; but, like all things Victorian, this elegant town is enjoying something of a revival as a resort of character. The old railway station is now a visitor centre.

On leaving Strathpeffer, join the A835 which, after **Garve**, winds through Strath Ben and **Achnasheen ㉘**. From here the southern leg (A890) through Glen Carron is the stuff of photomurals, with Kyle of Lochalsh at the end of the rainbow that leads across the sea to Skye. Achnasheen's northern leg (A832) points for 9 miles (14 km) to **Kinlochewe ㉙** at the head of **Loch Maree** and close to the National Nature Reserve of **Beinn Eighe**. In the pine forests there is a good chance of seeing rare and protected wildlife: deer, wildcat, pine marten and golden eagle. Nature trails begin in the car park.

BELOW: a ploughing contest near Inverness.

Changing times

Alternatively, from **Dingwall** – was Macbeth really born here? – road (A9) and rail cling to the east coast. At **Evanton** is the **Clanland and Sealpoint Centre**: (open daily; tel: (01349) 830000), an exhibition of Highland history and wildlife in a restored 18th-century building. There's a good chance of seeing seals on the shore walk. Near **Alness** ㉚, on a hill, is a replica of the Gate of Negapatam in India, which General Sir Hector Munro, hero of its capture, had built by local men. Today Alness is dormitory to **Invergordon** on Cromarty Firth, which offered shelter to Britain's navy through two world wars and suffered the closure of its naval base in 1956. The area has also seen dramatic changes since the choice of Nigg Bay for the construction of oil rig platforms.

Memories at **Tain** ㉛ are older, going back to 1066, when it became a Royal Burgh. Though St Duthac was born and buried here, it didn't save the two chapels dedicated to him from disastrous fires – or guarantee sanctuary. Today visitors can call in at the **Glenmorangie Distillery** (open Mon–Fri; tel: (01862) 892477) to see how the famous malt whisky is made and to try a sample.

From Tain, the A836 leads to **Bonar Bridge** and motorists have to adjust to negotiate single-track roads and the sheep that share them. This is Viking country, more Scandinavian than Scottish, with spectacular views of heather-covered moor and loch.

At **Invershin** is a superbly situated castle without a burden of history. Retainers, some heavy-laden, come and go beneath the towers and battlements with which it is over endowed. It was built as late as 1914 for the Duchess of Sutherland and is now a youth hostel.

"All roads meet at Lairg," it's said. Sometimes in August it seems all the sheep

Map, pages 270–1

Beinn Eighe is a fascinating geological "pudding" of old red sandstone topped with white quartzite.

BELOW: crofting is still a way of life in remote areas of the Highlands.

Dunrobin Castle is the Scottish home of the Dukes of Sutherland, who played a leading role in the Highland Clearances.

in Scotland do as well. **Lairg** ❸❷ is in the heart of Sutherland crofting country and the lamb sales identify it as a major market-place. Mirrored in the quiet waters of Loch Shin is an Iron Age hut circle on the hill above the village.

The eastern spoke (A839) from Lairg's hub reaches the coast at Loch Fleet and **Dornoch** ❸❸, where some regard Royal Dornoch, opened in 1616, as offering better golf than the Old Course at St Andrews. Dornoch Castle's surviving tower suffered the indignities of use as a garrison, court-house, jail, school and private residence. Now it's a hotel. The lovely Cathedral is also a survivor: badly damaged in a 17th-century fire, it was largely restored in the 1920s.

To the north is **Golspie,** which lives in the shadow of the Sutherlands. An oversize statue of the First Duke looks down from the mountain; a stone in the old bridge is the clan's rallying point; and nearby is the Duchess's **Dunrobin Castle** (open Apr–mid-Oct: Mon–Sat; tel: (01408) 633177), an improbable confection of pinnacles and turrets trying to be a schloss or a chateau. Formal gardens are a riot of colour in summer. The prehistoric fort at Carn Liath a little further along the coast is a nice antidote.

The goldrush that brought prospectors to the burns of **Helmsdale** ❸❹ in the 1860s was short-lived. Its main attraction today is the **Timespan Heritage Centre** (open Easter–mid-Oct: Mon–Sat and Sun pm; tel: (01431) 821327), which brings the history of the Highlands to life; there is also a large garden with a unique collection of medicinal and herbal plants. Intrepid visitors keep going north to **Caithness**, for centuries so remote from the centres of Scottish power that it was ruled by the Vikings. Trade links were entirely by sea and in the boom years of the fishing industry scores of harbours were built. The fleets have gone; the harbours remain.

The A9 to **Berriedale** twists spectacularly past the ravines of the Ord of Caithness and on to **Dunbeath**, where a few lobster boats are a reminder of past glories. Here too is the **Laidhay Croft Museum** (open Easter–Oct: daily; tel: (01593) 731244), a restored traditional longhouse with stable, house and byre all under one roof. **Lybster** ❸ offers more bustle, but at **Mid Clyth** leave the road at a sign, "Hill o' Many Stanes", for a mystery tour. On a hillside are 22 rows, each with an average of eight small stones, thought to be Bronze Age.

Herring were the backbone of **Wick**'s prosperity and come to life again in the **Wick Heritage Centre** (open June–Sept: Mon–Sat; tel: (01955) 605393). More than 1,000 boats once set sail to catch the "silver darlings". Now the near-deserted quays give the harbour a wistful charm.

Natural attractions

For cross-country record breakers, **John o' Groats** ❸, at the end of the A9, has a natural attraction – although, contrary to popular belief, it is not the northernmost point in Britain. A Dutchman, Jan de Groot, came here in 1500 under orders from James IV to set up a ferry service to Orkney to consolidate his domination over this former Scandinavian territory. A mound and a flagstaff commemorate the site of his house. Boat trips run from the harbour to Orkney and to **Duncansby Head**, 2 miles (4 km) to the east, where many species of birds nest on the dramatic towering stacks. From here a road runs to the lighthouse. West of John o' Groats, on the A836, is the **Castle of Mey**, the Queen Mother's home. Further on is **Dunnet Head**, the British mainland's most northerly point.

The approaches to **Thurso** ❸ are heralded by the Caithness "hedges" that line the fields, the flagstones that were once shipped from local quarries to every cor-

Jan de Groot's response to requests from his eight sons as to who should succeed him was to build an octagonal house with eight doors and with an octagonal table in the middle so that each sat at the "head".

Map, pages 270–1

BELOW: spectacular cliffs carved out by the sea at Duncansby Head.

ner of the old Empire. The streets of Calcutta were paved by Caithness. **Fisher-biggins**, the fishermen's old quarter, is a facsimile reproduction from 1940, but elsewhere there is pleasant Victorian town planning. **Scrabster** is Thurso's outport, with a ferry to Orkney. The site of Scotland's first nuclear power research station, now defunct, at **Dounreay** was partly chosen for its remoteness.

The furthest point

It's an odd feeling: nothing between you and the North Pole except magnificent cliff scenery. At **Tongue** ㊳ the sea loch pokes deep into the bleak moorland, and near **Durness** ㊴, which has some huge expanses of wonderful beach, the Alt Smoo River drops from the cliff into the Caves of Smoo. From Durness, a combined ferry and bus service travels to **Cape Wrath**. From here, the top left-hand corner of Britain, Orkney and the Outer Hebrides can be seen. Look out for cooties, sea cockies, tammies and tommienoories (puffins by another name).

The rich supplies of herring inspired the British Fisheries Society in 1788 to build fisher cottages at Ullapool and improve the harbour.

The return to Lairg can be made south from Tongue on the lovely A836 through **Altnaharra** ㊵, where crosses, hut circles and Pictish brochs abound. From Durness the A838 joins the western coast at **Scourie** ㊶, where mermaids are mistaken for seals and palm trees grow.

Ullapool ㊷, 52 miles (83 km) south of Scourie, is a resort for all seasons, beautifully situated on Loch Broom facing the sunset. The **Ullapool Museum and Visitor Centre** (open Mon–Sat; tel: (01854) 612987), in a former Telford church, has interactive displays on the history and people of the area. Today, a car ferry serves Stornoway in Lewis and trippers leave for the almost deserted but delightfully named **Summer Isles**. And smoking is good for you at **Achiltibuie** ㊸, where fish and game are cured by being steeped in spicy aromatic brines. ❑

Below: looking toward Suilven.

Peatland versus Profit

One person's wilderness is another's development potential. This age-old conflict of interests has been at the centre of a bitter dispute between conservationists and business interests in the Highlands as commercial foresters talk about expanding the 13 percent of Scotland that is tree-covered to 30 percent by the beginning of the 21st century.

At the centre of the controversy is the Flow Country of Caithness and Sutherland in the far north, so called because the peat bogs which cover it appear to be moving like a slowly advancing glacier. This extraordinary landscape, which is one of Europe's last remaining wildernesses, is a breeding ground for many of Britain's most important wading-birds such as the rare greenshank, the merlin and the black-throated diver. Yet vast new forests of lodgepole pine and sitka spruce are marching across the peatland, destroying the bird's habitats.

The forestry industry argues that the new plantations help cut Britain's import bill for timber, but the true propulsion for the accelerating afforestation is that it provides generous tax concessions for wealthy investors – such as London-based sportsmen, pop stars and television personalities.

So remote is this vast area of soggy open moorland and low, featureless hills that until recently only a handful of bird-watchers and fishermen realised the extent to which "tax-avoidance forestry" was advancing. Planting in Scotland requires no planning permission and the investment companies behind the schemes kept an understandably low profile. The other major planter, the Forestry Commission, has traditionally possessed such wide powers that it is known in the Highlands as "a state within a state".

The Flow Country, thanks to its magical landscape, provided a potent focus for pressure groups wishing to draw the media's attention to the problem. But elsewhere in Scotland huge numbers of conifers have been planted by forestry companies. About one-fifth of the southwest region of Dumfries and Galloway is now forested, and hill farms in the Borders area have also had to make way for trees. Islanders on Arran, in the Clyde estuary, began calling their island "Little Finland" as more and more of it disappeared under encroaching conifers.

The debate is far from one-sided, however. Many Scots, bemused to find that familiar areas have become "eco-systems", are impatient with the conservationists. The now defunct Highlands and Islands Development Board argued that a ban on forestry and other land uses would kill prospects for up to 2,000 local jobs and would jeopardise the economic future of whole communities. The Highland Regional Council agree: what was the point of having no trees, it asked, if it led to no jobs and no people?

The conservationists had an answer. Forestry employs relatively few people, they said, whereas tourism provides 100,000 jobs in Scotland. And tourists won't want to gaze at a landscape of lodgepole pine. ❑

RIGHT: the unspoilt Highlands.

HIGHLAND FLORA AND FAUNA

The wilderness of northern Scotland may appear to be older than living memory, but humans have actually had a big impact on its natural history

The symbol of Scotland – the thistle – is not tough enough for the Highlands. Heather, bilberry (*left*), bog cotton, asphodel and sphagnum moss (a springy, water-retaining plant that eventually rots down into peat) are the plant survivors here.

But ranging across this unrelentingly bony land are a couple of other particularly resilient symbols of Scotland – golden eagles and red deer.

Red deer in the Highlands are thought to number 330,000, a population which is barely restrained by the huge deerstalking industry. In the summer the herds are almost invisible to all but the hardiest walkers, but in the winter they descend into river valleys in search of food. The golden eagle is virtually invisible all year round, although the population is relatively stable in the mountains. Recent moves have re-established pairs of white-tailed sea-eagles on the island of Rum, though breeding hasn't yet been particularly successful.

Causing concern is the capercaillie, a turkey-sized game bird with the mating call of a brass band. Although it is no longer hunted, it has never learned to cope with modern deer fences: flying low through woodland, it crashes straight into them at speed.

Another distinctive Highland bird is also vanishing fast. The corncrake's unmistakeable rasping call is only heard in remote corners of the outer Hebridean islands.

CURSED WEE BEASTIE

One thriving specimen of Highland natural history is often omitted from the brochures: the biting midge. There are some 34 species of midge in Scotland. Only two or three attack humans, and *Culicoides impunctatus* (with distinctive speckled wings) does the lion's share. In the end, you have to laugh, or they'd drive you crazy. After all, as they say, midges are compassionate creatures: kill one, and a couple of thousand arrive for the funeral.

▷ **GOLDEN EAGLE**
Eagle pairs mate for life. A young eagle will stay with its parents for up to a year before setting off in search of new territory and a mate of its own.

▽ **WATER MAMMALS**
Seals are more timid than they used to be, thanks to aggressive fish farmers. Otters survive in wilder areas, and there are efforts to re-introduce beavers to a couple of rivers.

▷ **HERD INSTINCT**
The idea that deer are nomadic and range for great distances in search of food is a romantic misconception. A study project on the island of Rum proved that most animals remained "hefted" to the couple of square miles where they were born.

◁ **RED GROUSE**
The red grouse, a game bird tough enough to nest on open moorland, has suffered heavily from over-hunting by humans and by birds of prey. Intensive studies have so far failed to come up with a solution which will bring the numbers back up again. It is now officially an endangered species.

RETURN OF THE LONESOME PINE

△ PINE MARTEN
There are only 3,000 of these small nocturnal mammals left in Great Britain, all in Scotland, where they nest in hollow trees. Their numbers were drastically reduced by the fur-trade in the early 20th century.

◁ YELLOW SAXIFRAGE
The saxifrage is common in the Arctic, but it regularly adds a splash of colour to Scottish moorlands. The most colourful season in the Highlands is autumn, when the heather is in bloom.

Long ago, most of the now-desolate areas of the Highlands were forested. Over the centuries the trees were felled for timber and to accommodate livestock. Deer and sheep are very effective grazers, and tree shoots don't stand a chance. Stop at a loch to compare the growth onshore with that on offshore islands and you will see how destructive grazing animals can be.

Several decades ago the Forestry Commission, a government body, set about fencing off areas of moorland for re-forestation. To make the initiative economically viable they chose the fast-growing sitka spruce, which they planted in marching rows. The result is not particularly pleasing on the eye, and there has been controversy over the use of public money. There are also worries about the damage coniferisation causes to the unique habitats in many areas – like the areas of bogland in parts of Caithness.

Recently several initiatives to reforest large areas with native Scots pine (*above*) and deciduous trees have been started on privately-purchased land by charitable organisations such as the Royal Society for the Protection of Birds, John Muir Trust and Will Woodlands Trust. It will be many years before these large-scale plantings start to show themselves on the landscape.

ORKNEY

In few places in the world is the marriage of landscape and seascape so harmonious, nor is there such a profusion of archaeological wonders and variety of wildlife

Six miles (12 km) of sea separate the northeast corner of Scotland from an archipelago of 70 islands, about one-third of which are inhabited. This is Orkney (the word means "seal islands" in old Icelandic), which extends over 1,200 sq. miles (3,100 sq. km). If you believe there are more islands it may be because you have drunk too well of the products of Orkney's two distilleries or are counting seals – both common and grey – which abound in these waters.

The "ey" is Old Norse for islands and one should refer to Orkney and not "the Orkneys" or "the Orkney islands". It also announces an ancient affiliation with Norway, an affiliation historical rather than geographical, for Norway lies 300 miles (480 km) to the east. Orkney was a Norwegian appendage until the end of the 15th century and the true Orcadian is more Norse than Scot. With a rich tradition of sagas, it's no surprise that 20th-century Orkney has produced such distinguished literati as Edwin Muir, Eric Linklater and George Mackay Brown.

To Orcadians, Scotland is the "sooth" (south) and never the "mainland", for that is the name of the group's principal island: when inhabitants of the smaller islands visit the largest, therefore, they journey to **Mainland**, and when they travel to the UK they are off "sooth" to Scotland. Not that there are many of them to travel: the population is about 19,000, of whom one-quarter live in the capital, Kirkwall. Travel within the archipelago is by ferries and more often by planes. The Loganair flight between Westray and Papa Westray is the shortest commercial flight in the world. In perfect weather conditions, it takes only one minute.

LEFT: the 12th-century Kirkwall Cathedral, Orkney. **BELOW:** Kirkwall harbour: familiar to sailors in both world wars.

Ancient and modern

To wander these islands is, for the dedicated lover of archaeology, a taste of paradise. Orkney offers an uninterrupted continuum of mute stones from Neolithic times (about 4500 BC) through the Bronze and Iron Ages to about AD 700, followed by remains from the days when the islands were occupied successively by the Celts and the Vikings.

Kirkwall ❶ is dominated by the 12th-century **St Magnus Cathedral** (open Mon–Sat; free). Construction began in the Norman style but its many Gothic features attest to more than 300 years of building. Facing the cathedral is the ruined **Bishop's Palace** (open Apr–Sept: Mon–Sat and Sun pm; tel: (01856) 875461), a massive structure with a round tower reminiscent of a castle. In the 13th century the great Norwegian king, Haakon Haakonsson, lay dying here while Norse sagas were read aloud to him. Nearby is a third ancient building, the **Earl Patrick's Palace** (open as Bishop's Palace), a romantic gem of renaissance architecture. It is roofless: in the 17th century its slates were removed to build the town hall.

Other Kirkwall attractions are the **Tankerness House Museum** (open Mon–Sat and Sun pm; Oct–Apr: closed Sun; tel: (01856) 873191), which presents the complete story of Orkney from prehistory to the present; the **Orkney Library**, one of the oldest public libraries in Scotland; and a golf course.

War and peace

South of Kirkwall is the great natural harbour of **Scapa Flow**. Here, the captured German fleet was anchored after World War I and here the fleet was scuttled. Only six of the 74 ships remain on the bed of this deep, spacious bay, which is bliss for the scuba-diver, a peaceful cornucopia for the deep sea angler.

The island of **Flotta**, at the south of Scapa Flow, is a North Sea oil terminal through which 12 percent of Britain's oil passes. This is the Orcadians' only concession to black gold.

Fifteen miles (24 km) west of Kirkwall is picturesque **Stromness ❷**, Orkney's second town. A well on the main street testifies that, in the 17th century, Stromness was developed by the Hudson Bay Company, whose ships made this their last port of call before crossing the Atlantic. The **Pier Arts Centre** open Tues–Sat; free) houses a collection of 20th-century paintings and sculpture, and the museum (open May–Sept: daily; Oct–Apr: closed Sun; tel: (01856) 850025) has natural history exhibits, ship models and a feature on the scuttling of the German Fleet at Scapa Flow. For more active pursuits, there is an indoor swimming pool and a golf course.

Most of Mainland's major archaeological sites are to the north of Stromness. Crawl into awesome **Maes Howe ❸** (open Apr–Oct: Mon–Sat and Sun pm), the most magnificent chambered tomb in Britain, which dates from 3500 BC.

TIP

On average, every square mile (2.6 sq. km) on Orkney has three recorded items of antiquarian interest. The key to these is often kept at the nearest farmhouse and payment is made by placing money in an honour-box.

BELOW: One in six of all seabirds that breed in Britain nests in Orkney.

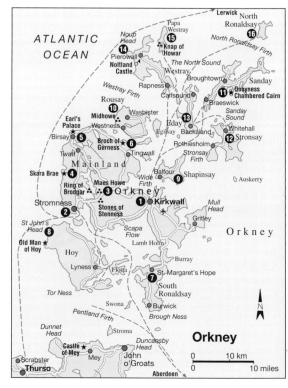

Within is a spacious burial chamber built with enormous megaliths; on some of these are incised the world's largest collection of 12th-century runic (Viking) hieroglyphics.

Near Maes Howe are the **Ring of Brodgar** and the **Standing Stones of Stenness**, the remains of two of Britain's most spectacular stone circles. When the former (whose name means "Circle of the Sun") was completed, about 1200 BC, it consisted of 60 standing stones set along the circumference of a circle about 340 ft (103 metres) in diameter. Today, 27 stones, the tallest at 14 ft (4 metres), still stand. The four giant monoliths of Stenness are all that remain of that particular circle of 12 stones, erected about 2300 BC.

Skara Brae ❹ (open Mon–Sat and Sun pm; tel: (01856) 874815), Britain's Pompeii, sits on the Atlantic coast alongside a superb sandy beach. The settlement, remarkably well preserved, consists of several dwelling houses and connecting passages and was engulfed by sand 4,500 years ago after having been occupied for 500 years. Skara Brae is a quintessential Stone Age site; no metal of any kind was found: all furniture – beds, chairs – are made of stone.

Five miles (8 km) north is **Birsay ❺** with the 16-century **Earl's Palace**. Opposite is the **Brough of Birsay**, a tiny tidal island (avoid being stranded); it is covered with rich remains of Norse and Christian settlements. A further 8 miles (13 km) east, and guarding Eynhallow Sound, is the **Broch of Gurness ❻** (open Apr–Sept: Mon–Sat and Sun pm; tel: (01831) 579478).

The principal southern islands are South Ronaldsay, Burray, Lamb Holm, Hoy and Flotta. Technically, the first three are no longer islands, being joined to Mainland by the **Churchill Barriers**. These were built by Italian prisoners during World War II after a German submarine penetrated Scapa Flow and sank

see map opposite

One stone in Maes Howe is surely the forerunner of today's graffiti. It says simply: "Ingigerd is the sweetest woman there is."

BELOW: Ring of Brodgar: 3,000 years ago there were 60 stones.

Brochs are Iron Age (100 BC to AD 300) strongholds built by the Picts. Unique to Scotland and ubiquitous in Orkney, they were circular at their base and their massive walls tapered gently inwards to a height of about 60 ft (18 metres).

the battleship *Ark Royal*. On **Lamb Holm** enter some Nissen huts and be astonished at the beautiful chapel built with scrap metal by these prisoners. The **Orkney Wireless Museum** (open June–Sept; tel: (01865) 874272) at **St Margaret's Hope ❼** on **South Ronaldsay** displays communication equipment from World War II.

Hoy, the second largest island of the archipelago, is spectacularly different. The southern part is low-lying but at the north stand the heather-covered Cuilags (1,420 ft/426 metres), from where all Orkney, except Little Rysa, can be viewed. A stroll along the 1,140-ft (367-metre) high **St John's Head ❽**, which teems with seabirds (beware the swooping great skuas) and boasts some rare plants, is sheer delight for the geologist, ornithologist and botanist or for those who just like to ramble. Immediately south of St John's Head is Orkney's most venerable inhabitant, the **Old Man of Hoy**, who, sad to say, appears to be cracking up. This 450-ft (135-metre) perpendicular sandstone column continues to challenge the world's leading rock-climbers.

Northward-bound

And so to the northern islands. Fertile **Shapinsay ❾** is so near Mainland that it is called suburbia. Also near Mainland, but further west and readily reached by local ferry are **Rousay ❿** and **Egilsay**. Rich archaeological finds have earned the former the sobriquet "Egypt of the North". Visit the remarkable 76-ft-long (23-metre) Neolithic **Midhowe** chambered tomb (open Apr–Oct: Mon–Sat and Sun pm), aptly named the "Great Ship of Death", which has 12 burial compartments each side of a central passage. Nearby is the magnificent **Midhowe Broch**. Ascend the summit of Mansemass Hill and stroll to Ward Hill

BELOW: The chapel built in Orkney by Italian prisoners during World War II.

for superb views of **Eynhallow**, medieval Orkney's Holy Island, between Rousay and Mainland.

On **Egilsay** an unusual round church, which has affinities with similar buildings in Ireland, marks the 12th-century site of the martyrdom of St Magnus.

Low-lying **Sanday**, with its white beaches, has room for a golf course but not to the exclusion of archaeological remains. Most important is the **Quoyness Chambered Cairn ⓫** (open Apr–Oct: Mon–Sat and Sun pm), standing 13 ft high (3 metres) and dating from about 2900 BC. It is similar to, but even larger than, Maes Howe. **Stronsay ⓬**, another low-lying island with sandy beaches, was formerly the hub of the prosperous Orkney herring industry. **Eday ⓭** may be bleak and barren, yet it is paradise for bird-watchers and has the customary complement of archaeological edifices.

Westray, the largest northern island, is unique in that its population is increasing. This is largely because of a successful fishing fleet which contradicts the allegation that the Orcadian is "a farmer with a boat". **Noup Head ⓮** is Westray's bird reserve and splendid viewpoint. The island also has a golf course and the ruined renaissance **Notland Castle**. **North Hill Nature Reserve** on **Papa Westray ⓯** is home to arctic terns and skuas. At **Knap of Howar** (open Apr–Oct: Mon–Sat and Sun pm) there are considerable remains of the earliest standing dwelling houses in northwest Europe (approximately 3000 BC). Their occupants, archaeologists have found, had "a strong preference for oysters".

On the most northerly island, **North Ronaldsay ⓰**, a dyke around the island confines sheep to the shore, leaving better inland pastures for cattle. Seaweed, the sole diet of these sheep, results in dark meat with an unusually rich flavour: an acquired taste. ❑

Map, page 300

BELOW: Orkney boasts the world's shortest commercial flight. It lasts one minute.

SHETLAND

Map,
page 308

*Remote and mysterious, the Shetland islands are a geologist
and bird-watcher's paradise, withstanding the pounding of the sea
and – more recently – the invasion of oil companies*

The writer Jan Morris called them "inset islands". In those two words she succinctly defined the mystery of the **Shetland Islands**, whose remoteness (200 miles/320 km to the north of Aberdeen) means that, in maps of Britain, they are usually relegated to a box in the corner of a page.

The 20 or so inhabited islands – nearly 80 more are uninhabited – are dotted over 70 miles (112 km) of swelling seas and scarcely seem part of Britain at all. The declining population (23,000) doesn't regard itself as British, or even as Scottish, but as Norse. The nearest mainland town is Bergen in Norway. Norwegian is taught in the schools. The heroes of myths have names like Harald Hardrada and King Haakon Haakonsson.

Spring comes late, with plant growth speeding up only in June. Rainfall is heavy, mists are frequent and gales (record gust: 177 miles/285 km an hour) keep the islands virtually treeless. It's never very cold, even in mid-winter, thanks to the North Atlantic Drift; and in mid-summer (the "Simmer Dim") it never quite gets dark.

The late-January festival of Up-Helly-Aa is loosely based on a pagan fire festival intended to herald the impending return of the sun. A procession of *guizers* (men dressed in winged helmets and shining armour) parades through the streets carrying burning torches with which they set fire to a replica of a Viking longship. It is an authentic fiesta for islanders only, but at other times the Shetlander is exceptionally hospitable and talkative. When he says, "You'll have a dram", it's an instruction not an enquiry.

PRECEDING PAGES:
Lerwick, Shetland's
capital.
LEFT: Britain's most
northerly lighthouse.
BELOW: Shetland
knitters at work.

Old and new settlements

Two check-in counters confront passengers at **Sumburgh Airport** on the main island, **Mainland**: one is for fixed-wing aircraft, the other for helicopters. North Sea oil generates the traffic and at one time threatened to overwhelm the islands. But the oil companies, pushed by a determined local council, made conspicuous efforts to lessen the impact on the environment and, although half of Britain's oil flows through the 1,000-acre (400-hectare) **Sullom Voe** terminal on a strip of land at the northern end of Mainland, they seem to have succeeded beyond most islanders' expectations. The 16 crude oil tanks, each holding 21 million gallons (95 million litres) were painted mistletoe-green, 124 species of birds have been logged within the terminal boundary, and outside the main gates a traffic-sign gives priority to otters.

A concentrated anthropological history of the islands is located at **Jarlshof ❶**, a jumble of buildings near the airport. Waves of settlers from the Stone, Bronze and Iron Ages built dwellings here, each on the ruins of its predecessor. The Vikings built on top of that and medieval farmsteads later buried the Viking traces. At

It's worth attending a folk concert in Shetland, as the islands are full of astonishingly accomplished fiddlers.

the end of the 19th century the site was just a grassy mound, topped with a medieval ruin. Then a wild storm laid bare massive stones in a bank above the beach and archaeologists moved in. Hearths were found where peat fires burned 3,000 years ago. Today old wheelhouses (so called because of their radial walls) have been revealed and an exhibition area, (open Apr–Sept: Mon–Sat and Sun pm; tel:(01950) 460112) fleshes out Jarlshof's history.

En route to the capital, Lerwick, 27 miles (43 km) to the north, the offshore island of **Mousa** is home to sheep and ponies, and also to a spectacularly well-preserved broch, a round dry-stone tower more than 40 ft (13 metres) high.

Lerwick ❷ looks no more planned than Jarlshof was. The old town has charm, with intimate stone-paved alleys leading off the main street of granite houses and dignified shops (no chain stores here). The windows of the baronial-looking **town hall** were presented to the town by Norway, Holland and Germany as thanks for Shetland's kindness to seamen.

The sea dominates the **Shetland Museum**, (open Mon–Sat; free; tel:(01595) 695057), sited above the library in Hillhead. Its theme is the history of life in Shetland from prehistory to the present. It has a collection of 5,000-year-old beads, pots and pumice stones found when excavating Sumburgh airport.

Six miles (10 km) from Lerwick is the old fishing port of **Scalloway ❸**, once Shetland's capital. Its main feature is the gaunt ruins of an early 17th-century castle built for Earl Patrick Stewart, a nephew of Mary Queen of Scots (open Mon–Sat; key from Shetland Woollens next door).

Deep voes (inlets) poke into the Shetland Islands like long fingers so that no part of the watery landscape is more than 3 miles (5 km) from the sea. As you drive across Mainland's moors, meadows and hills, dramatic sea views abruptly

LOCAL POPULATIONS

Sheep outnumber people on Shetland by eight to one. "They eat everything," says one islander. Shetland ponies are more loved. They were carefully bred to keep their legs short so that they could pull carts through Britain's coal mines, but these days they graze freely, or are sold as children's pets. But it's birds that dominate Shetland. Because of the lack of woodlands there are fewer than 50 breeding species, but no lack of numbers. Filling the sky and the cliff ledges are 30,000 gannets, 140,000 guillemots and 300,000 fulmars. There are over 3,000 pairs of great skua (known locally as bonxies). Puffins *(above)* begin to arrive in May and before long there are 250,000 of them. Take a small boat round the islands and, as well as the birds, you can find seal colonies, porpoises and dolphins.

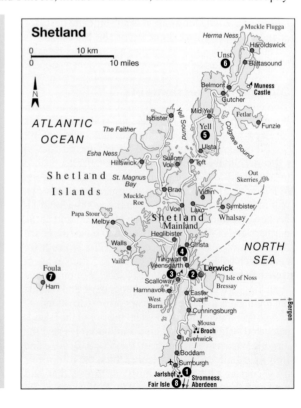

materialise. Shetlanders were always more sailors than farmers; but at **Tingwall** , north of Lerwick, an **Agricultural Museum** (open June–Aug: Mon–Sat; tel:(01595) 840344) lays out in an old farmyard a rare collection of old peat-cutting tools and cooking pots.

Remote places

Small ferries connect a handful of smaller islands to Mainland. **Yell ❺**, a peaty place, has the **Old Haa Visitor Centre** (open Apr–Sept: Tues, Wed, Thurs, Sat, and Sun pm; tel:(01957) 722339) which includes a display of the story of the wrecking of the German sail ship, the *Bohus*, in 1924, and a craft centre selling genuine rather than generic Shetland garments. **Unst ❻**, the UK's most northerly island, has an important nature reserve at **Herma Ness** with a visitor centre (open Apr–mid-Sept: daily; tel:(01957) 711278). From the cliffs at Herma Ness gaze out on rocky **Muckle Flugga**, the last land before the Arctic Circle. **Fetlar**'s name means "fat island", a reference to its fertile soil. **Whalsay** is prosperous, thanks to its notably energetic fishermen. The **Out Skerries**, a scattered archipelago, has a thriving fishing fleet. The peacefulness and abundant wild flowers of **Papa Stour**, a mile of turbulent sea west of Mainland, once attracted a transient hippy colony.

Foula ❼, 14 miles (23 km) to the west of Scalloway, must be Britain's remotest inhabited island and, most winters, is cut off for several weeks by awesome seas. The spectacular 1,200-ft (370-metre) cliffs are home to storm petrels, great skuas and a host of other seabirds. **Fair Isle ❽**, 20 miles (32 km) to the southwest, is home of Fair Isle sweaters, whose distinctive geometric patterns can be dated back 2,000 years to Balkan nomads. ❑

see map opposite

TIP

Keen ornithologists make for the Bird Observatory on Fair Isle, a major European centre set up to monitor birds all year round.

BELOW: a Viking festival sets Lerwick alight every January.

INSIGHT GUIDES
Travel Tips

Simply travelling safely

American Express Travellers Cheques

- are recognised as one of the safest and most convenient ways to protect your money when travelling abroad

- are more widely accepted than any other travellers cheque brand

- are available in eleven currencies

- are supported by a 24 hour worldwide refund service and

- a 24 hour Express Helpline service provides assistance and information when travelling abroad

- are accepted in millions of shops, hotels and restaurants throughout the world

AMERICAN EXPRESS

Travellers Cheques

CONTENTS

Getting Acquainted

The Place

Scotland, named after the Scotti, an Irish tribe who settled in western Scotland during the 6th century, is constitutionally part of the United Kingdom. Its total area is 30,405 sq. miles (78,772 sq. km). It extends 274 miles (441 km) from north to south, and is washed by the Atlantic Ocean on the west and north and by the North Sea on the east; England is to the south. It has a number of islands off its deeply indented coast, including the Inner and Outer Hebrides to the west and Orkney and the Shetland Islands to the north.

Topographically, there are three main regions:
● The Highlands make up the northern two-thirds. The highest mountain, is Ben Nevis (4,406 ft/1,343 metres), and the Grampian Mountains lie in the southern Highlands.
● The central area is a lowland region with isolated hills. It is the most densely populated area and contains Scotland's coalfields. The main cities – Edinburgh (the capital), Glasgow and Dundee – lie in this area.
● The Southern Uplands is a region of rounded hills covered by heather, bracken, and short grass. Sheep are reared here. Most lower ground, up to about 1,500 ft (450 metres), was once forested, but after centuries of clearing, little natural forest remains.

The main rivers are the Tay and the Forth, which rise in the Highlands and flow across the Central Lowlands to the sea, and the Clyde and the Tweed, which rise in the Southern Uplands. They are renowned for their fishing, including salmon.

The People

The worst insult to the 5.1 million Scots who still live in Scotland – millions more are scattered throughout the world – is to regard them as English. Their character is quite different, as are many of their institutions such as the church, the law and the education system. Their dialect, folklore, custom and architecture are all distinct from English equivalents.

It was the failure of the Romans to conquer Scotland (which they called Caledonia) that left its people free to develop their own Celtic identity. Gaelic is still spoken in the mountainous west by about 2 percent of the population. English, the official language, is spoken with a strong regional accent. Most Scots belong to the Presbyterian church.

Language

English in one form or another is spoken in Scotland. There are various regional dialects and local expressions used. In most parts of Scotland, the uninitiated could be forgiven that the name "Ken" was unusually popular; in fact, the Scots use "ken" at the end of sentences as the English are wont to use "do you know". The Scots have a tendency towards understatement, which is well illustrated by the phrase "it's not bad" – for which there is no greater compliment.

In the Highlands and the Islands, Gaelic is still spoken and is the first language of some of the older people. However, nowhere is it anyone's only language.

The Economy

Scotland's traditional coal-mining industry was overshadowed in the 1970s and 1980s by the offshore oil industry in the North Sea. This industry brought new wealth to Scotland's northern ports but is now declining, and it remains a bitter complaint of Scots nationalists that profits from "Scotland's oil" found their way south to the British government's coffers in London.

Since the Industrial Revolution of the same period, manufacturing has been located mainly in the Central Lowlands and along the east coast. Iron, steel and textiles once predominated, but have been largely replaced by modern high-tech industries, such as computers. The once important shipbuilding industry around the Clyde has almost gone. Whisky distilleries can be found mainly in the Highlands.

Fishing is a major industry, especially off the east coast. Farming resources are small: only 16 percent of the land is cropland, and two-thirds is useful only for rough grazing. Oats and fodder crops are grown, and sheep raising remains important; it was first introduced on a large scale in the late 18th and early 19th centuries when landlords forcibly evicted most of the Highlands' population.

Government

In a referendum in 1997 Scots voted in their own parliament, which will have its inaugural session in Edinburgh in summer 1999. Scotland will continue to be governed from Westminster, London, in matters such as defence, and will continue to be represented in the British Parliament by members from the Labour and Scottish Nationalist parties.

The legal and education systems are already separate from

those of the rest of Great Britain. For local government purposes, Scotland is divided into nine administrative regions.

Time Zones

Scotland, like the rest of the UK, follows Greenwich Mean Time (GMT). In spring the clock is moved forward one hour for British Summer Time (BST), and in autumn moved back again to GMT. Especially in the north of Scotland, this means that it is light till 10pm and after in June and early July.

When it is noon GMT, it is:
4am – Los Angeles
6am – Chicago and Winnipeg
7am – New York and Toronto
8am – Halifax
noon – London and Dublin
2pm – Cape Town
9.30pm – Adelaide
10pm – Melbourne and Sydney
midnight – Wellington

Climate

No matter what you say about Scottish weather, you are bound to be wrong. There are those who rave about the cloudless two weeks they spent on Skye; others have made several visits and have yet to see the Cuillins.

But it can be said that the west is generally wetter and warmer than the east. Summers are cool, with July temperatures averaging from 13° to 15°C (55–59°F), though often peaking above 20°C in the afternoon. Winters are cold, with January temperatures ranging from 3° to 5°C (37–41°F), frost at night, and the higher mountains sometimes remaining snow-covered for months. Rainfall is heavy, except on the east coast, and exceeds 2,540 mm (100 inches) in the Western Highlands.

January, April, May and June are usually drier months than July, August and September – but take an umbrella whenever you go.

Planning the Trip

What to Wear

Given the climate, it follows that you should never be without a raincoat or a warm sweater. Neither should you be without light clothes in summer. For those attracted to the excellent opportunities for hill-walking and rock-climbing, it is essential to come properly prepared. In the mountains the weather can change very quickly. Each year people suffer serious and needless injury through setting out without adequate equipment; the Highlands are no place to go on a serious hill walk in a T-shirt and tennis shoes.

Electricity

220 volts is standard. Hotels usually have dual 220/110-volt sockets for razors. If you are visiting from abroad, you will

Temperature Ranges

Edinburgh's highest/lowest daily average temperatures in Celsius (Fahrenheit in brackets) are:
● **January** 6°/1° (42°/34°)
● **February** 6°/1° (43°/34°)
● **March** 8°/2° (46°/36°)
● **April** 11°/4° (51°/39°)
● **May** 14°/6° (56°/43°)
● **June** 17°/9° (62°/49°)
● **July** 17°/9° (65°/52°)
● **August** 18°/11° (64°/52°)
● **September** 16°/9° (60°/49°)
● **October** 12°/7° (54°/44°)
● **November** 9°/4° (48°/39°)
● **December** 7°/2° (44°/36°)

probably need an adaptor to link other small electrical appliances to the three-pin sockets universal in Britain; it is usually easier to find these at home before leaving than in Scotland.

Health

It is advisable to have medical insurance. Citizens of European Union countries are entitled to medical treatment under reciprocal arrangements and similar arrangements exist with some other countries. No matter which country you come from, you will receive immediate emergency treatment free at a hospital casualty department.

Money Matters

Currency
The British pound is divided into 100 pence. The coins used are 1p, 2p, 5p, 10p, 20p, 50p, and £1. One of the minor pleasures of living in Scotland is that, although the £1 coin is widely used, £1 notes (issued by the Royal Bank of Scotland) still circulate along with notes of £5, £10, £20, £50 and £100. (Technically, Scottish notes are not legal tender in England and Wales, but many shops will accept them and English banks will readily change them for you.)

Traveller's Cheques
Eurocheques and Eurocard can be used at banks and travellers' cheques can be cashed at banks, *bureaux de change* and many hotels, though the best rates are normally available at banks.

Credit Cards
Access (or MasterCard) and Visa are the most commonly acceptable credit cards, followed by American Express and Diners Club. Small guest houses and bed-and-breakfast places may not take credit cards, preferring payment in cash.

Banks

Scotland has its own banks: the Royal Bank of Scotland, the Bank of Scotland and the Clydesdale Bank. They still issue their own notes – although the Royal Bank is the only one to issue the £1 note – which circulate alongside Bank of England notes.

Don't expect consistent opening hours. The Royal Bank and the TSB (Scotland) are open in the cities Monday–Friday 9.15am–4.45pm and until 5.30pm on Thursday. The Bank of Scotland is open 9.30am–4.45pm except on Thursday when it closes at 3.30pm, but re-opens from 4.30–5.30pm. The Clydesdale is slightly different again, opening from 9.15am–4pm each day except Thursday when it remains open until 5.30pm.

In rural areas, banks may close between 12.30pm and 1.30pm and may not be open later on Thursday. However, you will also find "travelling banks" – large trucks which go round the smaller villages at set times each week and can provide most banking services. These times are advertised locally.

Public Holidays

Local, public and bank holidays can be frustrating for visitors, but generally there will be a supermarket open somewhere during the major public holidays, which are **25** and **26 December**, **1** and **2 January** and **Good Friday**. If you are having difficulty, try petrol stations, which nowadays very commonly have good small shops on the premises and are open till late, or even for 24 hours.

Other national holidays in Scotland are **May Day** (first Monday in May), **Spring Holiday** (Monday in late May) and **Summer Holiday** (first Monday in August).

Getting There

By Air

There are excellent services from London (Heathrow, Gatwick, Luton and Stansted airports) and several English regional airports to Edinburgh, Glasgow, Aberdeen and Inverness. Some of these include no-book shuttle flights on which stand-by tickets are available at considerable reductions. Airlines flying these routes include **British Airways, British Midland** and **Air UK.**

Flying time between London and Edinburgh or London and Glasgow is about 70 minutes; and under two hours from London to Aberdeen or Inverness.

Two airlines, **Ryanair** and **EasyJet**, have introduced very low price, no frills flights into Scotland. EasyJet fly from London (Luton) to Glasgow and Edinburgh, while Ryanair fly from London (Stansted) to Glasgow Prestwick, and their fares are often less than half those of other airlines. **Aer Lingus** flies from Dublin to Glasgow and Edinburgh.

Scotland is reasonably well served by direct non-stop flights from the North American continent. The services offered at the time of writing were:
● Chicago to Glasgow: **American Airlines** (operate in summer only)

Airports

● **Edinburgh Airport** (Tel: (0131) 333 1000) is 6 miles (10 km) west of the city centre with good road access and a useful airlink bus service to the heart of town.
● **Glasgow Airport** (Tel: (0141) 887 1111) is 8 miles (13 km) west of the city centre alongside the M8 motorway at Junction 28. A coach service runs between the airport and

● New York JFK to Glasgow: **British Airways, Northwest Airlines** (via Amsterdam)
● Toronto to Glasgow: **Air Canada**

Using these flights, it is possible to make straightforward connections to a large number of other European and North American destinations.

Flights from Scotland to London connect with destinations worldwide.

By Rail

There are frequent InterCity services to Scotland from many mainline stations in England. On most trains the journey time from London (Euston or Kings Cross) to Edinburgh is slightly more than four hours and from London (Euston or Kings Cross) to Glasgow it is about five-and-a-half hours.

Sleeper and Motorail services run between London (Euston) and Edinburgh, Glasgow, Aberdeen, Inverness and Fort William.

Try to avoid travel on Sundays when services are often curtailed and engineering works mean that journeys can take much longer.

For current fares and timetables, and also for credit card sales and reservations, call (0345) 484950 or (0345) 550033. Information offices are open 8am–9pm daily while London, Edinburgh and Glasgow provide a 24-hour service.

Anderston and Buchanan bus stations, both in the heart of the city.
● **Aberdeen Airport** (Tel: (01224) 722331) is 7 miles (11 km) west of the city centre with excellent road access (A96). A coach service runs between airport and city centre.
● **Inverness Airport** (Tel: (01463) 232471) is about 10 miles (16 km) east of the town.

More colour
for the world.

HDCplus. New perspectives in colour photography.

http://www.agfaphoto.com

AGFA

Probably the <u>most</u> <u>important</u> TRAVEL TIP you will ever receive

Before you travel abroad, make sure that you and your family are protected from diseases that can cause serious health problems.

For instance, you can pick up *hepatitis A* which infects 10 million people worldwide every year (it's not just a disease of poorer countries) simply through consuming contaminated food or water!

What's more, in many countries if you have an accident needing medical treatment, or even dental treatment, you could also be at risk of infection from *hepatitis B* which is 100 times more infectious than AIDS, and can lead to liver cancer.

The good news is, you can be protected by vaccination against these and other serious diseases, such as *typhoid*, *meningitis* and *yellow fever*.

Travel safely! Check with your doctor at least 8 weeks before you go, to discover whether or not you need protection.

Consult your doctor before you go... not when you return!

By Road
There are good motorway connections from England and Wales. The M1/M6/A74 and M74 is the quickest route, though heavily congested at the southern end. The A1, a more easterly approach, is longer but may be a better bet if you plan to make one or two stopovers on the way. Edinburgh and Glasgow are about 400 miles (650 km) from London.

By Bus
Scottish Citylink (Tel: 0990 505050) and National Express (Tel: (0990) 808080) operate daytime and overnight coaches from England to Scotland. The journey takes about 8 hours from London to Edinburgh or to Glasgow. Coach travel may not be as comfortable or as fast as the trains, but it is a good deal cheaper.

Practical Tips

Emergencies

For emergency services such as police, ambulance, the fire service or lifeboat service dial 999.

Although Scotland isn't normally associated with mosquitoes, an aggressive breed of biting midge exists, especially in warm, humid conditions in parts of the west coast, and calls for a tough repellent from June to September.

Newspapers

There are two quality dailies. *The Scotsman*, printed in Edinburgh, and *The Herald*, printed in Glasgow, both have good coverage of Scottish and other UK news and foreign news, as well as material on the arts and business. Many of the London dailies have Scottish editions. Dundee boasts the quirky *Dundee Courier*. Much of the Highlands is covered by the *Press and Journal*, printed in Aberdeen. It tries to live down its reputation for excessive parochialism, epitomised by the spurious headline on what proved to be a story about the sinking of the *Titanic*: "Aberdeen man lost at sea".

The most popular is the tabloid *Daily Record*, a stablemate of England's *Daily Mirror*. English dailies circulate widely in Scotland, and some, such as the *Daily Express*, have distinct Scottish editions.

The four main cities each have evening papers. Scotland's most popular Sunday newspaper is the *Sunday Post*,

from the same stable as the *Dundee Courier*. It defies classification: perhaps the most helpful comment on it would be that it tries to be useful and inoffensive. *Scotland on Sunday* is the only quality Sunday.

Throughout Scotland, there are many local weekly papers which you may find both entertaining and informative if you are interested in a particular region, or simply interested in newspapers.

Magazines

Scotland is poorly served by magazines. However, the *Scottish Field* and the *Scots Magazine* are good-quality monthly magazines which deal with Scottish topics. The *Edinburgh Review* is a literary review of consistent quality. *The List*, an Edinburgh-based listings magazine which appears every two weeks, provides lively and comprehensive coverage of events in both Edinburgh and Glasgow.

Radio and Television

Radio and TV are excellent, for the most part. Radio Scotland is the main BBC radio service and national BBC radio stations also operate in Scotland; so it is possible to hear excellent Radio 4 (FM 92.4–94.6/LW 198) (a mixture of news, current affairs and light entertainment) as well as the classical music channel on Radio 3 (FM 90.2–92.4). Classic FM (FM 99.9–101.99) serves up the more familiar classics and some intriguing and challenging quiz games. Radio 2 (FM 88–90.2) concentrates on light entertainment and sport. Sports fans will tune in to Radio 5 Live (MW 693/909).

Radio 1 (FM 97.6–99.8), Virgin (MW 1215), Atlantic (LW 252) and local radio stations run by both the BBC and commercial companies offer wall-to-wall pop and light music, interspersed with terse news summaries. Local stations tend to provide an unimaginative diet of pop music but can be useful sources of local traffic news and other important information.

Television services are provided by BBC and commercial companies. BBC1 is a general TV service, mirrored (though with a more down-market emphasis) by the commercial ITV network on Channels 3 and 5. BBC2 and its commercial stablemate, Channel 4, recognise the existence of more specialist audiences and minority groups. Satellite channels are becoming much more widespread, and are proliferating at a great rate, as is cable TV. These channels are usually available on room TVs in the larger hotels.

Postal Services

Main post offices are open 9am–5.30pm Monday–Friday, and 9am–12.30pm on Saturday. Sub-post offices (which often form part of another shop) keep similar hours, though they usually close for one half-day during the week.

Telecoms

When dialling from abroad, the international access code for the UK is 44, followed by the area code (Edinburgh 131, Glasgow 141, Aberdeen 1224, etc).

To reach other countries from Scotland, first dial the **international access code 00**, then the country code (e.g. Australia 61, France 33, Germany 49, Japan 81, the Netherlands 31, Spain 34, US and Canada 1). If using a US credit phone card, dial the company's access number: Sprint 00 801 15; AT&T 00 801 10; MCI 00 801 11.

The minimum charge for a call made at a public telephone is 10 pence. Some telephones

accept only cardphone cards, which can be purchased at post offices and shops displaying the cardphone sign for £1, £2, £4 or £10, depending on the amount of telephone time they will provide.

Direct dialling is possible to most parts of the world.

Tourist Information

In Scotland

General postal enquiries should be made to the Scottish Tourist Board, 23 Ravelston Terrace, Edinburgh EH4 3EU. Tel: (0131) 332 2433.

The Scottish Tourist Board has its Edinburgh and Scotland Tourist Information Centre at 3 Princes Street in the centre of Edinburgh (tel: (0131) 557 1700). Other tourist information is provided by 14 area **Tourist Boards** throughout Scotland. Their main offices, with the areas covered, are:

Aberdeen and Grampian Tourist Board, Migvie House, North Silver Street, Aberdeen AB10 1RJ. Tel: (01224) 632727. Fax: (01224) 848805. (Aberdeen City, Moray and Aberdeenshire.)

Angus and City of Dundee Tourist Board, 4 City Square, Dundee DD1 3BA. Tel: (01382) 434664. Fax: (01382) 434665. (Angus and the City of Dundee.)

Argyll, the Isles, Loch Lomond, Stirling and Trossachs Tourist Board, 7 Alexandra Place, Dunoon, Argyll PA23 8AB. Tel: (01369) 701000.

Useful Numbers

- Directory enquiries **192**
- International directory enquiries **153**
- Assistance in making UK calls **100**
- Assistance in making international calls **155**
- Emergencies – police, fire and ambulance **999**

Fax: (01369) 706085. (Argyll and Bute, Clackmananshire, Dumbarton and Clydebank, Falkirk and Stirling.)
Ayrshire and Arran Tourist Board, Burns House, Burns Statue Square, Ayr KA7 1UP. Tel: (01292) 262555. Fax: (01292) 269555. (Ayrshire and the Island of Arran.)
Dumfries and Galloway Tourist Board, Campbell House, Bankend Road, Dumfries DG1 4TH. Tel: (01387) 250434. Fax: (01387) 250462. (Dumfries and Galloway.)
Edinburgh and Lothians Tourist Board, 3 Princes Street (Waverley Market), Edinburgh EH2 2QP. Tel: (0131) 557 1700. Fax: (0131) 557 5118. (City of Edinburgh, East Lothian, Midlothian, West Lothian.)
Greater Glasgow and Clyde Valley Tourist Board, 11 George Square, Glasgow G2 1DY. Tel: (0141) 204 4400. Fax: (0141) 221 3524. (City of Glasgow, East Dunbartonshire, Inverclyde, Lanarkshire, Renfrewshire.)
The Highlands of Scotland Tourist Board, Information Centre, Grampian Road, Aviemore PH22 1PP. Tel: (0990) 143070. Fax: (01479) 811063. (Caithness, Inverness-shire, Ross-shire, Sutherland and the Island of Skye.)
Kingdom of Fife Tourist Board, Kingdom House, 7 Hanover Court, North Street, Glenrothes KY7 5SB. Tel: (01592) 750066. Fax: (01592) 611180. (Fife.)
Orkney Tourist Board, 6 Broad Street, Kirkwall, Orkney KW15 1NX. Tel: (01856) 872856. Fax: (01856) 875056. (Orkney Islands.)
Perthshire Tourist Board, 45 High Street, Perth PH1 5TJ. Tel: (01378) 638353. Fax: (01738) 444863. (Perthshire and Kinross.)
Scottish Borders Tourist Board, Murrays Green, Jedburgh, Roxburghshire, TD8 6BE. Tel: (01835) 863435.

When you're
bitten by the travel bug,
make sure you're protected.

Check into a British Airways Travel Clinic.

British Airways Travel Clinics provide travellers with:
- A complete vaccination service and essential travel health-care items
- Up-dated travel health information and advice

Call **01276 685040** for details of your nearest Travel Clinic.

BRITISH AIRWAYS
TRAVEL CLINICS

New Insight Maps

Maps in Insight Guides are tailored to complement the text. But when you're on the road you sometimes need the big picture that only a large-scale map can provide. This new range of durable Insight Fleximaps has been designed to meet just that need.

Detailed, clear cartography
makes the comprehensive route and city maps easy to follow, highlights all the major tourist sites and provides valuable motoring information plus a full index.

Informative and easy to use
with additional text and photographs covering a destination's top 10 essential sites, plus useful addresses, facts about the destination and handy tips on getting around.

Laminated finish
allows you to mark your route on the map using a non-permanent marker pen, and wipe it off. It makes the maps more durable and easier to fold than traditional maps.

The first titles
cover many popular destinations. They include Algarve, Amsterdam, Bangkok, California, Cyprus, Dominican Republic, Florence, Hong Kong, Ireland, London, Mallorca, Paris, Prague, Rome, San Francisco, Sydney, Thailand, Tuscany, USA Southwest, Venice, and Vienna.

✕ INSIGHT GUIDES
The world's largest collection of visual travel guides

Fax: (01835) 864099.
(The Scottish Borders.)
Shetland Islands Tourism,
Market Cross, Lerwick,
Shetland ZE1 0LU. Tel: (01595)
693434. Fax: (01595) 695807.
(Shetland Islands.)
Western Isles Tourist Board,
26 Cromwell Street, Stornoway,
Isle of Lewis HS1 2DD.
Tel: (01851) 703088.
Fax: (01851) 705244. (Lewis,
Harris, N. Uist, Benbecula, S.
Uist and Barra.)

Most towns have **Tourist
Information Centres** (TICs);
not all are open in the winter
months. A selection is given
below. Those marked Δ are
open all year.
Aberdeen TIC, St Nicholas Hse,
Broad Street, Aberdeen AB9
1DE. Tel: (01224) 632727. Δ
Ayr TIC, Burns House, Burns
Statue Square, Ayr KA7 1UP.
Tel: (01292) 288688. Δ
Ballater TIC, Station Square,
Ballater. Tel: (01339) 755306.
Banff TIC, Collie Lodge, Banff
AB45 1AU. Tel: (01261) 812419.
Blairgowrie TIC,
26 Wellmeadow, Blairgowrie,
Perthshire.
Tel: (01250) 872960. Δ
Braemar TIC, The Mews,
Mar Road, Braemar.
Tel: (01339) 741600. Δ
Brodick TIC, The Pier, Brodick,
Isle of Arran KA27 8AU.
Tel: (01770) 302140. Δ
Callander TIC, Rob Roy &
Trossachs Centre, Ancaster
Square, Callander.
Tel: (01877) 330784.
Crieff TIC, Town Hall, Crieff,
Perthshire.
Tel: (01764) 652578. Δ
Dornoch TIC, The Square,
Dornoch IV25 3SD.
Tel: (01862) 810400. Δ
Dumbarton TIC, Milton (A82),
Dumbarton.
Tel: (01389) 820501. Δ
Dumfries TIC, Whitesands,
Dumfries DG1 4TH.
Tel: (01387) 253862. Δ
Dundee TIC, 4 City Square,

Dundee DD1 3BA.
Tel: (01382) 434664. Δ
Edinburgh Airport, Tourist
Information Desk.
Tel: (0131) 333 2167. Δ
Elgin TIC, 17 High Street, Elgin
IV30 1BG.
Tel: (01343) 542666. Δ
Falkirk TIC, 2-4 Glebe Street,
Falkirk SKi 1HX.
Tel: (01324) 620244. Δ
Fort William TIC, Cameron
Square, Fort William PH33 6AJ.
Tel: (01397) 703781. Δ
Gairloch TIC, Auchtercairn,
Gairloch, Ross-shire.
Tel: (01445) 712130. Δ
Glasgow TIC, 11 George
Square, Glasgow G2 1DY.
Tel: (0141) 204 4400. Δ
**Glasgow Airport, Tourist
Information Desk**.
Tel: (0141) 848 4440. Δ
Gretna Gateway to Scotland,
M74 Service Area, Gretna
DG16 5HQ.
Tel: (01461) 338500. Δ
Inverness TIC, Castle Wynd,
Inverness IV2 3BJ.
Tel: (01463) 234353. Δ
Lanark TIC, Horsemarket,
Ladyacre Road, Lanark ML11
7LQ. Tel: (01555) 661661. Δ
Linlithgow TIC, Burgh Halls,
The Cross, Linlithgow EH49
7EJ. Tel: (01506) 844600. Δ
Oban TIC, Argyll Square, Oban
PA34 4AR.
Tel: (01631) 563122. Δ
Paisley TIC, Town Hall, Abbey
Close, Paisley.
Tel: (0141) 889 0711.
Peebles TIC, High Street,
Peebles EÓ45 8AG.
Tel: (01721) 720138. Δ
Perth TIC, 45 High Street,
Perth PH1 5TJ.
Tel: (01738) 638353. Δ
Portree TIC, Meall House,
Portree, Isle of Skye IV51 9BZ.
Tel: (01478) 612137. Δ
St Andrews TIC, 70 Market
Street, St Andrews KY16 9NU.
Tel: (01334) 472021. Δ
Stirling TIC, 41 Dumbarton
Road, Stirling FK8 2LQ.
Tel: (01786) 475019. Δ
Ullapool TIC, Argyle Street,

Ullapool, Ross-shire.
Tel: (01854) 612135.
Wick TIC, Whitechapel Road,
Wick KW1 4EA.
Tel: (01955) 602596. Δ

In London
The Scottish Tourist Board runs
a Scottish Information Centre at
19 Cockspur Street, London, on
the southwest side of Trafalgar
Square. Tel: (0171) 930 8661.
Information about Scotland is
available through the British
Tourist Authority offices.

Outside of the United Kingdom
Australia, BTA, Level 16,
Gateway. 1 Macquarie Place,
Sydney NSW 2000.
Tel: (2) 9377 4400,
Fax: (2) 9377 4499.
Canada, BTA, 111 Avenue Road,
Suite 450, Toronto, Ontario
M5R 3J8. Tel: 416 925 6326,
Fax: 416 961 2175.
Ireland, BTA, 18-19 College
Green, Dublin 2. Tel: (1) 670
8000. Fax: (1) 670 8244.
New Zealand, BTA, Suite 305,
3rd Floor, Dilworth Building,
Corner Queen & Customs
Streets, Auckland 1. Tel: (9)
303 1446, Fax: (9) 377 6965.
South Africa, BTA, Lancaster
Gate, Hyde Lane, Hyde Park,
Sandton 2196 (visitors). PO Box
41896, Craighall 2024 (mail).
Tel: (11) 325 0343. Fax (11)
325 0344.
USA: Chicago, BTA, 625 N
Michigan Avenue, Suite 1510,
Chicago IL 60611 (personal
callers only). Toll free phone:
1-800 462 2743.
USA: New York, BTA, 7th Floor,
551 Fifth Avenue, New York, NY
10176-0799. 1-800-GO-2-BRITAIN,
or (212) 986 2200. Fax: (212)
986 1188.

Heritage Organisations

The National Trust for Scotland
The Trust is Scotland's premier
conservation body, and has in
its care over 100 buildings or
areas of significant heritage

interest. Its properties range from single boulders, such as the Bruce Stone in Galloway, through magnificent houses and castles including Culzean, Crathes and Fyvie, to large areas of outstanding countryside. The latter include Glencoe, Mar Lodge in the Cairngorms, Kintail and Goat Fell on Arran.

The Trust was formed in 1931 and currently has about 250,000 members, who gain free admission to its properties. Further information from 5 Charlotte Square, Edinburgh EH2 4DU (Tel: (0131) 226 5922).

Heritage Scotland
This is the government's own heritage body, principally for sites of historic or archaeological interest. Its portfolio of well over 300 properties ranges from the magnificent Borders abbeys up to Stone Age sites in Orkney and Shetland.

A "Friends of Historic Scotland" membership pass gives free admission to HS properties and brings other benefits. Further information from Longmore House, Salisbury Place, Edinburgh EH9 1SH (Tel: (0131) 668 8800).

Consulates

Australia, Hobart House, Hanover Street, Edinburgh EH2. Tel: (0131) 226 6271.
Canada, 3 George Street, Edinburgh EH2 2HT. Tel: (0131) 220 4333.
Malawi, 17 York Road, Edinburgh. Tel: (0131) 552 2519.
Malta, 139 Old Dalkeith Road, Edinburgh. Tel: (0131) 664 1070.
Pakistan, 137 Norfolk Street, Glasgow G5. Tel: (0141) 429 5335.
South Africa, 69 Nelson Mandela Place, Glasgow G2. Tel: (0141) 221 3114.
United States, 3 Regent Terrace, Edinburgh EH7 5BW. Tel: (0131) 556 8315.

Getting Around

By Air

There is a network of air services within Scotland which is especially valuable if going to the islands. Flying to these destinations saves a lot of time and also can give a different perspective on the countryside. The major carrier is Loganair (now known as British Airways Express). British Airways central booking number for all services is 0345 222 111.

By Rail

ScotRail offers a wide variety of tickets which permit unlimited travel throughout Scotland. Freedom of Scotland Rovers passes permit unlimited travel on eight or 15 consecutive days or on four out of eight or 10 out of 15 consecutive days. Area Rovers (choice of North Highlands, West Highlands, Heart of Scotland or Festival Cities) permit unlimited travel in any one of these regions for seven consecutive days or, in the case of Festival Cities for three out of seven consecutive days.

Scottish Travelpasses permit unlimited travel for 8 or 15 consecutive days on Scotrail and most of the Caledonian MacBrayne west coast ferries. Together with discounts on the P&O ferries and many buses and postbuses these are truly comprehensive Scottish travel tickets. Details can be obtained from Scotrail, Tel: 0345 484950 or 0345 550033.

A few routes to try are:

Glasgow to Fort William and Mallaig (164 miles/265 km). Train enthusiasts head for the West Highland line, which operates steam locomotives on Tuesday, Thursday and Sunday during the summer months from Fort William to the fishing port of Mallaig, from which a ferry departs for Skye. From Glasgow, the route passes alongside Loch Lomond, across the wild Rannoch Moor and, after Fort William, over the majestic Glenfinnan Viaduct and hillsides dotted with deer. For details, contact: ScotRail West Highland Transport Centre, Fort William PH33 6AN (Tel: (01397) 703791).
Glasgow to Oban (101 miles/163 km). The train branches off the Fort William route at Crianlarich and heads past ruined Kilchurn Castle and the fjord-like scenery of the Pass of Brander to Oban, "gateway to the Inner Hebrides".
Perth to Inverness (118 miles/190 km). The route, through forested glens and across the roof of Scotland, takes in Pitlochry, Blair Atholl and Aviemore. As well as being a ski centre, Aviemore is the departure point for steam trains on the 5-mile (8-km) Strathspey Railway line.
Inverness to Kyle of Lochalsh (82 miles/132 km). From mid-May until October (no Sunday service) this regular service on a twisting line with breathtaking scenery is enhanced by the Hebridean Heritage train having an observation car, while both it and the "Atlantic Heritage" train have a dining car service. A commentary is provided. The journey, which takes in lochs, glens and mountains from the North Sea to the Atlantic Ocean, is especially dramatic towards Kyle of Lochalsh from where the new bridge leads over the water to Skye.
Inverness to Wick or Thurso (161 miles/260 km). Passes by

castles, across wild moorland and on to Britain's most northerly rail terminals.

Steam Trains

Railway preservation societies are alive and thriving in Scotland. Apart from the popular West Highland line, half a dozen other lines operate steam trains of one sort or another.

The **Northern Belle**, a 10-coach touring train operated by Grampian Railtours, is available for two-, three- and four-day luxury rail land cruises of Scotland. These trips include all meals served at seat, accommodation in hotels and off-train visits. Information from Caledonian Heritage Tours, 11 Mavis Bank, Newburgh, Ellon, Aberdeenshire AB41 6FB. Tel/Fax: (01358) 789513.

The **Caledonian Railway** (Brechin), Angus, runs steam train rides every Sunday from June to September, and at Christmas and Easter, from Brechin to Bridge of Don. Brechin station is also open on Saturdays. Enquiries to Brechin Station, 2 Park Road, Brechin, Angus DD9 7AF. Tel: (01674) 810318.

The **Bo'ness & Kinneil Railway**, West Lothian, runs steam-hauled trains on most summer weekends (also six days a week through July and August, and at Christmas and Easter) on a 3-mile (5-km) branch line to Birkhill for a visit to the Avon Gorge and the Fireclay Mine. Historic Scottish locomotives, rolling stock and railway buildings. Enquiries to Bo'ness Station, Union Street, Bo'ness EH51 9AQ. Tel: (01506) 822298.

Strathspey Railway runs during the summer months for 5 miles (8 km) from Aviemore (Speyside) to Boat of Garten, providing good views of the Cairngorm Mountains. It is hoped to extend the line to Grantown-on-Spey. Enquiries to Aviemore (Speyside) Station, Inverness-shire PH22 1PS. Tel: (01479) 810725.

The **Mull & West Highland Railway** has steam and diesel trains running in summer on a narrow-gauge track for 1¼ miles (2 km) through superb mountain and woodland scenery from the ferry terminal at Craignure to Torosoy Castle and Gardens on Mull. Enquiries to Tel: (01680) 812494. Fax: (01680) 300595.

At the top end of the market is the **Royal Scotsman**, one of the world's most exclusive trains. This mobile hotel for just 32 passengers combines spectacular scenery with superb food and wine and impeccable service. A four-night Scotland tour visits Glamis Castle, Ballindalloch Castle, the Highland Wildlife Park and the island of Skye. Tours operate between April and October, departing from and returning to Edinburgh and costing £2,450 per person. Also offered are two-day Edinburgh to London and back tours costing £1,200 each, or a six-day Grand Tour which combines both elements at a cost of £3,40. Enquiries to the Great Scottish & Western Railway Company. Tel: (0131) 555 1344.

Ferries

Scottish ferries are great. On long routes, like the 5-hour Oban to Barra ferry, there are car decks, cabins, comfortable chairs, a restaurant and self-service. On others, such as the 7-hour round trip to the tiny island of Eigg, Muck, Rum and Canna, ferries are basic with wooden seats and minimal refreshments. These working boats, carrying goods and mail, as well as passengers, are mainly used by islanders, with some bird-watchers and the occasional curious visitors. Take note that unless you specify beforehand, disembarking for sightseeing is not allowed.

There is plenty of small private enterprise on the west coast. There are cruises from Arisaig on the mainland to Skye and Mull as well as to Eigg, Muck, Rum and Canna. Day trips to the National Trust for Scotland island of Staffa with Fingal's Cave, to the bird island of Lunga and the uninhabited Treshnish islands, start from the Ulva, Dervaig and Fionnphort, all of which are on Mull, while Staffa can also be reached from Iona. There is a virtual 10-minute shuttle service from Fionnphort on the southwest tip of Mull to Iona.

Caledonian MacBrayne Ferries

A must for the visitor who intends to explore the island-studded west coast – the Hebrides and the islands of the Clyde – is the Caledonian MacBrayne timetable, which can be obtained from: Ferry Terminal, Gourock, PA19 1QP, Scotland. Tel: (01475) 650100; reservations: (0990) 650000. This is as incomprehensible to the first-time visitor as a Chinese scroll. Locals whip through it with ease. Summer booking is vital to avoid the nerve-racking, time-consuming "standby" queue.

Caledonian MacBrayne, a fusion of two companies, grew out of the 19th-century passenger steamers and now has a near-monopoly on west coast routes. Its 30 vessels call at 53 ports on the mainland and on 23 islands. They sell island hopscotch tickets and, best value for visitors with cars – rover tickets for driver and one passenger, giving 8 or 15 days unlimited travel on most routes.

These trips allow some time ashore and there is no dificulty in finding out about such services when you arrive. Tourist information centres and many hotels have brochures.

In northern Scotland, the ferry services to Orkney and Shetland are a great deal easier to grasp than those to the Western Isles; for one thing, there are only two major islands and only two major companies. Summer booking is essential.

Orkney

There is just one vessel for cars to Orkney: the comfortable roll-on/roll-off *St Ola* run by P&O, which takes 2 hours to cross from Scrabster on the mainland to Stromness on Orkney. There is one sailing a day except Sunday in January, February, March and two or three sailings a day (only one on Sunday) throughout the rest of the year with extra services during high summer. There is a good car park on Orkney.

A passenger ferry runs from May to September from Gill's Bay, near John o'Groats, to Burwick on South Ronaldsay. There are two or three daily departures, including Sunday. The crossing takes around 40 minutes. Buses and coaches can be boarded on Orkney and there are cars for hire.

Once on Orkney, a dozen or so smaller islands can be visited by local ferries. The Kirkwall tourist office has more details.

Shetland

During the summer the P&O service, which takes 14 hours between Aberdeen and Lerwick, Shetland's main port, is doubled from one boat to two. Both ferries are modern roll-on/roll-off vessels with cabins, shops, restaurants and cafeterias. The second ferry makes the round trip, calling at Orkney, where it remains for 2 hours, on both the outward and the return journey.

Once again local ferries ply between the tiny islands of Yell, Unst and Fetlar. P&O Ferries brochures can be obtained from PO Box 5, P&O Scottish Ferries Terminal, Jamieson's Quay, Aberdeen AB9 8DL.
Tel: (01224) 572615.
Fax: (01224) 574411.

Pleasure Cruises

On Loch Katrine, which has supplied Glasgow with water since 1859, the *SS Sir Walter Scott*, Scotland's only screw steamer in regular passenger service, makes three daily round-trip voyages between the Trossachs and Stronachlachar piers from mid-April until the end of September. The morning trip permits a 15-minute landing at Stronachlachar, while the two one-hour afternoon trips are non-landing (no morning trip on Saturday). Enquiries to Trossachs Pier Complex, Loch Katrine, by Callander FK17 8HZ.
Tel: (01877) 376316.

From May until October the undistinguished *The Second Snark* and *Rover*, which are based at Greenock, make a variety of half- and full-day cruises visiting renowned beauty spots of the Firth of Clyde and permitting landings of 2–4 hours. Shorter cruises are made by the *MV Kenilworth*. (Clyde Marine Cruises, Princes Pier, Greenock PA16 8AW. Tel: (01475) 721281.) Similar cruises from Gourock, with longer time ashore, can be enjoyed from the end of April until mid-October on Caledonian MacBrayne craft. Tel: (01475) 650100.

From April to October the *Maid of the Forth* sails from South Queensferry, just outside Edinburgh, to Inchcolm Island with its ruined, medieval abbey. Sailing time on the Firth of Forth (seals are often seen) is 30 minutes and 1½ hours is spent ashore. (Maid of the Forth, Hawes Pier, South Queensferry. Tel: (0131) 331 4857.)

At Easter and from May to September the 130-passenger *MV Shearwater* sails each morning from Arisaig for a full day to the small islands (Rum, Eigg, Muck) of the Inner Hebrides or to Skye. Several hours are spent ashore. (Murdo Grant, Arisaig Harbour, Inverness-shire PH39 4NH. Tel: (01687) 450224.
Fax: (01687) 450678.)

During the summer months the *TSMV Western Isles* makes half-and full-day cruises from

The Hebridean Princess

The *Hebridean Princess*, more a stately country-house hotel on water than the usual run-of-the-mill luxury liner and accommodating only 49 passengers in elegant staterooms, makes a series of cruises from Oban from March until October.

The region covered is the northwest coast of Scotland,

Inner and Outer Hebrides, the Orkney and Shetland Islands and even St Kilda. The route varies from cruise to cruise and voyages last 6, 8, 10 and 15 days. In the words of the Captain Iain Cameron, "We are on a cruise: not on an expedition," and so the printed schedule may be altered to avoid bad weather.

An unusual feature of this luxurious ship is that cars can roll-on and roll-off, thus enabling travellers to explore independently at the various ports of call. (Bookings can be made through Hebridean Island Cruises Ltd., Acorn Park, Skipton North Yorkshire, BD23 2UE. Tel: (01756) 701338.)

Mallaig past dramatic scenery to surrounding lochs, or to the islands of Rum and Canna, or to Skye with landings. (Bruce Watt Sea Cruises, Mallaig. Tel: (01687) 462320 or (01687) 462233.)

From May to September daily sailings (weather permitting) are made from Anstruther to the Isle of May aboard the *May Princess*. The trip lasts about 5 hours, with 3 hours ashore to explore the island, whose cliffs, at least until July, are covered with breeding kittiwakes, razorbills, guillemots and shags. The ruins of a 12th-century chapel can also be visited. (Anstruther Pleasure Trips, Pittenweem Road, Anstruther, Fife KY10 3DS. Tel: (01333) 310103.)

From Easter until mid-October *Anne of Etive* departs from Taynuilt on 3-hour cruises into Loch Etive and to the mountains of Glencoe. The route covered is inaccessible except by boat. If fortune favours then seals on the rocks, the golden eagle of Ben Starav and deer on the crags will be seen. Morning and afternoon departures except at the start and finish of season. (Contact Donald Kennedy, Taynuilt. Tel: (01866) 822430.

Several companies run 2- to 4-hour cruises from Ullapool to the Summer Isles. Some are nature cruises, some are sunset cruises and some permit landing on the islands. (MacKenzie Marine, Green Pastures, Ullapool. Tel: 01854 612008.)

Summer Isles cruises also depart from Achiltibuie aboard the *Hechtoria*. These last about 4 hours and permit landing on the islands. (I. Macleod, Achiltibuie Post Office. Tel: (01854) 622200.)

Public Transport

By Bus
Major towns have their own bus services. In addition, there are bus services serving rural communities and linking the various towns. These are fairly good, and the visitor who intends to make frequent use of buses should investigate the various tickets which allow unlimited use of buses for specific periods. Details are available from bus stations and tourist offices.

An unusual delight and a superb way to meet the people and learn something of their customs is to board one of the Royal Mail Postbuses, which provide an essential post-and-passenger service in isolated parts of the country. To people in rural communities the familiar red Postbus is both a welcome friend and a lifeline to the world outside. The buses cover nearly 150 routes stretching from the Borders to the Outer Hebrides.

By Taxi
The major cities have sufficient taxi stands. Outside the cities, it will usually be necessary to telephone for a taxi.

Private Transport

Scotland has an excellent network of roads which, away from the central belt, are usually not congested. Driving on the left is the rule and passengers must wear seat belts. In urban areas, the speed limit is either 30 or 40 mph (48 or 64 km/h), the limit on country roads is 60 mph (97km/h), and on motorways and dual carriageways 70 mph (113 km/h).

In some parts of the Highlands and on many of the islands, roads are single track with passing places. The behaviour of drivers on these roads tends to show that good old-fashioned courtesy is not dead. On these narrow roads, please use the "passing places" to let oncoming vehicles pass, or others behind you to overtake.

Radio Scotland (FM 92.4–94.7/ MW 810) broadcasts details of road conditions throughout the day at the following times: Monday–Saturday 06.54, 07.28, 07.52, 08.28, 16.30, 17.30, Sunday 06.55 and 09.00. Details of particular problems, accidents or emergencies are broadcast as appropriate throughout the day. The broadcast travel information includes details of ferry, rail or air travel hold-ups or changes. Local stations also broadcast travel and road information.

In the Highlands and on the islands, it is wise to fill up on Saturday if you are planning to drive on Sunday. This is because, in some places, strict Sunday observance means that filling stations will be closed.

Car Rentals

Self-drive rental costs £20–£50 a day, depending on the type of car and the duration of the rental. The rates are reduced in the October–April off-season. For more detailed information, apply directly to the car rental companies. Main car rental companies are:

EDINBURGH
(Area code: 0131)
Arnold Clark, Lochrin Place, Tollcross. Tel: 228 4747.
Avis Rent-a-Car, 100 Dalry Road. Tel: 337 6363.
Budget Rent-a-Car, The Royal Scot Hotel, 111 Glasgow Road. Tel: 334 7739.
Europcar UK Ltd, 24 East London Street. Tel: 557 3456.
Hertz Rent-a-Car, 10 Picardy Place. Tel: 556 8311.
Little's Chauffeur Drive, 33 Corstorphine High Street. Tel: 334 2177.
Mitchell's Self Drive, 32 Torphichen Street. Tel: 229 5384.
National Car Rental, 39 Roseburn Street. Tel: 337 8686.
W.L. Sleigh Ltd (chauffeur-driven), 6 Devon Place. Tel: 337 3171.

Woods Car Rental,
Hilton International,
69 Bedford Road.
Tel: (01506) 858660.

EDINBURGH **A**IRPORT
Alamo. Tel: 333 5100.
Avis Rent-a-Car. Tel: 333 1866.
Europcar UK. Tel: 333 2588.
Hertz Rent-a-Car. Tel: 333 1019.
Woods Car Rental.
Tel: (01506) 858660.

GLASGOW
(Area code: 0141)
Arnold Clark,
Allison Street. Tel: 423 9559;
40 Hamilton Rd. Tel: 778 2979;
Crow Road. Tel: 434 0480;
Castlebank St. Tel: 339 9886.
Avis Rent-a-Car,
161 North Street.
Tel: 221 2827.
Budget Rent-a-Car,
101 Waterloo Street.
Tel: 226 4141.
Catherine's Chauffeur Drive,
28 Gavinton Street, Muirend.
Tel: 637 7036.
Europcar, 38 Anderston Quay.
Tel: 248 8788.
Hertz Rent-a-Car,
106 Waterloo Street.
Tel: 248 7736.
Little's Chauffeur Drive,
1282 Paisley Road West.
Tel: 883 2111.
Mitchell's Self-Drive,
47 McAlpine Street.
Tel: 221 8461.
National Car Rental,
76 Lancefield Quay.
Tel: 204 1051.

GLASGOW **A**IRPORT
Arnold Clark, Phoenix Park,
Linwood. Tel: 848 0202.
Avis Rent-a-Car,
St Andrews Drive.
Tel: 887 2261.
Budget Rent-a-Car,
Phoenix House, Inchinnan Road.
Tel: 0800 626063.
Europcar, Inchinnan Road.
Tel: 887 0414.
Hertz Rent-a-Car,
St Andrews Drive.
Tel: 887 2451.

Mitchell's Self Drive,
54 Glasgow Road, Paisley.
Tel: 887 7866.
National Car Rental,
Terminal Building.
Tel: 887 7915.
Woods Car Rental,
Inchinnan Road. Tel: 848 1559.

THE **S**OUTHWEST
AYR
Dalblair of Ayr,
27 Prestwick Road.
Tel: (01292) 269123.

PRESTWICK **A**IRPORT
Arnold Clark, Main Street.
Tel: (01292) 470545.
Avis Rent-a-Car,
Terminal Building.
Tel: (01292) 477218.
Europcar,
Terminal Building.
Tel: (01292) 678198.
Hertz Rent-a-Car.
Tel: (01292) 511281.

FORTH & **C**LYDE
STIRLING
Arnold Clark, Kerse Road.
Tel: (01786) 478686.
Europcar UK Ltd,
Mogil Motors Ltd, Drip Road.
Tel: (01786) 472164.
Finlay Guy Ltd,
11 Whitehouse Road.
Tel: (01786) 463137.
National Car Rental,
Borestone Crescent, St. Ninians.
Tel: (01786) 470123.

THE **W**EST **C**OAST
FORT **W**ILLIAM
Ace Car & Van Hire,
Tom-na-Faire, North Road.
Tel: (01397) 703348.
Budget Rent-a-Car,
Road to the Isles Filling Station,
Lochy Bridge.
Tel: (01397) 702500.

OBAN
**Argyll Motor Services (Oban)
Ltd**, Shore Street.
Tel: (01631) 563519.
**Fiat Rental, Hazelbank Motors
Ltd**, Lynn Road.
Tel: (01631) 566476.

INNER **H**EBRIDES
SKYE
Ewen MacRae,
West End Garage, Portree.
Tel: (01478) 612334.
Sutherland's Garage, Broadford.
Tel: (01471) 822225.

OUTER **H**EBRIDES
LEWIS
Lewis Car Rentals,
52 Bayhead Street, Stornoway.
Tel: (01851) 703760.
Lochs Motor Transport,
33 South Beach St., Stornoway.
Tel: (01851) 705857.
Stornoway Car Hire, Airport.
Tel: (01851) 702658.

BENBECULA
Ask Car Hire, Linicleat.
Tel: (01870) 602818/602862
night.
MacLennan Bros. (Motors) Ltd,
Balivanich. Tel: (01870) 602191.

SOUTH **U**IST
Laing Motors, Lochboisdale.
Tel: (01878) 700267.

CENTRAL **S**COTLAND AND **F**IFE
PERTH
Arnold Clark,
St. Leonard's Bank.
Tel: (01738) 442202.
Europcar UK Ltd,
26 Glasgow Road.
Tel: (01738) 636888.
Hertz Rent-a-Car,
405 High Street.
Tel: (01738) 624108.
Practical Car & Van Rental,
97 Crieff Road.
Tel: (01738) 620804.

THE **E**AST **C**OAST
ABERDEEN
Arnold Clark, Girdleness Road.
Tel: (01224) 249159.
Avis Rent-a-Car,
16 Broomhill Road.
Tel: (01224) 574252.
Europcar UK Ltd.,
121 Causewayend.
Tel: (01224) 631199.
Hertz Rent-a-Car,
Railway Station.
Tel: (01224) 210748.

Mitchell's Self Drive,
35 Chapel Street.
Tel: (01224) 642642.
National Car Rental,
46 Summer Street.
Tel: (01224) 626955.

ABERDEEN AIRPORT
Avis Rent-a-Car, Dyce.
Tel: (01224) 722282.
Europcar UK Ltd,
Terminal Building.
Tel: (01224) 770770.

Hertz Rent-a-Car,
Terminal Building Dyce.
Tel: (01224) 722373.

DUNDEE
Arnold Clark, East Dock Street.
Tel: (01382) 226521.
Budget Rent-a-Car,
Tayford Motor Co., Balfield Road.
Tel: (01382) 644664.
Hertz Rent-a-Car,
West Marketgait.
Tel: (01382) 223711.
Mitchell's Self Drive,
90 Marketgait.
Tel: (01382) 223484.
National Car Rental,
45–53 Gellalty Street.
Tel: (01382) 224037.

ELGIN
B & J Hire, Sandy Road.
Tel: (01343) 542625.

THE NORTHERN HIGHLANDS
AVIEMORE
**MacDonald's Self Drive Car
Hire,** Tiga Beag, 13 Muirton
Avenue. Tel: (01479) 811444.

INVERGORDON
Ken's Garage, Kildary.
Tel: (01862) 842266.

INVERNESS
Budget Rent-a-Car,
Railway Terrace.
Tel: (01463) 713333.
Cordiners Inverness Ltd,
Harbour Road.
Tel: (01463) 710000.
National Car Rental,
Shore Sreet.
Tel: (01463) 238084.

Europcar UK Ltd, Highlander
Service Station, Millburn Road.
Tel: (01463) 235337.
Hertz Rent-a-Car,
Railway Station.
Tel: (01463) 711479.
H.W. Jack (Car Hire) Ltd,
17 Henderson Drive.
Tel: (01463) 236572.
Kenning Car Rental, Unit 3,
Highland House, Longman Road.
Tel: (01463) 242400.
Arnold Clark,
47 Harbour Road, Inverness.
Tel: (01463) 236200.
Sharps Reliable Wrecks,
1st Floor, Highland Rail House,
Station Square, Academy Street.
Tel: (01463) 236684.

INVERNESS AIRPORT
Avis Rent-a-Car, Dalcross.
Tel: (01667) 462787.
Hertz Rent-a-Car,
Terminal Building.
Tel: (01667) 462652.

ORKNEY
KIRKWALL
Europcar UK Ltd,
Scarth Hire, Great Western Road.
Tel: (01856) 872601.
W.R. Tulloch & Sons Ltd,
Castle Garage, Castle Street.
Tel: (01856) 876262.

KIRKWALL AIRPORT
W.R. Tulloch & Sons Ltd,
Terminal Building.
Tel: (01856) 875500.

SHETLAND
LERWICK
Bolt's Car Hire, 26 North Road.
Tel: (01595) 693636.
John Leask & Son, Esplanade.
Tel: (01595) 693162.
Star Rent-a-Car,
22 Commercial Street.
Tel: (01595) 692075.
Stronach Gordon, Garthspool.
Tel: (01595) 693718.

SUMBURGH AIRPORT
Bolt's Car Hire.
Tel: (01950) 460777.
John Leask & Son.
Tel: (01950) 460209.

Where to Stay

A wide range of accommodation
is available in Scotland, from
hotels of international standard
to simple bed-and-breakfast
(B&B) accommodation. Prices
vary from under £20 a night for
bed-and-breakfast to over £100
at the most expensive hotel.

The Scottish Tourist Board
has recently introduced a new
system of grading accommodation concentrating on assess-
ment of quality (although symbols still indicate services available). Star gradings range from
one star (fair and acceptable) to
five stars (exceptional/world
class). These are applied to all
types of accommodation including hotels, bed-and-breakfasts
and self-catering.

You are, however, still likely
to come across places graded
by the old dual system. This
tells you first how extensive the
facilities are, from "listed" for
the most basic facilities up to
five crowns for those with the
most facilities. In addition, the
accommodation is graded for
quality into three categories to
include: "Approved",
"Commended" or "Highly
Commended".

If planning a caravan holiday,
look out for the Thistle logo.
The "Thistle Commendation" is
awarded by the industry and the
Tourist Board to parks which
meet the highest standards of
excellence in environment, facilities and the caravans.

Staying in bed-and-breakfast
accommodation is not only economical, it is also a flexible and
potentially interesting way to
see the country. Local tourist

offices operate booking schemes and, except at the height of the tourist season in July and August, it is not necessary to book in advance. Bed-and-breakfasts in the Scottish Tourist Board scheme will, at a minimum, be clean and comfortable. With luck you may find the proprietor friendly and a mine of local information with suggestions about the route to take or the things to see and do. Most of the better bed-and-breakfast establishments serve dinner on request, which is usually excellent and modestly priced.

Particularly good value are Campus Hotels, the name given to bed-and-breakfasts and self-catering facilities offered by the Scottish Universities in Aberdeen, St Andrews, Dundee, Edinburgh, Glasgow and Stirling. These are available during vacations. In addition to accommodation, they offer the use of university facilities such as tennis courts and swimming pools.

Information on all types of accommodation is available at the Scottish Tourist Board and local tourist information centres *(see page 316)*.

Except for the more expensive city hotels, prices quoted include breakfast. Approximate guides to prices per person per night in a double room are: £ = below £20; ££ = £20–£30; £££ = £30–£50; ££££ = £50–£70; £££££ = above £70. On occasions, the distinction between bed-and-breakfast establishments, guest houses and private hotels becomes blurred, especially when the former have en suite facilities and serve dinner.

Hotels & Guest Houses

EDINBURGH HOTELS
(Area code: 0131)
£££££ (above £70 per person)
Balmoral Hotel, Princes Street.
Tel: 556 2414. Fax: 557 3747.
189 rooms. Edinburgh's

premier hotel, built in 1862 and reopened in 1991 after a £23 million facelift. Many rooms with view of the castle. **£££££**
Caledonian Hotel, Princes Street. Tel: 459 9988. Fax: 225 6632. 236 rooms. The "Grande Dame" of Edinburgh hotels is constantly being upgraded. Many rooms with view of the castle. **£££££**
George Inter-Continental, 19–21 George Street. Tel: 225 1251. Fax: 226 5644. 195 rooms. Very central, well-established, grand old hotel, recently refurbished. **£££££**
Holiday Inn Crowne Plaza, 80 High Street. Tel: 557 9797. Fax: 557 9789. 238 rooms. A modern hotel situated on the Royal Mile. Well equipped leisure centre and undercover car park. **£££££**
Sheraton Grand Hotel, 1 Festival Square. Tel: 229 9131. Fax: 229 6254. 261 rooms newly refurbished. Set back from busy Lothian Road and close to city centre. Complete leisure club. **£££££**

££££ (£50–£70 per person)
Carlton Highland Hotel, 19 North Bridge. Tel: 557 2368. Fax: 556 2691. 197 rooms. Impressive Victorian building directly opposite offices of *The Scotsman*. Leisure centre, nightclub and 3 restaurants. **££££**
Channings, South Learmont Gardens. Tel: 315 2226. Fax: 332 9631. 48 rooms. A series of splendid Edwardian adjoining houses a few minutes from city centre. Comfortable reception area and lounges. Bedrooms individually furnished. **££££**
Howard Hotel, 34 Great King Street. Tel: 557 3500. Fax: 557 6515. 15 rooms. Three interconnected 18th-century town houses in the New Town result in a magnificent classical hotel. Garden. **££££**
Norton House Hotel, Ingliston. Tel: 333 1275. Fax: 333 5305. 47 rooms. Splendid country

house hotel close to airport and Royal Highland Show grounds. **££££**
Roxburghe Hotel, 38 Charlotte Square. Tel: 225 3921. Fax: 220 2518. 75 rooms. Distinguished hotel situated close to Princes Street. Recently refurbished. **££££**
Royal Terrace Hotel, 18 Royal Terrace. Tel: 557 3222. Fax: 557 5334. 93 rooms. Georgian terrace building on a cobbled street, minutes from east end of Princes Street. Leisure club and large private garden. **££££–£££££**

£££ (£30–£50 per person)
Bank Hotel, 1 South Bridge Road. Tel: 556 9043. Fax: 558 1362. 9 rooms. Former bank in midst of Royal Mile, now converted into cafe-bar with bedrooms above. **£££**
Bruntsfield Hotel, 69–74 Bruntsfield Place. Tel: 229 1393. Fax: 229 5634. 50 rooms. Well-established hotel 3 miles (5 km) from city centre. **£££**
Edinburgh Capital Moat House, Clermiston Road. Tel: 535 9988. Fax: 334 9712. 111 rooms. Well-appointed hotel 3 miles (5km) from city centre. Leisure club. **£££–££££**
Edinburgh City Travel Inn, 1 Morrison Link. Tel: 228 9819. Fax: 228 9836. 128 rooms. Interesting bid to provide economical, comfortable, no-frills accommodation in city centre. **££–£££**
Holiday Inn Garden Court, 107 Queensferry Road. Tel: 332 2442. Fax: 332 3408. 119 rooms. Friendly hotel 1½ miles (2.5 km) west of city centre. **£££**
Thrums Private Hotel, 14/15 Minto Street, Newington. Tel: 667 5545. Fax: 667 8707. 14 rooms. Detached Georgian house with garden, five minutes from city centre. **£££**

EDINBURGH GUEST HOUSES
££ (£20–£30 per person)
Advocate,
28 Northumberland Street.
Tel: 557 8036. Fax: 558 3453.
7 rooms. William Playfair's old home, a handsome Georgian town house in the heart of the city. **££**
Ashlyn Guest House,
42 Inverleith Row.
Tel/Fax: 552 2954.
8 rooms (5 en suite). Listed Georgian house. Close to Botanic Garden and five minutes from city centre. **££**
Meadows Guest House,
17 Glengyle Terrace.
Tel: 229 9559. Fax: 229 2226.
5 rooms (3 en suite). Comfortably furnished, close to city centre. **££**
Salisbury Guest House,
45 Salisbury Road.
Tel/Fax: 667 1264. 12 rooms (9 en suite). Georgian listed building, near Holyrood Palace and Royal Mile. **££**
Sibbet House,
26 Northumberland Street.
Tel: 556 1078. Fax: 557 9445.
5 rooms (4 en suite). Stay with the "Auld Alliance" (Scotland-France) in a home filled with antiques and family photographs in heart of New Town. **££**
Stuart House,
12 East Claremont Street.
Tel: 557 9030. Fax: 557 0563.
7 rooms (6 en suite). Refurbished Georgian house close to city centre. Non-smoking. **££**

£ (below £20 per person)
Joppa Turrets, 1 Lower Joppa.
Tel: 669 5806. 5 rooms (3 en suite). For those who must be by the seaside. On the beach at Joppa but close to bus routes and 5 miles (8 km) from city centre. **£–££**
Newington Guest House,
18 Newington Road.
Tel: 667 3356. Fax: 667 8307.
8 rooms (5 en suite). Lovely period furnishings in a Victorian house on the main road into the city from the south. **£**

GLASGOW HOTELS
(All phone numbers carry the code 0141)
£££££ (above £70 per person)
Hilton Glasgow, 1 William Street. Tel: 204 5555. Fax: 204 5004. 319 rooms. New 20-floor tower in the centre of the city, just off the motorway. Extensive health and leisure club. **£££££**
One Devonshire Gardens,
1 Devonshire Gardens.
Tel: 339 2001. Fax: 337 1663.
27 rooms. Exquisite West End hotel in residential district. Each room different, service deluxe and old-fashioned. **£££££**

What the codes mean
Approximate prices per person per night in a double room:
● £ = below £20
● ££ = £20–£30
● £££ = £30–£50
● ££££ = £50–£70
● £££££ = above £70

££££ (£50–£70 per person)
Charing Cross Tower Hotel,
10 Elmbank Gardens.
Tel: 221 1000. Fax: 248 1000.
282 rooms. Modern, well-appointed hotel west of city centre, close to motorway links. **££££**
Copthorne Hotel,
George Square.
Tel: 332 6711. Fax: 332 4264.
141 rooms. Situated in the heart of George Square next to Queen Street Station. **££££**
Forte Posthouse Glasgow City,
Bothwell Street.
Tel: 248 2656. Fax: 221 8986.
247 rooms. Five-minute walk from Central Station. **££££**
Glasgow Thistle Hotel,
36 Cambridge Street.
Tel: 332 3311. Fax: 332 4050.
302 rooms. First-class hotel in heart of the city. **££££**
Marriott Glasgow,
500 Argyle Street.
Tel: 226 5577. Fax: 221 7676.
298 rooms. Standard modern hotel just off the motorway.

Excellent health club with pool and two squash courts. **££££**
Moat House, Congress Road.
Tel: 306 9988. Fax: 221 2022.
264 rooms. One of the city's newest hotels, sited on the River Clyde next to the Scottish Exhibition Centre. **££££**
Town House Hotel, Nelson Mandela Place. Tel: 332 3320. Fax: 332 9756. 36 rooms. Grand, lavishly furnished hotel in the heart of the city. **££££**

£££ (£30–£50 per person)
Best Western Ewington Hotel,
132 Queens Drive.
Tel: 423 1152. Fax: 422 2030.
45 rooms. Well-appointed terrace hotel in leafy street beside Queen's Park. **£££**
Central Hotel,
99 Gordon Street.
Tel: 221 9680. Fax: 226 3948.
222 rooms. The city's oldest hotel is part of Central Station. Recently refurbished. Leisure centre. **£££**
Sherbrooke Castle,
11 Sherbrooke Avenue.
Tel: 427 4227. Fax: 427 5685.
25 rooms. Scottish baronial castle in own grounds on south side, about 3 miles (5 km) from city centre. Handy for the Burrell Collection and Pollok Country Park. **£££**
Stakis Glasgow Grosvenor,
Grosvenor Terrace.
Tel: 339 8811. Fax: 334 0710.
96 rooms. Hotel with striking façade near Botanic Gardens, University of Glasgow and trendy Byres Road. **£££**

££ (£20–£30 per person)
Boswell Hotel,
27 Mansionhouse Road.
Tel: 632 9812. Fax: 632 5987.
12 rooms. Small bustling hotel on south side of city with three busy bars. Near public transport. Family suites. **££**

GLASGOW GUEST HOUSES
££ (£20–£30 per person)
Iona Guest House, 39 Hillhead Street. Tel/Fax: 334 2346.

9 rooms (none en suite). Well-established and comfortable. Close to Botanic Gardens. ££

McClays Guest House, 268 Renfrew Street. Tel: 332 4796. 62 rooms (39 en suite). Well appointed, comfortable guest house only a few minutes from city centre. ££

The Town House, 4 Hughenden Terrace. Tel: 357 0862. Fax: 339 9605. 10 rooms. Elegantly refurbished Victorian townhouse in quiet conservation area in West End. ££

£ (below £20 per person)
Alamo Guest House, 46 Gray Street. Tel: 339 2395. 7 rooms (3 en suite). Situated on pleasant, quiet road alongside Kelvingrove Park. £

Kirkland House, 42 St Vincent Crescent. Tel/Fax: 248 3458. 5 rooms (all en suite). In the quieter part of a beautiful crescent. Close to the city centre. £

The Victorian House, 212 Renfrew Street. Tel: 332 0129. Fax: 353 3155. 40 rooms. Elegant guest house close to Royal Concert Hall, galleries and museums. No restaurant. £

THE BORDERS
Hawick
Kirklands Hotel, West Stewart Place. Tel: (01450) 372263. Fax: (01450) 370404. 12 rooms. Charming Victorian house with large garden. £££

Mansfield House Hotel, Weensland Road. Tel: (01450) 373988. Fax: (01450) 372007. 12 rooms. Victorian country house hotel in 10 acres (4 hectares). Glorious public rooms. £££

Innerleithen
The Ley. Tel/Fax: (01896) 830240. 4 rooms (all en suite). Victorian home set in 30 acres (12 hectares) of woodland. Beautifully furnished, superb dinners accompanied by good wine card. Open Feb–Oct. ££

Traquair Arms, Traquair Road. Tel: (01896) 830229. Fax: (01896) 830260. 10 rooms. Charming country house hotel with excellent food, close to historic Traquair House. £££

Kelso
Sunlaws House. Tel: (01573) 450331. Fax: (01573) 450611. 22 bedrooms. 18th-century country house, owned by the Duke of Roxburghe, 3 miles (5km) south of Kelso. Superb public rooms. 200 acres (81 hectares) of beautiful grounds. Fishing, clay-pigeon shooting, croquet, tennis, championship golf course. ££££

Cross Keys, The Square. Tel: (01573) 223303. Fax: (01573) 225792. 25 rooms. Old coaching inn set in town centre square with French character. £££

Melrose
Burts Hotel, Market Square. Tel: (01896) 822285. Fax: (01896) 822870. 21 rooms. Tastefully modernised old town house in main square, close to magnificent ruined abbey. £££

Peebles
Tontine Hotel, High Street. Tel: (01721) 720892. Fax:(01721) 729732. 35 rooms. Long-established hotel on graceful main street, with views from rear to the River Tweed. £££

Peebles Hotel Hydro. Tel: (01721) 720602. Fax: (01721) 722999. 137 rooms. Large imposing château-style hotel set in 34 acres (14 hectares) overlooking the River Tweed valley and Border hills. Leisure centre, excellent tennis, walking and riding. £££–££££

St Boswells
Dryburgh Abbey Hotel. Tel: (01835) 822261. Fax: (01835) 823945. 26 rooms. This graceful, renovated Victorian building is beautifully situated and stands immediately next to Dryburgh Abbey and the River Tweed. ££££

Selkirk
Glen Hotel, Yarrow Terrace. Tel/Fax: (01750) 20259. 8 rooms. Small, friendly hotel close to Ettrick Water, good food. £££

THE SOUTHWEST
Arran
Auchrannie Country House Hotel, Brodick. Tel: (01770) 302334. Fax: (01770) 302812. 28 rooms. Large mansion in 10 acres (4 hectares) of grounds near bay and castle. Full leisure complex, award-winning restaurant. £££

Kinloch Hotel, Blackwaterfoot. Tel: (01770) 860444. Fax: (01770) 860447. 44 rooms. Superb views of Mull of Kintyre. Leisure facilities include indoor pool and squash court. £££

Ayr
Jarvis Caledonian Hotel, Dalblair Road. Tel: (01292) 269331. Fax: (01292) 610722. 114 rooms. Town centre hotel close to all facilities and beach: many rooms with fine views. Leisure club. £££

Dumfries
Cairndale Hotel, English Street. Tel: (01387) 254111. Fax: (01387) 250555. 76 rooms. Family-owned hotel, regular live entertainment, full leisure club. £££

Gatehouse of Fleet
Cally Palace. Tel: (01557) 814341. Fax: (01557) 814522. 56 rooms. Magnificent public rooms and comfortable bedrooms in this Georgian mansion set in 100 acres (40 hectares) of forest and parkland. Extensive leisure facilities. £££

Murray Arms Inn, Ann Street.
Tel: (01557) 814207.
Fax: (01557) 814370.
13 rooms. Attractive 18th-century posting inn where Robert Burns wrote *Scots Wha Hae*. Comfortable bedrooms. £££

Girvan
Turnberry Hotel, Golf Courses & Spa, Turnberry. Tel: (01655) 331000. Fax: (01655) 331706. 132 rooms. For nearly 100 years a hotel of choice. Country club and spa incorporating 17 deluxe bedrooms. Elegance and gracious service obvious throughout, especially in the restaurants which provide superb views. Horse-riding, squash, tennis and, of course, golf. £££££

Moffat
Auchen Castle Hotel, Beattock. Tel: (01683) 300407. Fax: (01683) 300667. 25 rooms, of which 10 are in modern wing. Set in 28 acres (12 hectares) with spectacular views. £££
Beechwood Country House Hotel. Tel: (01683) 220210. Fax: (01683) 220889. 7 rooms. Elegant country house overlooking Moffat. £££
Moffat House Hotel, High Street. Tel: (01683) 220039. Fax: (01683) 221288. 20 rooms. An 18th-century Adam mansion set in own grounds. £££

Newton Stewart
Kirroughtree Hotel. Tel: (01671) 402141. Fax: (01671) 402425. 17 rooms. Cheerful, colourful Georgian mansion in 8 acres (3 hectares) of landscaped gardens. Strong Burns associations. Renowned for Scottish food. ££££

Stranraer
North West Castle Hotel. Tel: (01776) 704413. Fax: (01776) 702646.

71 rooms. Comfortable hotel on seafront. Indoor curling rink and full leisure centre with indoor pool. £££

Troon
Marine Highland Hotel, Crosbie Road. Tel: (01292) 314444. Fax: (01292) 316922. 72 rooms. Next to golf courses, close to sea. Health and fitness club, 2 restaurants. £££–££££
Piersland House Hotel, Craigend Road. Tel: (01292) 314747. Fax: (01292) 315613. 23 rooms. Built for Sir Alexander Walker of whisky fame, the hotel is adjacent to the golf courses. £££

What the codes mean

Approximate prices per person per night in a double room:
● £ = below £20
● ££ = £20–£30
● £££ = £30–£50
● ££££ = £50–£70
● £££££ = above £70

FORTH & CLYDE
Airth
Airth Castle Hotel. Tel: (01324) 831411. Fax: (01324) 831419. 75 rooms. Historic castle building, now converted to a fine hotel set in 17 acres (7 hectares) of grounds. Leisure club. ££££

Denny
The Topps, Fintry Road, Denny. Tel: (01324) 822471. Fax: (01324) 823099. 8 rooms. Working sheep farm in lovely location, 11 miles (18 km) south of Stirling. Non-smokers only. Superb cuisine. ££

Falkirk
Best Western Park Hotel, Camelon Road. Tel: (01324) 628331. Fax: (01324) 611593. 55 rooms. Well-appointed hotel close to Dollar Park and Mariner Leisure Centre. £££

Stirling
Garfield Guest House, 12 Victoria Square. Tel: (01786) 473730. 8 rooms. Large Victorian house in quiet square, close to town centre. B&B only. ££
Golden Lion Hotel, 8 King Street. Tel: (01786) 475351. Fax: (01786) 472755. 71 rooms. Recently refurbished hotel in town centre. £££
Park Lodge Hotel, 32 Park Terrace. Tel: (01786) 474862. Fax: (01786) 449748. 10 rooms. Part Victorian, part Georgian hotel in heart of town filled with antiques. Some rooms with 4-poster beds. £££
Stirling Highland Hotel, Spittal Street. Tel: (01786) 475444. Fax: (01786) 462929. 76 rooms. Recently restored, listed, former school with complete leisure centre in town centre. ££££
Stirling Management Centre, University of Stirling. Tel: (01786) 451666. Fax: (01786) 450472. 74 rooms (all en suite). Purpose-built conference centre/hotel on bucolic university campus 3 miles (5 km) from Stirling. £££
Terraces Hotel, 4 Melville Terrace. Tel: (01786) 472268. Fax: (01786) 450314. 15 rooms. Georgian house close to town centre. Friendly atmosphere, good food. £££

THE WEST COAST
Appin
Invercreran Country House Hotel, Glen Creran. Tel: (01631) 730414. Fax: (01631) 730532. 7 rooms. Unusual, isolated country house hotel in 25 acres (10 hectares) of woodland with superb views and individually designed bedrooms. Painted ceiling in dining room will get all talking. ££££

Arisaig
Arisaig House, Beasdale. Tel: (01687) 450622. Fax: (01687) 450626.

13 rooms. Handsome Victorian house set in 20 acres (8 hectares) of magnificent grounds which stretch down to the sea. Beautiful walled garden. Half-board only. Highly regarded contemporary cuisine. (Room rate puts hotel in ££££ category.)

Arrochar
Cobbler Hotel. Tel: (01301) 702238. Fax: (01301) 702353. 60 rooms. Superbly sited in landscaped gardens on shores of Loch Long, below the impressive mountain whose name it bears. £££

Crinan
Crinan Hotel. Tel: (01546) 830261. Fax: (01546) 830292. 22 rooms. Some rooms have private balconies; all have stunning sea views. Dine in Lock 16, the rooftop restaurant, and admire the seascapes and the activity on the canal below. ££££

Eriska
Isle of Eriska, Ledaig by Oban. Tel: (01631) 720371. Fax: (01631) 720531. 16 rooms. Welcoming hotel on private island joined to the mainland by a short bridge. Bedrooms vary in size and each has its own character. Lovely grounds with tennis, croquet. £££££

Fort William
Innseagan House Hotel, Achintore Road. Tel: (01397) 702452. Fax: (01397) 702606. 24 rooms (21 en suite). Comfortable, good food and great views of Loch Linnhe. Sited 1½ miles (2.5 km) south of town. ££–£££
Inverlochy Castle Hotel, Torlundy. Tel: (01397) 702177. Fax: (01397) 702953. 17 rooms. Possibly the grandest hotel in Scotland, with imposing public rooms. Impeccable service. Set in glorious grounds with views of Ben Nevis. Wonderful contemporary cuisine

and outstanding wine list. Snooker, tennis and game fishing. £££££
Moorings Hotel, Banavie. Tel: (01397) 772797. Fax: (01397) 772441. 24 rooms. 3 miles (5 km) from town at Neptune's Staircase at the start of the Caledonian Canal with superb views of Ben Nevis. £££

Gairloch
Old Inn. Tel: (01445) 712006. Fax: (01445) 712445. 14 rooms. Charming hotel in mountain and sea setting. Excellent food. £££

Glenelg
Glenelg Inn. Tel/Fax: (01599) 522273. 6 rooms. Lively pub with restaurant is the focal point of this waterfront inn. Bedrooms, which are individually and tastefully decorated, have grand views of Skye. £££

Inveraray
Argyll Hotel. Tel: (01499) 302466. Fax: (01499) 302389. 30 rooms, all en suite. Sited almost at the castle gates on the shores of Loch Fyne, hotel offers true Scottish cuisine and hospitality. £££

Kyle of Lochalsh
Lochalsh Hotel, Ferry Road. Tel: (01599) 534202. Fax: (01599) 534881. 35 rooms. Magnificently situated, comfortable hotel on the water's edge with superb views of Skye and the Cuillins. £££

Loch Awe
Ardanaiseig Hotel, by Taynuilt. Tel: (01866) 833333. Fax: (01866) 833222. 14 rooms. Elegant country house hotel far away from it all. Beautiful public rooms. Woodland garden. Hotel boats suitable for fishing, solarium, tennis, snooker. Half-board only. ££££
Taychreggan Hotel, by Taynuilt. Tel: (01866) 833211.

Fax: (01866) 833244. 20 rooms. Delightful hotel around a cobbled courtyard on a secluded part of Loch Awe. Game and coarse fishing, clay-pigeon shooting, boating. £££

Loch Lomond
The Lodge on Loch Lomond, Luss. Tel: (01436) 860202. Fax: (01436) 860203. 29 rooms. Lochside hotel with magnificent views. Sauna in every bedroom. £££
Ardlui Hotel, Ardlui. Tel: (01301) 704243. Fax: (01301) 704268. 11 rooms (8 en suite). Friendly country house hotel on loch shore, good atmosphere, fine food, excellent walking. £££

Loch Melfort
Loch Melfort Hotel, Arduaine. Tel: (01852) 200233. Fax: (01852) 200214. 26 rooms. A relaxed atmosphere prevails in this splendid hotel which looks out on magnificent scenery, 20 miles (32 km) south of Oban. £££

Oban
Caledonian Hotel, Station Square. Tel: (01631) 563133. Fax: (01631) 562998. 70 rooms. Imposing, recently modernised hotel. Close to the ferries to the islands. £££
Columba Hotel, Esplanade. Tel: (01631) 562183. Fax: (01631) 564683. 49 rooms. Well-established hotel on waterfront. £££
Knipoch Hotel, 6 miles (10km) south of Oban. Tel: (01852) 316251. 17 rooms. Peaceful, elegant paradise with delightful public rooms and well appointed bedrooms. Has its own smokery which contributes to the superb meals. Excellent wine list. ££££
Manor House Hotel, Gallanach Road. Tel: (01631) 562087. Fax: (01631) 563053. 11 rooms. Situated in own grounds on commanding promontory above Oban Bay. £££ (including dinner).

Willowburn Hotel, Clachan Seil, Island of Seil. Tel: (01852) 300276. 6 rooms. Delightful small hotel 10 miles (16km) south of Oban, reached by a single-span bridge "over the Atlantic". ££

Talladale
Loch Maree Hotel, Talladale, by Achnasheen. Tel: (01445) 760288. Fax: (01445) 760241. 20 rooms. Refurbished hotel situated on Loch Maree with a wonderful atmosphere; a fishermen's haven. Bedrooms somewhat small except for the one in which Queen Victoria stayed. £££

Tarbert (Loch Fyne)
Stonefield Castle Hotel. Tel: (01880) 820836. Fax: (01880) 820929. 33 rooms. Baronial mansion set in 56 acres (20 hectares) with magnificent views over Loch Fyne. Glorious gardens. Outdoor heated pool, sauna, solarium, snooker. ££££

Ullapool
Ceilidh Place, 14 West Argyle Street. Tel: (01854) 612103. Fax: (01854) 612886. 24 rooms (10 en suite). With bookshop, café, restaurant and concert hall, this is not only a good hotel but is also the cultural centre of Ullapool. Bunk House with 11 rooms is spartan but immaculate and great for families. ££–£££
Harbour Lights Hotel, Garve Road. Tel: (01854) 612222. 19 rooms. Well appointed, comfortable hotel close to ferry terminal. £££
Strathmore Guest House, Lochinver Road. Tel: (01854) 612423. 5 rooms (4 en suite). The upstairs en suite rooms with a private lounge are very pleasant and have commanding views of Loch Broom. ££

INNER HEBRIDES

Iona
St Columba Hotel. Tel: (01681) 700304. 26 rooms. Situated close to the famous abbey, the hotel enjoys fine views across the water to Mull. £££

Mull
Ardfenaig House, by Bunessan. Tel/Fax: (01681) 700210. 5 rooms (3 en suite). Isolated spot, perfect for relaxing and close to ferry for Iona. Set in 15 acres (6 hectares) of woodland and gardens. ££££ (includes dinner).
Druimard Country House Hotel, Dervaig. Tel/Fax: (01688) 400345. 6 rooms. Beautifully restored Victorian country house widely known for its interesting cuisine. Pleasant conservatory and informal atmosphere. £££
Pennygate Lodge, Craignure. Tel: (01680) 812333. 7 rooms (4 en suite). Former Georgian manse, in 5 acres (2 hectares) of gardens, close to the ferry terminal from Oban. ££

What the codes mean

Approximate prices per person per night in a double room:
- £ = below £20
- ££ = £20–£30
- £££ = £30–£50
- ££££ = £50–£70
- £££££ = above £70

Western Isles Hotel, Tobermory. Tel: (01688) 302012. Fax: (01688) 302297. 23 rooms. Gothic-style building magnificently situated above Tobermory Bay. £££

Raasay
Isle of Raasay Hotel. Tel: (01478) 660222. 9 rooms. Take the ferry from Sconser on Skye to the smaller island of Raasay for a real escape in beautiful surroundings. Superb walking and birdlife. £££

SKYE

Ardvasar Hotel, Ardvasar. Tel: (01471) 844223. 10 rooms.

Traditional white-washed hotel overlooks Sound of Sleat and Mallaig. One mile from Mallaig–Armdale ferry. £££
Atholl House Hotel, Dunvegan. Tel: (01470) 521219. Fax: (01470) 521481. 10 rooms. Former manse on the outskirts of village with superb views of Loch Dunvegan. £££
Cuillin Hills Hotel, Portree. Tel: (01478) 612003. Fax: (01478) 613092. 25 rooms. Situated just outside Portree with views over Portree Bay to the Cuillins. £££
Eilean Iarmain (Isle of Ornsay) Hotel, Sleat. Tel: (01471) 833332. 12 rooms. Friendly 19th-century inn by the sea featuring Gaelic hospitality. Six rooms are in the inn and six across the drive in the Garden House. Spectacular views. Renowned for its seafood. £££
Flodigarry Country House Hotel, Staffin. Tel: (01470) 552203. Fax: (01470) 552301. 19 rooms. Historic mansion beneath the Quiraing mountains offering glorious views. Separate house where Flora MacDonald once lived has been tastefully converted into rooms. £££
Ptarmigan, Broadford. Tel: (01471) 822744. Fax: (01471) 822745. 3 rooms. Delightful accommodation 8 miles (13km) from the ferry with grand views across Broadford Bay. Binoculars in bedrooms for bird-watchers. ££
Rosedale Hotel, Beaumont Crescent, Portree. Tel: (01478) 613131. Fax: (01478) 612531. 23 rooms. Comfortable, privately-owned waterfront hotel converted from former fishermen's houses. Some bedrooms are small and hotel is a regular warren. £££
Skeabost House Hotel, Skeabost Bridge. Tel: (01470) 532202. Fax: (01470) 532454. 26 rooms. Former hunting lodge in 12 acres (5 hectares) of secluded woodlands and garden on the shore of Loch Snizort.

Famous Sunday buffet lunch in sunny conservatory. £££

Sligachan Hotel,
Sligachan.
Tel: (01478) 650204.
Fax: (01478) 650207.
22 rooms. Famous climbers' hotel, fully modernised, with magnificent views of the Cuillins. Full of atmosphere. Campsite close by for spartans. £££

Viewfield House, Portree.
Tel: (01478) 612217.
Fax: (01478) 613517.
11 rooms (9 en suite). Idiosyncratic country house hotel in extensive wooded grounds overlooking the bay. Open mid Apr–mid Oct.Each room different: all large. Something of a time warp although bathrooms modern. An experience. £££

OUTER HEBRIDES

Barra
Castlebay Hotel,
Castlebay. Tel: (0871) 810223.
12 rooms. Overlooks the bay with its castle. Easy access to ferry terminal. £££

Harris
Scarista House,
Scarista. Tel: (01859) 550238.
Fax: (01859) 550277.
7 rooms. Former manse with superb views of beach and sea. Bedrooms, including those in the annexe, individually designed. No credit cards. £££

Lewis
Seaforth Hotel,
James Street, Stornoway.
Tel: (01851) 702740.
Fax: (01851) 703900.
68 rooms. Large, comfortable hotel close to ferry terminal and town centre. £££

North Uist
Lochmaddy Hotel,
Lochmaddy.
Tel: (01876) 500331.
Fax: (01876) 500210.
15 rooms. Conveniently placed close to the ferry terminal, and with lovely sea views. ££

CENTRAL SCOTLAND AND FIFE

Aberfeldy
Farleyer House, Weem.
Tel: (01887) 820332.
Fax: (01887) 829430.
15 rooms. A touch of luxury in the middle of the Perthshire highlands. A former dower-house dating back to the 16th century. £££–££££

Anstruther
The Spindrift, Pittenweem Road.
Tel/Fax: (01333) 310573.
8 rooms. A Victorian house B&B establishment. Non-smoking. ££

Auchterarder
Gleneagles Hotel. Tel: (01764) 662231. Fax: (01764) 662134. 216 rooms. Elegance is the name of the game here. Public rooms are very grand. Bedrooms are tastefully furnished and comfortable. Nightly dancing to live band in drawing room. Health spa and leisure centre. Activities include tennis and croquet courts, squash, clay-pigeon shooting, coarse and game fishing, horse riding and, of course, golf. £££££

Auchtermuchty
Ardchoille Farm Guest House, Dunshalt. Tel: (01337) 828414. 3 rooms. Elegant, modern farmhouse with superb views of Lomond Hills. Attractive dining room with fine china and crystal: excellent food. ££

Blair Atholl
Dalgreine, Bridge of Tilt.
Tel: (01796) 481276. 6 rooms (3 en suite). Charming large house close to Blair Castle, superb walking, snooker table available. ££

Blairgowrie
Altamount House, Coupar Angus Road. Tel: (01250) 873512. Fax: (01250) 876200. 7 rooms. Well appointed country house, 1 mile (1.5 km) south of the town. Excellent reputation for food. £££

Callander
Bridgend House Hotel,
Bridgend. Tel: (01877) 330130.
Fax: (01877) 331512. 6 rooms (5 en suite). 18th-century family-run hotel with magnificent views of Ben Ledi. £££

Highland House Hotel,
South Church Street.
Tel: (01877) 330269. 9 rooms (7 en suite). Non-smoking Georgian house. ££

Roman Camp Hotel, Callander.
Tel: (01877) 330003.
Fax: (01877) 331533.
14 rooms. Hunting lodge from 1625 set in beautiful gardens that sweep down to the River Teith, in which fishing is available. Renowned for its cuisine. ££££

Arden House, Bracklinn Road.
Tel: (01877) 330235. 6 rooms. A non-smoking house with superb views of the Trossachs. Renowned as the setting for the vintage BBC TV series *Dr Finlay's Casebook.* £££

Crieff
Crieff Hydro Hotel.
Tel: (01764) 655555.
Fax: (01764) 653087.
203 rooms, 11 suites. Magnificent Victorian building, in 800 acres (300 hectares) of grounds. Superb accommodation, food and leisure facilities. £££

Dunblane
Cromlix House, Kinbuck.
Tel: (01786) 822125.
Fax: (01786) 825450.
14 rooms. One of Scotland's great country house hotels. All rooms are large and splendid, and antiques abound. Magnificent conservatory. Noted for its superb food and extensive wine list. Trout and salmon fishing. Also riding, clay-pigeon shooting, tennis and croquet. ££££–£££££

Stakis Dunblane Hydro.
Tel: (01786) 822551.
Fax: (01786) 825403.
219 rooms. Hotel with Victorian façade in 44 acres (18 hectares)

grounds. Excellent sports and leisure facilities. £££

Dunkeld
Kinnaird Estate, Dalguise. Tel: (01796) 482440. Fax: (01796) 482289. 9 rooms. Be pampered in elegant surroundings in this country house hotel 4 miles (6 km) northwest of Dunkeld. Renowned for its cuisine and service. £££££
Stakis Dunkeld House. Tel: (01350) 727771. Fax: (01350) 728924. 85 rooms. Splendid hotel, former home of the Duke of Atholl, on the banks of the River Tay in 280 acres (112 hectares) of woodland. Extensive leisure facilities, clay-pigeon shooting and tennis. ££££

Falkland
Covenanter Hotel. Tel: (01337) 857224. Fax: (01337) 857163. 9 rooms. 17th-century coaching inn in conservation village, close to magnificent Falkland Palace. ££

Glenisla
Glenisla Hotel, Kirkton of Glenisla. Tel/Fax: (01575) 582223. 6 rooms. Friendly, comfortable hotel in magnificent setting in lovely glen. £££

Glenshee
Spittal of Glenshee Hotel. Tel: (01250) 885215. Fax: (01250) 885223. 49 rooms. Slightly eccentric but very friendly and lively hotel in wonderful setting. Regular live entertainment. ££

Killin
Dall Lodge. Tel: (01567) 820217. Fax: (01567) 820726. 10 rooms. Modernised Victorian mansion. Excellent food. Fishing, golf, walking, tennis, bowls. £££

Kinloch Rannoch
Loch Rannoch Hotel. Tel: (01882) 632201. Fax: (01882) 632203.

19 rooms. Converted shooting lodge in magnificent surroundings, excellent food, live entertainment, wide range of leisure activities. £££

Perth
Ballathie House Hotel, Kinclaven by Stanley. Tel: (01250) 883268. Fax: (01250) 883396. 27 rooms plus ground floor suite. Relaxing and civilized former shooting lodge on River Tay. Graciously proportioned public rooms and splendidly comfortable bedrooms. ££££

What the codes mean

Approximate prices per person per night in a double room:
- £ = below £20
- ££ = £20–£30
- £££ = £30–£50
- ££££ = £50–£70
- £££££ = above £70

Huntingtower Hotel, Crieff Road. Tel: (01738) 583771. Fax: (01738) 583777. 32 rooms. Country house hotel 3 miles (5 km) west of Perth, standing in its own beautiful grounds. £££
Iona Guest House, 2 Pitcullen Crescent. Tel: (01738) 627261. Fax: (01738) 444098. 5 rooms. Comfortable, semi-detached house with private parking close to city centre. £
Kinnaird Guest House, 5 Marshall Place. Tel: (01738) 628021. Fax: (01738) 444056. 7 rooms. Comfortable, friendly guest house, part of a Georgian terrace overlooking South Inch. Private parking. £
Murrayshall House Hotel, Scone. Tel: (01738) 551171. Fax: (01738) 552595. 26 rooms. Sumptuously appointed, elegant country house in 300 acres (120 hectares) of parkland, 4 miles (7km) north of Perth. Superb food and wine served in luxurious dining room. Has its

own challenging 18-hole golf course. ££££
Parklands, St Leonards Bank. Tel: (01738) 622451. Fax: (01738) 622046. 14 rooms. Classical Georgian town house, refurbished, overlooking the South Inch park. £££–££££
Queens Hotel, Leonard Street. Tel: (01738) 442222. Fax: (01738) 638496. 51 rooms. Recently modernised and with new leisure complex added. Situated close to the city centre. ££££
Salutation Hotel, 34 South Street. Tel: (01738) 630066. Fax: (01738) 633598. 84 rooms. One of Scotland's oldest hotels, where Bonnie Prince Charlie is said to have stayed. £££
Stakis City Mills Hotel, West Mill Street. Tel: (01738) 628281. Fax: (01738) 643423. 76 rooms. Comfortable hotel overlooking a 15th-century watermill, in the city centre. £££

Pitlochry
Atholl Palace Hotel, Atholl Road. Tel: (01796) 472400. Fax: (01796) 473036. 76 rooms. Majestic building set in 50 acres (20 hectares) and with health club. £££
Dunfallandy House Hotel, Logierait Road. Tel: (01796) 472648. Fax: (01796) 472017. 9 rooms. Georgian mansion set above the town, with glorious views of Tummel valley. ££
Killiecrankie Hotel. Tel: (01796) 473220. Fax: (01796) 472451. 11 rooms. Good country house hotel in beautiful setting overlooking the Pass of Killiecrankie, 3 miles (5 km) north of Pitlochry. £££
Knockendarroch House Hotel, Higher Oakfield. Tel: (01796) 473473. Fax: (01796) 474068. 12 rooms. Victorian mansion overlooking the town and Tummel valley. Two rooms have four-poster beds. ££

Pitlochry Hydro Hotel,
Knockard Road. Tel: (01796)
472666. Fax: (01796) 472238.
64 rooms. Refurbished hotel
with health club standing in own
grounds overlooking town. ££££
Scotland's Hotel, Bonnethill
Road. Tel: (01796) 472292.
Fax: (01796) 473284.
60 rooms. Traditional family-run
hotel with health and leisure
club near centre of town. £££

St Andrews
Argyle Hotel, 127 North Street.
Tel: (01334) 473387.
Fax: (01334) 474664.
16 rooms. Late Victorian
building 400 yards from Old
Course and beaches. ££
Cleveden Guest House,
3 Murray Place.
Tel/Fax: (01334) 474212.
6 rooms (5 en suite). Five
minutes' walk from Old Course,
beach and town centre. ££
Rufflets Country House Hotel,
Strathkinness Low Road.
Tel: (01334) 472594.
Fax: (01334) 478703.
25 rooms. Country house set in
10 acres (4 hectares) of beautiful gardens 2 miles (3 km) from
golf course and beaches. One
of the rooms has a queen-sized
four-poster. Cooking is light with
emphasis on fresh Scottish produce. ££££–£££££
Rusacks Hotel, Pilmour Links.
Tel: (01334) 474321.
Fax: (01334) 477896.
50 rooms. Grand, refurbished
Victorian hotel overlooking 18th
hole of the Old Course. Excellent
service. £££–££££
St Andrews Old Course Hotel.
Tel: (01334) 474371.
Fax: (01334) 477668.
125 rooms. Large, elegant
hotel overlooking the famous
17th "Road" Hole of Old
Course. Well equipped health
club. £££££
West Park House, 5 St Mary's
Place. Tel: (01334) 475933.
4 rooms (3 en suite). Listed
Georgian house close to all
activities. ££

St Fillans
Achray House Hotel.
Tel: (01764) 685231.
Fax: (01764) 685230. 9 rooms.
Welcoming small hotel with
superb views across Loch Earn,
serving excellent food. £££
Four Seasons Hotel.
Tel/Fax: (01764) 685333.
18 rooms. Comfortable,
unpretentious Scandinavian-type
hotel at eastern end of Loch
Earn. Excellent food. £££

THE EAST COAST
Aberdeen
Atholl Hotel, 54 Kings Gate.
Tel: (01224) 323505.
Fax: (01224) 321555.
35 rooms. Elegant granite
Victorian hotel in the west end.
Good reputation for food. £££.
Caledonian Thistle Hotel,
Union Terrace. Tel: (01224)
640233. Fax: (01224) 641627.
80 rooms. Recently refurbished
hotel in city centre. ££££
Copthorne Aberdeen,
122 Huntly Street. Tel: (01224)
630404. Fax: (01224) 640573.
89 rooms. City centre hotel with
all facilities. £££–££££
Craiglynn Private Hotel,
36 Fonthill Road.
Tel/Fax: (01224) 584050.
9 rooms (7 en suite). Victorian
elegance wth modern comforts.
£££
Forte Posthouse, Bridge of Don.
Tel: (01224) 706707.
Fax: (01224) 823923.
123 rooms. New, high standard
hotel next to the Exhibition and
Conference Centre on north
side of city. £££
Marcliffe at Pitfodels,
North Deeside Road, Cults.
Tel: (01224) 861000.
Fax: (01224) 868860.
42 rooms. Country house hotel
in western suburbs. Very well
appointed, excellent food. ££££
Marriott, Overton Circle, Dyce.
Tel: (01224) 770011.
Fax: (01224) 722347.
154 rooms. Luxurious hotel with
full leisure facilities, close to
airport. ££££

Westhill Hotel, Westhill.
Tel: 01224) 740388.
Fax: (01224) 744354.
50 rooms. Modern style, in the
city suburbs, 7 miles (11 km)
from city centre. £££

Aboyne
Hazlehurst Lodge, Ballater
Road. Tel: (01339) 886921.
Fax: (01339) 886660. 4 rooms.
Formerly the coachman's lodge
to Aboyne Castle, filled with
works of art by Scottish artists
of international repute. ££

Alford
Kildrummy Castle Hotel,
Kildrummy. Tel: (01975)
571288. Fax: (01975) 571345.
6 rooms. Baronial mansion with
lots of wood panelling,
tapestries and grand staircase
overlooking ruined 13th-century
castle. Glorious gardens.
Excellent food accompanied by
splendid wine list. ££££

Banchory
Banchory Lodge. Tel: (01330)
822625. Fax: (01330) 825019.
22 rooms. Large, well-furnished
rooms and log fires. The
Victorian furnishings create an
air of traditional luxury. On the
banks of River Dee with private
fishing. £££

Boat of Garten
Avingormack Guest House.
Tel: (01479) 831614. 4 rooms
(2 en suite). Great conversion
of a former croft provides
superb views of Cairngorms
through picture windows.
Specializes in vegetarian and
traditional meals. Non-smoking
house. £

Dundee
Discovery Quay Travel Inn,
Riverside Drive.
Tel: (01382) 203240.
Fax: (01382) 203237.
40 rooms. Friendly, informal
family hotel overlooking River
Tay and close to Discovery
Centre. £££

Old Mansion House,
Auchterhouse by Dundee.
Tel: (01382) 320366.
Fax: (01382) 320400. 6 rooms.
16th-century baronial house
7 miles (11km) north of Dundee.
Spacious bedrooms with excellent bathrooms; splendid service
and views. Outdoor heated pool,
tennis, croquet. £££

Shaftesbury Hotel, 1 Hyndford
Street. Tel: (01382) 669216.
Fax: (01382) 641598.
12 rooms. Refurbished Victorian
mansion in peaceful residential
area yet close to city and
University. £££

Stakis Dundee Hotel, Earl Grey
Place. Tel: (01382) 229271.
Fax: (01382) 200072.
104 rooms. Modern hotel with
good leisure facilities. Situated
on the banks of the River Tay
with views across to Fife.
£££–££££

Swallow Hotel, Invergowrie.
Tel: (01382) 641122.
Fax: (01382) 568340.
107 rooms. Victorian mansion
cleverly renovated and extended.
Has a leisure club and a
conservatory restaurant. £££

Elgin
Mansion House Hotel,
The Haugh. Tel: (01343)
548811. Fax: (01343) 547916.
22 rooms. Tastefully restored
and decorated baronial mansion
with castellated tower overlooking River Lossie. Many rooms
have four-poster beds. Leisure
centre with indoor pool. ££££

Grantown-on-Spey
Culdearn House, Woodlands
Terrace. Tel: (01479) 872106.
Fax: (01479) 873641. 9 rooms.
Elegant Victorian house. Great
selection of malt whiskies and
good wine list. Taste of
Scotland dinners. £££

Skye of Curr Hotel, Dulnain
Bridge. Tel/Fax: (01479)
851345. 8 rooms. Lovely old
house, nicely refurbished, in
secluded grounds. Excellent
food and wine. £££

Huntly
Old Manse of Marnoch, Bridge
of Marnoch. Tel/Fax: (01466)
780873. 5 rooms. Charming
1805 manse on banks of River
Deveron. Rooms large and individually furnished. Excellent food
and possibly the world's most
extensive breakfast menu. ££

What the codes mean

Approximate prices per person
per night in a double room:
● £ = below £20
● ££ = £20–£30
● £££ = £30–£50
● ££££ = £50–£70
● £££££ = above £70

Macduff
The Highland Haven, Shore
Street. Tel: (01261) 832408.
Fax: (01261) 833652. 24
rooms. Harbour-side hotel with
great views. Good food. Golf
and fishing available. £££

Montrose
Grey Harlings, Dorward Road.
Tel: (01674) 673980. 6 rooms
(2 en suite). Former golf clubhouse, now providing welcoming
accommodation. Beds and
breakfasts both king size. £

Park Hotel, John Street.
Tel: (01674) 673415.
Fax: (01674) 677091.
59 rooms. Family-run hotel with
high standards of accommodation and food. Situated in a
quiet location yet close to town
centre and beaches. £££

Nairn
Carnach House Hotel,
Delnies. Tel: (01667) 452094.
Fax: (01667) 452994.
8 rooms. Edwardian house
2 miles (3 km) west of Nairn in
8 acres (3.5 hectares) of wooded grounds. £££

Clifton Hotel, Viewfield Street.
Tel: (01667) 453119.
Fax: (01667) 452836.
12 rooms. The owner's theatrical interests are evident in this
unusual town house hotel with

sea views. Bedrooms are highly
individual. Excellent French
cuisine and a wine list with 75
champagnes. £££

Golf View Hotel, Seabank Road.
Tel: (01667) 452301.
Fax: (01667) 455267.
47 rooms. Imposing Victorian
hotel overlooking the sea and
the Black Isle. New leisure centre, tennis and near golf course.
£££–££££

Links Hotel, 1 Seafield Street.
Tel: (01667) 453321.
Fax: (01667) 456092.
10 rooms. Elegant Victorian
building with sea views. Log
fires. Inclusive golf packages
utilising 30 courses. £££

Newburgh
Udny Arms Hotel, Main Street.
Tel: (01358) 789444.
Fax: (01358) 789012.
26 rooms. Village pub with
great food and character.
Rooms tastefully furnished with
period furniture. Close to
Cruden Bay golf course. £££

Peterhead
Waterside Inn,
Fraserburgh Road. Tel: (01779)
471121. Fax: (01779) 470670.
109 rooms. On banks of River
Ugie and not far from the sea.
Full leisure facilities. £££

Portsoy
Boyne Hotel.
Tel/Fax: (01261) 842242.
13 rooms. Charming building in
beautiful fishing village. Golf,
fishing, whisky trail close by. £££

Spey Bay
Spey Bay Hotel.
Tel: (01343) 820424.
10 rooms. Beautiful setting on
Moray Coast. Own golf course.
Speyside Way path close by.
£££

THE NORTHERN HIGHLANDS
Achiltibuie
Summer Isles Hotel.
Tel: (01854) 622282.
Fax: (01854) 622251.

13 rooms. Simple but delightful hotel with glorious views over the Summer Isles. £££

Aviemore
Stakis Aviemore Coylumbridge Resort Hotel. Tel: (01479) 810661. Fax: (01479) 811309. 175 rooms. In the heart of the Grampians and an ideal centre for outdoor leisure. Complete leisure centre. £££
Stakis Aviemore Four Seasons Hotel. Tel: (01479) 810681. Fax: (01479) 810534. 89 rooms. Well appointed hotel with leisure centre in heart of Highlands. ££££

Ballater
Glen Lui Hotel, Invercauld Road. Tel: (01339) 755402. Fax: (01339) 755545. 19 rooms. Friendly country house hotel with superb views towards Lochnagar. Fishing, golf, skiing etc available. ££–£££
Netherley Guest House, 2 Netherley Place. Tel/Fax: (01339) 755792. 9 rooms (4 en suite). Family-run guest house in centre of village, high standards of service. ££
Stakis Royal Deeside Hotel, Braemar Road. Tel: (01339) 755858. Fax: (01339) 755447. 44 rooms. Excellent modern hotel with full leisure facilities. £££–££££

Beauly
Lovat Arms Hotel, High Street. Tel: (01463) 782313. Fax: (01463) 782862. 22 rooms. All rooms feature a clan tartan and many have canopied or half-tester beds. Produce from family farm served in dining room. £££
Priory Hotel, The Square. Tel: (01463) 782309. Fax: (01463) 782531. 23 rooms. Comfortable private-ly-owned hotel in an attractive village square next to priory ruins. Scrumptious afternoon tea. £££

Braemar
Invercauld Arms Thistle Hotel. Tel: (01339) 741605. Fax: (01339) 741428. 68 rooms. Historic building now offering high standards of accommodation and food. £££
Moorfield House. Tel: (01339) 741244. 7 rooms (1 en suite). Very welcoming and friendly family-run hotel at edge of famous Games Park. ££

Cromarty
Royal Hotel, Marine Terrace. Tel: (01381) 600217. 10 rooms. Comfortable, welcoming family hotel with great view of the Cromarty Firth where dolphins swim among parked oil rigs. ££–£££

Dingwall
Tulloch Castle Hotel, Tulloch Castle Drive. Tel: (01349) 861325. Fax: (01349) 863993. 19 rooms. Elegant country house hotel in superb surroundings, ideal for a relaxing break. £££

Dornoch
Royal Golf Hotel, Grange Road. Tel: (01862) 810283. Fax: (01862) 810923. 25 rooms. Mansion overlooking Dornoch Firth and playful dolphins. New leisure centre, 2 tennis courts and adjacent to championship golf course. £££

Drumnadrochit (on Loch Ness)
Borlum Farmhouse. Tel/Fax: (01456) 450358. 5 rooms (2 en suite). Extremely comfortable B&B accommoda-tion in 18th-century farmhouse with antique furnishings. Conservatory offers superb views of Loch and Glen. Horse-riding school next door. ££
Drumnadrochit Hotel. Tel: (01456) 450218. Fax: (01456) 450793. 20 rooms. Modern, attractive hotel close to Loch Ness and the visitor centres for "monster watchers". Also 4 travelodges opening 1999. ££

Fort Augustus
Lovat Arms Hotel. Tel: (01320) 366206. Fax: (01320) 366677. 21 rooms. Long-established hotel near centre of village, close to loch and Caledonian Canal. Big selection of malt whiskies. £££

Foyers
Foyers Hotel. Tel: (01456) 486216. 9 rooms. Hotel of good character on wooded slopes overlooking Loch Ness and near to Falls of Foyers. £££

Glen Shiel
Cluanie Inn. Tel: (01320) 340238. Fax: (01320) 340293. 11 rooms. Traditional Scottish Inn, now fully modernised, far away from it all on the main road to Skye. Roaring fires in public rooms. £££

Invermoriston
Glenmoriston Arms Hotel. Tel: (01320) 351206. Fax: (01320) 351308. 8 rooms. 200-year-old coaching inn nestling in lovely glen close to Loch Ness. ££

Inverness
Brae Ness Hotel, Ness Bank. Tel: (01463) 712266. Fax: (01463) 231732. 10 rooms. Non-smoking family-run hotel on the River Ness. Close to town. ££
Bunchrew House Hotel, Bunchrew. Tel: (01463) 234917. Fax: (01463) 710620. 12 rooms. Every inch a 17th-century Scottish baronial home yet very laid-back. Stands in 15 acres (6 hectares) of grounds on the Beauly Firth, 5 miles (8 km) west of Inverness. ££££
Columba Hotel, Ness Walk. Tel: (01463) 231291. Fax: (01463) 715526. 86 rooms. Refurbished hotel on banks of River Ness. Close to town. £££
Culduthel Lodge, 14 Culduthel Road. Tel/Fax: (01463) 240089. 12 rooms. Splendid

19th-century house overlooking the Moray Firth, Inverness and the Black Isle. Unusual circular drawing room. £££

Culloden House Hotel, Culloden. Tel: (01463) 790461. Fax: (01463) 792181. 25 rooms. An architectural gem 3 miles (5 km) east of Inverness, associated with Bonnie Prince Charlie and the Battle of Culloden. Magnificent public rooms, four-poster curtain-framed beds. Dine in the Adam Room to local produce cooked in the French manner. 40 acres (17 hectares) of lovely grounds. Tennis, sauna, solarium, snooker. £££££

Dunain Park. Tel: (01463) 230512. Fax: (01463) 224532. 14 rooms. Georgian country house, 1 mile from Inverness on A82, set in 6 acres (2.5 hectares) of gardens and grounds. Wide variety of bedrooms, some with four-poster beds. Auld Alliance (marriage of French and Scottish produce and skills) is served accompanied by a fair selection of wines. Indoor swimming pool, sauna, croquet. ££££

Jarvis Caledonian Hotel, Church Street. Tel: (01463) 235181. Fax: (01463) 711206. 106 rooms. Elegant city hotel alongside the River Ness with all facilities. £££–££££

Whinpark Hotel, 17 Ardross Street. Tel/Fax: (01463) 232549. 10 rooms. Victorian house situated in quiet area close to River Ness. ££

John o'Groats
John o'Groats House Hotel. Tel: (01955) 611203. Fax: (01955) 611408. 16 rooms (3 en suite). As far north as you can get on the mainland, overlooking the Pentland Firth and handy for the summer ferry to Orkney. ££

Kincraig
Osprey Hotel. Tel: (01540) 651242. Fax: (01540) 651633.

9 rooms. Pleasant, small Highland hotel just off the main road providing friendly service. Vegetarian meals. ££

Kingussie
Scot House Hotel, East Terrace. Tel: (01540) 661351. Fax: (01540) 661111. 9 rooms. Friendly, welcoming hotel in centre of village. £££

Lochinver
Albannach Hotel, Baddidarroch. Tel/Fax: (01571) 844407. 4 rooms. Delightful 19th-century house set in a walled garden. All comforts for those who enjoy the outdoors. Good home cooking and vegetarians welcomed. ££

What the codes mean

Approximate prices per person per night in a double room:
- £ = below £20
- ££ = £20–£30
- £££ = £30–£50
- ££££ = £50–£70
- £££££ = above £70

Inver Lodge Hotel. Tel: (01571) 844496. Fax: (01571) 844395. 20 rooms. A modern hotel with superb views of the loch. ££££

Newtonmore
Balavil Sport Hotel. Tel: (01540) 673220. Fax: (01540) 673773. 50 rooms. Refur-bished building on main street with excellent leisure facilities. £££

Pines Hotel, Station Road. Tel: (01540) 673271. 6 rooms. Beautiful building set in wooded grounds providing peaceful accommodation. £££

Scourie
Eddrachilles Hotel, Badcall Bay. Tel: (01971) 502080. Fax: (01971) 502477. 11 rooms. Beautifully maintained hotel on 320 acres (133 hectares) of waterfront property

with stunning sea views. Close to Handa Island bird sanctuary. Open March–October. £££

Strathpeffer
Strathpeffer Hotel. Tel: (01997) 421200. Fax: (01997) 421110. 35 rooms. Efficiently run hotel in village centre, close to all amenities. ££–£££

Dunraven Lodge, Golf Road. Tel: (01997) 421210. 11 rooms. Beautiful Victorian villa in extensive grounds overlooking the village, peaceful and relaxing. ££

ORKNEY
Albert Hotel, Kirkwall. Tel: (01856) 876000. Fax: (01856) 875397. 19 rooms. Traditional hotel in centre of town; recently refurbished. £££

Foveran Hotel, St Ola, Kirkwall. Tel: (01856) 872389. Fax: (01856) 876430. 8 rooms. Family-run hotel set in 35 acres (14 hectares) overlooking Scapa Flow. £££

Lynfield Hotel, Holm Road, Kirkwall. Tel: (01856) 872505. Fax: (01856) 870035. 8 rooms. Formerly the residence of the distillery manager: you can still sniff the "guid stuff" – and it's free. ££

SHETLAND
Broch House Guest House, Upper Scalloway. Tel: (01595) 880767. Fax: (01595) 880731. 3 rooms. Modern house in elevated position with excellent view over Scalloway. £

Buness House, Baltasound, Unst. Tel: (01957) 711315. Fax: (01957) 711815. 4 rooms (3 en suite). 17th-century building on island of Unst, most northerly of the Shetland islands. Close to Hermaness nature reserve and fine cliff scenery. Open Mar–Dec. £

Busta House Hotel, Busta, North Mainland. Tel: (01806) 522506. Fax: (01806) 522588. 20 rooms. Country house hotel

Campus Hotels

Excellent accommodation is available during summer and Easter vacations and, on several campuses throughout the year, at 8 universities. In total, more than 14,000 bedrooms, many but not all en suite and with no single supplement, are available, while self-catering accommodation in units suitable for 4–8 persons is also offered.

The standard of accommodation keeps improving, e.g. the Chancellor's Hall at Strathclyde has 231 rooms all with television and tea- and coffee-making facilities and a lounge area, while Dundee's West Park Centre is specifically designed to meet the needs of the disabled.

At Dundee, Glasgow, Heriot-Watt (in Edinburgh), St Andrews, Strathclyde (in Glasgow) and Stirling, accommodation is under £20, while at Aberdeen and Edinburgh it is between £20 and £25. These rates include breakfast.

Contacts are:
● Aberdeen – (01224) 272664
● Dundee – (01382) 344039
● Edinburgh – (0131) 667 0662
● Glasgow – (0141) 330 5385
● Heriot-Watt – (0131) 451 3110
● St Andrews – (01334) 462000
● Stirling – (01786) 467141
● Strathclyde – (0141) 553 4148

23 miles (37km) north of Lerwick, dating from 1588 and with private harbour and slipway. £££
Grand Hotel,
Commercial Street, Lerwick.
Tel: (01595) 692826.
Fax: (01595) 694048.
20 rooms. Oldest purpose-built hotel in Shetland, recently refurbished. Close to harbour and town centre. £££
Shetland Hotel,
Holmsgarth Road, Lerwick.
Tel: (01595) 695515.
Fax: (01595) 695828.
65 rooms. Modern hotel with leisure complex. Views of the harbour and Isle of Bressay. £££
Sumburgh Hotel.
Tel: (01950) 460201.
Fax: (01950) 460394.
32 rooms. Former laird's house, close to airport and Jarlshof ancient monument. Superb beaches nearby. £££

Youth Hostels

There are about 80 youth hostels, many of them in the Highlands. These hostels provide low-cost accommodation, usually with dormitory-type bedrooms. To join the Youth Hostels Association costs from £2.50–£6 and accommodation is between £3.65 and £12.50 a night depending on the facilities at the hostel.

For details contact the Scottish Youth Hostels Association (SYHA), 7 Glebe Crescent, Stirling, FK8 2JA. Tel: (01786) 891400.

Independent Hostels

Scotland has a growing network of excellent independent hostels which provide similar accommodation to the SYHA hostels but with the advantage that you don't have to join any organisation to use them. Prices are usually under £10 per night and the facilities are often surprisingly good. Moreover, many of these hostels are in remote locations. For more details, contact Independent Hostels Scotland, 13 Lower Breakish, Isle of Skye IV42 8QA.

Where to Eat

More than 50 years have elapsed since that distinguished travel writer H.V. Morton wrote: "Scotland is the best place in the world to take an appetite." The country has long been renowned for its produce from river and sea, from farm and moor. Fish is something of a speciality, with salmon being particularly good: kippers and Arbroath Smokies (haddock smoked over wood) are delicious too. Shellfish – lobsters, prawns, oysters, mussels – are unsurpassed and exported all over the world, while Aberdeen Angus beef and Border lamb are both renowned. Various dishes are distinctly Scottish, such as haggis – which is probably more enjoyable if you don't know what should be in it (the heart, lungs and liver of a sheep, suet, oatmeal and onion).

Over the past decade culinary skills have matched the quality of the produce and today it is possible to enjoy superb meals in Scotland served in the most elegant of restaurants as well as in simple small spaces with scarcely more than half-a-dozen tables. The hours at which restaurants, especially smaller ones away from the main cities, serve meals tend to be less flexible than in many other countries. High tea, usually served from 5 to 7pm, is an interesting meal consisting usually of fish and chips or an egg dish followed by lashings of scones and pancakes and all accompanied by gallons of tea.

Dr Johnson remarked that "If

an epicure could remove by a wish, in quest of sensual gratifications, wherever he had supped he would breakfast in Scotland." No doubt he would say the same today. There is surely no better way to start the day than porridge, Loch Fyne kippers and Scottish oatcakes.

On a more mundane level, there is no shortage of fast food outlets of one sort or another throughout Scotland. For a cheap and enjoyable take-away meal, you could do a lot worse than try the humble "chippie" (fish and chip shop).

The symbols at the end of each entry provide a rough guide to prices, based on the average cost of a three-course evening meal, excluding wine. £ = under £10; ££ = £10–£20 per head; and £££ = £20–£30 per head. Lunch is almost invariably considerably less expensive and nearly all restaurants serve table d'hôte meals, which are about half the price of an à la carte dinner.

Taste of Scotland

The *Taste of Scotland* scheme invites eating places to apply for membership, and states its purpose in its guidebook as "to help [the visitor] experience to the full the richness and diversity of Scottish cuisine". All members are inspected before being admitted to the scheme; the annual guide lists some 400 restaurants, bistros and cafés where quality, service and in many cases considerable innovation can be guaranteed.

For anyone interested in good food and drink, the *Taste of Scotland* guide would be a sound investment. It is available from larger Tourist Information Centres or from the Scottish Tourist Board direct (0131 332 2433), and in some bookshops. As membership varies from year to year, Taste of Scotland members are not indicated in this guide, but a

good selection of the places listed here are in fact members at the time of going to press.

Pubs and Bars

Many pubs in Scotland now sell "real ale", cask-conditioned beer in various strengths (60°, 70° and 80°) made by Scottish brewers, large and small. Ask for 80-shilling rather than "heavy" or you'll get the nasty, fizzy stuff. Connoisseurs should look out for Caledonian 70-shilling and 80-shilling, which are made using traditional methods in a Victorian brewery. Most pubs have a reasonable selection of malt whiskies and other spirits.

Licensing hours in the cities are liberal. If you try hard enough, so they say, you can drink for 22 out of 24 hours. Certainly, there is no shortage of pubs which are "open all day", which usually means from about 11am until 11pm or midnight (1am in the main cities). Sunday afternoons can be more difficult, but the desperate can always try a hotel bar. Areas where good pubs can be found in Edinburgh and Glasgow are suggested below.

EDINBURGH RESTAURANTS

(All phone numbers begin with the code 0131)

Scottish

Jackson's, 209–213 High Street. Tel: 225 1793. Atmospheric basement restaurant on the Royal Mile serving imaginative Scottish cooking in somewhat cramped space. Very popular with tourists. Set lunch an excellent bargain. £££

Stac Polly, 8 Grindlay Street. Tel: 229 5405 and 29 Dublin Street. Tel: 556 2231. Modern variations on traditional Scottish cuisine showing originality and excellence. ££

Contemporary & International

Martins, 70 Rose St North Lane. Tel: 225 3106. Difficult

to find, this small, well established restaurant is well worth the trouble. Limited but confident contemporary menu with best cheeseboard in town. Excellent discreet service. £££

The Abbotsford Restaurant and Bar, 3 Rose Street. Tel: 225 5276. Upstairs restaurant, separate from pub, serves splendid pub food in Victorian old-world charm. £

The Atrium, 10 Cambridge Street. Tel: 228 8882. Located in the foyer of the Traverse Theatre, this is the most stylish place in town and currently the "in" place. Sophisticated, imaginative menu served in mellow, contemporary ambience with excellent service. £££

The Witchery, 352 Castlehill, Royal Mile. Tel: 225 5613. Imaginative Scottish cuisine. Two restaurants, each with unusual atmosphere. Upstairs is dark and atmospheric – beams and oil lamps – while downstairs is bright with lots of greenery and small outdoor terrace. Excellent wine list. £££

Vintner's Rooms, The Vaults, 87 Giles Street, Leith. Tel: 554 6767. Dine either in a unique candlelit restaurant in old wine merchants' auction room or in a high functional space with a fire at one end and a bar down one side. Creative cooking of fresh produce, especially fish, is robust. Everything from the bread to the fudge with coffee is home-made. £££

Seafood

Café Royal Oyster Bar, 17A West Register Street, plus 8 other branches. Tel: 556 4124. An Edinburgh institution where the ambience is everything. Stained glass and polished wood; always bustling and seafood is preferred. £££

Creelers Seafood Bistro and Restaurant, 3 Hunter Square. Tel: 220 4447. Like its sister establishment on the Isle of

Arran, specialises in imaginative cooking of fresh seafood, plus game and vegetarian dishes. £–££

Marinette, 52 Coburg Street, Leith. Tel: 555 0922. Fish and chips as they should be but rarely are: cooked with Gallic flair; simply the best. ££

Skippers, 1A Dock Place, Leith. Tel: 554 1018. "Very fishy, very quayside, very French" with a somewhat nautical atmosphere. £££

Chinese

Chinese Home Cooking, 34 West Preston Street. Tel: 668 4946. Straightforward Cantonese cooking of consistently high standard. Bring your own bottle. £

Kweilin, 19 Dundas Street. Tel: 557 1875. Large space serving authentic Cantonese dishes, especially strong on seafood. Many think the best Chinese in town. £

Loon Fung Seafood Restaurant, 32 Grindlay Street. Tel: 229 5757. Genuine Cantonese cooking, specialising in varied and tasty fish dishes. £

Szechuan House, 12 Leamington Terrace. Tel: 229 4655. For those who like it hot and spicy. Basic surroundings, near the King's Theatre, serving authentic Szechuan dishes. £

French

Duck's at Le Marché Noir, 2–4 Eyre Place. Tel: 558 1608. Scottish/French menus served with excellent wines in restful ambience in a quiet corner of the New Town. £££

L'Auberge, 56–58 St Mary's Street. Tel: 556 5888. Successful marriage of Scottish produce and French culinary skills. Excellent fish dishes and wide selection of desserts. 600 wines, almost exclusively French, with numerous half-bottles. £££

Le Café Saint-Honoré, 34 N.W. Thistle Street Lane. Tel: 226

2211. Step into this pleasant bistro, leave Scotland behind and enter France. Good value lunch. Some imaginative dishes. Decent wine list. ££

Merchants Restaurant, 17 Merchant Street. Tel: 225 4009. Innovative and varied French cuisine in smart surroundings. £££

Pierre Victoire, 38 Grassmarket. Tel: 226 2442; 8 Union Street. Tel: 557 8451; 10 Victoria Street. Tel: 225 1721; 5 Dock Place, Leith. Tel: 555 6178; 17 Queensferry Street. Tel: 226 1890 and 10 Edinburgh Road, South Queensferry. Tel: 331 5006. Closed Sunday or Monday. All six restaurants have limited menus yet serve excellent food. Decent, moderately priced wines. Not a lot of space at each table and can be very crowded. £

Pompadour, Caledonian Hotel, Princes Street. Tel: 459 9988. Possibly Edinburgh's most elegant and formal dining room. Lunchtime features *Legends of the Scottish Table*, while in the evening the other member of the *Auld Alliance* (France) holds sway. Classic wines, impeccable service and soothing piano music. £££+

A simpler menu with, nevertheless, a good range of classic and some international dishes is served in **Carriages**, the Caledonian's 2nd restaurant. ££

Indian

Indian Cavalry Club, 3 Atholl Place. Tel: 228 3282. The paramilitary uniforms – some ill-fitting – of the staff should not be off-putting. This up-market Indian restaurant with an emphasis on steaming attempts, with a fair amount of success, to blend brasserie and Indian restaurant. Better than average wine list at reasonable prices. ££

Kalpna, 2 St Patricks Square. Tel: 667 9890. Gujerati and

southern Indian vegetarian food in a non-smoking restaurant. Decent, moderately priced wine list. £

Lancers Brasserie, 5 Hamilton Place. Tel: 332 3444. Rather elegant space with three rooms serving Bengali and north Indian cuisine. Renowned for curries. Modest wine list. ££

Shamiana, 14 Brougham Street. Tel: 228 2265. North Indian dishes served in this elegant Indian restaurant. Excellent Tandoori and curry. ££

Italian

Ferri's Pizzeria, 1 Antigua Street, Leith Walk. Tel: 556 5592. Good, reasonably priced food. Cheerful environment. £

Tinelli, 139 Easter Road. Tel: 652 1932. Small, unpretentious restaurant with a limited menu of superb north Italian food. Splendid cheese selection. ££

Mexican

Pancho Villas, 240 Canongate. Tel: 557 4416. Lively, informal atmosphere at affordable prices. £

Tex Mex, 47 Hanover Street. Tel: 225 1796. Just what the name suggests: reasonably priced and authentic. £

Viva Mexico, 41 Cockburn Street. Tel: 226 5145. Cosy restaurant that transports you back to atmosphere of old Mexico. Food (for some) on spicy side. Good selection for veggies. Great margaritas. ££

Thai

Siam Erawan, 48 Howe Street. Tel: 226 3675. The city's top Thai restaurant with authentic Thai food and laid-back waiters. Good wine list. ££

Vegetarian

Henderson's, 94 Hanover Street. Tel: 225 2131. Basement self-service eatery. Busy, especially at lunch, with a mainly young clientele enjoying excellent vegetarian cookery. Live music in evenings. £

Bistros
Doric Tavern, 15 Market Street. Tel: 225 1084. A brash upstairs bistro, a long-term favourite, with excellent wine. Strong on vegetarian dishes. Pleasant at lunch and trendy in the evenings. £

La Cuisine d'Odile, 13 Randolph Crescent. Tel: 225 5685. A simple bistro (no alcohol) in the basement of L'Institut Français d'Écosse serves a limited menu of delightful, inexpensive lunches (Tues–Sat, noon–2pm). £

Ryan's Bistro, 2 Hope Street. Tel: 226 7005. A pleasant, relatively small space below Ryan's bar at the west end of Princes Street. Small but imaginative menu and courteous staff. £

Waterfront Wine Bar & Bistro, 1c Dock Place. Tel: 554 7427. Moderately priced fish dishes and good choice of vegetarian dishes served in a conservatory on the dock. Excellent wine selection on blackboards. ££

Cafés
Buffalo Grill, 14 Chapel Street. Tel: 667 7427. American-style serving great inexpensive food. Bring your own wine. £

Gallery of Modern Art Coffee Shop, Belford Road. Tel: 332 8600. Delightful self-service café opening out into garden, serves delicious home-cooked lunches. Attracts many locals. Licensed. £

Laigh Coffee House, 117A Hanover Street. Tel: 225 1552. An old world stone-flagged basement kitchen which serves (self-service) glorious salads and cakes for which you would kill. Very popular. £

Queen Street Café, National Portrait Gallery, Queen Street. Tel: 557 2844. Good home-cooked food and excellent cakes (self-service) in a some-

what cramped space. Strong on vegetarian dishes. £

Pubs and Bars
Good areas to try include the Royal Mile, Grassmarket, Rose Street, Haymarket, London Road and West Register Street; but all over the city there is a good choice, and there are many excellent pubs in the suburbs and surrounding towns and villages, which diligent exploration will unearth.

What the codes mean

Average cost of a three-course evening meal per person, excluding wine:
- £ = below £10
- ££ = £10–£20
- £££ = £20–£30

NEAR EDINBURGH
Two top restaurants on the outskirts of Edinburgh are:
Champany Inn, Linlithgow, Lothian EH49 7LU. 17 miles (25 km) from Edinburgh. Tel: (01506) 834532. Has been called "the best steakhouse in Britain". Aberdeen Angus is the speciality and from the grill come entrecôte, pope's eye, porterhouse, sirloin and rib eye. The seafood is as excellent as the meat. A superb wine list, reasonably priced, with large selection of South African wines. £££+

The Champany Inn Chop and Ale House is an informal sister restaurant serving the same excellent – but smaller – steaks and consequently easier on the pocket. Hamburgers are made from the best ground beef and Boerwors sausages are mixed with lamb. ££

La Potiniere, Main Street, Gullane, Lothian EH31 2AA. 17 miles (25 km) from Edinburgh. Tel: (01620) 843214. A small, unpretentious shopfront exterior belies the joys, both of decor and of food, within. Imaginative

French cooking beyond compare – no choice – served on delicate Limoges china. The wine list is first-rate. No credit cards: no smoking: booking essential and best to book this year for next. Limited opening. £££+

GLASGOW
(Area code: 0141)
Scottish
Puppet Theatre, Ruthven Lane, off Byres Road. Tel: 339 8444. A series of small rooms in which great contemporary dishes are served. £££

Ubiquitous Chip, 12 Ashton Lane. Tel: 334 5007. Long-popular Glasgow restaurant in an attractive covered garden courtyard which suggests a hothouse. Traditional and original Scottish recipes make for a most enjoyable cuisine in a delightful atmosphere. Outstanding, competitively priced wine list. Upstairs is a more modestly priced separate restaurant. ££–£££

Seafood
City Merchant. 97–99 Candleriggs. Tel: 553 1577. Renowned fish restaurant, recently extensively refurbished and extended. Also oyster bar. Taste of Scotland member. ££

Rogano, 11 Exchange Place. Tel: 248 4055. A Glasgow institution which is the place for a special occasion. The 1930s Art Deco appearance gives a slightly austere feel. When the fish is good (other food also served) it is superb. Less formal, bistro-style restaurant downstairs and an oyster bar behind the main restaurant for lighter, more reasonably priced, rapidly served meals. £££

Two Fat Ladies, 88 Dumbarton Road. Tel: 339 1944. A fairly simple tiny restaurant serving large portions of excellent contemporary food, mainly fish and game. A very small, practically exclusively New World wine list, indicating the owner-chef's origins. Advisable to book. ££

International
Yes, 22 West Mile Street. Tel: 221 8044. International cuisine using fresh Scottish produce in elegant and stylish surroundings, often with pianist. Private dining room available. £££
Bourbon Street, 108 George Street. Tel: 552 0141. Jazz-orientated New Orleans-style bar and restaurant with live music and dancing. ££

Chinese
Loon Fung, 417 Sauchiehall Street. Tel: 332 1240. Cavernous room in which Cantonese dishes and a selection of *dim sum* are served throughout the day. Also vegetarian set dinner. Pleasant staff and good menu. ££

French
The Brasserie, 176 West Regent Street. Tel: 248 3801. Imposing pillared entrance leads to a dining area that suggests an exclusive club. Excellent food with a slightly *nouvelle* presentation. ££
Pierre Victoire, 91 Miller Street. Tel: 221 7565; 165 Hope Street. Tel: 221 9130. Just what one expects from Pierre Victoire restaurants: a Gallic ambience; no frills and good limited inexpensive French cuisine. £

Indian
Ashoka Tandoori, 108 Elderslie Street. Tel: 221 1761. The touchstone by which all other Glasgow Indian restaurants are measured. Seating upstairs is not as dark and gloomy as the large room below. ££

Italian
Café Qui, The Italian Centre, 17 John Street. Tel: 552 6099. A cleverly designed atmospheric

restaurant serving decent Italian food. Plus a bar downstairs. This is part of one of Glasgow's newest and most splendid complexes. ££
L'Ariosto, 92 Mitchell Street. Tel: 221 0971. An outstanding, long-established Italian restaurant. Regular dinner dances with live music. ££
La Parmigiana, 447 Great Western Road. Tel: 334 0686. Light modern ambience in a fairly formal, popular restaurant in the west end. Interesting food should be rounded off with crème brûlée alla Strega. Must book at lunchtime. ££
Ristorante Caprese, 217 Buchanan Street. Tel: 332 3070. Cheerful, small, well-established family restaurant. Good standard cooking with Neapolitan influence and few surprises. £–££

Mexican
Cantina del Rey, 10 King's Court (off King Street). Tel: 552 4044. Best Mexican food in town, renowned for its fajitas. Children eat free if in a party group. ££

Vegetarian
Granary, 82 Howard Street. Tel: 226 3770. Vegetarian food and excellent baking in a comfortable and friendly atmosphere in city centre. £

Bistros
Baby Grand, 3 Elmbank Gardens, Charing Cross. Tel: 248 4942. Crowded café-bar with continental atmosphere and grand piano. Especially –popular after theatre. ££
Belfry, 652 Argyle Street. Tel: 221 0630. Very comfortable and restful wine bar serving Scottish cuisine. Upstairs is its big brother, **The Buttery**, which is not such a good buy. ££
Fire Station, 33 Ingram Street. Tel: 552 2929. Intriguing conversion of part of Victorian fire station retaining many

original features. "Happy Hour" up to 7pm on pasta dishes. £–££
Froggies, 53 West Regent Street. Tel: 572 0007. Friendly and relaxing place offering good value. Adjacent New Orleans Bar has lively atmosphere and offers Cajun and Creole snacks. £–££
October Café, The Rooftop, Princes Square, Buchanan Street. Tel: 221 0303. A bright, cheery brasserie, the offshoot of the renowned October, where modestly priced food combines East and West cuisines. ££
Papingo, 104 Bath Street. Tel: 332 6678. Excellent value for money and high quality. Special pre-theatre meals, fixed price menu. £

Cafés and Tearooms
Café Gandolfi, 64 Albion Street. Tel: 552 6813. The grandfather of modern Glasgow café life. Tasty dishes mean it is busy at lunchtime. Half-a-dozen inexpensive wines are offered by glass or bottle. £
Willow Tearooms, 217 Sauchiehall Street. Tel: 332 0521; 97 Buchanan Street. Tel: 204 5242. The only Mackintosh tearooms still functioning. A feast for the eyes if not for the stomach. Invariably extremely busy at lunch. Not open for dinner. £

Pubs and Bars
The city centre offers a bewildering choice – try the Merchant City area, George Square, Argyle Street, Hope Street and Sauchiehall Street for starters. The suburbs and surrounding towns are also very well supplied with excellent pubs, many providing very good food as well.

NEAR GLASGOW
An outstanding restaurant on the outskirts of Glasgow is:
Gleddoch House Hotel, Langbank, Renfrewshire (near Glasgow airport). Tel: (01475)

540711. Elegant restaurant featuring Scottish dishes in a small hotel which has a first-class 18-hole golf course and a host of other facilities. Booking essential. £££. The hotel has 37 bedrooms, some with view of Loch Lomond.

THE BORDERS
Kailzie Garden Restaurant, Kailzie, Peebles. Tel: (01721) 722807. An unpretentious restaurant housed in the old stable square and carefully converted to retain as many original features as possible. Limited menu of good home cooking and baking with fruit and vegetables from the gardens. Homely atmosphere. Dinner on Saturday only. £–££
Le Provençale, Monksford Road, Newtown St Boswells. Tel: (01835) 823284. The *Auld Alliance* has got together here (René in the kitchen and Elizabeth in the front of the house) and the result is no-nonsense French cooking of the highest standard. No credit cards. £–££
Riverside Inn, Canonbie. Tel: (01387) 371512. An old white-painted inn overlooking the River Esk houses a jolly, idiosyncratic bar and restaurant. Both serve unusual – leek and parsnip soup, poached bantam egg in madeira jelly – dishes. Extensive wine list. £££. Inn has 8 bedrooms.
Simply Scottish, High Street, Jedburgh. Tel: (01835) 864696. Bistro-style restaurant with nice pine furniture using good local produce to produce imaginative and tasty meals. ££
Sunflower, 4 Bridgegate, Peebles. Tel: (01721) 722420. Tiny quality food store has a few tables and serves interesting snacks throughout the day. Some wines. Credit cards not accepted. £
Wheatsheaf Hotel, Main Street, Swinton. Tel: (01890) 860257. A small Berwickshire village yields

this genuine country inn with a surprisingly extensive and imaginative menu. Voted Macallan Hotel of the Year in 1997. ££. There are 5 bedrooms.

THE SOUTHWEST
Chapelton House, Stewarton-Irvine Road, Stewarton. Tel: (01560) 482696. An elegant turn-of-the-century mansion with panelled dining room. Ambitious contemporary cooking and wine list with nearly 200 bin numbers, including many half-bottles. Smart dress preferred. £££. There are 8 bedrooms.
Northpark House Hotel. Alloway. Tel: (01292) 442336. In the heart of Burns country, the restaurant offers cooking with flair but without pretension. Very extensive wine list. ££. There are 5 bedrooms.

What the codes mean

Average cost of a three-course evening meal per person, excluding wine:
● £ = below £10
● ££ = £10–£20
● £££ = £20–£30

FORTH AND CLYDE
Houston House, Uphall. Tel: (01506) 853831. Excellent Scottish food from local products served in the handsome dining room of a 16th-century house. A prodigious wine list with labels from around the world and a splendid selection of malts. ££–£££. The hotel has 30 rooms, some with four-posters, and stands in 20 acres (8 hectares) of grounds next to a golf course.
Kiplings, Mine Road, Bridge of Allan (near Stirling). Tel: (01786) 833617. An old Victorian building which was the pump room when Bridge of Allan was a spa. An imaginative menu served in a tastefully furnished semi-circular dining room. ££

Old Howgate Inn, Wester Howgate. Tel: (01968) 674244. Danish restaurant in a cosy 18th-century inn serving a wide choice of open sandwiches. A Danish speciality is offered each evening. Decent wine list at reasonable prices. £
Open Arms Hotel, Dirleton. Tel: (01620) 850241. Pleasant restaurant overlooking village green and ruined 16th-century castle. Interesting, well-presented menu concentrating on local produce. ££. The Hotel has 7 pleasant rooms.
Scholars, Stirling Highland Hotel, Stirling. Tel: (01786) 475444. Elegant dining room offering excellent selection, using local produce whenever possible. ££

WEST COAST
Airds Hotel, Port Appin. Tel: (01631) 730236. A charming old inn on edge of Loch Linnhe. Serves what many claim to be the best food in all Scotland. Excellent wine list. 12 comfortable and chintzy bedrooms for those who wish to stay over.
Loch Fyne Oyster Bar, Clachan Farm, Cairndow. Tel: (01499) 600236. Simply the finest of oysters served in this simple café-cum-restaurant, smokehouse and produce shop at the head of Loch Fyne. Those who can tear themselves away from the oysters will enjoy the langoustines and the products – eel, mussels, etc – of the smokehouse. Leave room for excellent Scottish cheese-board. Short good, inexpensive wine list. ££
Lock 16-Rooftop Seafood Restaurant, Crinan Hotel. Tel: (01546) 830261. (This must be distinguished from the hotel's main dining room on the ground floor.) A simple room with spectacular views, especially when the sunset puts on a show. A closer view is of the locks at the end of the Crinan canal and

the fishing fleet unloading its catch prior to it becoming the hotel's 5-course dinner (time of delivery noted on menu). Wordy wine list. Booking essential. Jacket and tie. £££. 22 bedrooms, each with a sea view. Some with private balconies.

SKYE
Kinloch Lodge,
Sleat. Tel: (01471) 833214. Lady Claire Macdonald, one of Scotland's best-known cookery writers, presides over the dining room, which offers a full 5-course menu each night, with variety and imagination to the fore. ££££. The lodge has 10 bedrooms.

Lochbay Seafood Restaurant,
Stein, Waternish. Tel: (01470) 592235. Halibut, shark, skate and ling may well be the specials in the atmospheric informal restaurant, which consists of two cottages, built in 1740. And if this be a wee bit too esoteric then there are always lobster, crab, scallops, oyster, wild salmon and… Peter Greenhalgh believes that the freshness of his fish would be diminished by elaborate saucing. No credit cards. ££

Three Chimneys Restaurant,
Colbost, by Dunvegan. Tel: (01470) 511258. Seafood platter and lobster feast are two of the most popular dishes served during a candlelit dinner in this atmospheric restaurant in what was formerly a croft. But do leave room for the scrumptious desserts. No smoking. ££

CENTRAL SCOTLAND
Kind Kyttock's Kitchen,
Cross Wynd, Falkland. Tel: (01337) 857477. Just opposite the palace, this small tearoom serves home-cured ham, free-range eggs, freshly baked bread and scones. Open Feb–Dec. No credit cards. £
Let's Eat, 77 Kinnoull Street, Perth. Tel: (01738) 643377. Also **Let's Eat Again** at

33 George Street. Tel: (01738) 633771. Exceptional bistro-style restaurant in city centre with a pleasant, relaxed atmosphere. Opened in 1996, it won Macallan Restaurant of the Year in 1997. ££
New Victoria,
2 Bruce Street, Dunfermline. Tel: (01383) 724175. A large upstairs room overlooking the abbey serving tasty, inexpensive, traditional food. Delicious sweets and puddings. No credit cards. £
Peat Inn,
Peat Inn by Cupar, Fife. Tel: (01334) 840206. An 18th-century village inn, only 6 miles (10 km) from St Andrews with an international reputation. A limited menu lists the very best of Scottish produce cooked imaginatively and served stylishly in beautifully furnished dining rooms. Superb wine list includes many half-bottles. Booking essential. £££+
The Residence has 8 luxury units (7 split-level) which maintain the excellence of the restaurant. £££
Pepitas,
11 Crails Lane, St Andrews. Tel: (01334) 474084. Good for snacks during the day as well as dinner in the evening. £
Perth Theatre,
High Street, Perth. Tel: (01738) 621031. A lively place for lunch and pre-theatre dinner. Good coffee bar. £
The Cellar,
24 East Green, Anstruther. Tel: (01333) 310378. Just off the harbour, a walled courtyard leads to an atmospheric restaurant serving some of the most splendid seafood around. Excellent wine list – French and New World bins – complements the food. Booking essential. £££
The Hollies,
Low Road, Auchtermuchty, Fife. Tel: (01337) 828279. Pleasant atmosphere and a chance to discover that the unlikely sounding Auchtermuchty is a real location. ££

THE EAST COAST
Ashvale Fish Restaurant,
44–48 Great Western Road, Aberdeen. Tel: (01224) 596981. A chance to visit an award-winning sit-down "chippie" serving not only great fish and chips but other fresh local dishes. ££
But'n'Ben,
Auchmithie, near Arbroath. Tel: (01241) 877223. Lunch, high tea and dinner are served in a traditional cottage with quarry tile floors and open fires in this out-of-the-way coastal village. The produce is local, cooking is traditional and the fish fresh from the Arbroath fleet. Vegetarian meals. ££
Cornerstone Coffee House,
118 Nethergate, Dundee. Tel: (01382) 202121. Plain cooking with no pretensions. Clean, pleasant café where a good inexpensive meal can be enjoyed. Open: Mon–Sat, 9am–4pm. £
Faraday's, 2 Kirk Brae, Cults, Aberdeen. Tel: (01224) 869666. Small, atmospheric restaurant in converted electricity sub-station offering Scottish cooking with various exotic influences. ££
Old Monastery, Drybridge, Buckie. Tel: (01542) 832660. The Grays' food is fit for the gods with the bar in the cloisters and the restaurant in the chapel, with original pitch pine ceiling and monk stencils. Extensive wine list. £££
Raffles Restaurant,
18 Perth Road, Dundee. Tel: (01382) 226344. Raffles, which overlooks the River Tay, serves pleasant, moderately price meals – coffee to dinner – in a relaxed atmosphere. Vegetarians welcome. Credit cards not accepted. £
Silver Darling,
Pocra Quay, North Pier, Aberdeen. Tel: (01224) 576229. Wonderful ambience just across from the fleet landing its catch. Soon it will be on your table, often cooked in the style of Didier Dejean's native Provence. £££

THE NORTHERN HIGHLANDS

Achin's Bookshop, Inverkirkaig, Lochinver. Tel: (01571) 844262. Simple, excellent home-coooking in Scotland's immaculate and well-stocked most northerly bookshop. Quality craft goods also on sale. £

Altnaharrie Inn, Ullapool. Tel: (01854) 633230. To get the full experience, book into one of the 8 bedrooms. Guests gather on the quay at Ullapool to be taken by boat to what has become an institution. Gunn Eriksen is the superb, imaginative chef in this tiny restaurant with 16 covers: Fred Brown is the host. Dinner is set except for a choice of desserts. Wines can be pricey. Closed: early November–Easter. £££

Anchor & Chain Restaurant, Coulmore Bay, North Kessock, near Inverness. Tel: (01463) 731313. Pleasant restaurant on the water's edge using fresh produce. £

Applecross Hotel, Applecross. Tel: (01520) 744262. Excellent local food in tiny restaurant with outside tables offering grand view of Skye. Reservations a must. ££

Badachro Inn, by Gairloch. Tel: (01445) 741255. Tiny, idiosyncratic, very popular pub on a sheltered bay with a garden by the sea. Wonderful prawns if available, and colourful hosts. £

Bayview Hotel, Russell Street, Lybster. Tel: (01593) 721346. A cosy bar and dining room popular with locals, who enthuse over 100 malt whiskies. Very friendly. ££

Bunillidh Restaurant and Tea Shop, Helmsdale. Tel: (01431) 821457. Lobsters and langoustines, home-made scones and shortbread. Full wine list. £

Dornoch Castle, Dornoch. Tel: (01862) 810216. Good Scottish food. ££

Dower House, Muir of Ord. Tel: (01463) 870090. An 18th-century house with an ornate dining room. The food, cooked in the modern style, is renowned for its taste as well as its presentation. Wine list with many half-bottles. £££. 5 bedrooms, all with Victorian-type bathrooms.

Green Inn, 9 Victoria Road, Ballater. Tel: (013397) 55701. In a village well-served with excellent, yet expensive, restaurants (Craigendarroch, Tullich Lodge), this granite building on the village green houses a more modestly priced restaurant serving imaginative dishes – baked crab with a chive and cheese sauce – prepared with local produce. £££. The inn has 3 bedrooms.

Kishorn Seafood and Snack Bar. Tel: (01520) 733240. An immaculate roadside snack shack which serves the freshest of shellfish prepared while you wait. £

What the codes mean

Average cost of a three-course evening meal per person, excluding wine:
- £ = below £10
- ££ = £10–£20
- £££ = £20–£30

Kylesku Hotel, Kylesku. Tel: (01971) 502231. Beautifully situated small restaurant with own smokery serves delicious moderately priced meals. ££. The hotel also has 6 rooms.

Seafood Restaurant, Tarbet, Scourie. Tel: (01971) 502251. As the name suggests, seafood dominates the menu, using produce caught from the restaurant's own boat in Loch Laxford. Open Easter–September, unlicensed. ££

The Cross, Tweed Mill Brae, Kingussie. Tel: (01540) 661166. Superb Scottish cuisine served in an old tweed mill recently converted into a delightful space. Superb wine list – clarets, half-bottles, dessert wines. Great cheese board. £££

Tigh an Eilean, Shieldaig. Tel: (01520) 755251. Excellent, traditional country cooking in a small restaurant in a small hotel on the shores of beautiful Loch Carron. ££. There are 12 rather small bedrooms, 9 en suite.

ORKNEY

Creel Restaurant, St Margaret's Hope. Tel: (01856) 831311. Historic seafront house offering innovative modern cooking with strong Orcadian influence. £££. There are 3 bedrooms available.

Ferry Inn, John Street, Stromness. Tel: (01856) 850280. Interior decor is that of a sailing ship, while the bar food ranges from marinated herring to Orkney pâté and Orkney cheese. £

Foveran Hotel, St Ola, Kirkwall. Tel: (01856) 872389. Scandinavian-style building offering outstanding seafood and wide variety of other dishes, including excellent vegetarian choice. Advance booking essential. £££

SHETLAND

Burrastow House, Walls. Tel: (01595) 809307. This peaceful, remote 18th-century house serves all local produce. Vegetarian choice available. £££. 5 en-suite rooms.

Busta House Hotel, Busta. Tel: (01806) 522506. Restaurant specialises in game, steaks, fish dishes. Good choice of vegetarian dishes. Open every day. Bar meals also available. ££

Pierhead Restaurant, Voe. Tel: (01806) 588332. Fresh seafood dishes plus good variety of other meals, lovely views across the Voe. Bookings essential in evening. ££

Nightlife

Music

Although scarcely a swinging country – other than when dancing the Highland Fling – Scotland has its fair share of after-dark activities.

The Royal Scottish National Orchestra and the Scottish Chamber Orchestra are excellent and give regular concerts in both Glasgow and Edinburgh as well as travelling to other parts of the country.

The Scottish Opera and Scottish Ballet have similar schedules.

Folk music abounds, with clubs in every town. Information is available locally and through newspaper advertisements.

Ceilidhs
In the Highlands and Islands, especially in isolated villages, the inhabitants hold occasional *ceilidhs*, which might be defined as informal social gatherings with folk music and formation dancing. Details of such "happenings" can often be obtained from local tourist boards.

Some regular and more commercial *ceilidhs*, which are tailored for tourists, are:

EDINBURGH
Carlton Highland Hotel,
19 North Bridge.
Tel: (0131) 472 3000.
May–September. Nightly at 7pm.
George Intercontinental Hotel,
19–21 George Street.
Tel: (0131) 225 1251.
May–September daily, except Friday and Saturday, 7–10pm.

Jamie's Scottish Evening, King James Thistle Hotel,
Leith Street.
Tel: (0131) 556 0111.
Mid-April–October. Nightly at 7pm.
Prestonfield House,
Priestfield Road.
Tel: (0131) 668 3346.
Mid-April–October. Sunday–Friday at 7pm.

INVERNESS
Cummings Hotel,
Church Street.
Tel: (01463) 233246.
Scottish Showtime, June–September, Monday–Saturday, 8.30pm.

LERAGS/OBAN
The Barn,
Cologins, Lerags (3 miles/5km) south of Oban.
Tel: (01631) 564501.
Thursday, summer only. 9.30pm.
MacTavish's Kitchens,
George Street. Oban.
Tel: (01631) 563064.
Mid-May–September, daily 8.30–10.30pm.

Other *ceilidhs* or live folk music sessions attended by locals and tourists are:

BALLATER
Victoria Hall.
Tel: (01339) 755865.
Late June–September, Friday until midnight.

EDINBURGH
Tron Ceilidh House,
Hunter Square.
Tel: (0131) 226 0931.
Behind the Tron church at the corner of High Street and "The Bridges". Every night. Folk music and jazz.

GLASGOW
The Riverside,
Fox Street (off Clyde Street).
Tel: (0141) 248 3144.
Every Friday and Saturday from 8pm. The place that started the *ceilidh* revival in Glasgow.

SKYE
Flodigarry Country House Hotel,
Staffin, Skye.
Tel: (01470) 552203.
Most Saturdays throughout the summer until 11.30pm (officially, but in reality often later).

Theatre

Theatre flourishes, with Glasgow's Citizens' Theatre and Edinburgh's Traverse Theatre being internationally renowned for their mounting of new plays and experimental works. Aberdeen, Dundee, Perth and Inverness are all home to first-class repertory theatres, while during the summer months the Pitlochry Festival Theatre mounts professional performances.

Commercial theatre too is still alive and kicking in the major cities. Its main venues are the Lyceum and Festival Theatre in Edinburgh and the King's in Glasgow.

ABERDEEN
Aberdeen Arts Centre,
33 King Street.
Tel: (01224) 635208.

DUNDEE
Dundee Rep Theatre,
Tay Square.
Tel: (013820) 223530.

EDINBURGH
Edinburgh Playhouse,
18–22 Greenside Place.
Tel: (0131) 557 2590.
Festival Theatre,
13–29 Nicholson Street.
Tel: (0131) 529 6000.
King's Theatre,
2 Leven Street.
Tel: (0131) 220 4349.
Royal Lyceum,
30B Grindlay Street.
Tel: (0131) 229 9697.
Theatre Workshop,
34 Hamilton Place.
Tel: (0131) 226 5425.

Traverse Theatre,
Cambridge Street.
Tel: (0131) 228 1404.

GLASGOW
Citizens' Theatre,
119 Gorbals Street.
Tel: (0141) 429 0022.
Kings Theatre,
297 Bath Street.
Tel: (0141) 227 5511.
Tron Theatre,
63 Trongate.
Tel: (0141) 552 4267.

INVERNESS
Eden Court Theatre,
Bishops Road.
Tel: (01463) 239841.

MULL
Mull Little Theatre,
Dervaig, Mull.
Tel: (01688) 400245.
The smallest theatre in Britain
(43 seats).

PERTH
Perth Repertory Theatre,
185 High Street.
Tel: (01738) 621031.

PITLOCHRY
Pitlochry Festival Theatre.
Tel: (01796) 472680.

ST ANDREWS
Byre Theatre,
Abbey Street.
Tel: (01334) 762888.

STIRLING
MacRobert Arts Centre,
University of Stirling.
Tel: (01786) 461081.

Casinos

Both Edinburgh and Glasgow
provide opportunities for you to
lose your money. The law
requires you become a member
of a casino about 48 hours
before you play. Membership is
free. Men are expected to wear
a jacket and tie. It is worth
checking the rules with the
casinos before your visit.

EDINBURGH
Stanley Berkeley Casino Club,
2 Rutland Place.
Tel: (0131) 228 4446.
Stanley Casino Martell,
7–11 Newington Road.
Tel: (0131) 667 7763.
Stakis Maybury Casino,
5 South Maybury Road.
Tel: (0131) 338 4444.
Stanley Edinburgh Casino Club,
Fork Place. Tel: (0131) 624 2121.

GLASGOW
Stanley Berkeley Casino Club,
Berkeley Street.
Tel: (0141) 332 0992.
Stakis Chevalier Casino,
95 Hope Street.
Tel: (0141) 226 3856.
Stakis Princes Casino,
528 Sauchiehall Street.
Tel: (0141) 332 8171.
Stakis Riverboat,
161 Broomielaw.
Tel: (0141) 220 6000.

Festivals

During the annual Edinburgh
International Festival in August –
and the concurrent Fringe, Jazz
and Film festivals – there is a
vast choice of quality cultural
events in the city every night,
ranging from opera and
experimental theatre to soon-to-
be-famous comedy talents *(see
also page 157).*
    Contacts are:
**Edinburgh International
Festival,**
tel: (0131) 473 2001 (enquiries);
473 2000 (bookings)
Edinburgh Fringe Festival,
tel: (0131) 226 5257 (enquiries);
(0131) 226 5138 (bookings)
Edinburgh Military Tattoo,
tel: (0131) 225 1188
**Edinburgh International Film
Festival,**
tel: (0131) 228 4051
**Edinburgh International Jazz
Festival,**
tel: (0131) 228 2202.

For an overview of other festivals
in Scotland, *see pages 101–103.*

Shopping

Most shops stay open
9am–5.30pm, with some shops
in the larger cities opening until
late on Thursday evenings. In
the smaller towns, there is
often an early closing day,
though few towns are without a
"wee shoppie" which stays
open at all hours and can provide food and drink and assort-
ed necessities. Supermarkets
are usually open to at least
8pm, later on Thursday and
Friday.

VAT refunds
Visitors to Scotland from non-EC
countries can obtain a refund of
value-added tax (currently 17.5
percent), which is normally
added to most purchases. Many
large stores will deduct the VAT
from purchases at time of sale
when the goods are being
shipped abroad directly from
the store. In other cases, visitors should obtain a receipt
which can be stamped by
Customs officers who will
inspect the goods at ports or
airports of exit; the receipt can
then be sent to the store, which
will mail a VAT refund cheque.

Sport

Participant Sports

Hill-walking, climbing, skiing, golf and fishing are some of the most obvious sports available, and are the subject of organised special interest holidays.

The Scottish Tourist Board has a useful free booklet, *Adventure and Special Interest Holidays in Scotland*. This includes details of various holidays, including not only the activities already mentioned, but also such diverse pursuits as leathercraft courses near Loch Ness and summer painting holidays in Perthshire.

Golf

Scotland is the home of golf and the game can claim to be the national sport.

There are hundreds of courses, most of them open to the public. Even the most famous courses, such as St Andrews, Carnoustie and Turnberry, are public courses, and anyone prepared to pay the appropriate fee and who can produce a handicap certificate (usually about 20 for men; 30 for ladies) is entitled to play on these courses.

It is advisable to book ahead at the "name" courses, although at St Andrews two-thirds of all start times on the Old Course (closed on Sunday) are allocated by ballot. To be included, contact the starter before 2pm on the day before you wish to play.

Walking

Scotland is a paradise for walkers, and walking is a rapidly growing tourism sector. There are 284 mountains over 3,000 ft (900 metres) – these are called Munros – and across the country you can find a wide range of climbs and walks suitable for the expert or the novice. The mountains, although not that high, should not be treated lightly. A peak which, when bathed in brilliant sunshine looks an easy stroll can, a few minutes later, be covered by swirling mist, and can become a death trap. The importance of proper equipment (compass and maps a must) and dress cannot be over-emphasised.

The Scottish Tourist Board (Tel: (0131) 332 2433. Fax: (0131) 315 4545) publishes an annual advice brochure, *Walk Scotland*. Scottish Natural Heritage (Tel: (0131) 447 4784. Fax: (0131) 446 2277) has free leaflets on long distance routes: the *West Highland Way*, from Glasgow to Fort William (95 miles/152 km) and the *Southern Upland Way* from Portpatrick to Cockburnspath (212 miles/340 km). Information on the myriad local walks can be obtained from tourist information centres.

Further Information
● The Mountaineering Council of Scotland, 4A St Catherine's Road, Perth PH1 5SE.
Tel: (01738) 638227.
Fax: (01738) 442095.
● Ramblers Association Scotland, 23 Crusader House, Haig Business Park, Markinch, Fife KY7 6AQ.
Tel: (01592) 611177.
Fax: (01592) 611188.

Fishing

Some of Britain's best fishing is found in Scotland. Rivers and lochs of all shapes and sizes can be fished for salmon and trout. Salmon fishing need not be as expensive as most people believe and trout fishing is available in far greater supply than is ever utilised. Local permits must be obtained; details of where to get these are available from tourist offices.

The salmon fishing season varies from river to river, starting from January in some places and as late as March in others and running until October. The trout season is from mid-March to early October. Fishing for migratory fish (salmon and sea trout) is forbidden on Sunday.

For general information contact the Scottish Tourist Board, 23 Ravelston Terrace, Edinburgh EH4 3EE. (Tel: (0131) 332 2433. Fax: (0131) 315 4545.)

Sea fishing is found around the entire coast, with the Orkney and the Shetland islands being a mecca. Shark, halibut, cod, bass, hake and turbot are just a few of the species that can be caught.

Skiing

Skiing has become increasingly popular as facilities have improved. The main centres are at Aviemore, Glencoe, Glenshee, Nevis Range (Fort William) and the Lecht.

There is also a large artificial ski slope at Hillend in the Pentland hills on the outskirts of Edinburgh.

Surfing

Few associate surfing with Scotland and yet enthusiasts claim that some of the world's best surfing is found around the Scottish coast.

The North coast, especially the eastern half (between Bettyhill and John o'Groats) has the most consistent of swells and variety of breaks, and

Thurso has been the scene of European championships. Other popular areas are the islands of the Inner Hebrides (Coll and Tiree).

Further Reading

Bird Watching

More than 450 species of birds have been recorded and the country's birdlife is unsurpassed. Some regions attract the rarest of species. Enormous seabird colonies can be seen on coastal cliffs and the islands. Outstanding are Shetland, Orkney, Handa Island, Isle of May, St Abb's Head, Bullers of Buchan. Birds of prey, from the buzzard to the merlin, are often seen in the Highlands, where golden eagles and the osprey can also be spotted.

Ornithological information can be obtained from the RSPB Scottish Office, 17 Regent Terrace, Edinburgh EH7 5BN. Tel: (0141) 557 3136. The Scottish Ornithologists' Club is at 21 Regent Terrace, Edinburgh EH7 5BT. Tel: (0131) 556 6042. The Scottish Wildlife Trust (Cramond House, Cramond Glebe Road, Edinburgh EH4 6NS. Tel: (0131) 312 7765) also manages many bird reserves.

Diving

Those who wish not only to go down to the sea but also under the sea won't be disappointed when they visit Scotland. Fish and plants abound in the clear waters which bathe the coast.

Outstanding sub-aqua areas with good facilities and experienced locals are the waters around Oban, the Summer Isles near Ullapool, Scapa Flow in Orkney and St Abbs Head on the southern part of the east coast. Information can be obtained from Scottish Sub-aqua Club, 16 Royal Crescent, Glasgow G3 7SL. Tel: (0141) 425 1021.

History

Fraser, A. *Mary Queen of Scots*.
MacLean, Fitzroy. *Bonnie Prince Charlie*. Canongate.
MacLean, Fitzroy. *A Concise History of Scotland*. Thames and Hudson.
Prebble, John. *Culloden and The Highland Clearances*.
Smout, T.C. *A History of the Scottish People 1560–1830*. Fontana.
Smout, T.C. *A Century of the Scottish People 1830–1950*. Fontana.
Steel, Tom. *Scotland's Story*. Fontana.

Poetry

Burns, Robert. Many editions available.
McGonagall, William. *Last Poetic Gems*. Winter/Duckworth. Scotland's (and perhaps the world's) worst poet, who has become something of a cult.

Miscellaneous

Allan, John R. *The Northeast Lowlands of Scotland*. Robert Hale.
Berry, Simon and Hamish Whyte. *Glasgow Observed*. John Donald Publishers.
Brogden, W.A. *Aberdeen, An Illustrated Architectural Guide*. Scottish Academic Press.
Cooper, Derek. *Road to the Isles*. Futura.
Cooper, Derek. *Hebridean Connection*. Futura.
Daiches, David. *A Companion to Scottish Culture*. Arnold.
Daiches, David (ed.). *Edinburgh: A Travellers' Companion*. Arnold.

Daiches, David. *Glasgow*. Andre Deutsch.
Dunn, Douglas. *Scotland: An Anthology*. Fontana.
Eames, Andrew. *Four Scottish Journeys*. Hodder & Stoughton.
Graham, Cuthbert. *Portrait of Aberdeen and Deeside*. Robert Hale.
House, Jack. *The Heart of Glasgow*. Richard Drew Publishing.
Johnson, Dr Samuel. *A Journey to the Western Isles; and James Boswell's Journal of a Tour to the Hebrides*. Two accounts of the same trip made in the 18th century by the great lexicographer and his biographer. Oxford University Paperbacks.
Morton, H.V. *In Search of Scotland*. Methuen.
Munro, Michael. *The Patter: A Guide to Current Glasgow Usage*. Glasgow District Libraries.
Exploring Scotland's Heritage. Her Majesty's Stationery Office.

Other Insight Guides

Among Apa Publications' range of more than 340 Insight, Compact and Pocket Guides are several titles on Scotland.

Companion volumes to the present book include *Insight Guide: Edinburgh* and *Insight Guide: Glasgow*. Both provide a complete cultural background, supplemented by stunning photography.

Compact Guide: Scotland is designed for portability; it is, in effect, a pocket encyclopaedia, packing in all the information you'll need, plus cross-referenced maps and photography.

Insight Pocket Guide: Scotland contains a local author's recommendations for places to go and things to do. It includes carefully timed itineraries and is designed for readers with limited time to spare.

ART & PHOTO CREDITS

Cartographic Editor **Zoë Goodwin**
Production **Mohammed Dar**
Design Consultant **Klaus Geisler**

Index

" I was first drawn to the Insight Guides by the excellent "Nepal" volume. I can think of no book which so effectively captures the essence of a country. Out of these pages leaped the Nepal I know – the captivating charm of a people and their culture. I've since discovered and enjoyed the entire Insight Guide series. Each volume deals with a country in the same sensitive depth, which is nowhere more evident than in the superb photography. **"**

Sir Edmund Hillary

The World of Insight Guides

400 books in three complementary series cover every major destination in every continent.